D1733421

RENEWALS 691-4574
DATE DUE

WITHDRAWN
UTSA Libraries

Collective Action and Community

Collective Action and Community

Public Arenas and the Emergence of Communalism in North India

Sandria B. Freitag

UNIVERSITY OF CALIFORNIA PRESS
Berkeley · Los Angeles · Oxford

University of California Press
Berkeley and Los Angeles, California

University of California Press, Ltd.
Oxford, England

© 1989 by
The Regents of the University of California

Library of Congress Cataloging-in-Publication Data

Freitag, Sandria B.
  Collective action and community : public arenas and the emergence
of communalism in north India / Sandria B. Freitag.
    p. cm.
  Bibliography: p.
  Includes index.
  ISBN 0-520-06439-9 (alk. paper)
    1. Communalism—India—Uttar Pradesh—History. 2. Riots—India—
Uttar Pradesh—History. 3. Uttar Pradesh (India)—History.
I. Title.
DS485.U64F74 1989
954′.2—dc19   88-36579
                                                 CIP

Printed in the United States of America
1 2 3 4 5 6 7 8 9

The paper used in this publication meets the minimum requirements of American National
Standard for Information Sciences—Permanence of Paper for Printed Library Materials,
ANSI Z39.48-1984.♾™

Library
University of Texas
at San Antonio

This book is dedicated to my parents:
to my mother, Joyce Saks, whose intellectual curiosity
started it all; and to my father, Robert Saks,
for encouraging the perseverance necessary
to finish.

Contents

List of Maps

Preface

This study has moved a great distance from its origins. It began as a dissertation focused on urban riots. In U.P. that generally meant riots between groups identified by religion. In the process of analyzing these riots, however, I made two important, unanticipated discoveries. The riots had all been characterized in the scholarly literature as "communal" in nature. Yet I discovered, when I looked at them closely, that those occurring in the late nineteenth century possessed characteristics that differentiated them in significant ways from those staged in the 1920s and 1930s. Given the general assumptions that accompany the way scholars use the term "communal," the burden of my dissertation was to distinguish the later riots that fit the term from the ones that had preceded them and that could not be accurately labeled in this way. In the elaboration of this argument, my dissertation traced the emergence of communalism.

While looking closely at the late nineteenth-century riots that preceded the development of communalism, however, I made a second discovery. The participants themselves had indicated that the riots functioned as one aspect of a much larger world of collective activities. The Muslim ex-kotwal Badr-ud-din, a key figure in the 1871 riots in Bareilly, vented his sense of grievance: "There never was such a Ramnaumi as there was this year. Such crowds, such music, such rites!" And in Agra in the following decade, memorialists protested to the provincial government:

Muslims were allowed to go in procession through the streets with tom toms beating, naked swords playing, and with burning sticks and zulfikar, that is to say a large number of swords arranged in line on a piece of wood . . . whereas the quiet and unobjectionable gaocharan ceremony of the Hindus was prohibited. Moreover, the Muslims are always allowed during their Muharram festival to mourn near Hindu temples and Hindu dwelling houses when marriage rites and ceremonies connected with child birth and so on are being performed. On such auspicious occasions the Hindus regard mourning as an omen of evil, yet the Muslims are not prevented from annoying the Hindus in this matter.[1]

In the present study, then, I am still interested in answering the question underlying my dissertation: what were the perceptions, values, and motivations that actuated north Indians—ordinary people, the nonelite, the illiterate or semiliterate populace—in the late nineteenth and early twentieth centuries? The focus has shifted, however, to the larger world of collective activities in public spaces, involving crowds and rites, music and swordplay, sacred space and sacred time. While the chief subject matter remains urban riots, this study argues that they can best be understood by placing them in a context provided by other collective activities—a world often labeled by scholars as "popular culture."

Part I sketches that context. It includes chapters that delineate each of the two key elements in the dynamic that quickens urban north Indian life: (1) the process by which constituent urban groups renegotiated their relationships through collective activities; and (2) the changing attitudes of the imperial state's provincial administration. Chapter 2 analyzes the attitudes of the provincial administration to the ongoing negotiations among urban groups. I have restricted the discussion about the British to this chapter, both to provide an extended backdrop to the chapters that follow and to limit the attention paid to them, for they are not my subject. Chapter 1 examines early examples of civic unrest prompted by changing relationships among Banaras's constituent groups. Because these examples include, within three years' time, both protest aimed against an imperial administration and conflict pitting Indian against Indian, they also illuminate a larger question that cannot

---

1. See chapters 3 and 4 for further discussion of these comments.

be fully answered in this study. The riots that form the subject of chapters 3 to 8 follow the pattern expressed in Banaras in 1809, when Indians attacked other Indians. In what circumstances might they, instead, have attacked the British directly? Because that mode was the exception rather than the rule in U.P., I have not fully addressed the question in this work. Essentially, I had to decide which context would be the most helpful in understanding the riots studied here: the world of collective activities, or the history of collective unrest and protest? I have judged the discussion of "popular culture" to be the best starting point, but I continue to work at creating a long-term view of unrest, as well.[2] In the meantime, the heart of the study commences at a point in time—the last third of the nineteenth century—in which protest activities in general had begun to target other Indians. Much of the discussion in Part II and Part III is devoted to discovering why.

The Introduction to Part I discusses at greater length the methodological assumptions underlying such a study, particularly my unwillingness to rely either on the interpretations penned by British administrators or on the vernacular didactic literature produced by the literate Indian elite, and the methodology informing an alternate focus on the *actions* taken collectively by the people in whom I am interested. The Introduction also initiates a discussion that continues throughout the work, in which this analysis is placed within a scholarly context provided by comparative history. Once I had identified what seemed to be the key points and characteristics in the narrative presented here, I became curious about the extent to which these themes also appeared in western European historiography. This curiosity was natural: much of the impetus for activities, particularly in the 1920s and 1930s in U.P., was explained by administrators and Indian elite alike as extensions of the worldwide development of nationalism. I wanted to see if these assumed similarities were accurate, and I sought out recent historical case studies (rather than theoretical works) that documented the connection between "popular culture" and the larger events figuring in English and French history. These European studies have been used here to frame the present study for two reasons. First, I think the studies on South Asia could prove very interesting to those who write European social history: it provides a depth of discussion that can only be achieved

2. See, for instance, my first speculations on this larger question, where I discuss various examples of unrest in one city in chapter 7, in Sandria B. Freitag, ed., *Culture and Power in Banaras* (Berkeley and Los Angeles: University of California Press, 1989).

through comparative history. To make this discussion more accessible for such readers, I have included a short summary of some of the constitutional and political events referred to but not described in detail in the text (see Appendix). Second, the evolution of the European nation-state differs in profoundly subtle but significant ways from the experiences in north India. Yet because it has shaped our underlying assumptions, it has tended to ensnare us as we look for explanations for developments in nineteenth- and twentieth-century India. I have tried to pinpoint both the important distinctions in the developments in the two regions, and the implications for Indian developments of the borrowing of this western European model.

Parts II and III form the heart of the study, in which changes begun in the late nineteenth century are traced through to their conclusions in the 1930s and into the postindependence period. The argument presented may seem unduly complex. But it proved impossible to convey the true nature of the dynamic involved without a nuanced analysis. Indeed, while identifying the underlying continuities of patterns throughout the U.P. area, I have tried in each chapter to tie the narrative carefully to the particularities of time and place, for these, too, matter. As I have tried to suggest in the conclusion, the nuances have become extremely important as the independent states of the subcontinent create new relationships with their constituent communities in the 1980s and beyond.

Prefaces provide the happy opportunity to thank those who participated in the lengthy process of turning a descriptive dissertation into an analytical monograph. To begin at the beginning is to acknowledge the extraordinarily helpful staff at the India Office. Over the last decade and a half they have provided highly professional guidance to the parts of the collection important for my work. More, several archivists have showed much ingenuity in successfully sleuthing out critical documents. I have been aided by the support and provocative criticism of a number of people. Ira Lapidus and David Arnold each gave my dissertation an extraordinarily detailed, careful scrutiny, for which I am very grateful. Others have been helpful with portions of the manuscript, including Gyan Pandey, Tom Metcalf, Kathy Ewing, Jim Masselos, Carol Breckenridge, and Arjun Appadurai. Special thanks must go to Keith Luria, whose detailed criticisms helped refine the manuscript to make it accessible to scholars of European history. Barbara Metcalf and Chris Bayly have been among my most helpful readers and critics, willingly subjecting themselves to various permutations of the text over many years. Lynne Withey, as sponsoring editor at the University of California Press, and David Lelyveld, as first reader, both provided constructive criticism that was empathetic to my intentions and that much strengthened the organization and exposition of my argument. To research assistants Christine Noelle, Steven Gilmartin, and Barbara Howell I owe special thanks for their careful attention to seemingly endless detail in readying the manuscript for publication. Finally, I would like to express my gratitude for being part of a larger intellectual community—represented particularly by David Gilmartin (my most faithful critic) and my students at the University of California at Berkeley—that has sustained my scholarly interest and commitment to this and other topics of north Indian social history.

A Note on Transliteration

Under the assumption that excessive use of diacritics and italics would distract from the readability of the text, Indian words have been treated as loan words whenever they appeared in *Webster's Third*. (As the reader will note, one might do a very interesting sociological study of American perceptions of India on the basis of that source!) If not available in *Webster's,* Indian words have been transliterated according to John T. Platt, *A Dictionary of Urdu, Classical Hindi and English,* except that *ć* and *ś* have been replaced with *ch* and *sh* so that nonspecialists will know the pronunciation. The few words not cited in either of these sources have been rendered according to popular English usage.

PART I

The Context

Local Communities and the State—Historiography and Methodology

Writers of European and South Asian social history have shared a similar central concern: the fate of "community," locally perceived and constructed, under the onslaught of an increasingly pervasive centralized modern state. Historians of Europe first expressed this interest through studies of collective protest activities (from food riots to working-class political mobilization); more recently they have focused on "popular culture" and leisure activities.[1] For historians of India, the concept of "community" has provided a fundamental mode of analysis. Conditioned by anthropologists (and nineteenth-century administrators[2]), community in the Indian context originally referred to village or

---

1. See, for instance, George Rudé, *The Crowd in History* (New York: Wiley, 1959); E. P. Thompson, "The Moral Economy of the English Crowd in the Eighteenth Century," *Past and Present* 50 (February 1971): 76–136; Natalie Zemon Davis, "The Rites of Violence: Religious Riot in Sixteenth Century France," *Past and Present* 59 (May 1973): 51–91; Eric Hobsbawm, *Primitive Rebels: Studies in Archaic Forms of Social Movements in 19th and 20th Centuries* (New York: Manchester University Press, 1967). Among more recent works on European popular culture, important contributions include Peter Burke, *Popular Culture in Early Modern Europe* (New York: New York University Press, 1978); and Eileen Yeo and Stephen Yeo, eds., *Popular Culture and Class Conflict, 1950–1914* (Atlantic Highlands, N.J.: Humanities Press, 1981). A contrary (and, in my judgment, somewhat unsophisticated) viewpoint is expressed in J. M. Golby and A. W. Purdue, *The Civilisation of the Crowd: Popular Culture in England 1750–1900* (London: Batsford, 1984).

2. Charles Metcalfe's observation is the most famous articulation of this administrative view: "The village communities are little republics, having nearly everything they want within themselves, and almost independent of any foreign relations. They seem to last where nothing else lasts. Dynasty after dynasty tumbles down; revolution succeeds to revolution; . . . but the village communities remain the same." Great Britain, *Parliamentary Papers* (House of Commons), 1830–1831, 11:331.

caste. More recent studies have broadened this definition, examining popular protest and cultural activities in terms similar to those used by scholars studying Europe.[3]

Although this is not the place to provide a definitive historiographical analysis of the term "community," we should begin by noting the shaping of the concept by Tönnies's contrast of *Gemeinshaft* and *Gesellschaft*. Of this opposition Macfarlane points out that "the contrast, as Tönnies described it, was between life based on bonds of kinship, geographical bonds and the sentiment of belonging to a group (blood, place, mind), which was termed 'community' [*Gemeinshaft*], and the modern phenomenon where all these links had been broken in what he termed 'society' [*Gesellschaft*]."[4] "Community" for many authors thus equaled the village, parish, or other bounded unit of premodern society.

Yet despite this ostensible effort to relegate the notion to premodern social constructs, the concept of "community" in each region has survived beyond the temporal dividing line of premodern and modern. As used for the more recent period, however, "community" has related primarily to the ideological expressions of social organization. For Europeanists, preconditioned by the impact of the Industrial Revolution, ideology has generally translated into expressions of class interests, particularly as they were reflected in the antagonisms between an emerging working class[5] and the alliance forged between state and middle class. The tenor of these studies may be most accurately reflected in a recent analysis of changes in English "popular culture," which argues that this relationship between local (lower-class) communities and the state should be characterized by "phrases like 'cultural revolution' or 'cultural imperialism' " rather than " 'incorporation' or 'social control.' "[6] By contrast, the scholarly discussion of British India still

3. See, for instance, Ranajit Guha, ed., *Subaltern Studies*, vols. 1–5 (Delhi: Oxford University Press, 1982–1985), and Rudrangshu Mukerjee, *Awadh in Revolt, 1857–1858: A Study of Popular Resistance* (Delhi: Oxford University Press, 1984).

4. Alan Macfarlane, "History, Anthropology, and the Study of Communities," *Social History* 2, no. 5 (May 1977): 631. Macfarlane is referring to Ferdinand Tönnies, *Community and Association (Gemeinschaft und Gesellschaft*, 1887), trans. C. P. Loomis (London: Routledge and Paul, 1955). For further discussion of historical use of the concept of community, see C. J. Calhoun's reply, "History, Anthropology, and the Study of Communities: Some Problems in Macfarlane's Proposal," *Social History* 3, no. 3 (October 1978): 363–73; and David Sabean, *Power in the Blood* (Cambridge: Cambridge University Press, 1984), introduction.

5. The seminal study, of course, is E. P. Thompson, *The Making of the English Working Class* (New York: Vintage Books, 1963).

6. Stephen Yeo, "Ways of Seeing: Control and Leisure Versus Class and Struggle," in Yeo and Yeo, eds., *Popular Culture and Class Conflict*, p. 137. As the Introduction to Part

bears the imprint of the most traumatic event of its recent history, its partition in 1947 into two independent nations—India and Pakistan—on the basis of religion. Where Europeanists have tended to see community ideology expressed as class, then, Indianists have favored religion as community ideology.[7]

This divergence of terminology and cultural specifics has masked similarities of process,[8] a term that in this case refers to the evolving relationship between communities and the state. Certainly the ways in which community identity came to be constructed and expressed, particularly in urban settings in India and Europe, seem to share significant common characteristics. Most prominent of these have been the symbolic enactments of events and rituals that simultaneously delineated common values and drew on shared historical moments and locally significant cultural referrents. In the urban cultures of both regions, these can be found in religious ceremonial occasions as well as civic events. Significantly, much the same kinds of symbolic rhetoric and codes of behavior have also carried over into the collective violence that punctuated urban life.[9] From such common experiences have emerged perceptions, definitions, and constructions[10] of shared community. Not coincidentally, this process of constructing ideological communities in both regions marked the periods of transition leading to a modern, industrialized nation-state. Social historians will find much of value in a comparison of this process as it developed in Europe and in South Asia.

The first step in understanding the process must focus, then, on the ways by which such constructed communities emerged. Equally significant is the second step—understanding the extent to which communities have withstood, and have been redefined under, the pressure of

---

III of this volume explores, a close connection between state interference and community as nation has been posited by many of these scholars.

7. Marxist analysts have long used this vocabulary for India, but with less convincing results. Recently, a creative effort to combine these analytical approaches has been attempted by the self-styled Subalternist school (see below). The most sustained expression of their attempt to deal with class and religion within the same analytical framework is Ranajit Guha, *Elementary Aspects of Peasant Insurgency in Colonial India* (Delhi: Oxford University Press, 1983).

8. In addition, it has prompted a number of social historians of South Asia to try to draw parallels not only through methodology but also through analyses dependent on identical class developments.

9. See works of authors such as Natalie Davis, Keith Luria, and John Bohstedt. Relevant work for India has been contributed, for instance, by Anand Yang, Dipesh Chakrabarty, and Gyan Pandey.

10. The word "construction" is used to convey the active and aware participation by those involved in defining elements of identity.

an expanding, centralized state and the resulting altered relationship with such an interventionist state. While the processes involved in western Europe and South Asia are similar, important regional differences do emerge in sociopolitical structures and in developments that significantly affected the relationship of state and community. Not least among these differences have been patterns of industrialization, which affected the areas under discussion unequally. But most important, imperialism created a framework for historical events that led South Asia in a very different direction from that taken in Europe. Many writers, however, have so underscored the differences (either by placing an emphasis on the cultural mode of South Asian society[11] or by measuring developments in South Asia against their supposed models in Europe and attributing any shortcomings to imperialism) that the comparison often has seemed impossible. By focusing here on community and state, we may establish an analytical framework that permits comparison while allowing us to use a similar vocabulary and methodology to delineate significant but subtle differences.

In trying to understand the changing relationship between the imperial Indian state and its constituent communities, this study looks to the realm in which community has been expressed and redefined through collective activities in public spaces. It develops an analytical framework that characterizes this realm as a coherent, consistent one of symbolic behavior—a realm of "public arenas." Such a realm impinged simultaneously on two worlds—that encompassing activity by locally constituted groups, and that structured by state institutions. Key to both worlds, this realm of public arenas came, in the late nineteenth and early twentieth centuries, to occupy a unique position in British north India. Originally just the realm in which collective activities were staged, it became an alternative world to that structured by the imperial regime, providing legitimacy and recognition to a range of actors and values denied place in the imperial order.

In tracing the history of this politico-cultural meeting point of populace and state, the narrative for India departs from the similar pattern we might trace for England or France. Delineating the ways in which it departs yields, as well, a history of the emergence of communalism in north India—that phenomenon we might define as a politicized community identity, or the "consciously-shared religious heritage which becomes the dominant form of identity . . . in which are fused a reinter-

---

11. See Louis Dumont, *Homo Hierarchicus: An Essay on the Caste System,* trans. Mark Sainsbury (Chicago: University of Chicago Press, 1970).

preted history, coupled with a new conceptualization of the world and the position of the identity group in that world."[12] Implicit in an examination of the development of communalism, therefore, is a desire to identify the unique elements that distinguish the direction taken in north India within a process whose outlines otherwise have been shared with European history. The contrast between these historical processes is sketched in the introductory sections that precede each of the three parts to this study. These introductions are meant not as definitive statements but rather as suggestive discussions prompted by comparative history.

Part I provides the context for understanding the story of the development of communalism in the area in which it proved particularly strong, the north Indian area of U.P. (now the state of Uttar Pradesh; at that time the administrative area that came to be known as the United Provinces [of Agra and Oudh]), located in the Gangetic plain and the foothills above it. This context includes several facets, among the most important being the basic premises, attitudes, and changing circumstances imposed by British administrators (chapter 2). To understand these imperial constraints, it is necessary to examine, as well, the north Indian world within which they acted, as it evolved from the Mughal Empire through the eighteenth-century Successor States period. For this purpose, chapter 1 uses as illustration the experience of Banaras, one of the five most important urban sites of the area. Banaras at this time served as the center of a small quasi-independent successor state and was among the first of the large urban centers to experience the impact of the British Raj. Analyzing events there helps to trace the central role played by collective activities in redefining the relationship among a state's urban communities.

South Asian Historiography

Both the Indian and British actors come to us, however, filtered through a very particular set of historiographical assumptions and certain kinds of sources. These, too, must be discussed before the context of a study such as this can be fully understood. We turn to these sources before beginning chapter 1 to provide both a statement of methodology and a rationale for the analytical framework used in this study.

---

12. Kenneth W. Jones, "Communalism in the Punjab: The Arya Samaj Contribution," *Journal of Asian Studies* 28, no. 1 (November 1968): 39–54.

1. Subcontinent of South Asia. (U.P. shaded).

We have noted that the ideological component of "community" for analysts of South Asia has related, generally, to religion. Current discussions of the significance of religious "community"—and the communalism that emerged in the twentieth century from its politicized constructions—inevitably have been shaped by the historiographical dialogue that preceded them. Regarded as self-explanatory, the term "communalism" was read back from the 1947 experience of partition and

2. Districts in U.P. (Bhojpuri region shaded).

independence; it has been applied to every earlier confrontation between participants who have, consequently, been labeled "Hindu" and "Muslim." By implication, it has been treated by scholars and participants alike as a phenomenon arising full-grown from the natural state of South Asian society. Such assumptions have shaped interpretations of eighteenth- and nineteenth-century events into very particular molds.[13] This self-explanatory approach to the subject is a historiographical

13. A recent demonstration is the volume edited by Mushirul Hasan, *Communal and Pan-Islamic Trends in Colonial India* (New Delhi: Manohar Publications, 1981). The volume includes a sophisticated essay by N. C. Saxena, "Historiography of Communalism in India," on the nature of communalism and the care that must be taken when using the term. Yet, ignoring Saxena's argument, Hasan's own essay in this volume, "Communal and Revivalist Trends in Congress," uses the term "communal" as though it not only provides an explanation for the actions of prominent leaders but actually has some valid, universal meaning.

outgrowth of political and constitutional history, the predominant form of analysis that evolved from the efforts of British administrators to understand the territory they ruled. In shaping historical interpretations, such politically focused historiography has fostered a tendency to see only those issues deemed important in the 1947 transfer of government structures from the British to Western-educated Indians.

The result has been a very special form of history, which has treated the relationship of state and community by emphasizing only certain aspects—those perceived as significant for the partition of the subcontinent. When discussing the late nineteenth century, for instance, such historians have emphasized the agitation over positions for Muslims in the administration and in schools. They have looked primarily at the promotion of Western education among Muslims, especially the efforts of Sir Sayyid Ahmad Khan and his evolving university at Aligarh; they looked as well at points of conflict like the Nagari-Urdu controversy over the adoption of the Devanagari script for use in the courts and administration.[14] When discussing "Hindus," historians have emphasized the establishment in 1875 of the reformist Arya Samaj and the experiments introduced by B. G. Tilak in Bombay linking nationalist rhetoric to what had been a private religious observance of the Ganpati festival. This historiographical approach addressed what were seen as the central problems of modern South Asia: the development of political structures to carry the nationalist movement, and the repeated and ever more successful attempts to involve the masses in these structures. It was natural in this approach, then, to emphasize the formation in the 1880s of the Indian National Congress and, twenty years later, of the Muslim League.[15]

14. See Christopher R. King, "The Nagari Pracharini Sabha (Society for the Promotion of the Nagari Script and Language) of Benares, 1893–1914: A Study in the Social and Political History of the Hindi Language," Ph.D. diss., University of Wisconsin, 1974, and "Forging a New Linguistic Identity: The Hindi Movement in Banaras, 1868–1914," in Sandria B. Freitag, ed., *Culture and Power in Banaras: Community, Performance, and Environment, 1800–1980,* (Berkeley and Los Angeles: University of California Press, 1989), pp. 179–202. Agitation in favor of Hindi was at least partially successful, and the governments of the Central Provinces and Bihar made provisions in the late 1860s to allow the use of Hindi alongside Urdu. Leading Muslims in U.P. were active in anti-Nagari organizations in the 1870s and again at the turn of the century to prevent this from happening in U.P. But in 1900, seemingly in response to a "Hindu" petition and without consulting these activist Muslims, the provincial government decided to accept Hindi as a lingua franca equal to Urdu in law courts and government offices. This decision broadened the number of people capable of carrying on official business with the government, but it was also seen as a threat to the literary culture that had developed around Urdu.

15. For a recent example of this type of emphasis, which dominated previous general histories, see Stanley Wolpert, *A New History of India* (New York: Oxford University Press, 1977).

With nascent nationalism the focus, it was relatively easy even to link the new Congress with such puzzling movements as the Cow Protection movement, which boasted networks to collect funds, circulated stump orators, and printed and disseminated propaganda in various parts of the country. By tracing the overlap between Congress and Cow Protection networks, it was possible, at least obliquely, to credit Congress with the ability to mobilize popular support for elite issues such as simultaneous examinations for aspiring Indian administrators and increased council participation by Indian notables.[16]

In the twentieth century, the rise of Pan-Islamism—culminating finally in the Khilafat movement of the 1920s—was used to explain Muslim participation in evolving political structures. Touchstones along the way included the Bengal Partition and its rescission;[17] the introduction, through the Morley-Minto Reforms of 1909, of separate electorates to protect Muslim minority interests; and the Lucknow Pact of 1916, which incorporated the minimum demands made by both the Muslim League and the Indian National Congress into a nationalist program for independence. By the early 1920s, according to this construction of events, all the components that would lead, less than three decades later, to independence and partition were in play. These components ranged from the personality of Mohandas K. Gandhi, with his genius for casting the nationalist struggle in a vocabulary accessible to the masses, to the identification by many Muslims with a cause that required special protection in an independent India; from the constitutional provisions laid down in the Government of India Act of 1919, which enlarged the franchise and turned over to Indians ever larger areas of power and patronage, to the reorganization first of the Congress and then of the League into agencies capable of mobilizing mass support.

One corrective to this political and constitutional slant has been to focus on intellectual history. Some of the best work on Muslims, for instance, has placed great emphasis on the writings of leading reform-

---

16. See John McLane, *Indian Nationalism and the Early Congress* (Princeton: Princeton University Press, 1977), p. 273: "The disturbances were connected with Congress-Muslim disagreements over legislative reforms passed in 1892. . . . The Congress demand for representative government and the cow protectors' call for legal measures against slaughter appeared to Muslims to be closely related threats."

17. The Bengal Partition alike provided Hindu activists with proof of the success of agitational politics and Muslims with a lesson in the failure of progovernment tactics. See Appendix, "Chronology of Political Events in U.P. and the British Empire."

ers[18] and on the educational efforts launched within the community.[19] Such work *is* a useful corrective, for it explores the sources for the ideological component that infused life into the organizations so thoroughly studied by those interested in political narrative. A second corrective has been the range of studies produced in the 1970s— primarily by those known as the Cambridge school—analyzing these general events in a local setting. Though still heavily preoccupied with political history, these analyses have helped highlight the unevenness, variety, and local character of developments during the late nineteenth and early twentieth centuries.

Although the constitutional and intellectual aspects are clearly important in tracing the history of the relationship between the state and its constituent communities, they have produced an incomplete explanation for the emergence of communalism. Moreover, these historiographical approaches have had important analytical ramifications. First, emphasis consistently has been placed on organizations,[20] since these figure as the primary actors on a political or constitutional stage. If we extrapolate values and meaning from organizations alone, we shall be seriously misled about the nature and development of communal consciousness. Second, and equally important, has been the tendency to make a distinction (perhaps subliminal) between popular—often violent—reactions to issues and the elite reactions of petition and institutionalized protest. Implied in this distinction is a value judgment that renders popular protest suspect, less than legitimate, or even irrational: the "insensate violence" of the bazaars and *muḥalla*s (neighborhoods).[21] Perhaps more problematic has been the related tendency of scholars to consider movements to have failed whenever they addressed "parochial" (i.e., local) issues rather than national ones or turned to violence in pursuit of their goals.[22]

18. See Peter Hardy, *The Muslims of British India* (Cambridge: Cambridge University Press, 1972).

19. David Lelyveld's *Aligarh's First Generation: Muslim Solidarity in British India* (Princeton: Princeton University Press, 1978) is an especially skillful and sensitive integration of social and intellectual history. Less work has been done on the Hindu side. Kenneth Jones's work on the Arya Samaj, *Arya Dharm* (Berkeley and Los Angeles: University of California Press, 1976), stands out; he has been working on the Sanatan Dharm Sabha as well.

20. Although other parts of the book do balance out this tendency, see Hardy, *The Muslims of British India,* esp. pp. 139–46, for a representative treatment.

21. F. C. R. Robinson, *Separatism Among Indian Muslims* (Cambridge: Cambridge University Press, 1974), p. 6. For a similar dismissive viewpoint on collective violence, see Bipan Chandra, *Communalism in Modern India* (New Delhi: Vikas [Vani Educational Books], 1984), p. 5.

22. See Gail Minault, *The Khilafat Movement: Religious Symbolism and Political*

It has seemed useful, therefore, to shift the focus from elite associations and publications to popular attitudes and actions as these were expressed in the realm referred to here as "public arenas." This change of focus rehabilitates popular protest as an expression of motivating values and perceptions seldom found in written sources. By delineating the relationship between collective activities and those elements studied earlier—particularly organizations and ideology—this new focus renders more explicable the popular support garnered by the political organizations of the 1920s and 1930s that had figured so prominently in the historiography.

Behavior as "Text"

One result of this shift in focus is to change rather dramatically our view of the development of communalism. Key to understanding the underlying connections among organizations, ideology, and popular participation is the process by which participants constructed the respective "communities" for which they acted. In this process certain shared values and behaviors were self-consciously chosen for emphasis: participants simultaneously defined their own community and created an "Other" encompassing those outside the boundaries they drew. The articulation of these constructions, in turn, calls to our attention the universe in which community came to be expressed. As the Banaras examples will suggest, that universe included both the formally constituted organizations studied before and a wide range of more informally organized activities, such as anjumans that brought together those interested in singing *marsiyas* during Muharram processions, or *akhāṟās* for physical fitness (based on guru-chela relationships and expressed in fictive-kin terms). All of these activities, in which group interests were pursued or expressed, share significantly similar characteristics. The more formal of them encompassed voluntary special-interest organizations (political agencies as well as neighborhood shrine committees).[23]

Mobilization in India (New York: Columbia University Press, 1982), p. 113; Minault considers it damning that "calls for nonviolence and self-discipline . . . were drowned out by a welter of appeals based on local economic grievances and sectarian religious sentiments."

23. Work on Banaras suggests that in addition to studying the elitist voluntary organizations pursuing special interests (e.g., the Urdu Defence Association) and caste association movements, scholars should begin looking for their equivalents among the lower castes in the collective actions taken by *shringār* committees and *akhāṟās* for everything from physical fitness gymnasiums to musical troupes. See Freitag, ed., *Culture and Power in Banaras.*

Public ceremonials or other collective activities, including those of protest, used more informal lines of organization. Taken together, these activities expressed community. Yet the focus in previous historiography on more formal activities, particularly those of special-interest groups organized by the professional elite, has obscured the continuity of those activities with events occurring informally in public spaces. By studying these together, we can identify more easily the rhetoric and shared values that unite the formal and informal worlds. Moreover, by examining the behavior of participants moving between realms previously treated as discrete, we can discern that these public arena activities encompass actions at once "political" and "religious," expressing both elite concerns and popular values. Indeed, to focus on the interplay between these realms allows us, ultimately, to explain a central development of twentieth-century history: the increasing significance attributed to acts of the ordinary person within north Indian power and political relationships.

This study is meant to suggest new historical interpretations made possible through an analysis of collective activities, including collective violence. It is based on the premise that such actions are not "insensate" but quite rational; that they can be subjected to careful scrutiny to yield evidence about the values and motivating forces of the crowd; and that, moreover, crowd behavior should not be seen as peripheral to the dynamics of historical change but is, in fact, at its very heart.[24] In this respect the events of history may be seen as emerging from the interplay between the collective acts of individuals and the larger economic and political forces of a world organized around an imperial order.[25]

Crowd behavior, however, is a problematic historical topic, for we cannot know the thoughts of the individuals who make up a crowd. Some written source materials are provided by the records describing speeches and other activities of those who take leadership roles before the crowd. But many of those at the head of crowds emerged at the moment. Often illiterate, like those they led, they may not have found the written word appropriate or necessary. In any case, the extent to

---

24. These historiographical assumptions coincide with those espoused by social historians of France and England and the Subalternist school in India. Notes, below, will indicate the extent to which I disagree with, or depart from, the Subalternists' implications of making this historiographical statement into a politico-scholarly philosophy.

25. I take Giddens's discussion on structuration theory, while much abstracted, to call for a similar set of methodological assumptions. Anthony Giddens, *The Constitution of Society: Outline of the Theory of Structuration* (Berkeley and Los Angeles: University of California Press, 1984), esp. pp. 288–327.

which such written sources would have reflected the values and opinions of the followers remains unclear. We must look elsewhere for our evidence. From materials available for the later decades of the twentieth century, we know that the best sources for the views of these actors would be publicly posted placards, folksongs, oral history, "popular painting" such as illustrations utilized by itinerant storytellers or works depicting local scandals and activities.[26] Two intriguing studies suggest what might be possible were such sources available for most urban centers. Majid Siddiqi has used folksong to much enrich a social history of unrest in Mewat. Gyan Pandey profitably contrasts the identification of significant events in two "histories" of an eastern U.P. *qaṣba* (urban center) to suggest both the overlap and the dissimilarities of viewpoint between two authors of very different background and training.[27] Unfortunately, although administrators cum amateur anthropologists assiduously collected folksongs and folktales for the rural areas in the late nineteenth century, virtually none of these sources may be taken, without special care, to reflect accurately the values or social organization of the north Indian urban world. Nor have we yet uncovered a wide range of local histories penned by the urban inhabitants of nineteenth-century north India.

In general, the closest we can come to primary source materials that connect, at least tangentially, to the popular perceptions and values of the city are newspapers and petitions. Newspapers, particularly the vernacular press, although written by a literate elite, functioned to "report" happenings, including collective activities. Petitions submitted to the authorities, written by that same elite in English as well as a vernacular language, attempted to "explain" collective action. Nevertheless, even where useful, these written sources remain ancillary to the main activities being studied. Roger Chartier and Jacques Revel, for instance, have argued convincingly for early modern France that such written sources are very problematic. To begin with, the implicit polemical agenda of the producers of these sources may differ radically from the values held by the intended audience. Moreover, the levels and nuances of meaning attributed to written documents may vary dramati-

26. See examples given in Mildred Archer, *Indian Popular Painting in the India Office Library* (London: HMSO, 1977).
27. Majid Hayat Siddiqi, "History and Society in a Popular Rebellion: Mewat, 1920–1933," *Comparative Studies in Society and History* 28, (1986): 442–67; Gyanendra Pandey, " 'Encounters and Calamities': The History of a North Indian *Qasba* in the Nineteenth Century," in Ranajit Guha, ed., *Subaltern Studies*, vol. 3 (Delhi: Oxford University Press, 1984), pp. 213–70.

cally among consumers of the documents, depending on the extent of each one's literacy and the popular cultural matrix of values brought to the materials.[28] We must look beyond north India's written sources, then, for information that reveals the core motivations and values of the crowd.

Given the paucity of primary sources that accurately reflect the values and perceptions of participants in collective action, particularly for the nineteenth and early twentieth centuries, those interested in the crowd must analyze primarily its *actions*. The premise informing this approach is that the values and motivations attributed to the actors can be explicated by analyzing the symbolic language expressed through action. The caveat, of course, is that such attributions may be ascribed only to the collectivity. Individuals within the crowd may have had very different motivations from one another and from the group as a whole.

Methodologically, the sources needed for this kind of approach must also be chosen with great care. They can be somewhat problematic, for we require not polemical explanations for crowd behavior (which characterize most vernacular primary sources related to this subject) but accurate descriptions of crowd action. Perversely enough (given the historiographical mistrust that has developed for these sources), administrative accounts, particularly of protest actions—if sufficiently detailed and written soon after the fact by someone relatively familiar with the locale—often prove the most valuable sources. Even then their descriptions must be used judiciously, often by reading between the lines to distinguish what a crowd actually did from what an administrator thought about those actions. Thus the historian must treat administrative accounts like any other primary source, taking care to distinguish what they *describe* from what they attempt to *explain*.[29]

As a technique, this approach of the study of crowd behavior owes much to what Victor Turner has called "comparative symbology." It is

28. See the essays by Revel (on the elites' polemical agendas) and Chartier (on varied meanings attributable to printed materials) in Steven L. Kaplan, ed., *Understanding Popular Culture* (New York: Mouton, 1984): Jacques Revel, "Forms of Expertise: Intellectuals and 'Popular' Culture in France (1650–1800)," and Roger Chartier, "Culture as Appropriation: Popular Cultural Uses in Early Modern France."

29. The use of British administrative sources admittedly flies in the face of the scholarly prejudice that has developed in America in favor of vernacular source materials. I am not arguing that administrative sources are better than vernacular ones. But neither the appropriate vernacular sources nor the checks necessary for using them judiciously are available for a study of crowd behavior. (Clearly, vernacular materials are available, and would be more appropriate, for discussion of other, related topics—such as the Arya Samaj's campaign for Cow Protection, or the Deobandi efforts to reform Muslim practices. Although that literature tangentially affects the world inhabited by the crowds with which I am concerned, its authors are not my subjects.)

the symbolic behavior of the crowd, as discerned through judicious interpretation of administrative accounts, that provides our historical "text." To analyze this text, the scholar must investigate "the relationships between symbols and the concepts, feelings, values, notions etc. associated with them." Administrative descriptions penned at the time provide us with information that enables us to consider carefully the full range of actions taken collectively. These actions possess the potential to speak to us through their shared symbolism, the general ambiance of the public spaces they occupy, and their methods of mobilization.

Particularly for the historian, changes over time in the meaning imputed to these symbols prove central to the analysis, for symbolic actions express "social and cultural dynamic systems, shedding and gathering meaning over time and altering in form."[30] Thus the meaning attributed to the symbols must be carefully situated in the specific historical context. As the power relationships and the cultural experiences of the participants change, symbolic meaning changes as well. In particular, this methodology is intended to emphasize the "structure-in-process" elements (to use Victor Turner's term) inherent in this world. No world of stasis, public arenas depend on processual elements that affect, and become reflected in, structure that changes with each iteration.[31] Analyzing such process involves looking at the full range of activities that infuse meaning into symbolic behavior. As Turner puts it, the ritual symbols of this world must be studied "in relation to other 'events', for symbols are essentially involved in social process. . . . Performances of ritual [are] distinct phases in the social processes whereby groups became adjusted to internal changes . . . and adapted to their external environment. . . . From this standpoint the ritual symbol becomes a factor in social action, a positive force in an activity field."[32]

30. Victor Turner, *Process, Performance and Pilgrimage: A Study in Comparative Symbology* (New Delhi: Concept, 1979), pp. 12–13.

31. See Arjun Appadurai, *Worship and Conflict Under Colonial Rule: A South Indian Case* (Cambridge: Cambridge University Press, 1981), pp. 1–6, for a general discussion of the methodological and analytical context into which Turner's work fits, including particularly its connections to the work of Geertz, Lévi-Strauss, and Edmund Leach. As the key spokesman for processual analysis, however, Turner is the one who has most carefully elaborated the analytical framework used here.

32. Turner, *Process, Performance and Pilgrimage*, p. 13. In its emphasis on "social process" this approach differs from that of Guha and others of the Subalternist school. Symbolic action expresses for them a fundamental opposition of upper and lower class, of oppressor and oppressed (which can, therefore, generally be read backward or forward in time). By contrast, I think the evidence shows that while on some occasions the symbolism did indeed express such opposition, this is not always the case. Instead, I would argue, the interpretation of symbolic action must be carefully contextualized.

The text of symbolic crowd behavior is most fully elaborated in collective activities that expressed popular values and worldviews. These activities—ceremonies, popular entertainments and performances, even violent protests—all took place in shared (therefore public) places, expressed through similar symbolic behavior and rhetoric. To understand the behavioral text, we must examine the symbolic vocabulary expressed in the realm we have designated "public arenas." It is to this shared world that we now turn in order to define fully, through example and analysis, what we mean by that term.

CHAPTER 1

Community and State in Public Arenas: The Banaras Example

To set the context for this study, as well as to illustrate the nature of public arenas, this chapter analyzes collective activities staged in public spaces in early nineteenth-century Banaras. Juxtaposing these examples illuminates the common core of characteristics that define public arenas—a world of ritual, theater, and symbol. It is a universe that sometimes reinforces hierarchy, providing roles for those occupying various positions within society, and at other times expresses conflict among unequals; it may even do both simultaneously. Most important, it is a world that is tied closely to the social and political contexts of its locale and hence accommodates and reflects change.[1]

The historical experience of Banaras, during initial encounters with an interventionist ruler in the guise of the East India Company, provides an important paradigm for this study of public arenas in north India. The early nineteenth-century public actions taken by Banarsis show us clearly the range of options available at that time and suggest the inherent significance of public arena activity. As a consequence, the Banarsi experience will also provide a foil for Part II, as we see how the potential inherent in public arena activity was restricted and reshaped

1. Unlike Habermas's concept of the "public sphere," we are not examining a universe that emerged only with the coming of national and territorial states, nor one based on free and equal participation conditioned by access to information and the impact of public opinion. Cf. Jürgen Habermas, "The Public Sphere: An Encyclopedia Article (1964)," *New German Critique* 3 (Fall 1974): 49–55. For a fuller explication of the contrasts and similarities between public spheres and public arenas, see the Introduction to Part III.

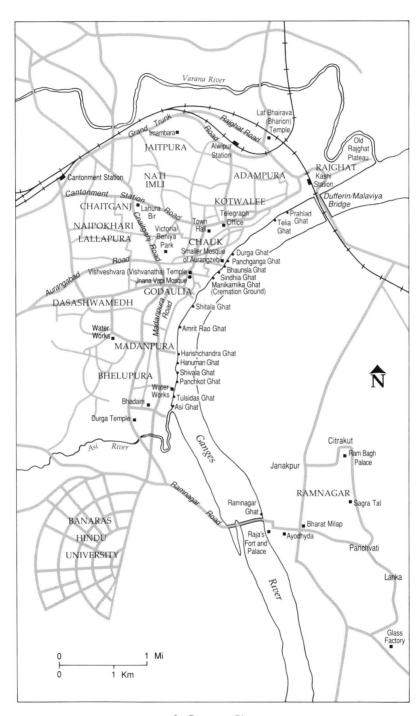

Varana River

Grand Trunk Road

Rajghat Road

Lat Bhairava
(Bharion)
Temple

Imambara

JAITPURA

Alwipur
Station

Old
Rajghat
Plateau

Cantonment Station

NATI
IMLI

ADAMPURA

RAJGHAT

Kashi
Station

Cantonment Station

KOTWALEE

Dufferin/Malaviya
Bridge

CHAITGANJ

Lahura
Bir

Telegraph
Office

Prahlad
Ghat

Telia
Ghat

NAIPOKHARI

Victoria

LALLAPURA

Beniya
Park

Town
Hall

CHAUK

Durga Ghat

Road

Smaller Mosque
of Aurangzeb

Panchganga Ghat

Bhaunsla Ghat

Aurangabad

Vishveshvara (Vishvanatha) Temple

Sindhia Ghat

Jnana Vapi Mosque

Manikarnika Ghat
(Cremation Ground)

GODAULIA

DASASHWAMEDH

Shitala Ghat

Water
Works

Amrit Rao Ghat

MADANPURA

Harishchandra Ghat

Hanuman Ghat

BHELUPURA

Shivala Ghat

Panchkot Ghat

Water
Works

Bhadaini

Tulsidas Ghat

Asi Ghat

Durga Temple

Asi River

Ganges

Citrakut

Ram Bagh
Palace

Janakpur

RAMNAGAR

Sagra Tal

Ramnagar
Ghat

BANARAS

HINDU

UNIVERSITY

Bharat Milap

Raja's
Fort and
Palace

Ayodhya

Panchvati

Lanka

River

Glass
Factory

N

0   1 Mi

0   1 Km

3. Banaras City.

by policies and events of the late nineteenth century. Banaras, as one of the premier pilgrimage sites in the subcontinent, has been understood primarily in terms of auspiciousness, in light of its location on the niche of land where the Ganges and Varana rivers meet and its role in Hindu cosmology. It also functioned, however, as the largest urban center in the eastern Gangetic plain, supported by a densely populated hinterland enjoying a high level of agricultural production. As the center of the Bhojpuri cultural region, Banaras also provided a focal point for a vernacular language-based culture encompassing eastern U.P. and western Bihar.[2] The city's population grew rapidly in the last half of the eighteenth century, numbering about two hundred thousand for much of the nineteenth and early twentieth centuries and remaining a good-sized urban site in the days following the decline of the largest Mughal imperial centers.

The eighteenth century witnessed new configurations of power relationships in Banaras, expressed through concomitant social and cultural structures.[3] Located at the apogee of this political structure was an alliance of ruling interests, encompassing a local dynasty from the Bhumihar caste (who laid claim to the title of Raja)[4] and the overlapping urban corporations formed by merchant-bankers and mendicant soldier-traders.[5] We must say a word about each of the members of this power triumvirate if we are to understand the political economy of the area.

2. For a discussion of the Bhojpuri cultural region, see, for example, Gyan Pandey, "Rallying Round the Cow: Sectarian Strife in the Bhojpuri Region, c. 1888–1917," in Ranajit Guha, ed., *Subaltern Studies,* vol. 2 (Delhi: Oxford University Press, 1983), pp. 60–129.

3. For a more detailed discussion of this phenomenon, see the Introduction in Sandria B. Freitag, ed., *Culture and Power in Banaras: Community, Performance, and Environment, 1800–1980* (Berkeley and Los Angeles: University of California Press, 1989).

4. This twice-born caste enjoyed high status throughout north India, where its members were prominent landowners and tenants with favorable terms. They exercised much influence, particularly in the rural areas, and were often involved (as were the Rajput clans) in the eighteenth-century migrations to which C. A. Bayly attributes the creation of many new commercial centers (*Rulers, Townsmen and Bazaars* [Cambridge: Cambridge University Press, 1983], pp. 95–96). The increasing power of the dynasty also helped to entrench the power of the Bhumihar clan in the area, particularly vis-à-vis Rajput and Maratha groups.

5. "Corporation" is used in the sense defined by C. A. Bayly, "an occupational or religious organization which transcended the bounds of 'caste' in the sense of jati. It would therefore include commercial or priestly associations . . . as well as certain types of ascetic [groups] which integrated urban or rural society and acted as self-regulating entities de facto. . . . [Thus] Indian society produce[d] dynamic, multi-caste institutions in the context of growing monetisation and the weakening of central state power" (*Rulers, Townsmen and Bazaars,* p. 163n).

Like the rise of other rural-based powerholders in north India, the political fortunes of the family who became the Rajas of Banaras followed an established pattern. Starting from a relatively small estate, this landlord family gained a position as tax official for the Nawabs of Awadh. They then utilized this position to consolidate a zamindari holding that extended to most of the Banaras province. By the 1750s Balwant Singh had gained the title of Raja for the family and, functioning as the virtually independent regional-level ruler, paid only a lumpsum tax or tribute to Awadh.[6] Indeed, the forces of his successor, Chait Singh, constituted in the 1780s some 10 percent of Banaras's population.[7] In recognition of the Raja's power and independence, the British East India Company did not attempt to rule the area directly when it took Banaras over from the Nawab of Awadh in 1775. The British did, however, establish a Resident, whose powers increased steadily over the next two decades. The Company's control was officially recognized when a young and epileptic Raja signed away his authority in an agreement in 1794. His successor, Oditya Narayan Singh, proved unsuccessful in his attempts to have the agreement set aside.[8]

Although the Rajas of Banaras successfully exploited their rural holdings and Bhumihar caste connections for political aggrandizement, they faced a variety of competitors. The Nawab of Awadh possessed ostensible control over the area: while paying lip service to the Nawab as regional power, the Rajas resisted his demand for hegemony and revenue as they entrenched themselves. At the local level, moreover, Rajput clans enjoyed long-held power, particularly in the surrounding countryside. Other groups, too, especially the large number of Marathas

6. Not least among the factors contributing to the family's success was its ability to profit from the changing economic and legal circumstances affecting control of land, particularly that introduced by the British. See Bernard Cohn, "The Initial British Impact on India: A Case Study of the Benares Region," *Journal of Asian Studies* 19, no. 4 (1960): 418–31. Unlike in European ruling families, primogeniture did not necessarily figure in the selection of the next generation's claimant to the title. The first two Rajas were Mansa Ram (1730–1738) and his son, Balwant Singh (1738–1770). The longevity of Balwant Singh doubtless proved significant in consolidating the power of the family. Chait Singh succeeded to the *gaddi* (throne, or seat of authority) in 1770 but was replaced in 1781 by Mehip Narayan when Chait Singh "rebelled" against Warren Hastings's exorbitant demands for money to help fight the French. Little differentiated the claims to the throne of Chait Singh and Mehip Narayan.

7. Bayly, *Rulers, Townsmen and Bazaars,* p. 114.

8. Oditya Narayan Singh ruled from 1795 to 1835. For aspects of the dynasty's history, see Cohn, "Initial British Impact"; "A History of the Province of Benares," Part I (London: India Office, 1873); H. R. Nevill, *District Gazetteer,* vol. 26, *Benares* [hereafter *Benares Gazetteer*] (Allahabad: U.P. Government Press, 1909); Bhola Nath Singh, ed., *Benares, a Handbook,* prepared for the Seventy-eighth Session of the Indian Science Congress, 1941.

resident in the city, nurtured similar pretensions to local power. The meaning, however, of the labels "Rajput" and "Maratha"—used by all the contemporary informants—remains somewhat opaque to us. We do know that "Rajput" (meaning prince, or son of a king) referred to martial lineages who had settled in the area during the eighteenth century. The term encompassed members of a "dispersed caste category united by a claim to a common attributional rank and a common life style," not members of an endogamous caste group.[9] While these Rajputs still occupied "an important position in the district" in the nineteenth century, "their former predominance" had been destroyed "by the rise of the Benares Rajas."[10] Those known as "Marathas" probably included at least three different groups—agents and relatives of the Maratha nobility or chiefs from the Deccan, pandits knowledgeable in Sanskritic texts, and merchants with useful trading ties to the western region.[11] It is likely that Maratha aristocratic kin, if not merchants as well, had also suffered from the shifting political and economic circumstances favoring the Bhumihar dynasty and its allies.

Indeed, in the face of such competition, the political strategies of the Bhumihar dynasty depended heavily on the alliances it had forged in the Banaras region. These alliances came to be expressed primarily through a new emphasis on a devotional form of Hindu culture that simultaneously emphasized military prowess and cast the dynasty as representa-

---

9. Thomas R. Metcalf, *Land, Landlords, and the British Raj* (Berkeley and Los Angeles: University of California Press, 1979), p. 4.

10. Nevill, *Benares Gazetteer,* p. 53.

11. We do not, of course, know what the label "Maratha" refers to, beyond the point of origin of this immigrant group from the Deccan and the presumption that they spoke Marathi. The interests of the ruling Marathas in the Deccan stemmed from the strong trading and military ties maintained between the Deccan and the pilgrimage centers in north India. For instance, the military collaboration of the Maratha chiefs with the Nawabi against the Rohillas included the condition that in return for their military support the Marathas would acquire control over Mathura, Prayag (Allahabad), Banaras, and Gaya (Singh, ed., *Benares, a Handbook,* p. 27). Although Maratha desire to exercise direct political control was thwarted by the British takeover, "Marathas" remained important in Banaras, numbering almost thirty thousand by the end of the eighteenth century (Bayly, *Rulers, Townsmen and Bazaars,* p. 137). They were culturally important in the city as well: "Deccani pandits," for instance, contributed substantially to Sanskritic studies from the sixteenth century on (Singh, ed., *Benares, a Handbook,* p. 23). Their economic impact may be judged by a document prepared for the East India Company by C. W. Malet, dated August 1788, which provided an unfavorable analysis of the trade deficit with the Maratha empire (India Office Library and Records Office, V 14484, U.P. Government, *Benares Affairs, 1788–1810*). Reflecting their intellectual as well as trading interests there, Marathas financed much of the eighteenth-century Hindu reconstruction of the city, which encompassed such charitable activities as erecting dharmshalas (rest houses) for pilgrims, building temples and feasting to support Brahmin priests, and constructing palaces for themselves and their local kin and agents (see Singh, ed., *Benares, a Handbook,* p. 28).

tives of the less Mughalized culture of the eastern region. Critical to the success of this effort was an alliance with the merchant-bankers of Banaras.[12]

Reflecting the economically strategic position enjoyed by Banaras in its location on the main west-to-east trade route, the merchant-bankers of the city exercised great influence through their connections both to their far-flung urban centers of origin and to surrounding "rural men of substance." To regulate their complex trading and banking world, they had organized into a corporate pyramid, at the top of which sat the Naupatti (the Society of Nine Sharers, a collection of mercantile families), which had become "a self-perpetuating oligarchy of status which no aspiring family could enter." Below the Naupatti other merchants and bankers grouped themselves, establishing linkages based variously on organization within a particular trade, among those trading in a particular region, or among those performing a particular function in the trading structure. A corporation of interests, merchants shared as well common conceptions of status and mercantile honor. These conceptions, in turn, had important implications for patterns of patronage, particularly those relating to religious ceremonies, sacred spaces, and practitioners.[13]

Connected to the merchant corporation were the mendicant soldier-traders known as Gosains. The largest owners of urban property in Banaras in the late eighteenth century, the Gosains possessed other characteristics that ensured their great influence with the denizens of Banaras. They formed "a religio-commercial sect, militarized to some degree, and organized according to the guru-chela principle."[14] They recruited without regard to caste and thus "admitted any person of abilities among them." This combination of religion, trade, and military power proved useful for mercantile activity: since "long distance trade needed armed protection, the dividing line between trading and soldiering must have been a thin one."[15] At the same time, the sect maintained pilgrimage routes and rhythms that enabled its members to combine trade with piety, giving them a commercial edge as well. They amassed the capital needed for trade through inheritance procedures that differed

12. For examples of occasions when the bankers provided the Raja with large sums of money, see IOL & R, L/PS/10, vol. 173 for 1910, file 876: Winter to Dane, p. 2.

13. Bayly, *Rulers, Townsmen and Bazaars*, pp. 177–80.

14. D. H. A. Kolff, "Sannyasi Trader-Soldiers," *Indian Economic and Social History Review* [hereafter *IESHR*] 8 (1971): 213–18. See also Stewart Gordon's comment on this article (pp. 219–20), and Bernard Cohn, "The Role of the Gosains in the Economy of Eighteenth and Nineteenth Century Upper India," *IESHR* 1, no. 4 (1964): 175–82.

15. Gordon, "Comment," p. 219.

from Hindu familial ones in permitting them to pass on a larger share of the inheritance to one chela.[16] To these advantages they added their religious position in Banaras, which linked them to a considerable body of *sadhus* (holy men) in the city.[17] Indeed, they constituted "a body of brokers between different social groups. They attracted veneration from the mass of the people and also had a close hand in the running of the merchant communities."[18]

The populace constituting this "mass of people" included a variety of groups responsible for its main industries or production activities. Preeminent among these were artisans, religious specialists, and scholars. Most of the literature on Banaras emphasizes the latter two groups,[19] but artisans constituted the most numerous. Especially important among their wares were silk products, brassware, and wooden toys. Of these producers, we may judge the weavers, virtually all Muslims, to be the most important—in part because of their number (more than a quarter of the population), and in part because of the collective role they played in the life of the city.[20] Whether artisans, religious specialists, or scholars, these inhabitants all occupied positions both dependent on, and interacting with, the powerholders of the city. The collective activities of the urban center suggest how this interdependence operated.

Political Relationships in Public Arenas

Collective ceremony—processions, festivals, and the like—was the genre of public activity in which collective experience was the most regular, sustained, and repetitive. As such, it tended to set the patterns, and often the symbolic rhetoric or vocabulary, for all public activities. Banaras's various communities doubtless participated in myriad activities limited to one or another more narrowly defined group. But a number of revealing references to collectively observed ceremonies

16. Cohn, "Role of the Gosains," pp. 175–82.

17. The magistrate in the early nineteenth century counted the Gosains as one-fourth of the city's inhabitants; to reach this figure he must have included all those who appeared to be mendicants. See IOL & R, Board's Collections, F/4/365, no. 9093 for 1812–1813 [hereafter "Board's Collections no. 9093"], p. 298.

18. Bayly, *Rulers, Townsmen and Bazaars*, pp. 181–84.

19. For scholars and priestly groups, see Singh, ed., *Benares, a Handbook,* and Diana Eck, *Banaras: City of Light* (Princeton: Princeton University Press, 1982). Jonathan Parry's work on the death specialists of Banaras adds another dimension entirely to the literature; see, for instance, "Death and Cosmogony in Kashi," *Contributions to Indian Sociology,* n.s., 15, no. 1–2 (1981): 337–65.

20. See especially Nita Kumar, "Popular Culture in Urban India," Ph.D. diss., University of Chicago, 1984; also Nevill, *Benares Gazetteer,* for references to the impact of weaver activity, and essays in Freitag, ed., *Culture and Power in Banaras.*

emerge from the sources for the early nineteenth century. Although these sources are fragmentary, they suggest a world in which the referents, ostensibly religious (e.g., Hindu idols and enactments of events from Hindu sacred epics), nevertheless attracted participation by most of the population, including that 25 percent composed of Muslim artisans. For instance, a source noted in 1809 that annual observance of "the marriage of the Laut" (a sacred pillar located on the periphery of the city) had involved participation "for some years" by "the lower classes of Hindus and Muhammedans," who "have divided the offerings between them." Other references note frequent Muslim participation "in offerings presented to the idols" located in a space shared by a mosque and a temple.[21]

One of the more important ceremonies observed citywide, the *Bhārat Milāp*, had begun as a neighborhood-based reenactment. This staging of the reunion of *Rām* with his brother *Bhārat* brought together lower-class participants and celebrants with their upper-caste patrons and audience. The effigies were carried in by Ahirs (or Yadevs, as they now call themselves),[22] while wealthier citizens of the city jockeyed for places on the surrounding balconies and rooftops to view the procession.[23] Like most citywide observances in north India, this celebration built on other kinds of unities. Members of an athletic *akhāṛā*, for instance, would march as one of the constituent groups in the "armies" that paraded with *Rām* and *Bhārat*, as would members of a particular neighborhood or dependents of a wealthy patron.[24]

21. Board's Collections no. 9093, pp. 168, 262A. The extent of common participation by Hindus and Muslims was suggested by Acting Magistrate Bird in 1809 when he noted that "the religious ceremonies of the Muhammedans and Hindus are so inseparably blended" that any attempt to "disunite them" would constitute a "new arrangement" (p. 269A).

22. The Ahirs were a populous ("cowherding") caste of laborers who had migrated to the city from the surrounding Bhojpuri countryside.

23. For more detailed discussion of this celebration, see N. Kumar, "Popular Culture," and Sandria B. Freitag, "State and Community: Symbolic Popular Protest in Banaras's Public Arenas," in Freitag, ed., *Culture and Power in Banaras.* Kumar also provides an insightful analysis of the general history of ceremonial activities in the city of Banaras, with very useful details of many ceremonials, particularly for the period beginning in the 1930s.

24. Neighborhoods in nineteenth-century Banaras were organized on two patterns. Particularly in the heart of the city, they tended to include a number of retainers around the *hawelī*s (great houses) of wealthy merchants; the more far-flung neighborhoods, which looked and functioned almost like villages, sheltered lower-class or caste groups of the same or related occupations. Cf. Bayly, "Indian Merchants in a 'Traditional' Setting: Banaras, 1780–1830," in C. Dewey and A. G. Hopkins, eds., *Imperial Impact: Studies in the Economic History of Africa and India,* (London: University of London, 1978), and Kumar, "Popular Culture."

Such collective ceremonials shared certain key characteristics. Usually relating to a corpus of Hindu Great Tradition "religious" themes and figures, they referred simultaneously to sites and urban markers (such as architecture) of specific local and subcontinent-wide significance. The act of sharing these sites for collective activities led participants to perceive them as public places available to all. These collective activities incorporated a wide range of local groups who often participated as units and whose corporate identities partially dissolved during the observance. Liminal experience provided a model for emulation, as well as an example, of a common neighborhood or civic identification—an identification that proved more important than the competing, more specialized identities that had originally brought participants to the event. Moreover, while patronage and participation in such ceremonies, by their form, often underscored hierarchical values, the experience nevertheless also illustrated common values that united the urban population across caste and class lines.

A final example suggests the extent to which even ceremonials drawing on a Great Tradition apparently significant only to a minority of the population fit into this larger pattern. The ceremony of Muharram took place over the first ten days of the month of Muharram. Set aside as the period of mourning in memory of the Prophet's grandson, Husain, and his followers, the observance commemorated their massacre in a battle over the line of succession. Despite this reference to events important only to Shi'as, Muharram functioned in early nineteenth-century Banaras as a ceremonial expression of "Islam" in which many members of the city nevertheless participated. This collective claim to Islamic identity was exercised by a group, where 90 percent of the Muslim participants were Sunni, not Shi'i, and very substantial numbers were Hindu.[25] The observance possessed several significant characteristics even beyond its broad-based crowds.[26] Like the style of observance in other

25. As late as 1895 the local vernacular press could comment, "Mohurram passed off without disturbance. . . . When it is Hindus who mostly celebrate this festival, what fear can there be?" (*Bharat Jiwan*, July 8, 1895, p. 1, quoted in Kumar, "Popular Culture," p. 316).

26. Evidence is relatively scanty about the details of the observance in the early nineteenth century. Crowd behavior in the 1809 riot suggests that the experiences of Muharram provided certain shared references of symbolic behavior, and the observance had proved sufficiently prominent in the early nineteenth century to serve as subject of a tourist's illustration (see the illustration of an early nineteenth-century procession on the book jacket of Juan Cole, *Roots of North Indian Shi'ism in Iran and Iraq: Religion and State in Awadh, 1722–1859* (Berkeley and Los Angeles: University of California Press, 1988). Reckoning from oral history, Nita Kumar has characterized the Muharram observances as among the oldest of the Banarsi ceremonials observed today and has dated them as extending back some two centuries (Kumar, "Popular Culture," pp. 309–17).

areas where the crowd preponderantly featured non-Shi'i participants,[27] the ceremonial emphasis in the Banarsi Muharram focused on its processional elements, as shoulder-born replicas of Husain's tomb (tazias) were paraded throughout the neighborhoods of the city. Popular participation encompassed a range of behaviors—from those "who chant, cheer, lament and physically torture themselves to express their grief," to those organized specifically to sing or provide stylized sword and stick fighting[28]—and thus enabled Hindus and Muslims disinterested in the original martyr motif to participate fully. Significantly, these "Muslim" ceremonies were organized at a very localized level and were characterized by competition among neighborhoods (*muḥallas*) and patrons. In all these characteristics they closely resembled ostensibly "Hindu" observances of the city's shared ceremonial life. Thus, while the frame of reference for particular observances might be that of either the Hindu or the Islamic Great Tradition, this distinction did not significantly affect the style of activities and popular values characteristic of all collective ceremonials in Banaras.

Into this ceremonial world of Banaras the Bhumihar dynasty introduced its own enactment of *Rāmlīlā* (the play, or sport, of *Rām*)—an observance that in the elaborated version popular by the early nineteenth century came to dominate the city's collective ceremonies.[29] Based on Tulsidas's version of the *Rāmāyan*, the *Rāmcharitmānās* (or *Mānās*), this celebration recounted the high points in *Rām*'s history as dispossessed king who must reclaim his kidnapped wife Sita and his kingdom. Though *Rāmlīlā* performances were ubiquitous throughout north India, the Banarsi royal version that evolved during the eighteenth century is particularly revealing as a locally contextualized and changing symbolic activity.[30] Based in the Raja's capital of Ramnagar (located

27. See chapter 8 on variances between the style of observance among Sunnis and Shi'as in Lucknow, especially the alterations occasioned in these observances during periods of change. See also the discussion of Muharram in Bombay city in Jim Masselos, "Change and Custom in the Format of the Bombay Mohurram in the Nineteenth and Twentieth Centuries," *South Asia*, n.s., 5, no. 2 (1982): 47–67, and in Sandria B. Freitag, "The Roots of Muslim Separatism in South Asia: Personal Practice and Public Structures in Kanpur and Bombay," in Edmund Burke III and Ira Lapidus, eds., *Islam, Politics, and Social Movements* (Berkeley and Los Angeles: University of California Press, 1988), pp. 115–45.

28. Kumar, "Popular Culture," pp. 310–11.

29. For detailed discussions of the Ramnagar *Rāmlīlā*, see Richard Schechner and Linda Hess, "The Ramlila of Ramnagar," *The Drama Review* 21, no. 3 (1977); Anuradha Kapur, "Actors, Pilgrims, Kings and Gods: the Ramlila at Ramnagar," *Contributions to Indian Sociology*, n.s., 19, no. 1 (1985): 57–74; and Freitag, ed., *Culture and Power in Banaras*.

30. It is not known precisely when the Ramnagar *Rāmlīlā* began; as noted by Kapur,

across the Ganges from the city of Banaras, and the next largest urban center in the Bhojpuri region), the observance became elaborated in very distinctive ways. From the usual ten-day celebration it was lengthened to a thirty-one-day festivity. The main locales of the story—for example, Ayodhya and Sri Lanka—came to be symbolized through permanent architectural installations erected throughout Ramnagar: a replication of the world, encompassed within the kingdom of the Raja. Many of the residents of Banaras came to have virtually year-round tasks associated with the staging of the *Rāmlīlā*, from artisans crafting goods needed to embellish the presentations, to actors and vyas (narrators) who studied their parts for many months. A key element of the observance (and a significant portion of the expense) involved the feasting of *sadhu*s who came to Banaras for the month. This charity reflected not only South Asian piety (particularly appropriate for rulers) but also the political alliance made between the dynasty and mendicants. Perhaps most significant, the actual staging of the event was altered to provide a role for the Raja that was symbolically, as well as physically, equal to that assigned to *Rām*. The two figures simultaneously portrayed god-kings (*Rām* was an incarnation of Vishnu; the Raja ruled Banaras, the earthly residence of the god Shiva). They often anchored the scenes by their placement, on platforms, at opposite ends of the field. The very rhythm of the staging was set by the entrances and exits of the Raja, particularly when he departed in the middle of the evening's observance to perform his puja, and no action took place until he returned. Indeed, the final day's ceremony pointed up the complex position of the Raja, when the *swarup*s (boy actors personating the gods) visited the court at Ramnagar, where they received from the Raja both adulation and symbolic payment for their performances.[31]

By the early nineteenth century the Ramnagar *Rāmlīlā* had become the preeminent collective ceremony observed by Banarsis. Its staging helped set a calendrical rhythm to the year; its locales reproduced the significant geographic places from the whole of the subcontinent in its environs; its appeal attracted thousands to the paired cities (some events boasted one hundred thousand spectators), particularly those represen-

---

descriptions in James Prinsep's *Benaras Illustrated in a Series of Drawings* (1833) suggest it was fully developed by that time (Kapur, "Actors, Pilgrims," p. 59).

31. This certainly provides an illuminating example for Clifford Geertz's argument about "the inherent sacredness of sovereign power." But by tying together through physical juxtaposition the actual acts of the Raja and the representations of the act of *Rām*, it goes beyond the meaning considered by Geertz. See Clifford Geertz, *Local Knowledge* (New York: Basic Books, 1983), chapter 6.

tatives of ritual power, the *sadhu*s and mendicants.[32] Most important, its processions and rituals enacted statements of political and cultural power, for they reinforced the collective attitude toward the Raja: "The Maharaja, in the words of informants, *is* the people and the kingdom, and his exchange with Rama is symbolic of that of the necessarily anonymous masses [who] throng to the spot."[33] These collective observances expressed, as well, the cultural values supported by the ruling alliance of the city.[34]

For our purposes, the role of these ceremonials as symbolic expressions of political power and cultural values provides crucial historical evidence. As Richard Schechner and Linda Hess have observed, the "key attributes" of the Ramnagar *Rāmlīlā* emphasized the "relationship between government, Maharaja, and ordinary people." In the world represented by the Ramnagar theater, "the Maharaja [was] as much a mythic figure as Rama." Throughout the *Rāmlīlā*, his actions and attire reflected his mythic kingly role as "upholder of religion, repository of tradition and authority," patron of the arts and learning. At the same time he had a second mythic role, that of representative of Shiva, the lord of ancient Kashi. As the story unfolds over the thirty-one days, "the boundaries between Rama's world and the Maharaja's world" dissolved.[35] Presentation of the dynasty in this light, as of *Rāmlīlā* patronage itself, was quite deliberate, coinciding with its emergence from under the control of the Nawab of Awadh to be a virtually independent line of rulers. As Philip Lutgendorf has noted:

> The Banaras rulers' growing involvement, in the latter part of the eighteenth century, with the Rām tradition . . . reflected among other things their need to cultivate an explicitly Hindu symbol of royal legitimacy, and thus to achieve ideological as well as political independence from the Nawabs . . . they turned not to the figure of Krishna (whose legend had, during preceding centuries of Muslim ascendancy, come to be almost exclusively focused upon a pastoral and erotic myth), but to that of Rām,

32. Kapur notes recent statistics suggesting that an average of twenty thousand now watch every day; on especially popular days there may be between forty thousand and one hundred thousand spectators (Kapur, "Actors, Pilgrims," p. 61, citing the 1965 Banaras *District Gazetteer*, p. 506). Norvin Hein suggests similar figures for the 1940s in his book *The Miracle Plays of Mathura* (Delhi: Oxford University Press, 1972).

33. Kumar, "Popular Culture," p. 266.

34. For detailed discussions of each of these groups, see the Introduction to Freitag, ed., *Culture and Power in Banaras*.

35. Schechner and Hess, "The Ramlila of Ramnagar," pp. 65, 77.

whose myth had retained a strong martial/imperial and socio-political dimension, expressed most clearly in the vision of Rām-rāj or the golden age of Rām's universal rule, and in the hero's role as exemplar of *maryādā*, a term that implied both personal dignity and social propriety.[36]

Other, internally significant political ends also were served by this elaboration of a popular observance—ends that reinforced the relations with the lower classes of Banaras, frequently Muslim, through the focus on the Raja as ruler of all. The emphasis in Tulsidas's version of the *Rāmāyan* on devotion over orthodoxy, on shared brotherhood over community and caste divisions, enabled the dynasty to use this event to express the integrative nature of the kingdom, encompassing even Muslim weavers. Indeed, as participants in Banaras's dominant Hindu culture—processionists representing an influential patron, or makers of ceremonial decorations, costumes, and pilgrims' souvenirs—members of the lower classes became integrated through the world of Banarsi public arenas, regardless of their other forms of identity.

Beyond this symbolic integration, however, the dynasty quite deliberately pursued other political ends. That is, choosing *Rāmlīlā* as the event to patronize proved significant in asserting the Hindu values that bound together those possessing power in Banaras—the Bhumihar dynasty, the Gosains and other priests and mendicants, and the merchant-bankers. *Rām* "fulfills his destiny . . . as the bearer of Hindu culture."[37] At the same time, by using a martial Hindu symbolic rhetoric, the dynasty robbed the competing Rajputs and Marathas of exclusive ownership of a political language they would otherwise have claimed as their own.

Values and Worldviews in Public Arenas

A brief examination of other performance genres that emerged in this period suggests that such Hindu values, supported by merchants, mendicants, and the Raja, represented the dominant culture of this urban area. Recent research on two very different forms of entertainment—*kathā*, or exegesis, of Tulsidas's *Mānas*, and street theater performances—provides insights into the values and worldviews of their audi-

---

36. Philip Lutgendorf, "Rām's Story in Shiva's City: Public Arenas and Private Patronage," in Freitag, ed., *Culture and Power in Banaras*, p. 41.

37. Schechner and Hess, "The Ramlila of Ramnagar," p. 54.

ences.[38] Indeed, these forms show that the urban culture expressed through collective activities in public spaces encompassed overlapping (though not identical) values, worldviews, venues, and occasions for both literate elite and lower-class patrons.

Taking our two examples to bracket the continuum of performance genres, we may see *kathā* as illustrative of activities patronized by merchant and other Banarsi elite groups, and street theater and recitations as representative of lower-class entertainment. Comparison of the two is thus instructive. *Kathā* enjoyed strong patronage and encouragement from the Ramnagar-based dynasty, beginning with Oditya Narayan Singh's reign in 1796 and extending through his successor's reign for much of the nineteenth century.[39] In that period, *kathā* performances occurred throughout the year in virtually every neighborhood. Vyas (exegetes) provided learned commentary on the *Mānas*, a text familiar and beloved in most Banarsi households. They performed usually in the late afternoon (although, under merchant patronage, performances came to be pushed back into the evening, after the shops had closed). Thus they provided accessible entertainment perceived as familiar and local. They might take as their text a particular passage, or a particular word used throughout the text. In this period, they usually recited as supporting evidence only the *Mānas* itself (although this, too, changed under what Lutgendorf has characterized as a "Sanskritizing" tendency to cite more orthodox sources). This style of presentation reinforced other ritualized and even informal uses of the *Mānas;* it was a text familiar to all, even the most illiterate family. Performers tended to be from the upper castes (increasingly, in recent years, to be Brahmins). Extended, locally based relationships were established between patron, vyas, and audience, for performers could be asked to continue the series of the afternoon discussions until they had completed the entire epic, an undertaking likely to last two years or more. They performed in shared and accessible quasi-public spaces, such as temple courtyards, ghats, or the verandas of well-to-do patrons.

---

38. Research cited in following notes. That we can draw these conclusions relates to the fact that the performance genres are by definition active, not passive, exercises. Audiences participated in a variety of ways: they rhythmically completed favorite lines started by the *kathā* exegete or interrupted to applaud a particularly skillful example of commentary; as consumers, they shaped both style and message of svang theatrical productions and judged the "competition" between the stagings mounted by the *akhāṛa*s of different performers.

39. For a full analysis of *kathā*, see Lutgendorf, "Ram's Story," and his "The Life of a Text: Tulsidas' *Rāmčaritmānās* in Performance," Ph.D. diss., University of Chicago, 1987.

By contrast, early nineteenth-century street performances seem to have included both ascetic storytellers, whose oral recitations concentrated on stories of "saintly personages," and performers of svang (an early form of street theater that came to be known late in the century as nautanki).[40] These performers were organized in traveling troupes structured as *akhāṛā*s, a form of voluntary organization quite familiar to Banarsis, given their passion for physical fitness gymnasiums. Voluntarily recruited, *akhāṛā*s nevertheless expressed connections between members in fictive kinship or familial terms and used variations of the guru-chela relationship to connect teachers-leaders to members-followers.[41] They performed in open public spaces, such as fairgrounds, crossroads, and bazaars. The actors were often of low or untouchable status, while the musicians were Muslims. In contrast to the increasing concern of *kathā* sponsors to appear legitimate through the inclusion of references to orthodoxy, street performances virtually depended for their popularity on their ambiance of moral "looseness." As Hansen argues, the perception of street performance as "low" or "lewd" stemmed not so much from its texts, which pointed to a maintenance of the status quo in "a highly moral universe, where good deeds and truthfulness are rewarded," but from its presentation "in the common tongue, in an open, exhibitionistic theatrical milieu."[42] Yet after the audience had enjoyed these reversals for the duration of the performance, the "fundamental orientation" of this street theater concluded with conservative messages, "reinforcing traditional attitudes toward social class, women, and the law."[43]

Thus, despite the tangible differences in style, the underlying values of these two performance genres reinforced each other.[44] Through vernacular presentations both emphasized two kinds of values simultaneously. On the one hand, they conveyed an egalitarian, devotional, and martial tradition that provided a space for every aspiring participant

---

40. For a discussion of svang, see Kathryn Hansen, *"Sultana the Dacoit and Harishchandra:* Two Popular Dramas of the Nautanki Tradition of North India," *Modern Asian Studies* 17, no. 2 (1983): 313–31, and "The Birth of Hindi Drama," in Freitag, ed., *Culture and Power in Banaras.*

41. For a further discussion of the importance of *akhāṛā* organization for popular culture activities, see Introduction to Freitag, ed., *Culture and Power in Banaras.*

42. Hansen, "The Birth of Hindi Drama," p. 74.

43. Hansen, *"Sultana the Dacoit,"* p. 331. This is consistent with findings for European popular culture as well.

44. Not least among their similarities was the absence of women as audience and actors in both genres, at least until recently.

member of the audience. On the other hand, much of the message conveyed by the *Mānas* as well as by street plays reinforced a hierarchical status quo that denigrated the powerless—particularly women and untouchables—and revered Brahmins and mendicants.[45] Most important, these values were reconciled in Banaras through a court culture that focused on the figure of the Raja, a ruler who expressed, through his patronage and participation in activities of popular culture, the cultural and political integration of the realm.[46]

Much of the debate by analysts of so-called popular culture turns on the degree to which such culture demarcated the lower classes from the elite. In Banaras, while the materials of popular culture provided the potential for the lower classes to separate out and invert the values and ordering of the elite world, this potential proved more inherent than real in the early nineteenth century. Indeed, through a kind of ripple effect, even the ostensibly orthodox and elite activities indirectly patronized efforts more popular in appeal: folk music performers were incorporated into merchant-supported annual renewal ceremonies for temples (*shringārs*); street theater preceded or followed *Rāmlīlā* enactments; the originator of the folk music genre *birahā* even performed at *kathā* events. These shared messages and venues, then, communicated cultural values and worldviews that overlapped, if they did not coincide.

Perhaps the most important similarity, however, related to the process, rather than the substance, activating the different performance genres. This was a process in which competition played a central role in the structuring and presentation of performances. What we may call a "conflict mode" ordered the way the performers perceived themselves, as one *akhāṛā* pitted itself against another for a performance. Indeed, such competition animated the performers and shaped the rhetoric by which they appealed to the gods for assistance as they did artistic "battle."[47]

45. For a fuller discussion of these complex messages, see Linda Hess, "The Poet and the People," revised version of paper presented at the University of Washington, Winter 1986.

46. For a similar discussion for Hindu polities in the South, see Burton Stein, "Mahanavami: Medieval and Modern Kingly Ritual in South India," in his *All the King's Mana: Papers on Medieval South Indian History* (Madras: New Era, 1984), and chapter 8 of Pamela Price, "Resources and Rule in Zamindari South India, 1802–1903: Sivagangai and Ramnad as Kingdoms Under the Raj," Ph.D. diss., University of Wisconsin, 1979.

47. See Hansen, "The Birth of Hindi Drama," and Scott Marcus, "The Rise of a Folk Music Genre: *Birahā*," in Freitag, ed., *Culture and Power in Banaras,* to illustrate this point.

Most significant, competition functioned to bring the audience, as participants, into the confrontation—both to pronounce the "winners" among competing *akhāṛā*s and to express symbolically their positions in the competition through the very act of attendance. Thus, popular support of these cultural activities—popular patronage, as it were—became a conscious, public act performed in a competitive context to further one's own, chosen group against an "Other." The implications of audience participation for public arena activities are obvious. Popular participation both extended the mode of conflict and conveyed the sense to each individual that she or he made a public statement when participating in this competitive situation. Competition could provide the basic motivating force underlying these public performances because all players—including the patrons and the audience—shared a basic understanding of the rules of competition. At the same time, therefore, elite patronage also engaged a conflict mode: those organizing and supporting processionists and floats competed against each other to acquire additional status.

Public arena activity thus provided a structure through which other kinds of social and political competitions could be expressed. The symbolic behavior of this arena made it ideal for such purposes. When we speak of the integrative nature of the dominant Hindu culture, then, we do not mean to suggest that it precluded conflict or competition in Banaras. Rather, such competition—for instance, that among the communities of Bhumihars, Rajputs, and Marathas for leadership of Banarsi society—was contained within the framework of acceptable behavior because it was expressed through public arena activity.

For several reasons public arenas proved especially important as the venues for both competition and consensus during periods of change. First, the symbolic actions staged there served as ways to renegotiate power relationships and their social expressions; as a result, public arenas possessed the potential for expressing the conflict between upper- and lower-caste or -class culture or between competing elites who sought to have status both conferred and confirmed through their patronage of public arena activities. Second, because public arenas expressed symbolically the worldviews of their inhabitants, they also conveyed a legitimacy deemed important to participants. Finally, the fact that public arenas offered the occasion and place for expressing the legitimate order and simultaneously provided opportunities for channeling competition and conflict made them the logical avenue for protest when the social and political order appeared violated.[48] Such occasions arose most dramatically in Banaras between 1809 and 1811.

Community, the State, and Collective Violence

Through the experiences of two very different sets of conflicts—one between groups of Banarsis in 1809, the other between the residents of Banaras and the British Raj in 1810–1811—a style and symbolic rhetoric of protest emerged in Banaras that would influence public conflict there for more than a century.[49] Although we cannot treat either of these riots in close detail,[50] they illuminate important alterations in the relationship between the state and its constitutent communities in Banaras.

These alterations focused particularly on two interrelated aspects of rule—the maintenance of public order, and the urban forms of financing the structures of order. As Bayly has noted, the functioning of the kotwal (head of police) and the qadi (law officer) was essential to the well-being of an urban central place. The kotwal, in particular, functioned as a hinge figure in the political order. Responsible to the Mughal Emperor for maintaining order and providing important information on

48. In this emphasis I disagree fundamentally with Bipan Chandra, who argues that communal riots "are not the main form or content of communalism." He goes on to note that "the communal riot was sudden and spasmodic, was an aspect of social pathology, and its causation lay either in the prevalence of a communal atmosphere generated by communal politics and communal ideology or in conjunctural causes, involving religious feelings alone or combined with some particular local interests, which could be effectively handled by efficient administrative or police action and secular public opinion. It is communalism as politics and ideology which can be and perhaps should be the subject of analysis as also of ideological-political struggle" (Bipan Chandra, *Communalism in Modern India* [New Delhi: Vikas (Vani Educational Books), 1984], p. 5). By focusing on public arena activity, I would argue, we can see quite clearly that it is impossible to separate politics from ideology *or* violent crowd behavior.

49. Several overlapping sources have been used for these riots, particularly for the House Tax Protest of 1810–1811. At the India Office, a large and detailed file, F/4/323, Board's Collections no. 7407 [hereafter Board's Collections no. 7407], is composed of petitions by the participants, as well as dispatches prepared by Acting Magistrate Bird on the spot. These items can be supplemented with observations by the acting third judge, J. D. Erskine, and the collector, W. O. Salmon, from various sources as noted. Excerpts from all of these observers' documents have been included both in Dharampal, *Civil Disobedience and Indian Tradition* (Varanasi: Sarva Seva Santgh Prakashan, 1971)— which, unfortunately, does not contain the texts of any of the petitions—and in an excellent article by Richard Heitler, "The Varanasi House Tax Hartal of 1810–11," *IESHR* 10, no. 3 (1972): 239–57. Where possible I have cited the latter two sources, since they will be most accessible to readers.

50. For more complete discussion of the political and social structures in Banaras, as well as full analytical descriptions of each of these riots, see Freitag, ed., *Culture and Power in Banaras*.

the urban development of Banaras,[51] he also had to command the confidence of all communities resident in the city in order to prevail on them to pledge " 'reciprocal assistance and [bind] them to a common participation of weal and woe.' "[52] Evidence suggests, however, that in Banaras by the turn of the nineteenth century the preexisting relationship between kotwal (as representative of the state) and communities had begun to erode.

Perhaps the first indicators emerged in 1803, when the British instructed the kotwal to become involved in the administration of the phatakbandi tax. This tax was levied by *muḥalla* leaders and expended by them on watchmen (chaukidars) who patrolled locally. Based in the neighborhoods, the system operated, in theory, without reference to the city administration. When, however, in 1803 the British magistrate discovered that some *muḥalla*s had failed to provide chaukidars, he assessed the value of the dwellings himself and instructed the kotwal to collect the tax he had determined. The measure was "stoutly resisted."[53] In the developments of the riot of 1809, too, we see evidence that the kotwal had lost the confidence of Banarsis. His inability to effect compromise and consensus was viewed by all (including himself) as a measure of the erosion of his power and position.

Like the kotwal, the Raja of Banaras had suffered significant losses. Beyond the rebuffs the East India Company dealt to his efforts to reclaim his dynasty's independent authority, he had also lost face in negotiations over changes in rural revenue-collecting structures. An 1810 document, for instance, notes that "in the late Tahsildari arrangements . . . the Rajah has been expressively disappointed and chagrined and . . . fancied himself degraded in dignity."[54] Given that much of the family's power stemmed from its rural position as one of the largest landowners of the area, this diminution in the degree of freedom the family enjoyed to act as intermediary revenue collectors represented a a substantial loss of face. As we shall see, it was so perceived by the Raja's competitors, the leaders of the Rajput and Maratha communities of Banaras.

51. For instance, the kotwal maintained census records; see Ishwar Prakash Gupta, *Urban Glimpses of Mughal India: Agra, the Imperial Capital, 16th and 17th Centuries* (Delhi: Discovery Publishing House, 1986), p. 28.
52. Bayly, *Rulers, Townsmen and Bazaars*, p. 308.
53. Nevill, *Benares Gazetteer*, p. 166.
54. IOL, Bengal Revenue Proceedings, P/55, vol. 37 (Proceedings for 11 January 1811). The reference is to British changes in the rules governing revenue collection at the tahsil level (i.e., that intermediary level between the district and pargana levels).

Superficially, the riot of 1809 has little to do with the structures of the state or the related erosion of power and influence of kotwal and Raja. It has always been identified as a religious riot. Certainly it was a clash over sacred space, and groups identified as "Hindu" were arrayed against groups identified as "Muslim."[55] However, by analyzing this 1809 riot together with the one that followed fourteen months later, we see that they emerged from the same set of changing circumstances. The symbolic behavior reveals different relationships, attitudes, and, consequently, behavior patterns by the various groups within the putative "Hindu" and "Muslim" communities of Banaras. Even more important, the behavior conveys other messages that reveal a social fabric undergoing great stress; the riots, then, can be seen as ritual behavior intended to renegotiate power relationships among these groups in their urban setting.

The site of the original dispute was a neutral area between the pillar known as the Lat Bhairava and a neighboring *imāmbārā*.[56] The neutrality of the area is underscored by the fact that weavers insisted in their 1809 petition that the idols set up on this ground were removed by the Brahmin in charge "when the Muslims met together for the purpose of prayer. . . . If there happened to be any which could not be conveniently taken away, they were carefully concealed with grass."[57] While this version of events probably exaggerates the transitoriness of Hindu claims to the ground, it does explain the strong reaction of the weavers to the act of devotion that, in their view, completely changed the nature

---

55. Indeed, this identification of the conflict as a "religious" one, although accepted by participants and observers—both at the time of the riot and in retrospect—also has been perceived as unprecedented. As a petition submitted at the time put it, this was "a disturbance of a more alarming nature than has ever been witnessed in this country. . . . For three days this city was filled with rapine, fire and murder" (IOR, Board's Collections no. 9093, p. 220). The petition was submitted by the qadi and *mufti* (the law officers of the Nizamat Adawlut, who resided in Banaras), requesting that they be permitted to withdraw from ruling on the government's case against the riot's "ringleaders."

56. The Lat, or staff, of Bhairava ("popularly known as the police chief of sacred Kashi") is located at the northern end of Banaras. The pillar, removed from a Hindu temple complex when Aurangzeb destroyed it, was left intact, but had once been much taller (Eck, *Banaras: City of Light*, p. 196). An *imāmbārā* is a building used particularly to store the tazias, or floats, paraded during Muharram. For the interesting historiography of the place of origin of this riot, see the conclusion to this chapter. The description presented here is based on documents prepared by Acting Magistrate Bird and others on the spot at the time of the riot and uses petitions presented to the government by residents of Banaras. Virtually every version of events written thereafter is inaccurate.

57. Board's Collections no. 9093, p. 169.

of the area. For into this shared space came a worshiper of Hanuman, who in fulfillment of a vow attempted to replace the statue's sheltering mud structure (perceived by Muslims as more "temporary" in nature) with one made of stone.

Apparently viewing the citywide celebration of *Bhārat Milāp* on 20 October 1809, as too significant a collective exercise to disrupt, the Muslim weavers postponed their protests until after the conclusion of that ceremony. Then they gathered to violently remove the stone structure and inflict damage on nearby sacred objects.[58] In this way they denied both the pilgrim's claim of sacredness for the spot and the new permanence of Hanuman's shelter. Word of the attack brought indignant Rajputs to the site, along with the kotwal and the British Acting Magistrate. No overt violence occurred in their presence. Once they had departed, however, the Rajputs damaged the *imāmbārā*. In response, the weavers drew both on their training in sword and stick performances (acquired at physical fitness *akhāṛa*s) and on the symbolic acts they performed during Muharram: "Collecting in considerable numbers armed with swords and clubs, [they] hoisted a standard and, exclaiming Imam Hossein and beating their breasts, marched towards the city."[59] Continuing their symbolic action, they marched to the temple of Vishveshvar (often transliterated Bisheshwar), which stood next to a mosque Aurangzeb had erected on the site of an older temple; the contiguous architectural sites were both known as Jnana Vapi (often transliterated Gyanbafi). Those left behind invoked religious symbols as well: after pulling down the pillar and breaking it into pieces, they "slaughtered a [sacred] cow at the foot of the Laut and sprinkled [the broken column] with the blood of the animal."[60] The language used in this exchange of protest and counterprotest strongly evoked such religious symbols as sacred space and concepts of pollution and purity. The public statements of religious community solidarity were tied to actions and places of historical significance, reinterpreted in this new context.

Beyond these initial actions and spontaneous responses, however, the complexity of the behavior of the participants reflects the urban political economy as much as it refers to overtly religious causes. Rajputs, slowly

58. This action, too, suggests that the position of kotwal and qadi had been eroded. Prior to Bhārat Milāp the weavers had indicated their willingness to submit the grievance to these two officers; after the observance, however, they took action directly, instead.

59. Board's Collections no. 9093, p. 45.

60. Ibid., p. 47.

gathering force, invoked symbols appropriate to their military culture and their relatively remote rural landlord base.[61] Late the next morning they gathered together again and returned to the *imāmbārā*. After destroying it completely and murdering the caretaker's family, they countered the blood purity and desecration symbolism of the slaughtered cow by killing a hog (an unclean animal in Muslim eyes) near the principal tomb. From the *imāmbārā* they moved on to destroy the Dargah of Fatima and then turned to the weavers' quarters. Their destruction of domestic spaces and their mutilation of Muslim bodies make it clear that the Rajputs, dependent on rural landholdings for their wealth, did not need good relations with the Muslim lower classes of the city.

Other "Hindus" reacted differently. Among the mendicants, the "brahmins and superior orders" gathered at the ghats and fasted. Another crowd, this one composed of Gosains, concentrated their attention on Muslim sacred spaces (rather than on their domestic quarters, as the Rajputs had done) and began pulling down the Jnana Vapi mosque.[62] "The whole of Benaras," the Acting Magistrate observed, "was in the most dreadful uproar and confusion. The temples were shut, and multitudes of armed Hindus were assembled in every quarter, directing their rage chiefly against the lives and properties of the Joolahers [*Julāhās*, i.e., weavers] and the Butchers"; indeed, "the whole quarter of the Joolahers was a scene of plunder and violence."[63] In this way the Gosains laid claim to the leadership role that had become theirs in the city during the previous century. By enlarging the Hindu sacred space of Jnana Vapi at the expense of one of Aurangzeb's mosques, they proclaimed the centrality to the cityscape of their own peculiar com-

---

61. Their petition describes it thus: "We, the Hindus, being informed of what had happened went all night from house to house vociferating, exclaiming and beating our breasts til it was day. (It was a mourning, which for us was like to the last day.)" (Board's Collections no. 9093, p. 155). Marginal notations at the India Office indicate that the last, parenthetical sentence was included only in the Persian (i.e., the official-language) version of the petition, not in either the Sanskrit or vernacular versions.

62. Information on the composition of the crowd is not as clear as it might be. Although this tidy division between Rajputs and Gosains is described by eyewitnesses, the petitions that followed imply that each crowd was composed of a mixture of "Hindus." The petitioners may have had different reasons for clouding the identities of the crowds this way—the "Hindu" petition because it would suggest that "Hindus" were united, the "Muslim" one because it would suggest that all Hindus attacked them. In any case, regardless of the precise composition of the crowd, the eyewitness accounts may be trusted to have accurately delineated the leadership and the majority of the body of each group in their caste identifications.

63. Board's Collections no. 9093, pp. 48–51.

bined roles of mendicant, soldier, and trader. At the same time, however—since this mosque was, in fact, very seldom used by any Muslims of Banaras—they did not imperil the lives or livelihood of this substantial sector of the urban population.

In contrast to these violent acts, the very lack of action by the Raja also seems significant. The Raja disarmed his men voluntarily and removed them from the city during the violent period. He remained aloof, withdrawn from the violence, an exemplar of the appropriate behavior expected of an integrative ruler. In the aftermath of the riot, he worked to restore peace, working with the British administrators, on the one hand, and with the leadership of various *muhalla*s, on the other.[64] In this way he reiterated his regal presence and function in the face of substantial social unrest—an ironic statement, given the threats to the dynasty's position presented by the English East India Company.

For it was the political changes introduced by the British, indicators of the Bhumihar dynasty's loss of power, that lay at the heart of the conflict. Against these, both Marathas and Rajputs used the riot to claim, through symbolic behavior, new power and leadership roles.[65] Such claims necessarily imperiled the relationships already established in the city—the influence and control exercised by the triumvirate of the dynasty, the Gosains, and the merchant-bankers, as well as the interdependence of the weavers and merchants that was expressed culturally through the figure of the Raja. In this context, the important identifiers of community, as expressed in the public arena, were not "Hindu" and "Muslim," but Maratha, Rajput, Gosain, and Julāhā. The real locus of the conflict, that is, was *within* the putative community of "Hindu," where the behaviors of Marathas, Rajputs, Gosains, and even Bhumihars were all designed to claim exclusive status for each group as "defender" of Hinduism.

The riot of 1809 represented, then, a first phase in a process by which Banarsi symbolic structures expressed, even as they enabled adjustments to, momentous political change. Fundamental community identities—

64. This active role may also suggest that the increasing dominance of the Bhumihar dynasty in the late eighteenth century had begun the process, soon taken over by the British, of undermining the role of the kotwal in the city.

65. In the course of this riot, the leader of the Marathas appeared anxious, on the one hand, to fill the role of Hindu avenger, and at key moments led his supporters in aggressive acts. On the other hand, he had pretensions to the style of exemplary leadership practiced by the Raja and intermittently tried to intervene with Banarsi crowds at the behest of the British. This behavior contributed much to the exasperation of the Acting Magistrate, who saw his actions as vacillating.

based on caste, occupation, place of origin of immigrants to the city, even mother tongue—became channels for mobilizing competition for cultural dominance in the urban environment. Religious symbols were used in this conflict because these drew on the vocabulary of public arenas, the realm in which status had come to be defined. This vocabulary also invoked the values and worldviews presented as legitimate in the performance genres occupying many of these same public spaces. It seems clear that as the state changed the rules governing expression of such dominance, Banaras's constituent communities began exploring new ways of relating to each other. In 1809 those explorations took place within a symbolic framework signposted by religious vocabulary.

The result of the 1809 riot, however, in fact reiterated the existing power structure, in which the triumvirate symbolized by the Raja maintained its dominance. The relationship *among* the communities of Banaras had been renegotiated, and the triumviate and its Hindu merchant-style cultural expression retained control. Yet given the ongoing changes being introduced by the East India Company, the riot could not clarify the relationship *between* these communities and the state.

In the second phase, therefore, the locus of conflict shifted, and so did the symbolic rhetoric. As opposed to the 1809 riot, in which Indians had attacked Indians, the collective action of 1810–1811 pitted Banarsis against the British Raj. From a dispute over a sacred site, the action shifted to protests against imposition of a new form of taxation. Underlying these differences in locale and rhetoric remained the context of uneasy power relationships and changes in the structures of urban rule.

Not least among the causes of unrest were the actions taken by the British Raj in the wake of the 1809 riot. These actions first affected the policing arrangements for the city. Significant further erosion of the kotwal's position is described in some detail in the documentation of the 1809 riots. The Acting Magistrate noted that the kotwal was able to do very little over the three days of violence.[66] The refusal of rioters to recognize his authority in the following days contributed much to the level of violence; the kotwal acknowledged this diminution in his popular support by requesting that he be allowed to retire.

British schemes to alter both the composition and the organization of the urban police force followed on this discussion of the kotwal's

---

66. Indeed, in their petition Hindu leaders began their list of grievances by noting that the kotwal (a Muslim) had released someone apprehended for slaughtering a cow. Since the grievance in fact bore no relation to the conflict, it must be taken as a symbolic statement of their sense that the kotwal was not protecting their most dearly held values (Board's Collections no. 9093, p. 74).

retirement. The reorganization plans included hiring more "Hindus" to counterbalance the overwhelming number of "Muslim" police—this number being responsible, the Acting Magistrate felt, for the fact that the police did not prevent the initial damage to Hindu sacred architecture. He went on to propose the creation of a new supervisorial layer of police (thanadars), attached to particular areas of the city, which would take over much of the responsibility previously held only by the kotwal.[67]

The changing relationship between the state and its constituent communities was affected most significantly by the administration's decision that certain persons be "brought to trial not for the outrages each had committed against the other, but one common offence against the peace . . . as an offence against the State." The government chose to prosecute only a few of the rioters, arguing that these men could represent their entire communities. The persons selected as appropriate for trial were chosen because "from acts and circumstances which have come to light, [these were the people who] appear to have instigated and encouraged, purely upon religious principle, the disgraceful excesses which were committed, or who were themselves personally concerned in the commission of some overt act of violence and outrage."[68] Such a trial, of persons possessing "considerable respectability," was recognized even by the British as an unprecedented act by the state. It excited throughout the city "a lively interest" (as the Acting Magistrate understated it).[69]

The Role of the State in Public Arenas

With these trials and the changes affecting police reorganization, the administration introduced measures to ensure closer control over collective gatherings,[70] and in December of 1810 it attempted to introduce a

67. Board's Collections no. 9093, p. 267. The original proposal from Bird called for abolition of the position of kotwal completely and assumption of many of his responsibilities by the Magistrate himself. The Board of Revenue decided instead to retain the position but to reassign much of its responsibility as noted.

68. Board's Collections no. 9093, pp. 272–77.

69. To qadi and *mufti,* law officers of the court in which the trials would be conducted, this aberration of practice proved truly alarming. In the normal course they would have been expected to issue a *fatwa* (decision interpreting the law) on the cases. But in this case it would be particularly awkward for them to do so, as they were residents of Banaras too. "These disturbances have been so general that our interference must raise thousands of enemies against us, and as our families reside in the city, we may justly apprehend both their and our total destruction."

70. This control operated more in public awareness than in actuality, for the Magistrate was instructed to exercise broad tolerance in permitting collective gatherings.

new house tax that would provide greater revenues to fund the expanded control apparatus.[71] Taken together, these interventions represented an unprecedented level of interference by government in the processes of neighborhood or local self-rule. In particular, the alterations in the ways in which urban revenues were raised and decisions were made about their expenditure implied significant change in the relationship of communities to the state.

That Banarsis perceived these implications is made clear by their behavior in the House Tax Protest of 1810–1811. Their reaction pitted the neighborhoods and occupational groupings of the city against the administrative officers of the emerging British Raj in a conflict that lasted for several months. Both sides in the protest recognized and agreed on the issues under dispute. These included control over the collection and dispersal of resources; the objects and persons appropriately subject to taxation; and, ultimately, the legitimacy of the protest itself. Significantly, structures of community organization provided critical means of mobilization: while "all ranks and description of Banarsis joined in the protest,"[72] the initial petitions were submitted by each neighborhood or *muḥalla*.[73] Occupations as well as neighborhoods provided organizational networks, as the administration recognized when it tried to negotiate with occupational *chaudharī*s (headmen). The form of protest followed a time-honored merchant pattern described as "sitting dharna," in which one attempts to turn public opinion against an opponent by sitting openly in protest until the opponent acquiesces to one's demands.

The values expressed by these localized communities also related to assumptions about the appropriate behavior expected of the state and communities in an urban environment. The protestors, for instance, pointed out that they were already paying other taxes such as stamp, transit, and town duties, over which the administration had direct control. In addition, the cost and responsibility for policing the neighborhoods was addressed by the existant phatakbandi form of taxation. The contrast between the proposed house tax and the phatakbandi clearly illuminates the issues. The phatakbandi operation had been organized locally within each *muḥalla*. The substantial sums, collected by the inhabitants themselves, then were used to pay chaukidars, who

---

71. Regulation 15 of 1810 called for a levy of 5 percent on the "annual rent" of all dwellings and 10 percent on that of all shops.

72. Acting Magistrate R. M. Bird, quoted in Dharampal, *Civil Disobedience*, p. 6.

73. Board's Collections no. 7407, p. 94; Heitler, "The Varanasi House Tax," p. 241.

were also chosen and supervised by the inhabitants. By contrast, the British proposed collecting the taxes on each dwelling for the city treasury; British officials would then decide what sums to expend in support of the revised police force. Thus the new taxation arrangements would have represented a very substantial infringement on neighborhood self-rule.

Similarly, the protestors objected to the notion of a tax on dwellings. Their arguments put the case clearly, aiming not at the rate of the tax but at the very legitimacy of the form of demand. Their petition noted that

> in the Shera and Shaster, together with the customs of Hindostan . . . houses are reckoned one of the principal necessaries of life, and are not accounted disposable property. . . . In this country, in the times of Mohamedan and Hindoo princes, houses were never rendered liable to contributions for the service of the state.[74]

They objected, as well, to the notion that representatives of government should go into their houses to determine the value to be taxed: while it is likely that their resistance expressed concerns about pollution and the seclusion of women, it also clearly implied their rejection of the right of the state to have intimate knowledge of their personal circumstances. Finally, as the petitions make clear, Banarsis viewed this new taxation as an intrusion into their customary charitable practices. The city was filled, they noted, with widows, Brahmins, and other poor who were housed in structures that could not be maintained if taxes had to be paid on them as well. Threats to this practice undermined basic tenets on which, the petitioners presumed, Banaras had been established: "In this holy city the rajas of ancient times from a principle of virtue and in the hopes of everlasting fame built houses and fixed salaries and settled perpetual donations for the subsistence and residence of brahmins, paupers and mendicants, there are hundreds of such houses appropriated to brahmins."[75]

Perhaps most significant, however, was the very form assumed by the protest. Taking oaths to shut down the bazaars and withdraw their services until "the outcry and distress" in the city induced the Magistrate to accede, more than twenty thousand inhabitants "sat dharna" in

---

74. Quoted in Heitler, "The Varanasi House Tax," p. 253.
75. Board's Collections no. 7407, pp. 106–13.

an open field in the city. Thus symbolic behavior in this protest reenacted what the participants viewed as ideal urban rule, in which every community had its place in the tent city assembled on the edge of the town. Within this collectively constituted and occupied space, each community had responsibility for organizing itself. Caste panchayats not only maintained order, they also "coerced" those whose support wavered for this "panch" form of protest.[76]

> Vast multitudes came forth in a state of perfect organization:
> each caste trade and profession occupied a distinct spot of
> ground, and was regulated in all its acts by the orders of its own
> punchayat, who invariably punished all instances of misconduct
> or disobedience on the part of any of its members. This state of
> things continued for more than a month; and whilst the authority
> of the British Government was, in a manner, suspended, the
> influence of the punchayat was sufficient to maintain the greatest
> order and tranquility.

> Several thousands of people continue day and night collected at
> a particular spot in the vicinity of the city where, divided accord-
> ing to their respective classes, they inflict penalties upon those
> who hesitate to join in the combination.[77]

Civic constructions of community, in this context, encompassed divisions of caste and occupation, as demonstrated by the ability of the protestors to bring to the field representatives of most families in Banaras and its rural environs:

> The Lohars, the Mistrees, the Jolahirs [*Jūlāhas*], the Hujams, the
> Durzees, the Kahars, the Bearers, every class of workmen en-
> gaged unanimously in this conspiracy, and it was carried to such
> an extent that during the 26th, the dead bodies were actually cast
> neglected into the Ganges, because the proper people could not
> be prevailed upon to administer the customary rites. These sev-
> eral classes of people [have been] attended by [a] multitude of
> others of all ranks and descriptions.[78]

76. Contrary to the impression conveyed by Heitler's article, these tactics are never characterized in the petitions as hartals (strikes). Rather, the terms used are "panch" and "sitting dharna."

77. The first observation is that of J. D. Erskine, Acting Third Judge of the Court of Appeal and Circuit for the Division of Banaras, in *Selections of Papers from the Records of the East India House,* . . . 2:89, quoted in Heitler, "The Varanasi House Tax," p. 246; the second is from Bird, quoted in Dharampal, *Civil Disobedience,* p. 8.

78. Bird, quoted in Dharampal, *Civil Disobedience,* p. 6.

Money was raised to support family members whose wage earners had withdrawn to the field: "The individuals of every class, contributed each in proportion to his means, to enable them to persevere, and considerable sums were thus raised."[79]

The legitimacy of the protest, then, stemmed in part from the fact that it had widespread support from virtually all levels of society, and in part from the fact that it was ordered by mechanisms reflecting local community organization. Even when the government decided to exempt religious buildings and lower-class dwellings from the house tax, the protest remained general. Indeed, the protestors proved willing to do more. When, after more than a month's protest in the field, they learned that the government refused to rescind the new tax, they vowed to march in a body all the way to Calcutta, stopping en route in each of the British-controlled cities "subject in common with ourselves to the grievance" of the house tax.[80] Administrators focused on the protestors' inability to carry out this threat. We may see it as a symbolic statement of alliances with the various communities in other urban centers against the state.

Furthermore, both rhetoric and action deliberately posed an indigenous system of community self-rule as legitimate against state perceptions of appropriate behavior. In their final petition to government, the protestors insisted they had not created a "disturbance," as the Magistrate charged, but had registered a complaint in a legitimate manner. They noted that

> the manner and custom in this country from time immemorial is this: that, whenever any act affecting every one generally is committed by the Government, the poor, the aged, the infirm, the women, all forsake their families and their homes, expose themselves to the inclemency of the seasons and to other kinds of inconveniences, and make known their affliction and distress.[81]

Another petition continued this sense of legitimate grievance. With "style and contents" characterized as "disrespectful" by the judges of

79. Letter from Collector W. O. Salmon, quoted in Dharampal, *Civil Disobedience,* p. 15. Landlord connections can be inferred from the extensive holdings possessed by Banarsi bankers; see descriptions in Nevill, *Benares Gazetteer,* pp. 117 et seq. Connections in the opposite direction (i.e., from moneylenders located in the countryside who helped contribute to the trading activities centered in Banaras) are discussed in Bayly, *Rulers, Townsmen and Bazaars,* pp. 103–6. For further references to fundraising, see Bird, quoted in Dharampal, *Civil Disobedience,* p. 13.

80. Bird, quoted in Dharampal, *Civil Disobedience,* p. 30.

81. Quoted in Heitler, "The Varanasi House Tax," p. 250.

the Provincial Court to which it was addressed, this petition baldly declared the "deadly evil" that the tax represented. Indeed, it went on, "if our bad fortune be such, that you are induced to wish our leaving this for other countries, we trust that you will be pleased to order what we have expended in buildings to be paid to us out of your treasury."[82]

This reluctant willingness to completely abandon the city suggests the depth of this profound clash between local community conceptions of how they should govern themselves and the new claims made by an intrusive state. The changes introduced in Banaras by the British administration over the preceding three decades had called into question the existing roles and influence of indigenous powerholders such as the Raja, the qadi, and the kotwal. But even more significant in impact was the changing role the state decreed for itself. The system of urban governance that had emerged from the eighteenth-century transition from Mughal to Successor State rule, while requiring the ruler to play only an indirect role in community self-rule, did call for his direct presence in public arena activities. The British desired a system that reversed both these points.

To understand the implications of this clash, we should look in some detail at the points on which communities and the new state disagreed. The petition of "Hindus" in 1809 described how they had canvassed from house to house, "vociferating, exclaiming and beating our breasts til it was day," at which time they all met in a large outdoor gathering. In contrast, such public discussions were characterized by the exasperated Acting Magistrate as the "abuse of that privilege which the Natives have been permitted to enjoy, of assembling among themselves to deliberate on questions of common interest." Further, in condemning the Rajput leader, he added that "it is clear from the whole tenor of his conduct that he considered this a dispute in which the public authority had no business to interfere. That as the injury had been offered to the Hindus at large it was for them alone to determine the measure of their revenge and unite in the common resolution of inflicting it."[83] Moreover, as the house tax conflict of the following year demonstrated, the ability and inclination of Banarsi communities to gather and decide collectively on courses of action directly threatened British perceptions of state authority. The Banarsi view, stated in the petition of 1809, was that "immemorial" time and custom validated their right to "make known their affliction and distress" to the government.

82. Board's Collections no. 7407, p. 203.
83. Board's Collections no. 9093, pp. 261, 295.

Equally important, Banarsis insisted that the state express its relationship to their respective communities in public venues and through appropriately symbolic behavior. During 1809, for instance, Acting Magistrate Bird proved willing to work unceasingly behind the scenes, where he repeatedly relied on personal, face-to-face relationships with the leaders of each community. But he disliked having to act publicly, having to place his own person physically in public arena spaces for symbolic purposes. Yet this was what Banarsis insisted on. His perception of the audacity of one demand in 1809 is apparent when he notes that "on the morning of the 24th the [leaders who became] prisoners assembled with the whole body of goshains and seating themselves upon the ghats remained there in spite of all remonstrance until . . . *I was compelled to go in person* to remove them; for this conduct they . . . collected not like the brahmins on the 23rd for religious principles, but for the purpose of obtaining concessions."[84] Again in 1810–1811, the protestors underscored their insistence that the representative of the state interact with them in public arenas. After persisting in their tent city for some weeks, they agreed that "they were willing to disperse, providing [the Acting Magistrate] *came to them in person* [in the field where they were residing] to request it."[85] The Acting Magistrate flatly refused.

Instead, the emerging British Raj chose another strategy—one that preserved its aloof authority in the face of the communities of Banaras but that, perhaps unintentionally, also satisfied the cultural expectations of these communities. Into this public arena the Raja of Banaras was sent as intermediary for the state:

> [He] proceeded with all the distinctions of his rank to the place where the people were collected, the mob soon listened to his exhortations, and returned to their homes, and the Rajah, selecting from among them, fifty of the persons principally concerned in the disturbance, brought them to [the Acting Magistrate] to acknowledge their offences; while the Rajah himself interceded in their behalf and solicited [the Acting Magistrate] to endeavour to procure both for themselves and for the subject of their complaint, the indulgence of the Government.[86]

---

84. Ibid., p. 304, emphasis added. Bird's perception was seconded in London, where the India Office copy has been underlined, with indignant marginal notes.

85. Bird, quoted in Dharampal, *Civil Disobedience*, p. 30; emphasis added.

86. Bird, quoted in Dharampal, *Civil Disobedience*, pp. 32–33.

The role of the Raja in this process thus served a critically important function. While his power was doubtless bounded by the British government, his behavior matched public expectations for a traditional ruler. Indeed, the figure of the Raja proved essential in focusing and expressing the continued cultural integration of Banaras. On the one hand, he could represent symbolically the culture shared by upper and lower classes, by Hindus and Muslims, and by Gosain, merchant, and Rajput alike. On the other hand, he provided the only symbol of authority on which both Banarsis and British could agree—the only figure who could operate both in public arenas, expressing the reformulated system of self-rule emerging in Banaras, and as an intermediary judged legitimate by the British administration.[87]

Conclusion

The literature on the Banaras riots of 1809 and 1810 provides a dramatic example of the ways in which administrative and scholarly assumptions about communalism have colored our understanding of north Indian history. Despite the fact that the scale of collective involvement proved much greater in the House Tax Protest of 1810, histories of Banaras inevitably emphasize the religious riot of 1809, not the civic protest. (See, for example, both the classic, if obviously intemperate, treatment of Banaras by M. A. Sherring, published in 1868, and the next most popular history, produced by E. B. Havell in 1905.)[88] Moreover, the prejudices of popular histories combined with administrative presumptions to provide a legacy almost inescapable for modern scholars. The early twentieth-century *Gazetteer* for Banaras, for instance, asserts:

---

87. We might note that his symbolic role as intermediary between state and community continued even after he convinced the residents to abandon their tent city. Once the crowds had dispersed and business and services had resumed, the Raja returned to the Magistrate. On this visit he again acted on behalf of Banarsi residents, bearing their petition to the Governor General in Council. Moreover, these representations by the Raja continued to be buttressed by expressions of ongoing public discontent; indeed, householders greeted the assessors with such "sullen silence" that the government could never actually collect the tax. While the administration delayed facing the inevitable, in part to save face and in part to await the decision of the India Office in London, eventually they acceded to public pressure. The tax was abandoned late in 1811; not until 1860 did the British dare to institute a house tax in Banaras.

88. M. A. Sherring, *Benares, Past and Present* (Delhi: B. R. Publishing Corporation, 1868; Delhi: Oxford University Press, 1975); E. B. Havell, *Benares, the Sacred City* (London: Blackie & Son, 1905). Havell, in turn, cites the Reverend William Buyers, *Recollections of Northern India* (London: John Snow, 1848). Buyers's version is appallingly inaccurate, with misplaced actions and invented cause-and-effect relationships.

The history of Benares during the first part of the nineteenth century is mainly a record of administrative development under British rule. . . . The only disturbance of the public peace occurred in 1809 *and the following year,* when the city experienced one of those convulsions which had frequently occurred in the past owing to the religious antagonism of the Hindu and Musalman sections of the population.[89]

This official interpretation of the 1809 riot (and, by implication, its warping of the events of 1810 to turn them into an extension of that riot) has been replicated, in turn, in a recent scholarly treatment regarded as the definitive picture of Banaras.[90]

These treatments of the 1809 riot as religiously motivated are perpetuated through use of a religious symbolism that is as astonishingly inaccurate as it is revealing. E. B. Havell, quoting William Buyers, explained in 1905 that the riot resulted from the clash of Muharram and Holi processions in the streets.[91] The 1909 *District Gazetteer* (and all subsequent discussions) emphasized the attacks on sacred space but identified this space as the mosque located at Jnana Vapi, the structure known (not coincidentally, for these symbolic purposes) as "Aurangzeb's mosque." Each account then goes on to note sagely the legacy that Aurangzeb's bigotry has fostered in this Hindu pilgrimage site. The assumption underlying this use of sacred space symbolism as spurious documentation of the riot is that "Hindus" and "Muslims" formed immutable communities in Banaras. We know, however, that less than fourteen months later these same communities had combined to present an integrated civic protest against new intrusions by the state. We know, further, that the original site was not Aurangzeb's mosque at all, but the Lat pillar located at the northern edge of the town (see map 3). The conflict itself expressed not so much timeless hostility between immutable communities of Hindus and Muslims as the readjustment of power relationships in an urban site undergoing significant political change.

If the constructed identities of "Hindu" and "Muslim" communities were not immutable, why was a religious idiom utilized by the participants? We have seen that public arena activities were permeated by such

89. Nevill, *Benares Gazetteer,* p. 207. Emphasis added.
90. See Eck, *Banaras: City of Light,* p. 196.
91. Holi is a spring festival of renewal; Havell characterizes it in this explanation as a "somewhat licentious celebration very popular with the lower classes of Hindus," and he goes on to describe both processions as "inflamed with religious excitement, *bhang* (a beverage laced with cannabis), and alcohol" (*Benares, the Sacred City,* p. 205).

an idiom, which often conveyed a shared civic identity as well. Given the nature of public arenas, this religious idiom became the vocabulary in which competition was expressed and through which adjustments were made in the social and cultural fabric. This process was heightened during periods of change, particularly change initiated by alterations in the relationship between the state and its constituent communities. Such change had emerged dramatically in the early nineteenth century in Banaras, but it underlay many of the events of the next century throughout north India. Before examining that century of change in some detail, we must look at the British Raj's perceptions of its own role.

CHAPTER 2

The Colonial Context: "Natural Leaders" and the State Under the British Raj

By the late nineteenth century the Banaras experience had been replayed in some fashion in all the major urban sites of U.P. While the process was uneven, occurring at different times in varying intensity for each locale, the result proved consistent throughout the province. Not only had the British colonial state substituted itself for indigenous rulers. More, the indigenous system of community self-rule had been turned on its head. Where earlier the ruler had been required to play only an indirect role in this self-rule, the imperial state now designed a system that was much more intrusive. Through the institutions of the state, the British Raj established a structure of rule that interfered, even though it would not participate, in an extraordinary range of activities related to the public arena. Yet where earlier the ruler had fully participated in public arena activity to establish his legitimacy, the imperial state had now withdrawn. In its place it had deputed certain local powerholders to act as its intermediaries. The extent to which these deputies could operate as successfully as had the Raja of Banaras is examined in more detail in Part II. Here it will suffice to note British intentions. For if we are to understand the constraints within which public arena activity developed in the late nineteenth century, we must first examine the framework of policy and behavior established by the provincial administration.

The fact that the administration perceived its own role differently at key moments between the 1870s and the 1940s makes its contribution more complex to analyze. Nor was the imperial administration mono-

lithic in its positions: the priorities of the Government of India sometimes clashed with those of the provincial government, and local officers
did not always uniformly interpret, or agree with, provincial policy.[1]
Still, at the provincial level it is possible to trace consistently articulated
policies regarding community issues—policies that changed significantly between the 1870s and the 1940s. To highlight the nature of these
changes, we will look first at the behavior of provincial administrators
as actors in this state theater. Equally important is the changing relationship between imperial administrators and their chosen intermediaries, as reflected in British assessments and reactions to the series of
events that form the narrative of this study. This chapter therefore
analyzes briefly the British role in the major events of the period, which
are described more fully in the chapters that follow on Bareilly in the
1870s, Agra in the 1880s, the Cow Protection movement in the 1890s,
innovations in Ramlila and the Kanpur Mosque Affair of the 1910s,
agitation in the 1920s, and the Kanpur Riot of 1931.

British Intervention in Public Arena Activities

Although the imperial structure precluded their direct participation in
public arenas, British administrators nevertheless proved an important
third party in conflicts, often affecting the nature as well as the outcome
of clashes between communities. It was inevitable that the administration should play so integral a role, for official approval was required for
virtually every facet of corporate religious life—from the shape, height,
and use of a building to the format of a religious procession. In the case
of the latter, all routes had to pass government scrutiny and receive prior
approval. The timing of an observance—the day chosen, the time of day,
and the duration of the exercises—was also administratively controlled.
Much attention was paid to the size and nature of the festivities: what
kinds of music, chants, and shouts would be permitted, and where; how
many groups would be allowed to participate; what size floats might be
used; and so on.[2]

---

1. For a detailed discussion of these differences in Madras administration, see Brian
Stoddart, "The Changing Face of Colonial Administration in South India," unpublished
paper, 1978.
2. This is not to say that, under the Mughal Empire, Mughal officials did not
intervene. Although the evidence is indirect, it appears that the kotwal negotiated agreements among communities over timing and spaces used for processions. (See, for instance,
I. P. Gupta, *Urban Glimpses of Mughal India: Agra, the Imperial Capital, 16th and 17th
Centuries* [Delhi: Discovery, 1986], esp. pp. 49–50.) However, the scale of intervention
seems to have changed significantly with British rule. Moreover, in contrast with prag-

Such administrative decisions profoundly affected the relationship between groups of participants, particularly when rites overlapped. The impact was much the same whether unintentional, deliberate, or the result of competing British interpretations of "custom."[3] Even if an administrator strove to remain impartial, he often had to arrange a new compromise to accommodate escalating demands, and his very action altered the equation.[4] Sometimes the mere presence of a new administrator could prompt a petition, upsetting the equilibrium.[5] The act of issuing an order and then changing it was almost sure to prompt reactions from both disputants, for each then had been made winner and loser. In an 1893 pamphlet presenting the arguments in favor of Cow Protection, Bishan Narayan Dar protested validly that "all the religious disturbances of the last ten or twelve years appear, to my mind, to have been brought about, in no small measure by the meddlesomeness of the Anglo-Indian official in our affairs."[6]

Although officials would have denied "meddling," provincial policy certainly changed over the decades, and this change was bound to have an effect. Policy in the 1870s treated such disturbances as sectarian and without political significance to the government. By the 1890s, however, this type of unrest was perceived as a direct threat to British control and consequently was put down with great severity. From that point on, though the administration maintained that it was only a disinterested arbiter between opposing camps, religiously focused unrest began to be treated as a security issue. Intelligence was gathered about these activi-

---

matic recognition by Mughal officials of power relationships in different urban places (for instance, the ascendancy of Hindu rituals in Banaras and of Muslim ones in Bareilly), the early British policy of "evenhandedness" treated competing communities as equals, regardless of local power structures.

3. One of the primary causes of the 1893 riots was public misinterpretation of actions taken by Azamgarh's Officiating Magistrate. For instance, his order that Muslims should register plans to sacrifice made no reference to customary usage—thus implying that anyone who requested to sacrifice would receive government approval (see chap. 5). In Agra during the 1880s the Magistrate deliberately pursued a policy of prohibiting the celebration of Hindu fairs during Muharram (see chap. 4). In Mau during the 1860s and 1870s the Magistrate persisted in asserting that Muslims were at liberty to slaughter, while the judge just as frequently held that the practice had been forbidden.

4. Typical was the decision during the 1880s to move all Muslim sacrifices of kine to the slaughterhouse in Delhi, whereas earlier they had taken place in private homes. The result was an unprecedented number of kine being killed under the new arrangement (*Alam-i Taswir*, 24 Aug. 1888, *Selections from the Vernacular Newspapers for the North-Western Provinces [SVN], 1888*, pp. 562–63).

5. This was, in part, the cause of the decade-long struggle in Agra in the 1880s (see chap. 4).

6. Bishan Narayan Dar, *An Appeal to the English Public on Behalf of the Hindus of the N.W.P. & O. . . .* (Lucknow: G. P. Varma, 1893), p. 1.

ties first by the Thagi and Dacoity Department and then by its successor, the Criminal Investigation Department (CID). By the 1920s the government considered religious issues to be hopelessly confounded with nationalist agitation. The tone of distrust in administrative references thenceforward was pronounced.

Administrators' perceptions of their own roles also changed in these decades. From a policy based on preservation of the status quo—what they called "customary practices"—the British turned to an "even-handed" approach. When equal treatment proved unsuccessful, the government began denying that administrative decisions were pronouncements about "rights": these "rights," they contended, could only be affirmed or denied by the courts. Thus, by the 1920s officials had abdicated the sense of responsibility they had previously felt. A similar withdrawal of face-to-face involvement by administrators in maintaining civil peace accompanied this abdication; the most pronounced characteristic of the Kanpur Riot of 1931 proved to be the complete lack of rapport and local knowledge possessed by city officials.

As the Banaras paradigm suggested, an effort to work through Indian intermediaries, whom the British characterized as "natural leaders," provided the key to the state's attitude toward public arenas. Officials only slowly lost faith in this approach, the linchpin of administrative policy before the turn of the century. Nevertheless, though the British realized eventually that much of their understanding of Indian social organization was either faulty or outdated, they seem always to have blamed "natural leaders" when mass enthusiasm for community issues resulted in violence.

"Natural Leaders" and the Imperial Hierarchy of Control

The British Raj drew its intermediaries from several sources. Some staffed the lower echelons of the administrative structure, continuing a tradition of government service established in preceding Indian empires. Perhaps more influential were local notables. In hopes of ingratiating themselves into the existing system of community self-rule, provincial administrators extended recognition and additional signs of status to such leaders through local institutions, such as honorary magistracies. In this way, leaders regarded as "natural" also performed an important function by integrating within their official roles activities of the public arenas with those of the state structure.

The use of such intermediaries seemed to validate British conceptions of the state: the Raj would maintain face-to-face and ceremonial relationships with "natural leaders" through the institutions of the state; in turn these leaders would reinforce their connections with constituent groups of Indian society in public arenas. Since community leaders were visible in public activities, the British did not need to be. Though absent from the public arenas created and valued by their subjects, however, the imperial regime did not devalue symbolic ritual. On the contrary, it created an array of appropriate rituals of state[7]—but these related to the British, not the Indian, view of imperial hierarchy. Referring as they did to values and worldviews rooted in western European notions of rule, these state rituals in their own way denied the legitimacy (and certainly the centrality) of the rituals of public arenas.

Nevertheless, in the process of inverting the previous relationships of rule, British administrators hoped to ensure social stability through their intermediaries—for there was an official assumption that these "natural leaders" stood at the apex of hierarchical networks through which social control could be exercised. Leaders who enjoyed personal and reciprocal contacts with officials in turn were to require and reward cooperation by lesser figures in their localities. The relationship between Indian intermediaries and the British thus was conceptualized as a reciprocal one, each side receiving benefits for the cooperation it extended.

Yet the administrative view was too sanguine; connections were unlikely to be that solid or that neatly hierarchical in shape. Particularly in activities enacted in public arenas, a variety of leaders laid competing claims to legitimacy. Most important in the divergence of this reality from the administrative theory was the fact that the British, in their search for influential intermediaries, concentrated on those practicing a certain type of leadership. They looked for those exercising power through personal, patron-client relationships, whether operating through residential, occupational, caste, ritual, or extended kinship networks. Such a British construction of leadership was framed in part because administrators thought they had discerned it in local society from such experiences as those in Banaras and in part because it coincided with expectations based on their own cultural background.

---

7. See Bernard S. Cohn, "Representing Authority in Victorian India," in Eric Hobsbawm and Terence Ranger, eds., *The Invention of Tradition* (Cambridge: Cambridge University Press, 1983), pp. 165–210.

Thus the men identified as "natural leaders" were raises or magnates of high status: in U.P. the term "rais" was applied equally to prominent traditional "headmen," commercial men of the urban areas, and to rural large landowners.

One urban study has traced the influence of such raises through a series of ever-broadening concentric circles. At the center were connections based on members of the immediate family, who ran trades and services allied to the primary business interests of the magnate. In the second circle were "the patron's most intimate contacts in the maintenance of his ritual, social and political status." In the outer circle were clients generally connected through economic dependence: "tenants, debtors and bonded workers of the patron." Indeed, religious and charitable activities provided a significant measure of the impact of such men on their urban environment. In Allahabad, for instance,

> Ram Charan Das and his nephew Bisheshwar Das constructed new bathing places on the rivers Ganges and Jumna. The related Chunni Lal family built a temple and a charity house in the market. Someshwar Das, another Tandon, aided Malaviya in the foundation of a Hindu orphanage. . . . The big Agarwal families also dotted the town with temples and rest houses, patronized the Ramlila committees, and became presidents of orthodox religious bodies in the neighborhood.[8]

As with the commercial men, traditional caste and occupational headmen fulfilled leadership positions that dispensed patronage and participated in public arena activities supporting religion and charity. Many of these activities, in turn, required cooperation with British officials to be effective. In Bareilly, for instance, throughout much of the nineteenth century a particular family of Brahmins—that of Chaudhuri Bussunt Ram—possessed responsibility for staging the *Rāmlīlā* festival. With the Tibri Mahunt they shared sponsorship of the *Rāmnaumī* procession as well. And in Agra's Juljhulni festival we will see that a variety of occupational headmen (*chaudharīs*) cooperated to bring together components of the assorted *muḥalla* processions. The value of control exercised by these men can be seen, as well, in the panchayats of elders who enforced behavioral standards on at least some of the commensal groups residing in an urban site.[9]

8. C. A. Bayly, *Local Roots of Indian Politics: Allahabad, 1880–1920* (Oxford: Clarendon Press, 1975), p. 73.

9. For Bareilly and Agra, see chapters 3 and 4; for Banaras, see C. A. Bayly, "Indian Merchants in a 'Traditional' Setting: Benares, 1780–1830," in C. Dewey and

The sources provide glimpses of the ways British administrators worked through leaders and their ties to communities. The Magistrate of Pilibhit, for instance, noted in March 1871 that since "taking out the Taziahs is opposed to [the Lieutenant Governor's orders] the Police is directed to warn the public accordingly, and obtain the signatures of the *Meer mohullahs,* showing that the prohibitory order has been made known to them."[10] Thus the act of signing the orders made clear to neighborhood leaders their responsibility for publicizing and implementing government instructions.

From the Mutiny/Revolt of 1857 the British took the lesson that in the countryside the landowners had the same sort of impact and influence as the leaders in the towns. They went to some length, therefore, to cement good relations with these "natural leaders"— especially with the talukdars (largest landholders), on whom the "Oudh Policy" depended heavily.[11] This effort involved not only issuing sanads (deeds) recognizing the exclusive right of a particular list of landlords to the title of talukdar but also introducing such legislation as the Encumbered Estates and Court of Wards acts to protect talukdari holdings. As a recent study of Lucknow suggests, the British administration so appreciated the role played by these landlords that it tried to transfer their influence to the urban environment as well, turning talukdars into an urban elite by settling them in Lucknow's Kaiserbagh and encouraging them to invest in urban real estate.[12]

At least one scholar has argued that the British also pursued a cooperative policy with those they collectively termed "Muslims."[13] This categorization is somewhat misleading, however. As suggested above, there were only certain Muslims regarded by the British as "natural leaders." Those leaders, such as the mujtahids of Lucknow or

A. G. Hopkins, eds., *Imperial Impact: Studies in the Economic History of Africa and India* (London: Athlone Press for the Institute of Commonwealth Studies, 1978).

10. IOR, Judl. (Criml.) Progs. for 1871, June, index no. 15, progs. no. 37, appendix E in vol. P/92 (emphasis added).

11. The "Oudh Policy" was the name given to pro-landlord strategies. It was first enunciated by W. C. Benett in the introduction to the 1877 *Imperial Gazeteer*, and its chief spokesman was Sir Harcourt Butler, author of *Oudh Policy—The Policy of Sympathy* (1906).

12. Veena Talwar Oldenburg, "Peril, Pestilence and Perfidy: The Making of Colonial Lucknow, 1856–1877," Ph.D. diss., University of Illinois, 1979, pp. 213–14. Now published as *The Making of Colonial Lucknow, 1856–77* (Princeton: Princeton University Press, 1984).

13. F. C. R. Robinson, "Consultation and Control: the United Provinces' Government and Its Allies, 1860–1906," *Modern Asian Studies* 5, no. 4 (Oct. 1971): 313–36.

the Muslim talukdars, who could exercise their influence through channels other than purely religious ones, were most likely to be considered "natural." But the British refused to recognize significant sources of leadership in indigenous society. The exceptions, which did not fit into British formulas, all possessed an appeal, often ideological, that could transcend patron-client relationships and a functional role that awarded leadership status even to lower-caste individuals. Among Muslims, for instance, emotional or ideological ties drew them to the *sajjāda nishīn*s of the urban *dā'ira*s (tombs of Sufi pirs). Similarly, lower-class taziadars (organizers of tazia processions) could confidently announce that without governmental concessions they would prevent Bareilly's tazias from being taken out during the 1872 Muharram.[14]

The British myopia when looking for leaders of Indian society may have been prompted in part by their own cultural conditioning, but essentially it expressed an imperial philosophy of rule. Only in a society ordered and controlled through networks based on personal ties—exercised face-to-face by powerful patrons—could room be found for representatives of the paramount power as well. Indeed, British administrators generally prided themselves on their good personal relations with powerholders in the localities.[15]

The way to rule a city, then, was to set up a hierarchical pyramid, topped by interaction between government officials and "natural leaders." Consultation, inducement, and compulsion characterized this interaction. As the provincial administration officially extended signs of status, recognition, and rewards to leaders they consulted regularly, they also compelled such leaders in return to control their dependents, thus preserving civic peace and stability. Putting British personnel at the top of the pyramid would not have been possible in a society where leaders expressed their power through ideological and class appeals. No available niche could be offered to an administrator, in the Qur'anic world organized by self-sufficient ulama or in one where power and status came from the function as taziadars. Similarly, the Cow Protection movement offered its greatest perceived threat in the degree to

14. See Bayly, *Local Roots,* and Nita Kumar, "Popular Culture in Urban India: The Artisans of Banaras, c. 1884–1984," Ph.D. diss., University of Chicago, 1984, for references to *sajjāda nishīn*s; the taziadars are discussed in Statement of Elliot Colvin, Magistrate of Bareilly, 17 Apr. 1871, Judl. (Criml.) Progs. for 1871, index no. 24, prog. no. 42A.

15. See, for instance, James S. Meston's justifications in the Kanpur Mosque Affair of 1913 (discussed below) and his warm personal correspondence with prominent Muslims, IOR, European Ms. Coln., f136/15.

which it created alternatives to government structures—courts, cattle pounds, even taxation through the collection of *chuṭkī* (handful of rice). The increasing disdain of British officials for those pleaders and publicists who expressed a nationalist ideology may be attributed partly to the activists' earlier subservience to "natural leaders" and partly to their exercise of an ideological appeal.[16]

Those possessing alternate sources of legitimate authority, in fact, often worked through traditional channels of social organization; but the British refused to recognize their legitimacy when they did so. This refusal may well have stemmed from the fact that such ideological appeals constituted a currency originally exchanged in public arenas; when it came to be used in state institutions as well, it broke with conventions on which the British relied so heavily.

The British did not refuse to recognize the significance of religion but brought it into service for the imperial state only in very specialized ways. As their recruitment of Banarsi policemen in 1810 suggests, they used the labels "Hindu" and "Muslim" in their institutional structures in ways that belied the Indian reality behind the terminology, and they created by administrative fiat a set of circumstances that encouraged for state purposes the establishment of identity by religion. Administrative decentralization—prompted by the need to broaden the financial base of government—had led to early forms of self-government, particularly the Municipalities Acts of 1868 and 1883. These acts pulled into the state structures a variety of leaders whose defined constituencies and influence varied widely but whose support was essential. More subtly, the British identified and labeled these constituencies by categories familiar to their western European experience but not necessarily reflective of Indian social organization. The broad terms "Hindu" and "Muslim" denote but the most obvious of these categories. As time passed and certain groups received rewards or penalties by virtue of their supposed identities, the labels came to possess a persistent institutional reality they had lacked earlier. Police recruitment throughout the province used this principle in the 1860s to alter the number of "Muslims" in the police force; attempts to fix the percentages of "Hindus" and "Muslims" in the revenue and judicial administrations followed in the next decade.

16. For the patronage by urban raises of these newly emerging professionals, see Bayly, *Local Roots,* especially pp. 74–75. For an extended discussion of the imperial philosophy of rule and its reliance on personal patron-client networks, see David Gilmartin, *Empire and Islam,* (Berkeley and Los Angeles: University of California Press, 1988), chap. 1.

Administrative choices seriously affected these categories in other ways, too. Stipulations of educational prerequisites for administrative employment—in a society where vernacular education differed dramatically depending on the student's religious and linguistic affiliation—represented but one such choice. Another was the language and script designated by the administration for official purposes, where agitations advocating the replacement of Persian with the Devanagari script (derived from Sanskrit) filled much of the last half of the century. Such choices had an indirect impact as well, for they were prompted by a shift from what C. A. Bayly has shown to be an "administrative contract" system to a rationalized, institutionally consistent administration, one that partially replaced caste and kin connections as employment criteria with measurable skills and training.

In other words, the provincial administration, while withdrawing from activities that would symbolically express in public the connections between community and state, nevertheless attempted to invoke community identity in the state structures it created. At the same time, however, it constructed institutions that worked only when the participants acted through power relationships based on much narrower and more localized bonds. These developments led to a paradoxical situation: though the British created circumstances in which ideological appeals would gain increasing credence, their implicit philosophy of rule denied legitimacy to activists who invoked such an idiom. In the nineteenth century that paradox could be resolved simply, by keeping the activities of the public arenas very separate from institutional ones. But in the twentieth century the inherent tension between these different ways of expressing identity proved central to the kinds of conflicts that emerged. We must look first at the changing role played in these events by the British Raj itself.

"Government Now Steps In to Mediate": 1871–1890

Our outline begins with the circumstances leading to the 1871 riot in Bareilly. Preparatory to the staging of an 1870 *Rāmnaumī* procession, administrators worked variously through their chosen intermediaries. They first consulted the widow of the man whose family had traditionally led Hindu festivals in the town. Through her agent she laid down the route she wanted for *Rāmnaumī*; this proposal was submitted to "some of the most influential among the Muslims," who studied the prescribed route "inch by inch, and said it was a most excellent route and would give satisfaction to everyone."[17] On the day of the procession Honorary Magistrates, of the same religion as the processionists, assisted the police and civil administrators in keeping order. When the outburst occurred, the Magistrate expected the leading Muslims, especially the Honorary Magistrates, to report immediately to him, and he used their laxity as evidence of their complicity in the riot. Once they finally did report in, he instructed them to return to their neighborhoods and maintain order.[18] Those leading citizens, and especially Honorary Magistrates, who behaved as expected received recognition through laudatory notices in the reports of local officials and in the acknowledgments returned by the Lieutenant Governor of the province.[19] Administrators also strongly castigated those who did not live up to expectations and reminded leaders of their responsibility for the good conduct of others. They issued threats of severe penalties should order break down on the next occasion.[20]

The use of Indians as intermediaries extended to the courts. Heavy use of Indian assessors, for instance, marked the trials of the 1871 rioters. (Drawn from the ranks of landowners, bankers, and traders, the designation "assessor" had become yet another way the administration could convey or recognize status.) Administrators took care to assign one "Hindu" and one "Muslim" assessor to each of the 1871 cases.[21] Finally, the provincial government quartered an extra police force in the troubled area as a punitive measure. The level of disaffection that remained, however, is implied by the renewal of the 1871 force for a second year.[22] At least some of this disaffection in 1872 must be

17. Statement of Elliot Colvin, Judl. (Criml.) Procs. for 1871, June, index no. 24, no. 42A; Statement of Lt-Colonel Earle, Superintendent of Police, 15 Apr. 1871, Judl. Progs. for 1871, index no. 25, prog. no. 42B.

18. Report of F. O. Mayne, Judl. Progs. for 1871, index no. 43, prog. no. 60, par. 22 [henceforth Mayne Report]. There were three classes of Honorary Magistracy, of increasing responsibility, with which the British could reward loyal and "influential" citizens.

19. Mayne Report, par. 32. In fact, these "leading Muslims" left town the next year.

20. Final Reports on Mohurram Riots at Moradabad, from Commissioner, Allahabad Division to Commissioner, Rohilkhund (no. A), 5 Nov. 1872, Judl. Progs. for 1872, index no. 15, prog. no. 5, par. 14.

21. *Report* on the Administration . . . for the Year ending 31 March 1873 named 1,902 "landowners" and 1,287 "bankers or traders" as assessors for the year. On occasion the assessors split along religious lines in their recommendations, but usually they did not. Though the judge generally agreed with at least one assessor, he also made finer distinctions in the counts than did they. The judge agreed with the assessors in 1,269 out of 1,472 cases (p. 98, par. 106). Since there could be as many as three assessors who might not agree on one case, this figure is misleading—the judge need only have agreed with one of them.

22. *Report* on the Administration . . . 1873, p. 86, par. 81; and *Report* on the Administration of the Police of NWP, statement D, pp. 6C and 7C.

attributed to administrative miscalculations about the roles and effectiveness of intermediaries. Whereas administrators relied on a Hindu family that had risen to prominence in the 1830s and on "natural leaders" among Muslims, by 1871 a number of new Hindus had emerged to compete with the widow of Naubut Ram for public arena leadership. Among Muslims, too, sources of power and influence extended beyond the "natural leaders" identified by the British. Magistrate Colvin issued the strongest condemnation:

> I believe the Mohammedan population generally were under the complete influence of Nawab Kazim Ali Khan, Shaikh Badr-ood-deen, Altaf Ali Khan, and Rahmut Hossein Khan. [He also names other men in the old city and new, who were "the next most influential men."] These men, whether for good or for evil, were the men to whom people looked for giving a lead, and it is to their influence I attribute the good order which attended the taking out of all the Mohammedan processions; and if they could keep order during these processions, it is proof to my mind that their influence is so great, that without their knowledge and consent, . . . no section of the Mohammedan population, however small, could have succeeded in making and concealing the intention of the attack of the Hindu procession.[23]

But was Colvin correct? That the Muslims named indeed functioned as leaders in their community is indisputable. Members of wealthy landowning groups, they traditionally wielded great power based on their pre-British positions in the Rohilkhund administration.[24] Moreover, members of this group, as representative "Muslims," brought suit in court to enforce an 1853 agreement on *Rāmnaumī* and Muharram.[25]

Despite Colvin's angry denunciation, however, there is nothing to connect any of his "influential Muslims"—save Badr-ud-din—to the 1871 riots. Of all the statements given by these leaders, only Badr-ud-din's conveys any sense of grievance. "There never," he said, "was such a Ramnowmee as there was this year. Such crowds, such music, such rites!"[26] Although the other "leading Muslims" left town before the

23. Statement of Elliot Colvin, Judl. Progs. for 1871, June, index no. 24, prog. no. 42A.

24. E.g., the Kumbohs cited in the court petition as "maafidaris": ibid., index no. 22, prog. no. 41, appendix J.

25. Nevertheless, none of these prominent Muslims was linked as plaintiff in a related suit on the unauthorized construction of a Hindu temple in a Muslim *muḥalla*.

26. Statement of Sheikh Badr-ud-din, 11 Apr. 1872; Judl. Progs. for 1872, index no. 35, progs. no. 52. The admitted connection between him and Amir Khan, the budmash (bad character) suspected of murdering the Tibri Mahunt, implicates Badr-ud-din, as does

1872 Muharram, thus admitting that in fact they could not prevent a riot from erupting, Badr-ud-din stayed on.[27] It is significant that the other "leading Muslims" demonstrated, by their retreat, that they could not exercise control. Moreover, W. A. Forbes, Commissioner of Allahabad Division, faced evidence suggesting that influence resided elsewhere: "Of the two deputations which waited upon me, professing to be 'taziadars' of Bareilly, every member was of the very lowest class. They demanded that the Mohurram arrangements [for 1872] might be revised." When Forbes insisted that the arrangements would remain as designated, he warned the taziadars of the results to those who dared oppose them: "Upon this they professed their satisfaction. Up to that date not a single tazia had been prepared in the city or neighboring town but by the evening and on the following days they were brought and carried to the towns and villages in the hundreds. Not a single theft, or quarrel, or offence of any kind against rules or law occurred on the great day."[28]

Contrary to British expectations, then, leadership and popular influence in an Indian city could be exercised by other than prominent patrons with extensive networks of clients. Those in positions such as taziadar or *mīr muḥalla* that conveyed legitimate authority even to "the very lowest classes" exercised significant influence as well. Should persons in such positions feel aggrieved, a riot could ensue—even if the "influential citizens" did not identify with, or support, these grievances. British calculations depended solely on "natural leaders" as intermediaries in public arenas. But within these popular culture activities, leaders legitimized in other ways also exercised influence. Without recognizing this fact, British administrators imposed severe measures in 1872 to force "natural leaders" to serve as their intermediaries.

Despite this severity, however, the government did not yet attach political significance to the popular unrest. When the special officer deputed to Rohilkhand recommended in disgust that all future proces-

---

the fact that Amir Khan notified him of the murder before the riot had broken out. That the police inspector responsible for provoking the Hindu crowd galloped directly to Badr-ud-din's compound is equally suspicious. It is possible that a factional fight— between Badr-ud-din directly (or his police henchman by proxy) and opponents—incited the Muslim side of the riot (ibid., par. 8, and index no. 28, progs. no. 45).

27. Those who left town are listed in Report from Lieutenant Colonel Earle, District Superintendent of Police, Bareilly, to Personal Assistant to Inspector General of Police, NWP (no. 232), Bareilly, 27 Mar. 1872, Judl. Progs. for 1872, index no. 27, progs. no. 78, par. 8.

28. Final Report on the Mohurram Riots at Moradabad, ibid., par. 15.

sions be stopped in the troubled areas, the provincial government disagreed, insisting that

> the riots originated purely in the ancient antagonism between the two religions. To punish the city, *as if for a political offence against the British Government,* would alter the whole colour of the proceedings. *Government now steps in to mediate* between the two sects inflamed one against the other. By visiting the city with a penalty, as for a political offence, Government would interpose as the injured party, and would draw upon itself some part, at least, of the ill-will and animosity which is now spent in mutual recrimination.[29]

Thus, in the latter part of the nineteenth century the British Raj saw itself as mediator. It could assign itself such an aloof and benign position because it had refused to exercise an active role in public arena activities. Instead, it could enforce on its chosen intermediaries the obligation of maintaining public order through a hierarchy of organization in which its own decidedly selective definition of "community" operated. As mediator, however, the imperial government could still see itself in a nonadversarial relationship with the society it controlled. As the nature of public arenas changed, however, this became less and less possible.

"Compelling the People to Control Each Other": 1893–1910

Indeed, within two decades the administration's neutral and nonpolitical viewpoint had disappeared forever. Not only the scale of the Cow Protection riots of 1893 but also their presumed connection with the impressively organized and highly influential Cow Protection Societies (Ga'orakshini Sabhas) established a direct, antagonistic relationship between community activities and the state. Concerned with the threat to its authority posed by the Cow Protection riots, the administration reacted swiftly and vehemently. Directing its ire primarily at the talukdars and other large landholders, it pointed out that the riots had occurred in rural areas supposedly under their control. These concerns of the government focused on the fact that its intermediaries placed

---

29. Confidential correspondence from C. A. Elliott, Officiating Secretary to Government, NWP, to Secretary to Government of India, Home Department (no. 1779A), Naini Tal, 5 Oct. 1871, Judl. Progs. for 1872, index no. 16, progs. no. 43, par. 4 (emphasis added).

more emphasis on their roles in public arenas than on their responsibilities to the state:

> In the recent events in these Provinces, nothing has caused more concern to the Lt-Governor than the secrecy with which the combined movements of large numbers of persons for an unlawful object have been arranged and carried out. Owing to various causes, the present law which binds landholders to give information . . . has become ineffectual.
>
> There can be no doubt whatever that some large landholders and others of smaller importance who do not reside in the disturbed districts or tracts have been responsible, not perhaps for the riots, but for the unlawful machinery which has made them possible, and for the mischievous agitation which has led to them. They and their agents must of course have known what was going on, and cannot have been ignorant of the letters which were being circulated and of the unlawful assemblies which were being arranged.[30]

Providing the "unlawful machinery" that was causing such concern were the Ga'orakshini Sabhas. The danger stemmed not only from their ability to call up thousands of supporters at relatively short notice. More particularly, danger lay in their arrangements for levying support payments from members:

> *Rule no. 4* [of the Ga'orakshini Sabha in Gorakhpur District, 1890]: For the protection of the Gao Mata [Mother Cow] each household shall every day contribute from its food supply one chutki, equivalent to one paisa, per member. . . . The eating of food without setting apart the chutki shall be an offence equal to that of eating a cow's flesh [for which the offender could be outcasted].[31]

As one administrator noted, "The contribution of a chutki . . . of foodstuff per member of a household at each meal daily seems a trifle when looked at as a single heap, but when the daily heaps of a whole village are brought together and these begin accumulating for a month, the total proceeds are immense." The Cow Protection Societies presented other dangers as well. In the eyes of U.P.'s Lieutenant Governor, Sir

---

30. Confidential letter no. 105/4 of 1893 from Chief Secretary to Government, NWP & O, to Secretary to Government of India, Home Department, Naini Tal, 18 Sept. 1893, IOR, L/P&J/6, vol. 367 for 1894, file no. 298, pars. 3 and 4.

31. Note on the Cow Protection Agitation in the Gorakhpur District [by A. Hoey], L/P&J/6, vol. 365 for 1894, file no. 84, pp. 2, 4 [henceforth Note . . . Gorakhpur].

Charles Crosthwaite, an offense against the law was an offense against the state.[32] Government officials noted hints even of the "inflammable and seditious character of utterances indulged in at Cow Protection meetings."[33]

From the administration's perspective, perhaps the greatest danger emerged from the efforts of some Sabhas to form an alternate state structure. According to the imperial administration, peasants encouraged to bring their cattle to a Sabha pound would reject the government-run pound. Evidence collected for the provincial Advocate General from several Sabha-conducted "trials" loomed large in Crosthwaite's mind when he characterized the Sabha as "a very dangerous organization which threatens in some districts to become the government de facto of the country."[34] In the "court" case of "Gao Mahdrain (Cow Empress) v. Sita Ram Ahir of Haidi," for instance, the Sabha "court" found that for impounding to the government pound a cow that was then sold to a butcher, Sita Ram had first to buy back the cow and then to stand trial. "The Court was formally held in ——'s house in ——. Sita Ram pleaded guilty and was sentenced to Rs. 4.8.0 fine." When he refused to pay, the court sentenced him to twenty-four days outcasting and various religious penalties.[35]

We can discern in such actions by Cow Protection Societies echoes of the community self-rule exercised in Banaras at the beginning of the century. No doubt because of this similarity, the imperial state distinguished sharply between voluntary withdrawal of the provincial government from active participation in public arenas and the attempt by organizations originally based in public arena activities to take on functions within the state structure. Consequently, the U.P. government

---

32. Speech at Ballia Durbar. Printed in full in the appendix to Dar, *An Appeal to the English Public*, p. 8.

33. The examples given by the Special Branch of the Thagi and Dacoity Department, however, do not seem especially frightening. There was, for example, the appeal made by Ga'orakshini Sabha lecturer Sriman Swami in Nepal, where he was said to have asked for three lakhs of rupees to overthrow the British Government; and the case of "the half-witted sadhu [who] was noticed going about Amritsar telling the people that, as the English mistreat cows, he intended to kill them." The Special Branch added ponderously that "it was suspected that he was tutored by one Bawa Narain Singh, pleader, well known to be disloyal" (Strictly Confidential Note on the Agitation Against Cow Killing, by the Special Branch of the Thagi and Dacoity Department, IOR, L/P&J/6, vol. 367 for 1894, file no. 257, pp. 11, 5, 7).

34. Confidential letter no. 105/4 of 1893, IOR, L/P&J/6, vol. 367 for 1894, file no. 257, p. 4, par. 4.

35. Strictly Confidential letter to Advocate General from C. J. Lyall, Secretary to Government of India, Home Department, IOR, L/P&J/6, vol. 367 for 1894, file no. 298.

worked through several avenues to reassert its sole hold on institutional mechanisms of rule and to manipulate those through whom it achieved social control. First, the rioters had to be punished. Though the leaders could not be proved guilty, Crosthwaite hoped to punish them by charging them for the costs of the punitive police force. In a series of special durbars, he met face-to-face with such leaders and charged

> the Hindu landholders of this district with having failed in their duty. Not one of them came forward to tell the officers of Government what was going on. Not one of them, so far as I know, lifted his hand to prevent his people from joining in the riots. Not one of them has assisted the Magistrate to trace out and convict the ringleaders. Now it is my duty to warn you earnestly against the dangers. . . . I ask you earnestly to desist from promoting and supporting societies which . . . cannot fail at the present time to keep alive the flame of religious animosity. . . . The cost of the additional force . . . will fall, and fall justly, on the landowners, who as I believe, are much to blame for what has occurred. It will depend on the endeavours you make to restore unanimity and good will whether I shall be able to relieve you of this burden after a shorter or longer period.[36]

Prudent and distrustful, the government also punished the talukdars by suspending their licenses to possess arms, denying them both status and the means to resist.[37]

By investigating minutely the workings of the Sabhas, the government demonstrated that through detailed knowledge it gained further control. The British marched a company of native infantry and a troop of cavalry through the area: "This was done because European soldiers have not been seen in the district since the Mutiny."[38] Finally, to bridge the gap it had created between public arenas and state institutions, the administration set up special Conciliation Committees in Azamgarh and elsewhere. These committees performed as quasi-institutional bodies composed of equal numbers of "leading Hindu and Muslim notables." They received instructions to take up individually the cases of each town or village and to arrive at a unanimous description of the "custom" that had previously pertained. They also took on responsibility for inducing

36. Crosthwaite's speech to Azamgarh Durbar, appendix to Dar, *An Appeal to the English Public,* p. 11.
37. Notes on *An Appeal to the English Public,* by J. LaTouche, Chief Secretary to Government of NWP&O, for the Under Secretary of State for India, 24 Jan. 1894, p. 3. Included in L/P&J/6, vol. 367 for 1894, file no. 298.
38. Notes on *An Appeal,* p. 1.

local Muslims and Hindus to abide by this carefully delineated "custom."[39]

The government proved completely successful in its attacks on the Sabhas, which soon atrophied from lack of patronage. Neither the influential "natural leaders" nor activists in the pay of the government dared to support them. The last issue of the *Godharm Prakash*, the chief vernacular newspaper dedicated to Cow Protection, soberly "thanked all those who had supported it since it was started in August 1886" and remarked that "as the Cow Protection movement had received a severe check, and its advocates had been brought into difficulties, the paper which entirely depended on them for its support could not possibly survive."[40] The aims of the U.P. government thus proved unmistakable. By the combination of these various "firm and fearless actions" the administration could reestablish "the true way of administering India"—that is, "by enforcing village responsibility and *compelling the people to control each other,* or if they cannot, to inform the authorities and enable them to do it."[41]

No longer benignly remote, the state nevertheless maintained its indirect relationship with public arena activity. Despite evidence that the use of intermediaries could not vitiate the intrinsic appeal of public arenas for the populace, the government persisted in its effort to isolate and downgrade their importance. Although the state had glimpsed through the Cow Protection movement the potential of public arena ideology for presenting an alternative to the state, a combination of raw power and precisely targeted political pressure proved sufficient to sustain its mechanisms of indirect control.

"A Definite Attack upon the Traditions of Our Administration": 1913–1920

Only two decades later the British government had despaired of "compelling" Indians to "control each other." Such despair emerged first from experiences such as the agitation surrounding the partition of Bengal. But it resulted as well from an expansion of activities in public

---

39. NWP&O Government Gazette, Instructions to the Conciliation Committees in the Azamgarh District, from Chief Secretary to Commissioner, Gorakhpur Division, 31 Aug. 1893, reprinted in the *Tribune* (Lahore), 11 Oct. 1893.

40. *Report* on the Administration . . . 1895, p. 212.

41. Confidential letter no. 105/4 of 1893, p. 4 (emphasis added).

arenas—activities that had drawn new types of leaders into full-scale involvement in urban affairs. These new men presented competing claims for popular leadership, which they generally couched in an ideological vocabulary. Perhaps because the Raj exercised such tight control over access to state institutions, these new leaders often concentrated, instead, on demonstrating their prestige in public arenas through religious and charitable activities involving sacred spaces and rites. The Kanpur Mosque Affair of 1913 portrays graphically the extent of participation by these new leaders and the predicament they presented to the provincial government's policies regarding public arenas and the state.

When the siting of a new municipal road forced the relocation of a *dālān* (bathing place) for an unpretentious mosque serving lower-class *Bisātīs* (peddlers), the government received reassurances from a "number of respectable and orthodox Muhammedans" that the action would not provoke major objections.[42] Although others did protest, the administration destroyed the *dālān*. So confident was the government that it enjoyed the support of those intermediaries who mattered that the Lieutenant Governor, Sir James Meston, later lamented that "an unfortunate feature of the present" situation prevented him from "publish[ing] their names in support" of his decision. Such publication, he had to admit, would have led to them being "immediately vilified in certain organs of the press." Yet, he continued, "I have a sufficient number of trustworthy and good Muhammedans among my old personal friends to feel perfect confidence that their advice in matters of this kind may safely be followed."[43]

Nevertheless, by mid-May the protests had become more widespread, and in an important precedent the reactions received extensive support from public arena activity staged beyond the confines of Kanpur. New collective leadership was exercised, as well, through an expanded mosque committee (mutawalli) drawn from throughout Kanpur. The press exercised its own sort of agitational leadership. These experiments of collective leadership represented significant innovations

---

42. Narrative based on "Minute by the Lt. Governor [James S. Meston] on the Cawnpore Mosque and Riot," 21 Aug. 1913, IOR, L/P&J/6, vol. 1256, file 3374 for 1913, p. 11 (also located in IOR, European Ms. Coln., F136/15) [henceforth Meston, "Minute"]. The account is corroborated (except as noted) by stories in the vernacular press in 1912 and 1913; see *SVN* for those years.

43. Meston, "Minute," p. 12.

in public arena activity. But the fact that the protestors expressed their grievances through activities in public arenas led administrators to consider their actions unimportant—even illegitimate.

Instead of legitimate leaders, Meston saw a dangerous coalition arrayed against the state. Analyzing local participants, he characterized "Azad Subhani and a few fellow-fanatics" as being moved by feelings of "outraged religion": Sobhani he described as "an insignificant maulvi of the old school, a teacher in an Arabic seminary, with a gift of fiery theological exhortation."[44] He warned that these local "fanatics" had become allied to an even more dangerous type: "The troubles of Turkey have . . . brought to the front a type of young Muhammedan in India who will always be a problem to us. He has little to do, and little to live upon; a poor education and no stability of character. Excitement is everything to him, and agitation provides a congenial and frequently remunerative employment." A third and the most dangerous group joined the other two: "energetic, clever, ambitious, sometimes personally embittered men, *whose aim is to displace the natural leaders* of the Muhammedan community, and to become for a time the leaders themselves."[45] (Although some scholars have taken Meston's analysis of the dangers in this leadership at face value,[46] more complex issues underlay the Kanpur Mosque Affair. These issues are discussed at some length in chapter 6.)

In precise terms, then, Meston laid out the ways in which the Kanpur Mosque Affair trammeled the British philosophy of rule. Though he argued that his decisions had been based on "the broad administrative considerations which underlie the maintenance of law and order, and the neglect of which would mean misgovernment and chaos,"[47] Meston took the conflict much more personally. Not only was the Affair a "trial of strength between [the Young Muhammedan party] and Government," it also constituted a *"definite attack upon the traditions of our administration* and upon the good relations subsisting between the officers of Government and the great mass of the Muhammedan people."[48]

---

44. Ibid., pp. 35–36.
45. Ibid., p. 37 (emphasis added).
46. See F. C. R. Robinson, *Separatism Among Indian Muslims* (Cambridge: Cambridge University Press, 1984), p. 215.
47. In response to a deputation led by the Raja: ibid., appendix 2.
48. Ibid., pp. 39, 17 (emphasis added).

Thus, to the administration the agitators lacked legitimacy; their claims on fellow Muslims, being ideological—hence "fanatical" and outside the realm of approved, institutionalized community politics—could only be viewed as self-serving. The state perceived such men to be very different from the "natural leaders" on whom the government relied, and championship of their cause could only be explained as an unscrupulous use of ideological appeals to undermine the legitimate power of their social betters. Significantly, these ideological appeals had to be seen as a rejection of the state in favor of public arena values, a substitution of ideology for those all-important personal ties between administrators and "natural leaders." As a consequence, the government felt compelled to refuse recognition to those involved in the agitation and to deny their cause legitimacy. Meston could see no other explanation for the bewildering notoriety the government received in the Affair.

But the state had been caught unsuspecting in the changing constructions of community held by Kanpuri and other Indian Muslims.[49] As significant as the changes in leadership patterns reflected in the agitation was the locus of the agitation in north India's public arenas. And certain ironies emerged from the inflexible government interpretation of the Kanpur situation. In later years Meston—probably through the personal relationships he had established with Muslims—proved more sympathetic than many administrators to Muslim ideological concerns. Moreover, by the end of the Affair a great many "natural leaders," such as the Raja of Mahmudabad, had been pulled into the agitation. It therefore came to possess legitimacy even in the administration's own terms. This confounding of participation by "natural" and new-style leaders heralded the impotence in subsequent decades of the old administrative tactics of control through reliance on intermediaries.

In administrative mythology, the Kanpur Mosque Affair looms unduly large in retrospect. The following year, for instance, the case was cited, if re-created, by a Punjab administrator when the Government of India solicited information from the various provinces on the utility of

49. It seems clear, for instance, that although local practice had tolerated the wearing of shoes in the *dālān*, once this became common knowledge it proved an embarrassment to the Muslim community in general—and for this reason the new citywide committee of mutawallis made it their first act to try to find the culprits. Similarly, an agreement to relocate part of the mosque might be possible to arrange quietly, locally; but once the cause received some publicity, in an atmosphere already heavily laden with despair over the position of Islam, relocation became impossible.

conciliation committees. He noted that "the great danger lies in the mob throwing its leaders overboard. This is what happened in the Kanpur riot case in which a measure which had repeatedly received the approval of the representatives of the community concerned in the Municipal Committee was unexpectedly assailed at the bidding of agitators from outside."[50] This dangerous and unpredictable influence of "outsiders," such a view implied, rendered useless the old relationship between the state and intermediaries chosen to represent its subject communities.

But what alternatives presented themselves? The state turned once again to the use of conciliation committees. They had been suggested in the 1890s and would again be suggested in the 1920s. Indians or the Government of India always proffered the suggestion, however—never the local administrative officer. In part he ignored such committees because he had little faith in them, fearing that any formal arrangement would provide just another arena for conflict and might limit his space to maneuver. But more significance underlay administrative resistance than this. As the Bombay Commissioner of Police candidly observed in 1914, "an admission on the part of Government that Conciliation Boards have become necessary is really tantamount to an admission that the power of the local executive official . . . has ceased to be effective, and that the local officials no longer possess the ability or the capacity to control the forces of disorder."[51] Such an admission would have been tantamount to a capitulation of the state to the terms and values embraced in public arena activities.

As administrators saw their favorite tactics founder on the ineffectiveness of "natural leaders," they also viewed with alarm the efforts by the new leaders who emerged in public arenas to claim many of these state-sanctioned responsibilities. For instance, by the early 1920s local political figures had begun to patrol during nationalist agitations, though the government ignored their efforts.[52] Meanwhile, provincial administrators, having recognized the difficulties in working through intermediaries, advised local officials to maintain firm control whenever

50. Miles Irving (Senior Secretary to Finance Commission) to J. P. Thompson (Punjab Revenue Secretary), 9 Nov. 1914, Punjab Board of Revenue, file 441/260. My thanks to David Gilmartin for this reference.

51. Letter from S. M. Edwardes, Commissioner of Police, to Secretary to Government of Bombay, 24 Sept. 1914, IOR, General Administration Proceedings for U.P., Jan. 1916, vol. P/9931, prog. no. 11, serial no. 16.

52. In 1914 a provincewide committee appointed by Meston reconstituted itself as a conciliation committee. It foundered, at least in part, because of the lack of government support (Meston papers, European Manuscript Collection, F136/15).

religious claims had to be arbitrated by administrative fiat. Reliance thus shifted from intermediaries to detailed police surveillance through the CID. No longer willing to arbitrate, the government aimed instead at freezing current usage, labeling it time-honored "custom." As early as 1911, in a covering letter to a CID report detailing the "political" uses that infused the Hindu *Rāmlīlā* festival, the administration firmly instructed its district officers "to enforce the principle that innovations must be prevented."[53] To prevent innovation, officers compiled copious records on "customary" forms of religious celebrations. Perhaps the government had learned its lesson too late, for its instructions reminded district officers that "there is rather a tendency to confine [the record book listing 'influential' men of the area] to people of rank and position, whereas a vast amount of influence for good or evil may be wielded by men of low social status, and even of known criminal disposition."[54] Such tacit recognition of the power and influence of public arena activities, however, proved hopelessly inadequate. In the intervening years of neglect by the state, public arenas had greatly enlarged their capacity to express popular sentiments and values. These could no longer be encompassed within the structure of the state: they now constituted a virtual alternative to it. The imperial regime had paid a high price for separating the two worlds of political action.

"The So-Called Leaders Do Not Lead": 1920–1930

For several years the repression of innovation, along with other factors, prevented new collective outbursts on a significant scale. Almost a decade passed before communal riots exploded again in the mid-1920s. The riots of 1923, 1924, and 1925 had several special characteristics. This series of riots made it clear that the British could no longer rely on their intermediaries to maintain control, yet several familiar tactics continued to be used for lack of better alternatives. In 1924 in Allahabad, for instance, although the "leading men" of the town had appointed a committee of nonofficials to accompany the *Chehlum* and *Rāmlīlā* processions, most of its members left Allahabad during the *Rāmlīlā*. Indeed, it appears that at no time during the unrest did "influential men" proffer any assistance.

53. Confidential file no. 325 for 1911, IOR, Genl. Admin. Confl. Progs., July 1911, vol. P/8649, prog. no. 5, serial no. 1, p. 1.
54. Confidential file no. 351 for 1914, IOR, Genl. Admin. Confl. Progs., Jan. 1915, vol. 11.

In response to yet another query from the Government of India about conciliation committees, the Commissioner of Lucknow expressed forcefully the lesson learned in this decade of rioting: "*So-called leaders do not lead, and no decision of theirs would carry any weight with the masses.* The leaders, moreover, are split up by personal and party jealousies, e.g. amongst the Hindus both Swarajists and Liberals are bent on preventing the other from getting the credit of effecting a settlement . . . the leaders of today are the nobodies of tomorrow."[55] These conclusions were seconded by the Chief Secretary to the provincial government: "Political rivalry, always latent, is now the dominant factor. . . . Causes of dispute are capricious and local, and can only be dealt with on the spot. In modern conditions, moreover, the influence of individuals changes with kaleidoscopic rapidity."[56]

British use of intermediaries had been nullified because the locus of political activity had shifted. By the 1920s the state could no longer keep public and state structures separate or control leaders by limiting their access to approved institutional outlets. Instead, new claimants attempted to influence the state by demonstrating their effectiveness in public arenas. British strategies hopelessly foundered in the face of these changes.

Complaints that "so-called leaders do not lead," that their influence changed rapidly and thus proved unreliable, reflected the frustrations of the government. Because administrators found it increasingly difficult to build personal relationships with prominent Indians into links that successfully reached down into local society, they had changed significantly their assessments of their own role in Indian society. The psychological distance they had traveled since the 1870s is measured strikingly in this 1926 discussion of the power and duties of the executive branch:

> The Governor in Council has of late received a number of applications from one side or another asking for a pronouncement by the Executive Government of this province on the respective rights of the two great communities. These requests appear to him to be based on a misconception of the powers and duties of the executive. It is for the civil courts alone to adjudicate upon all questions of civil rights. . . . *The local and temporary*

---

55. Bombay Confl. Progs., vol. 71, progs. no. 1, serial no. 6, p. 3, par. 3 (emphasis added).

56. Ibid., pp. 4–5, pars. 5 and 6.

orders of the magistrates and police are in no sense a pronouncement upon rights; they are limited in their operation to particular occasions and particular periods; and the restrictions or regulations which in the interests of the public peace they may impose, are determined entirely by the special circumstances of such occasion or period. Orders so limited in scope, purpose and duration should not be mistaken for an attempt to adjudicate upon the question of title.[57]

State action matched its tone. After refraining from prosecutions and punitive action for two years, the government insisted in 1926 that "the point had been reached at which further leniency would be misplaced." In future it would unhesitatingly "prosecute offenders against whom evidence was available" and would impose punitive police in select localities.[58]

At the same time, the government confidentially denied its district officers the ability to pronounce on rights: "A mere protest by members of another community is not in itself sufficient ground for the passing of orders." For instance, it was not enough for "certain Muslims" to protest against a procession with music passing a mosque. "It is clearly also necessary that the district authorities should be satisfied that the protesting party feel the matter so keenly that they are likely to break the peace if the protest is ignored." Moreover, the "apprehension of a riot, which it would not be beyond the powers of the police to suppress, would not justify a Magistrate in yielding to every protest or demand, however preposterous." This new refusal to adjudicate, in turn, created a new view of "custom" and the government's role vis-à-vis "innovation." Custom and previous practice might prove relevant, but they no longer were conclusive considerations when passing orders. As for innovation, "the existing state of tension between the two communities [was] itself a new factor." In these new circumstances administrators would find it impractical "to decide the disputes of today solely with reference to past records."[59]

The provincial administration, then, had essentially despaired of its technique of maintaining a status quo to buttress its chosen intermediar-

57. Open Letter from Chief Secretary to Government, U.P., to all Commissioners of Divisions and District Magistrates, Naini Tal, 15 June 1926, Bombay Confl. Progs., vol. 71, progs. no. 1, serial no. 6 (emphasis added).
58. Ibid., pp. 3, 2.
59. Ibid., pp. 3, 4.

ies. Although the administration held itself aloof from the Indian society it precariously ruled, it remained bitter about the ineffectiveness of "natural leaders." A report to the Legislative Assembly on the Delhi riot in 1924 dryly noted that "the Honorary Magistrates did not embarrass the official authorities," and in 1925 the Magistrate of Aligarh snidely commented of the local *Rāmlīlā* committee that "for complacency in disastrous failure their attitude is hard to beat."[60] Faced with perceived complacency and lack of cooperation, the administration relied entirely on the exercise of raw power: "If there is no further opportunity for persuasion or conciliation, District Magistrates need not hesitate . . . to use Section 144, Criminal Procedure Code, freely. This section is intended to preserve the public tranquility, and if it has to be frequently used, that is because its use is forced upon the authorities."[61]

Thus, by the 1930s a number of changes in official policy had been introduced. A redefinition of "leadership" in the urban context, as well as a continued denial of legitimacy to public arena activity, underlay these changes. If government still played an important role in the development of events, it was by lack of action rather than by direct attempts to influence Indian intermediaries to adopt certain policies. Officials had come at last, though grudgingly, to recognize the effectiveness, if not the legitimacy, of the type of leader who espoused an ideology based on certain constructions of community. They tried to turn these ideological appeals to their own advantage, playing on community divisions that had become obtrusive in U.P. society. They even used Indians (in government posts or as members of opposition organizations) to make their appeals. A Muslim journalist of Kanpur, for instance, recalled that "The Collector tried to throw nets around me. He tempted me with everything including title, Honorary Magistracy, and service. A very big Hindu officer of the province . . . offered me Rs.150 p.m., besides traveling expenses, for delivering in the villages of Cawnpore district only four speeches against the Congress, every month."[62]

<hr>

60. CID Report, IOR, Genl. Admin. Confl. Progs., July 1926, prog. no. 3(a), series no. 3, p. 10, par. 12.

61. Open Letter from Chief Secretary to Government, U.P., 1926, p. 4.

62. All-India Congress Committee 68/1931, typescript of "Report of Cawnpore Riots Enquiry Committee," p. 180, cited in Gyan Pandey, *The Ascendancy of the Congress in Uttar Pradesh, 1926–34* (Delhi: Oxford University Press, 1978), p. 129.

"No Self-Respecting Man Would Like to Provoke Them": 1930–1947

British withdrawal from direct, personal relations with Indian leaders had special significance in the 1931 debacle in Kanpur. In general terms, it made imperative a different philosophy of rule. Because the power behind ideological appeals could no longer be ignored, administrators pointed to such appeals as evidence that Indians, divided into two warring camps, could not rule themselves. Not a new view of Indian society, such an interpretation now provided virtually the only rationalization for imperial rule; a British government seemed essential because neither Muslim nor Hindu would trust the other to rule.

The reinterpretation of the Kanpur Mosque Affair in this period illustrates the new rationalization. Though in 1913 the Affair had rallied Muslims against the government without any direct participation by Hindus of the city, by 1931 the District Magistrate could explain that "there was that feeling about the mosque and [nearby Teli] temple that dates from the time of Sir James Meston. The trouble was that the temple was allowed to stand, a part of the mosque was allowed to be demolished. During these [1931] riots the first thing that *of course* happened was the burning of that temple."[63] Even as late as 1927 such a view of communal relations and the significance of the Affair had not seemed a matter "of course" during another Hindu-Muslim riot: neither mosque nor temple had been injured. By 1931, however, such a view of warring camps had become essential to justifying British rule.

In this changed environment, two characteristics of British rule emerged dramatically from the evidence presented to the official Enquiry Committee. First, officials, such as the collector, demonstrated a remarkable lack of knowledge about the course of the riot that was unprecedented. In part this resulted from a strategy of establishing a headquarters near a telephone and remaining within it. His predecessors had always traveled around the city, trying to maintain a personal presence. In 1931, however, the collector repeatedly stated that he "did not know" about events and that the committee "must ask the police and military." Since the police superintendent pleaded similar ignorance, the administration clearly had no grasp of occurrences in the

63. IOR, L/P&J/7/75 for 1931, Commission of Inquiry Report on the Cawnpore Riot of 1931, Evidence, p. 11 [henceforth "Evidence"]. Testimony of District Magistrate Sale (emphasis added).

city.[64] This ignorance stands in sharp contrast, for instance, to the detailed report prepared on riots in 1893 (which even listed collectors of *chuṭkī* and their superiors in several districts). It is debatable whether these earlier administrators really understood the dynamics of the society in their charge. Nevertheless they possessed a certain confidence in their ability to understand and in the power of detailed knowledge to give them control. Such confidence had eroded completely by 1931.

Also destroyed was the personal relationship between British officials and Indian leaders. When asked incredulously if he had called "any prominent gentlemen for assistance," Collector Sales replied, "I did not ask them during the crisis time of the riot. After that people came and said 'Shall we help you,' I said, 'Do rescue work or that sort of thing. . . . ' I can only say we did not particularly think of them in the first two days of the riots." Some officials reacted in more surly and threatening ways when leaders, particularly Congress activists, requested government assistance in controlling riot actions in particular *muḥalla*s. One such leader sadly observed, *"No self-respecting man would like to provoke them."*[65] Indeed, patterns established during Civil Disobedience campaigns haunted Kanpur in 1931; they were evident in the "go slow" policy practiced by police and the adversarial relationship between administrators and Indian leaders.

Though government inactivity infuriated Indian leaders, it expressed well the altered philosophy of rule: the administration now saw itself as outside of, and remained aloof from, the communal bitterness. Collector Sale listed the reasons for the unrest at Kanpur in 1931, including the demographic balance between Hindus and Muslims, the lawlessness engendered by the Civil Disobedience campaign, and the long tradition of ill-will between the two communities.[66] For none of these causes would the state take responsibility. The relationship between imperial state and communities had atrophied completely.

Conclusion

In curious ways the position taken by administrators in 1931 can be seen as a mirror image of the posture taken in the 1870s. Then the state saw itself as outside the society of constituent communities and hence as a

64. See, for instance, "Evidence," pp. 20–40.
65. Ibid., pp. 585–86 (emphasis added).
66. Ibid., pp. 11–12.

mediator. Such a state did not perceive riots and religious violence as a threat to either the government or its philosophy of rule, because the administration did not see itself as having a vested interest in activities confined to public arenas. But in the intervening years the imperial ruler had been first pulled into public arenas, by virtue of feeling threatened when "natural leaders" did not maintain social stability as expected, and then pushed out again, as its ability to induce and coerce those in leadership positions waned. After the 1920s, when indigenous leadership often proved transitory and "kaleidoscopic," the government once again saw itself as outside north Indian society, this time not as arbiter but as armed guard.

In the absence of the state, presumed or real, the activities of public arenas had expanded dramatically. They had been refined by participants to express the sense of community experienced by urban dwellers of U.P. In Parts II and III we examine the process by which such activities, by invoking shared values and symbols, united people beyond their urban locality. Such activities came to challenge the very structure of the imperial state by presenting, in an alternative arena, a different national-level ideology—that of communalism.

Construction of Community

"Community" in the Late Nineteenth Century— Structure and Communitas

New conceptions of state-community relations, and alternative symbolic expressions of restructured urban relations: these provided the early nineteenth-century context for the development of communalism. For communalism to develop, however, new meaning had to be infused into collective action. Symbols of fellow feeling thus took on new meaning as they emerged from the constructions of community used to express the changed circumstances of north Indian urban life.

To understand this process, we must seek the basis of the collectivity. Thus, we begin Part II by examining the comparative historiography relating to the notion of "community." With the exception of Tönnies, scholars have seldom precisely defined the term.[1] Dealing with a culturally or geographically bounded entity often eased the task for the Europeanist, as studies of preindustrial village life attest.[2] In South Asia, too, studies rather easily defined "community" when the analyst began

---

1. See the discussion of Tönnies and citations for Macfarlane and others in the Introduction to Part I. Relative to the points made here, see C. J. Calhoun, "Community: Toward a Variable Conceptualization for Comparative Research," *Social History* 5, no. 1 (January 1980): 105–29.

2. See David Underdown, *Revel, Riot and Rebellion: Popular Politics and Culture in England, 1603–1660* (Oxford: Clarendon Press, 1985), and David Sabean, *Power in the Blood: Popular Culture and Village Discourse in Early Modern Germany* (Cambridge: Cambridge University Press, 1984). As noted below, however, though both authors begin with bounded communities, they do modify their definitions of "community" in significant ways.

with a specific village or a particular jati (subcaste) or adivasi (tribal) group.[3]

Although the task becomes infinitely more complex when analyzing urban areas, scholars have, often unself-consciously, carried over assumptions based on the geographically- or socially-bounded unit. For early modern England, for instance, John Bohstedt blames rapid urbanization for destroying a sense of village-based community (and, ultimately, prompting growth of a new "community" constructed by the working class) in large towns like Manchester.[4] Perhaps the most sustained effort to treat a European urban area as a community has been attempted by Charles Phythian-Adams, who characterizes his examination of the "desolation" of sixteenth-century Coventry as a "community study."[5] Carrying over the notion of village as community to the preindustrial provincial town, Phythian-Adams examines the "whole urban area," with chapters treating "formal groups" such as the household, craft fellowship, guilds, and councils, and "informal groupings" reflected through the extended family, apprenticeship, and other aspects of social stratification. What united these formal and informal units into a single whole, however, was the urban residents' "image of the city," whose "history was expressed in myth [while its] ideal of its contemporary structure [was expressed] in ritual. . . . Together [myth and ritual] served to identify and explain what made Coventry different from anywhere else." As the "mirrors of the community," Phythian-Adams argues, myth and ritual served not only to distinguish the town from its surrounding countryside but also to identify the urban area "with the

3. Adivasis, in particular, have received much scholarly attention; see the *Subaltern Studies* series (Oxford University Press), especially volumes 2, 3, and 4. For efforts to determine how these basic kinds of identities could then be expanded ideologically and politically, see such studies of caste movements as Robert Hardgrave, *The Nadars of Tamilnad* (Berkeley and Los Angeles: University of California Press, 1969); for a more recent exploration of how the definition of community (and the label) of "Maratha" was changed to convey something very different—a non-Brahmin identity—see Rosalind O'Hanlon, *Caste, Conflict and Ideology: Mahatma Jotirao Phule and Low Caste Protest in Nineteenth Century Western India* (Cambridge: Cambridge University Press, 1985).

4. John Bohstedt, *Riots and Community Politics in England and Wales, 1790–1810* (Cambridge, Mass.: Harvard University Press, 1983), especially chapters 6, 7, and 9. Bohstedt also suggests, however, without presenting much evidence, that other towns that had grown slowly over the preceding period might still possess an all-encompassing sense of community.

5. Charles Phythian-Adams, *Desolation of a City: Coventry and the Urban Crisis of the Late Middle Ages* (Cambridge: Cambridge University Press, 1979). The term "community study" suggests another historiographical process not discussed here: that of historians drawing on the analytical constructs and methodologies pioneered by anthropologists. Both Phythian-Adams and Macfarlane discuss this process explicitly.

nation."[6] In some senses, however, this evocative urban picture has not moved far beyond that presented by Tönnies a century earlier. "If the Reformation represented a line drawn under the long and evolving tradition of medieval urban community, it also signalised a final disruption of cultural assumptions. . . . For many citizens such changes must have been bewildering; for others, the ideal of the corporate community had long been replaced by an acceptance of a wider pluralistic society."[7] By contrast, Garrioch's study of Paris insists that scholars making such arguments have not looked for evidence of community in the smaller and more localized areas within cities, such as neighborhoods.[8]

Thus, the Tönniesean juxtaposition of premodern community and modern society has predominated. Indeed, it is striking to note the extent to which European historiography clusters on each side of the great divide of 1800. The clear implication is that no single narrative can unite the preindustrial and industrialized worlds.

In South Asia, historians attempting to find the meaningful referent for urban community have discussed groups identifying themselves as members of a minority religion,[9] as residents of particular *muḥalla*s (neighborhoods),[10] and even as migrant mill workers.[11] Two studies of

6. Ibid., pp. 170, 174, 172. Phythian-Adams makes the fascinating point that half the ritual year was devoted to reinforcing local ties within the city, the other half with articulating connections between the city and the world outside (p. 179).

7. Ibid., p. 275.

8. David Garrioch, *Neighbourhood and Community in Paris, 1740–1790* (Cambridge: Cambridge University Press, 1986), p. 6 and thereafter.

9. But see the debate between Paul Brass and Francis Robinson on what precisely this identity was supposed to mean, in David Taylor and Malcolm Yapp, eds., *Political Identity in South Asia* (London: Curzon Press, 1979). The debate is overblown; what mattered was not whether Muslims were motivated to so identify themselves because they were part of some "primordial" community (Robinson's position), or because they perceived their social and economic position to be in decline (Brass's position), but the extent to which they drew on both of these lines of argument—and *why* they did so. As we shall see, that question can be answered more convincingly by looking to public arena activity than by either of these authors' arguments.

10. See, for instance, Nita Kumar, "Popular Culture in Urban India: The Artisans of Banaras, c. 1884–1984, Ph.D. diss., University of Chicago, 1984, and Sylvia Vatuk, *Kinship and Urbanization: White Collar Migrants in North India,* (Berkeley and Los Angeles: University of California Press, 1972).

11. For migrant mill workers, the attributes of "community" could be defined simultaneously in a number of overlapping ways: by the nature of labor itself; by hierarchical relationships associated with labor; by linguistic identity, i.e., as speakers of Hindi in a non-Hindi city; etc. See Raj Chandavarkar, "Workers' Politics and the Mill in Bombay Between the Wars," *Modern Asian Studies* 15, no. 3 (1981): 603–47, but also Dipesh Chakrabarty, "Trade Unions in a Hierarchical Culture: The Jute Workers of Calcutta, 1920–50," in Ranajit Guha, *Subaltern Studies,* vol. 3 (Delhi: Oxford University Press, 1984). It is worth noting that the authors are both discussing, in the main, up-country workers who migrated to the mills of Bombay and Calcutta from the U.P. area.

special interest advance our understanding of community construction in South Asia. Arjun Appadurai, in *Worship and Conflict Under Colonial Rule,* has documented the extent to which requirements imposed by an Anglo-Indian law court affected the self-definition of the "Tenkalai community of Triplicane" as it served as the basis for electing trustees of the Sri Partasarati Svami Temple in Madras. In this study, "Tenkalai" became defined variously by reference to subsect (identified by caste marks), neighborhood of residence, and even (at one point) economic status. Gyanendra Pandey's recent analysis of "histories" penned by two very different residents of an eastern U.P. *qaṣba* compares the definitions of community proffered, respectively, by a member of a local Muslim zamindari family, who perceives the urban center itself as the community, and a weaver, whose shifting "consciousness of community was an ambiguous one, straddling as it did the religious fraternity, class, qasba and mohalla."[12]

As this summary review suggests, two quite different definitions of "community" have been used, more or less self-consciously, by social historians. First, some studies have identified elements of community in very localized expressions, leading to a definition of community based on social bonds—what Sabean calls "a series of mediated relationships," which we will term a "relational" form of community.[13] Although this form of community is often buttressed by *ideas* of overarching connection—notably kinship models or hierarchies relating to social order—it refers to personalized connections among participants rather than to abstracted ideological connections. Such connections, transacted through face-to-face relationships, reflect geographical proximity, economic and political ties, and the like. Second, other studies have isolated ideologically-based identities,[14] in which "community" has operated in broad terms to include participants through abstracted ideological appeals and terms of reference.[15]

---

12. See Arjun Appadurai, *Worship and Conflict Under Colonial Rule: A South Indian Case* (Cambridge: Cambridge University Press, 1981), esp. pp. 178–211; and Gyanendra Pandey, "'Encounters and Calamities': The History of a North Indian *Qasba* in the Nineteenth Century," in Guha, ed., *Subaltern Studies,* vol. 3, pp. 252, 269.

13. See Nita Kumar, especially "Work and Leisure in the Formation of Identity: Muslim Weavers in a Hindu City," in Freitag, ed., *Culture and Power in Banaras.* For insights on the relational definition of community, see Sabean, *Power in the Blood,* p. 28, and Garrioch, *Neighbourhood and Community,* p. 3.

14. See O'Hanlon, Brass, and Robinson for South Asia; and the implications embedded in Bohstedt's and Garrioch's discussions of broader communities in European urban areas.

15. Relevant to these two definitions of community for English studies is the debate around the nature of the "moral economy" as expressed by participants in eighteenth-century riots in England. For E. P. Thompson, originator of the term, notions of shared

Localized and relational, or broad-based and inclusive: these appear to be two very different notions of community. They are not necessarily contradictory, however, for they may simply represent different forms or levels, or different historical moments and configurations. We will attempt to define the notion of "community" more precisely; but we should note first that however imprecise the analytical formulations may have been, these studies supply sufficient historical evidence to indicate that collective action is indeed motivated by participants' perceptions that they belong to some kind of collectivity, whether relational or ideological.

To refine a definition of community beyond this basic point becomes more problematic. Although localized community may be taken as a given, its nature must still be analyzed. A variety of forms of social organization enable us to do this. In chapter 3, for instance, we discuss neighborhood, *akhāṛā*s, and temple or festival managing committees. Beyond those forms, however, lie other questions for analysis. To what extent do relational forms of community possess the capacity either to enlarge into, or to link up with, ideological expressions of community? Answers to that question enable us to gauge, as well, the degree of politicization an ideological movement is capable of undergoing. For whereas local constructions of community obviously have implicit political implications (in the broadly defined sense of power relationships), only movements capable of more encompassing and ideological potential carry overt political messages and perform explicitly political roles (in the more narrowly defined sense of politics). That issue must be borne in mind as we analyze the events of the late nineteenth century.

Efforts to discover linkages between these two types of constructions, or levels, of community have been relatively rare for South Asia. Work on Europe, by contrast, has found that examinations of popular culture activities often provide the evidence necessary to determine the existence of such a linkage. For example, David Underdown—in an effort to understand the extent and nature of popular support for the Roundheads and the Cavaliers during the period of the English civil war, from 1640 to 1660—has focused on the "cultural conflict" emerging from

---

values based on assumptions of a paternalistic moral economy constituted an ideology that united the lower classes throughout most of England. Bohstedt, by contrast, argues that the extent to which rioters and their local rulers jointly recognized such values very much depended on the social relationships and political culture of the locality. (E. P. Thompson, "The Moral Economy of the English Crowd in the Eighteenth Century," *Past and Present* 50 (February 1971): 76–136, and John Bohstedt, *Riots and Community Politics*.

efforts by certain members of the "middling sorts" to suppress "ancient feasts and popular recreations," such as church ales and street theater.[16] (In a contrast that has fascinating implications for the differences in the directions taken during the two revolutionary periods, Isherwood's study of theater in France documents an opposite trend, in which the audience for elite and popular theater coalesced just before the French Revolution.)[17]

These studies also modify significantly notions of community in both countries. For England, Underdown argues that the level of resistance to suppression of popular culture varied according to ecological region, with the greatest resistance by villagers in relatively stable areas of arable cultivation, and the least by the more loosely affiliated populations of dairying and cattle-grazing districts and the towns. The former areas, Underdown argues, were "trying to preserve the cultural and religious forms in which more traditional notions of community were expressed." For instance, defending the revel feast held in Rangeworthy during Whitsun week, villagers declared that "by all the time whereof the memory of man is not to the contrary," the feast was held for "the allaying of strifes, discords and debates between neighbour and neighbour." Thus the concept of "community" functions for Underdown as the antithesis of individualism and represents a collective vision, often nostalgic, of a social past of harmonious, vertical integration.[18] Putting together Isherwood's study (which concludes with the importance of the mingled audiences of street theater created by the great love of Parisians for "the promenade") with Garrioch's, we see for Paris a similar modification in the definition of community, whereby popular culture activities could simultaneously support a very localized sense of neighborhood and—albeit only intermittently—the sense of a broader world

---

16. Underdown, *Revel, Riot and Rebellion*, p. 49.

17. Robert M. Isherwood, *Farce and Fantasy: Popular Entertainment in Eighteenth-Century Paris* (New York: Oxford University Press, 1986). Lynn Hunt's related analysis of the attempts made during the Revolution to build a symbolic political language from, but defining itself against, popular culture is discussed in more detail in Part III.

18. Underdown, *Revel, Riot and Rebellion*, pp. 235, 63. Underdown uses the term "community" to characterize what is being signified during a period of major change. He has attempted to nuance the previous historiography on popular culture by showing that the conflict represented more than an attempt by a reforming middle class to suppress lower-class pastimes; it also should be seen, he believes, as reflecting two increasingly diverse regional cultures in seventeenth-century England. The emerging culture of the "clothing parishes of the cheese country" emphasized "moral reformation, individualism, the ethic of work and personal responsibility." In contrast, arable villages clung much longer to a conception of society that stressed "tradition, custom, and the cooperative, harmonious 'vertical' community."

that mocked the bureaucracy of an unresponsive state as well as pretensions based on birth.

Communitas and Structure

Methodologically similar to the recent work on Europe, the present study uses public arena activities to evaluate the extent to which such a link connected the localized perceptions of community to more encompassing ideological constructions in north India.[19] Part II compares late nineteenth-century collective activities with those that preceded them, in order to trace the development of this linkage.

Before turning to such an analysis, however, we must begin by asking how collective activities served to express constructions of community. The answer to that question demonstrates that popular culture activities provide our best evidence for tracing the ultimate development of communalism. We are asking, that is, how collective festivities and entertainments functioned to achieve this sense of shared community. Victor Turner proposes that as they come together for collective observances, participants experience a liminal state.[20] He calls this state "communitas," that "intervening liminal phase—betwixt and between the categories of ordinary social life . . . the direct, immediate, and total confrontation of human identities which tends to make those experiencing it think of mankind as a homogenous, unstructured and free community." Turner does not argue, of course, that this process is completed—that society becomes unstructured or that the experience lasts beyond its appointed moment. He discusses the interplay of caste and communitas during a pilgrimage in western India, showing us that in every society communitas must stop short at the cultural boundaries imposed by the structure of social organization.[21] This happens, in large part, because the conditions leading to the experience of communitas can only occur where "structure" organizes to produce the liminal experience. Neither structure nor communitas can exist without the

19. For a similar approach, see Susan Bayly's work on goddess worship among Muslims otherwise identified as reformist: the popular culture activities around goddess shrines have helped her to measure the extent to which "Muslim" as an identity marker referred not so much to the content of their religious practices as to other conceptions of community ("Islam in Southern India: 'Purist' or 'Syncretic'?," a paper presented at the Conference on Islam in South Asian Society, Ohio State University, April 1983).

20. Victor Turner, *Dramas, Fields and Metaphors: Symbolic Action in Human Society* (Ithaca: Cornell University Press, 1974).

21. Ibid., p. 285.

other: Turner's model is an indivisible whole held together by its own inherent tension. In contrast to the profound fellow feeling of communitas, then, structure in this model is "all that which holds people apart, defines their differences, and constrains their actions . . . those cognitive, linguistic and ideological, as well as physical and social structures—it is, in brief, that which confers order and regularity on phenomena."[22] As phenomena that imply both structure and communitas, the collective observances of early modern Europe and colonial South Asia simultaneously required structure (which led to division and separation) in order to occur, even as they created a liminal state that emphasized the underlying similarities uniting their participants.

Imbued with communitas, yet expressing structure: these characteristics typify public arena activities. They enable the scholar to gauge the nature of the "community" to which participants perceived themselves as belonging, as well as the values being perpetuated and protected. Underdown, for instance, examines the types of sports played, as well as the complaints levied against those who persisted in church ales, to illustrate the values for which the participants fought. Garrioch's study of local community in Paris underscored which social relationships continued to dictate acceptable models of appropriate behavior. Even Bohstedt's comparison of riots in three different types of British locales concluded by using the riots as a gauge. Where riots could still operate as a "negotiated political process," they characterized areas sufficiently integrated to function as all-encompassing, vertical "communities" (compared with areas that began to express concepts of community organized horizontally).

In a similar way, we will use riots and allied popular culture activities occurring in late nineteenth-century U.P. to reveal the sinews of north Indian urban life—sinews that provided the basic elements of community. Chapter 3 examines the structural side of communitas in the north Indian *qaṣba* of Bareilly—from the ties of neighborhood to those of voluntary associational activity related to sociability and ritual observances; from the ties prompted by occupation of the same shared, public space to elements of social competition. Chapter 4 analyzes observances, especially those in Agra during the 1880s, to identify elements that contribute to the communitas of Turner's model. Finally, chapter 5 examines a major occasion in the 1890s when elements of communitas and its attendant structures worked to link loosely an ideological move-

22. Ibid., pp. 274, 287.

ment, on the one hand, and localized protests against changes in relational communities, on the other.

Riots in North India

A major riot, or cluster of events including a riot, provides the focal point for each of the chapters in this study. The use of such riots opens up a series of windows into the social history of those places and moments, presenting the equivalent of stop-action photographs of all the players. Though the choice of riots was in part dictated by the availability of source materials, this was not necessarily an artificial constraint: the most prominent and thoroughly documented riots were also those with the greatest historical and social impact.[23] That the scale and nature of these moments of conflict underwent substantial change in the 1870s made that decade a logical starting point for Parts II and III of this study. Focusing on actions of the crowd and its leadership and on the conditions in which a riot would erupt in the subcontinent tells us much about the social context as well as the motivating values and ideals behind the events. There were, of course, occasional riots that exploded spontaneously from an altercation between individuals in the street or bazaar. Generally, however, these outbursts were staged by gatherings of people assembled for other purposes.

Much attention, therefore, has been devoted in the following pages to the nature of such gatherings—to the elements of communitas and structure that shaped them. Especially susceptible were occasions when participants had gathered for public ceremonial processions, public protest meetings, or Friday prayer or other religious observances. Participants had been attracted to these gatherings by a variety of social ties, emotional appeals, and other methods of mobilization. These riots thus played an integral part in the popular activity of public arenas. Indeed, rather than present a "spasmodic view of popular history,"[24] this study contends that the riots are significant precisely because they constituted an essential component in a framework of social interaction that regarded violence as one of a range of legitimate options of group action. It was an option located at the far end of the spectrum, however: the riots are especially useful because they signal heightened tension

---

23. The social impact may be measured, for instance, by the symbolic reenactment of these events in later riots. See especially Kanpur for evidence of this, as discussed in chapters 6 and 7.

24. E. P. Thompson, "Moral Economy," p. 76.

and, therefore, reflect points of significant change. Moreover, taking a cue from Bohstedt, we may also consider that riots—to the extent that they functioned as a form of "political negotiation"—also measured the extent to which public arenas remained a viable forum for renegotiation and expression of urban sociopolitical relationships.

The pattern made by riots thus allows us to trace high points of a historical process over a period of decades.[25] If, for instance, riots large enough in scale to be included in various administrative and historical surveys are plotted on a map of the province, it becomes clear that the riots studied in this section—particularly those of the 1870s and 1880s—occurred almost exclusively in the western region, particularly in the Rohilkhand area of middle-sized towns. The riots then move from the Rohilkhand–upper Doab area down into the Gangetic valley, and thence throughout the province. Tensions continued intermittently at the turn of the century, a period particularly marked by efforts to infuse public festivals with new meaning, but the only riot of significance before the 1920s was the one in Kanpur in 1913. By the 1920s, violent activity on behalf of community had spread over much of the province. Despite their ubiquitousness, the riots in the 1920s were less significant than their predecessors, as their scale and nature were very circumscribed—more often small-scale, staged confrontations than massive collective expressions of public opinion. The 1930s tell another story: the roster of urban centers experiencing communal violence again expanded, and the scale of riots (in terms of damage and deaths) also began to rise. By the 1940s, communal identity as a cultural force, and collective violence in pursuit or protection of such identity, had become widespread in the province, and the pattern, as well as the motivation, for communal riots had become well established. Although the scale certainly escalated after 1940—particularly in 1947—it is possible to end the present study in 1940 because the process leading to communalism had essentially run its course by the beginning of that decade.

Parts II and III concentrate on events of the late nineteenth and early twentieth centuries. The riots that occurred then differ both quantitatively and qualitatively from those that preceded them. Perhaps the most obvious difference is the numerical increase in the incidence of riots. Since most of these riots took place in urban centers, we may presume

25. For a more detailed discussion, see Freitag, "Hindu-Muslim Communal Riots in India: A Preliminary Overview," in *Berkeley Working Papers on South and Southeast Asia,* vol. I (Berkeley: Center for South and Southeast Asia Studies, 1977).

one cause of the increase to be the rapid urbanization that took place during the nineteenth century.[26] More significant are differences in the nature of these riots: while studies of the earlier events argue that they do not relate to each other in any concrete way, it is clear that those of the late nineteenth century do begin to form an important new pattern.

The early nineteenth-century Banaras riots, examined in some detail in chapter 1, typify patterns characteristic of the eighteenth and early nineteenth centuries.[27] In tracing these patterns, Bayly suggests that they tended to occur when local rulers altered the circumstances surrounding religious ceremonials, or because of disputes relating to control over sacred spaces—circumstances that reflected changed relationships among the participating communities and/or with the state. But by the early nineteenth century, the context of such changes generally related to the intrusion of a new style of state embodied in the English East India Company, and reflected the altered position of urban officers who had previously represented the state: we saw what this meant in Banaras as the British administration changed the status and functions of kotwal and police.

As Bayly has noted, the riots occurring throughout the nineteenth century and into the twentieth century *appear* much the same as these earlier riots. They continue to invoke a symbolic rhetoric rich in religious signification. They occupy many of the same urban spaces. But significant differences between these riots and their predecessors have been obscured by analysts like Bayly who have ignored the changing meaning behind this religious symbolism—that is, who have overlooked the "processual" element urged on us by Turner's discussion of symbolic behavior.[28] The present study argues that there is a significant difference between these early events and those of the late nineteenth century. In the eighteenth and early nineteenth centuries—as we have seen in Banaras—religion provided the vocabulary for expressing a

26. See ibid.
27. For elaborations and examples of this pattern, see C. A. Bayly, "The Prehistory of 'Communalism'? Religious Conflict in India, 1700–1860," *Modern Asian Studies* 19, no. 2 (1985): 177–203. However, it should be noted that the remainder of this discussion takes issue with Bayly's conclusions, many of which would seem to be belied by his own work on urban culture. See references in chapter 3, especially, to the insights of *Rulers, Townsmen and Bazaars* (Cambridge: Cambridge University Press, 1983).
28. Following Bayly's lead, another study that has ignored the changing processual nature of meaning behind symbolic behavior is Juan Cole, *Roots of North Indian Shi'ism in Iran and Iraq: Religion and State in Awadh, 1722–1859* (Berkeley and Los Angeles: University of California Press, 1988).

variety of conflicts that arose around public arena activities. This vocabulary often indirectly suggested, as well, the relationship of localized communities to each other and to the urban political economy as a whole. But in the late nineteenth century, while the venue and symbolism remained unchanged, the meaning inferred by this symbolism came to be reinterpreted. In particular, the changes related to efforts made by participants to express, and even to define through such vocabulary, a shared sense of community.

A religious vocabulary became, that is, a sustained way of imbuing collective expressions of localized, relational community with a more ideological and broad-based definition of the collectivity. Although we do not mean to suggest a hard and fast periodization for this process, it occurred, for most parts of U.P., during the late nineteenth century. And in the early twentieth century the use of religion to express community became linked to overtly political activity by individuals whose concerted action had implications beyond the locality—or "communalism" in the sense in which analysts now use the term. Again, we do not mean to imply a series of lockstep developments, but to distinguish analytically between two very different parts of a process that was certainly in motion after the mid-nineteenth century and was beginning to bear fruit by the 1920s. In any case, at no time before the 1920s can the term "communalism"—as it is currently understood and used—be employed to describe accurately these earlier events.

In Part II we concentrate on the circumstances surrounding public arena activities that give them the potential to connect with each other, and the process by which this happened. In Banaras, public arena activities expressed a still vigorous court-centered culture that doubtless had been paralleled during the eighteenth century in Awadh, Rohilkhand, and other Successor State areas. By the late nineteenth century, however, very little of this court culture remained in the urban centers of north India outside Banaras.[29] Instead, we find that a new set of relationships had emerged to shape public arena activities. These relationships reflected a context that changed significantly as imperial administrators replaced the princely courts, as the fortunes and influence of courtier classes declined, and as the status and cultural

29. For a discussion of the significant differences this change made for Banaras, see Freitag, "State and Community: Symbolic Popular Protest in Banaras's Public Arenas," in Freitag, ed., *Culture and Power in Banaras*. Another exception may have been the Rohilla princely state of Rampur; see Lance Brennan, "A Case of Attempted Segmental Modernization: Rampur State, 1930–1939," *Comparative Studies in Society and History* 23, no. 3 (July 1981): 350–81.

domination of other urban groups (most notably Hindu merchants and their allies) increased.

What distinguishes this process in British north India particularly is the extent to which the state withdrew from direct patronage and participation in such collective activities. The contrast with early modern Europe is instructive. In both India and western Europe, community activities faced "an innovating, intruding state." Yet in England, this state remained active in public arenas, attempting to substitute its own approved rituals for those previously created by the local community.[30] In north India, the provincial government, although still intrusive in its efforts to regulate public arenas, nevertheless withdrew from exercising an active presence there. Instead, it concentrated its energies and resources on state institutional structures: it created its own rituals for this venue,[31] and developed relationships within state structures with those it deemed "natural leaders." By contrast, perhaps the most striking feature of Underdown's study of seventeenth-century England is the continuing, close alignment between developments in the national political arena and those in the local, popular cultural one. In late nineteenth-century British India, however, the two diverge increasingly, and Indian actors focus more and more on the realm remaining to them—that of public arenas. As they do, the violence that grew out of competitive activity began to take on a different character than it had possessed previously. This profound difference between the process as it emerged in Europe and that of north India lies at the heart of our historical comparison. We turn now to examine this process more closely.

30. Underdown, *Revel, Riot and Rebellion,* p. 216 and thereafter.
31. See Bernard S. Cohn, "Representing Authority in Victorian India," in Eric Hobsbawm and Terence Ranger, eds., *The Invention of Tradition* (Cambridge: Cambridge University Press, 1983), pp. 165–210.

CHAPTER 3

Bareilly in the 1870s: Community and Conflict Expressed Through Structure

Riots in Bareilly provide a useful focal point for tracing changes from the north Indian urban society in Banaras in the 1810s to that characteristic of the late nineteenth century. This century of change, in a city of significance to Mughals, Rohillas, and British alike, marked the "turbulent" urban history that characterized western U.P.[1] We may use two earlier riots, relating to religion, which took place in Bareilly in 1816 and 1837, to trace the important changes in urban structure during this transitional period under the British, and then compare them with the riot of 1871. The 1871 riot, in particular, illustrates the potential of public arena activity for fostering communitas.

We concentrate here on the essential characteristics of "structure" in Turner's model of communitas. "Structure" in this case refers most obviously to social and physical structures—to social changes affecting Hindu merchants and scribal groups as well as Muslim landowners and artisans, and the consequent changes in relations among these groups. It refers as well to changes in the physical context of urban places like the *qaṣba* of Bareilly; to the more localized affinities through which urban residents organized their lives; and to the network of symbols that expressed their values and worldviews.

---

1. Nevill writes that the city had long functioned as the center for "Mughal fiscal and diplomatic activity in the region." The British, too, used it as their administrative base for the Board of Commissioners, who oversaw the ceded districts. H. R. Nevill, *District Gazetteers of the United Provinces of Agra and Oudh*, vol. 13, *Bareilly* (Allahabad: U.P. Government Press, United Provinces, 1911) [henceforth *Bareilly Gazetteer*], p. 166.

The "Nature" of Urban Central Places

Rapidly expanding urbanization in north India provided the first and most obvious characteristic of the structure of communitas. That the locale of most U.P. "communal" riots was urban suggests that cultural identity as it developed in city sites like *qaṣba*s proved especially significant. (Only during the Cow Protection riots of 1893 did the settings become more rural, and even here "rurban" centers played a critical hinge role in fostering Cow Protection ideology in the country-side.)[2] One scholar writes, "Primarily . . . communal rioting has been an urban phenomenon in the United Provinces. . . . Its cities along the Gangetic plain have contributed . . . to the surge of riots in all the peak periods."[3]

U.P. was not unique in possessing a riotous urban context: cities proved important in the communal history of the Punjab, Bombay, and south India as well.[4] But the distribution of urban centers in the province, and the proportion of the provincial population that could be termed urban,[5] were unusual and may have led to the pattern of distinct urban styles that emerged there by the mid-nineteenth century (see map 4). So, too, may the pace of urbanization, for the number of urban centers increased substantially between 1850 and 1880. After 1860, a newfound stability followed rapid urbanization for those cities strategically located along the rail routes. Increasing specialization among urban centers, a rapid rise in urban property values, and widespread "refurbishing of towns and zamindari palaces" accompanied these developments. Merchants and brokers followed business to the rail-heads, while new industrial sites like Kanpur became stabilized and service personnel congregated in the new government center at Al-

2. Moreover, both major spates of Cow Protection activity were prompted by urban events, most notably court decisions that changed the legal status of the cow in terms of civil rights. See chapters 5 and 6.

3. Richard D. Lambert, "Hindu-Muslim Riots," Ph.D. diss., University of Pennsylvania, 1951, p. 229. See also Freitag, "Hindu-Muslim Communal Riots in India: A Preliminary Overview," in *Berkeley Working Papers on South and Southeast Asia,* vol. 1 (Berkeley: Center for South and Southeast Asia Studies, 1977).

4. See Sandria B. Freitag, "The Roots of Muslim Separatism in South Asia: Personal Practice and Public Structures in Kanpur and Bombay," in Edmund Burke III and Ira Lapidus, eds., *Islam, Politics, and Social Movements* (Berkeley and Los Angeles: University of California Press, 1988); and Freitag, "Religious Rites and Riots," Ph.D. diss., University of California, Berkeley, 1980, chap. 8.

5. Although no one center can compare statistically with Calcutta, these trends, described by O. H. K. Spate and Enayat Ahmad ("Five Cities of the Gangetic Plain: A Cross Section of Indian Cultural History," *The Geographical Review* 40) refer to the province as a whole.

4. Urban centers in U.P.

lahabad.[6] As a result of these activities, the nature of urban centers had become established in the latter half of the nineteenth century. By then the province contained over one-third of the largest cities (population greater than 250,000) in the subcontinent—more than any other province—and almost one-fifth of the next largest cities (100,000 to 250,000). Of its five largest urban centers (Agra, Kanpur, Lucknow, Allahabad, and Banaras) all but one came to dominate the "communal" history of the region (see table 1).[7]

6. C. A. Bayly, *Rulers, Townsmen and Bazaars* (Cambridge: Cambridge University Press, 1983), pp. 436–37.
7. Spate and Ahmad ("Five Cities," pp. 260–78) base their generalizations on statistics of the 1941 census. These were always the largest centers in U.P., though their relative population size alternated. Why Banaras did not figure more prominently in U.P.

TABLE 1   POPULATION OF U.P.'S LARGEST CENTRAL PLACES

City	1911	1941	Percentage increase
Lucknow	260,000	387,000	49
Benares	209,000	263,000	26
Agra	182,000	284,000	56
Kanpur	174,000	487,000	180
Allahabad	168,000	260,000	55

SOURCE: *Census of India* for years indicated.

Although this is not the place to discuss in detail the evolution of these cities and market towns, it is important to note the nature of north Indian urban life. The smallest urban centers surviving the economic and agrarian crises of the 1830s fit into two distinct "social formations" that proved to be of great significance thereafter in shaping the character of U.P. towns and cities. These two, to use C. A. Bayly's terms,[8] comprised "corporation" towns dominated respectively by Hindu merchants (*ganj*s) and by Indo-Islamic "service gentry" (*qaṣba*s). Not surprisingly, the urban nature of these central places found form and expression through the cultural practices of local society. The resulting distinctive urban styles will prove significant in the following narrative.

The Islamic service *qaṣba*s that developed in clusters around centers of Muslim power in Rohilkhand and the upper Doab were dominated by a literate and homogeneous elite, who embraced a distinctive Indo-Persian style of culture. This service gentry, performing clerical and military service for the Mughal empire and its successor states, also invested in land. Their cultural and literary patronage and the attendant high rate of literacy (resulting from a developed educational infrastructure) meant that such urban places continued—even after their political decline—to act as preservers of Indo-Persian traditions and values.

"communal" history is discussed indirectly in Parts II and III; it forms the subject of my essay, "State and Community: Symbolic Popular Protest in Banaras's Public Arenas," in Freitag, ed., *Culture and Power in Banaras: Community, Performance, and Environment, 1800–1900* (Berkeley and Los Angeles: University of California Press, 1989).

8. Bayly, *Rulers, Townsmen and Bazaars*. Although the extremely useful terminology and historical outline are Bayly's, his article "The Prehistory of 'Communalism'?" (*Modern Asian Studies* 19, no. 2 [1985]: 177–203) suggests that I am more willing than he to push the implications of his arguments.

Indeed, it appears that "the most durable urban functions [of such *qaṣba*s] have proved to be those associated with culture and religion."[9] Nevertheless, the service gentry's attempts to buttress their fortunes through landholding did not save them from suffering often severe financial declines during the nineteenth century. Their rights to agricultural resources often proved precarious, and they did not have their local caste fellows to fall back on, as did the other landed gentry, the Rajputs.

*Ganj*s in U.P. formed two variants. In the eastern districts particularly, Rajput-dominated "rurban lineage settlements" had developed as low-level administrative and land-revenue centers in areas lacking other kinds of central or intermediate places. They were "usually small, functionally simple, and lacking in the services, crafts and special institutions usually deemed consonant with city life." Organized by the dominant lineage of the area, they also lacked the typically urban characteristics of "occupational diversity, ethnic heterogeneity, impersonality, universalistic criteria and secularism."[10] Yet they did perform important functions that distinguished them from the surrounding countryside, including "military and protective functions, market activities, caste leadership and determination of caste rank." In addition to providing low-level administrative services for the state, they also performed important hinge functions between state/central place culture and that of the more parochial countryside. But though they attempted to mimic the style and manner of royal and princely courts, in fact their value systems and social institutions more closely duplicated rural patterns.[11] Indeed, their most important cultural functions preserved and mediated local caste and religious values through ritual enactments as well as economic and social acts aimed at preserving local status hierarchies.

The other variant of the *ganj* provided a cultural style that came to dominate most U.P. urban places after the mid-nineteenth century. Though frequently modified by the presence of Muslim *muḥalla*s, this style took its shape from the values and corporate activities of the Hindu merchant class. Significantly, this urban culture became unified through

9. C. A. Bayly, "The Small Town and Islamic Gentry in North India: The Case of Kara," in K. Ballhatchet and J. Harrison, eds., *The City in South Asia* (London: University of London, 1980).

10. Richard G. Fox, "Rurban Settlements and Rajput 'Clans' in Northern India," in Fox, ed., *Urban India: Society, Space, and Time,* Program in Comparative Studies on Southern Asia, monograph no. 10 (Durham, N.C.: Duke University Press, 1970), p. 176.

11. Ibid., pp. 180, 169.

a Hindu religious revival that "provided standards of orthodox behavior to which all who participated in the moral community of the merchants were constrained to respond." Moreover, "in the commercial bazaars, Hindu and Jain religion provided the solidarities out of which corporations and a sense of urban, even political identity was forged."[12] (The significance of the increasing dominance of Hindu merchant-styled urban culture provides an important strand in the following narrative and is a focal point of chapters 4, 5, and 6.)

Bayly's model, formulated to describe the nature of small urban centers, also suggests the character of larger central places as well. The cultural styles of *ganj* and *qaṣba,* replicated in neighborhoods existing side by side in the larger places, jockeyed for dominance. However, in the nineteenth century at least, this proximity and potential competition did not lead to sustained friction. Instead, in this period the most significant characteristic was shared by both styles—the development of the intermediary roles played by "corporations" of urban U.P. residents.

Indeed, what marked the late eighteenth and early nineteenth centuries, particularly, was the performance of civic or corporate functions by intermediary bodies on behalf of their constituents. In so doing, leaders of these intermediary bodies—Rajput lineage leaders, Hindu merchant raises, and their equivalent within Muslim neighborhoods (the *mir muḥalla*)—provided a certain embodiment of community. Development of this intermediary function, it is important to emphasize, related only partly to the new imperial regime and much more to indigenous developments. "The early colonial period," Bayly notes, "saw the further consolidation of a merchant and service class between the state and agrarian society. It was as much the product of the slow commercialization of political power which had gathered pace in the late Mughal period as of the export of trades and land market of colonial rule. . . . An indication of the persistence of an indigenous social change, it was no less important because its idiom remained 'traditional.' "[13]

The first characteristic of late nineteenth-century community structure, then, related to urbanization of a very particular type. This urbanization led to the development of two potentially competitive cultural styles, fostered by elites who, in similar corporate manner, acted on behalf of their fellow urban residents.

---

12. Bayly, *Rulers, Townsmen and Bazaars,* pp. 371, 348.
13. Ibid., pp. 344–45.

Riots in Rohilkhand

Bareilly, as a major center in Rohilkhand—one of the most highly urbanized areas of India—provides an instructive case in point for understanding how these cultural styles ultimately came into conflict. While the power of the Mughal empire declined during the eighteenth century, bands of Pathan adventurers called Rohillas created a number of chiefdoms in the area situated between the Himalayan foothills, the Ganges, and Awadh. In a "Muslim conquest style" that emphasized town-building and trade, the Rohilla newcomers not only defeated local Rajput brotherhoods to establish chiefdoms but also converted their rurban lineage centers into *qaṣba*s.[14] Despite this conflict-ridden beginning, however, the Rohilla chiefs created and maintained cordial relations with their subjects, including Hindus: they forged close ties with the Rajputs remaining in their areas and attracted dependent Hindu merchants to their burgeoning urban centers. Nevertheless, the dominance exercised by the literate Muslim service gentry set the style of these urban sites. Indeed, with 15 to 20 percent of its population located in *qaṣba*s, by the mid-eighteenth century Rohilkhand possessed an urban culture that reflected the mutual interdependence of Muslim tribal ruler and Hindu merchant.[15] Efforts by the Nawab of Awadh (as well as the Marathas) to wrest control over the area little affected this urban culture. Although the Nawab finally proved successful in 1784, he soon lost the area to his erstwhile ally in the struggle, the British East India Company, which forced him to cede Rohilkhand in 1801.[16]

The urban center of Bareilly proved as important to the British as it had been to the Rohillas, not least for its legitimizing role. But the British did not find it easy to maintain order in Bareilly. A house tax protest centered there in 1816 closely resembled the Banaras protest of 1810: "public clamour" brought the assessment process to a halt, "business was at a standstill, the shops were shut, and crowds assembled at the cutcherry to petition against the impost."[17] Mufti Mohamed

14. See Lance Brennan, "Social Change in Rohilkhand 1801–1833," *Indian Economic and Social History Review* 7 (1970): 443–65, and "A Case of Attempted Segmental Modernization: Rampur State, 1930–1939," *Comparative Studies in Society and History* 23, no. 3 (July 1981): 350–81; see also Bayly, *Rulers, Townsmen and Bazaars*.

15. Bayly, *Rulers, Townsmen and Bazaars*, pp. 15, 23, 120.

16. The exception was the princely state of Rampur, which remained a focal point for Rohilla control (Brennan, "A Case of Attempted Segmental Modernization," p. 354).

17. Nevill, *Bareilly Gazetteer*, p. 167.

Ewaz, "a man of great age and reputed sanctity, who was held in profound veneration throughout Rohilkhand," headed the protest. He described himself in his petition by noting that "whenever I interceded on behalf of the people they [i.e., previous rulers, first Rohilla Hafiz Rehmat Khan and then the Nawab of Awadh] consented to my request."[18] In fact, crowd perceptions that the mufti was in danger led to the initial outburst. The structures of mobilization used in this 1816 riot befitted a *qaṣba:* cooperation among neighborhood leaders (*muḥalladar*s) linked up with "an informal religious organization based on the mosques of the *mohullas* and the teacher-pupil relationship of the city's major Sufi orders."[19]

More precisely, descendants of the Rohilla chiefs, along with the Hindu merchants they had attracted to the *qaṣba,* dominated the *muḥalladar* structure. They were joined by prominent ulama—in Bareilly, these ulama belonged to the Barelwis, an ulama-sufi order distinctive for its defense of customary practice[20]—who greatly influenced the lower-class urban inhabitants (many of whom were Muslim). The lower class, described as artisans and day laborers, included "dyers, weavers, shoemakers and bricklayers."[21] As in Banaras, then, the alliance previously responsible for directing urban life continued to hold influence even some fifteen years after the British had acquired direct control of the area. "The Bunneans and Saokars were from the beginning particularly active in forming a band of union among themselves which should resist an individual application (for payment) and defeat every effort to divide or persuade them."[22] Indeed, through the pull of such urban alliances, leading Hindu merchants and members of the Muslim lower classes participated in the riot even though the protest related particularly to the sharp decline experienced by many of the Muslim Rohilla landholders, whose control of land had become imperiled under the British administration.[23] (This group in decline included not only the

18. Ibid.
19. Bayly, *Rulers, Townsmen and Bazaars,* pp. 324–25.
20. See Barbara Daly Metcalf, *Islamic Revival in British India: Deoband 1860–1900* (Princeton: Princeton University Press, 1982).
21. Lance Brennan, "The Local Face of Nationalism: Congress Politics in Rohilkhand in the 1920s," *South Asia* 5, no. 2 (December 1975): 10. The description of lower-class groups is from Bareilly Committee's Report, 25 October 1816, quoted in Bayly, *Rulers, Townsmen and Bazaars,* p. 327.
22. Bareilly Committee's Report, 25 October 1816, quoted in Bayly, *Ruler, Townsmen and Bazaars,* p. 326.
23. See Brennan, "Social Change in Rohilkhand."

Rohilla descendants but also significant numbers of Khatris and Kayasths—Hindu scribal groups who had long participated in Indo-Persian culture).[24] Ultimately their decline, and the attendant prosperity enjoyed by new merchants attracted to the area, would dissolve the urban coalition that still operated in 1816.

Indeed, a riot in 1837, though on a smaller scale than that of 1816, serves as a measure of how quickly this dissolution would occur once it had begun. The economic opportunities, particularly of the sugar boom in the 1820s and revenue-farming advantages offered by the British to moneylenders, had attracted new and wealthy Hindu merchants to Rohilkhand urban centers. As Bayly notes, the mercantile newcomers "had little connection with the patronage of the earlier Muslim rulers" and often proved "unwilling to acquiesce in a continued ceremonial inferiority." A test presented itself in 1837, when the timing for *Rāmnaumī* and Muharram observances overlapped.[25] Reflecting the new balances of power within such towns, British administrators reversed previous orders, which had been designed to protect Islamic service-gentry interests, and permitted full-scale observances of the *Rāmnaumī*.[26] When this prompted unrest among Muslim inhabitants of the *qaṣba,* members of the Indo-Persian elite led the crowds to the *karbalā*.[27] In this way they tried to contain collective action within the confines of a Muslim sacred space and, in the process, turn Muslim attention inward to prevent public protest from being directed at Hindus. Thus,

24. See Bayly, *Rulers, Townsmen and Bazaars,* p. 337, and Brennan, "The Local Face of Nationalism," p. 15.

25. Bayly, *Rulers, Townsmen and Bazaars,* p. 337. *Rāmnaumī* commemorates the birth of *Rām* (the seventh divine incarnation of Vishnu) and is the most important festival of Vaishnavite Hindus. Temples are decorated and the image of *Rām* is adorned and paraded; the *Rāmāyan* is read in temples, and nautches (Anglo-Indian transliteration of the word for dance performances) take place at night (H. R. Roe, Assistant to Deputy Inspector-General of Police, Criminal Investigation Department, U.P., *Guide to Muhammadan and Hindu Festivals and Fasts in the U.P.* [Allahabad: U.P. Government Press, 1934], p. 24). Muharram, at this period in the U.P., was observed by both Shi'as and Sunnis as a period of mourning in memory of Husain and his followers; the first ten days in the month cover the period in which the massacre at Karbala took place. "The Shias, who attach greater value to Ali as a Khalif than the Sunnis, observe this commemoration with fervour; during these first ten days they hold Majlis (mourning meetings in their houses and imambaras), but both communities take out processions with tazias (copies of the tombs of Husain) and alams (copies of the flag of Husain) on several of these days, especially on the 10th Mohurram, when the tazias are conveyed to the local Karbala and the tops of them there buried" (Roe, *Guide,* pp. 8–9).

26. See the discussion for nearby Shahjahanpur in Bayly, *Rulers, Townsmen and Bazaars,* p. 337.

27. The *karbalā* was a field traditionally set aside to symbolize the original battlefield of the events commemorated during Muharram.

many "went out to the Kurballa and remained there til the Ramnowmee procession was over," the leaders having first disarmed the crowd and locked up the weapons they had collected.[28]

On behalf of their fellow Muslims, leaders then negotiated a compromise, which obligated Muslims to refrain from killing cattle in the bazaar on Hindu festival days in return for keeping the days of Muharram free of Hindu processions. The very terms of this agreement suggest that major changes were under way. It was not so much that the issues involved were new—Cow Protection, like sacred space around Muharram processions, had long represented important values. Rather, the ability of Hindus to have their ceremonial rights recognized in a *qaṣba* measured their new clout in this urban setting. Recognition of such rights, in turn, permitted Hindus to negotiate recognition of their demands to limit or prevent the slaughter of cattle.

The agreement indicates, as well, the extent to which the old order held, although under great strain. While the new Hindu merchant and Brahmin arrivals pushed for expanded recognition of their religious values and ceremonials, the remnant of the old order led the search for a compromise. Most prominent in meeting with Muslim leaders had been Chaudhari Basant Rai, "one of the leading Brahmans of the city" from a family "whose experience of Muslim rule predated the Rohillas," and in the 1830s, as representative of the old order, he carried the day.[29] Nevertheless, although adhered to the following year, the agreement was imperiled by the decline in influence this family had experienced. A Muslim carpet maker murdered Basant Rai a few years later, and when *Rāmnaumī* and Muharram again overlapped in the early 1850s, his son had great difficulty extending the agreement of 1837.

During the middle third of the nineteenth century, then, the economic well-being and related urban power of the residents of the *qaṣba* of Bareilly shifted significantly. Although sufficient "social glue" remained in these decades to prevent wholesale changes in the ceremonial life of the area, certain shifts had taken place, and the glue had virtually dissolved by 1870. A description of the riot that occurred that year illuminates the new elements of structure that replaced the eighteenth-century pattern.

---

28. Report of F. O. Mayne, Officer on Special Duty, to Officiating Secretary to Government NWP, dated Bareilly, 27 Apr. 1871. IOR, Judl. (Criml.) Progs. for NWP for 1871, index no. 43, prog. no. 60, par. 10.

29. *Bareilly Gazetteer*, pp. 168–69; Bayly, *Rulers, Townsmen and Bazaars*, p. 338.

Declaring themselves no longer bound by earlier agreements, Bareilly Hindus announced in 1870 that they would take out the *Rāmnaumī* during Muharram.[30] Attempting a new form of compromise, the British administration divided the day between the Hindu and Muslim processions.[31] Seemingly satisfied, Muslims carried out their *ʿalam*s (copies of flags of Husain, often in brass) as requested, but Hindus closed their shops for four days and refused to hold their procession. In the same spirit of protest, some Hindus laid the foundation stone of a temple near an "ancient" Muslim mosque, in a quarter that was "inhabited principally by Muslim residents" and was known as an area where butchers slaughtered cattle.[32]

When the government issued new orders decreeing that in future all processions must avoid the *chauk* (market) or main city roads, Muslims turned to the courts to enforce the earlier agreements. Instead, the Civil Court decreed that the contracts had been binding only on those who signed them and for the occasions for which they were made.[33] Hindus, continuing their own protests, began a boycott, refusing to buy from, or sell to, Muslims, to employ Muslim servants and musicians, to lend money to Muslims, to eat food killed by Muslims, or to allow vakils (lawyers) to take up Muslim legal causes.[34]

30. Although participants are referred to collectively as "Hindus" and "Muslims" in the sources, we do not mean to suggest that *all* Hindus or Muslims were involved.

31. The newspaper *Akbar Alam* (21 April 1870) credits a joint meeting of Hindu and Muslim raises with designing this compromise, which was then approved by government. No mention of this occurs in official sources (*Selections from the Vernacular Newspapers for the North-Western Provinces [SVN], 1870*, p. 165.

32. Regular Appeal no. 178 of 1870, Sheikh Taj Muhammad et al., plaintiffs vs. Moolchund and Thakoory . . . defendants. IOR, Judl. (Criml.) Progs. for NWP for 1871, June, index no. 133, prog. no. 42, Appendix K. The temple was constructed despite the prohibition by the court and was sabotaged by neighboring Muslims. The plaintiffs tore the walls down, stole the idols, and brought another suit. The judgment cited said that the temple could be built, but the judge issued a permanent injunction against the use of musical instruments. Even this last inhibition was struck down in an appeal six months later. (The ground of that appeal is interesting, as well: the appellate judges insisted that "the plaintiffs have no recognized position nor are in any other matter entitled or authorized to represent the Muhammedan community of the quarter where the temple stands," and that the judge's earlier decree prohibiting musical instruments was an illegal infringement [ibid.].)

33. Judgment of Mr. H. Vansittart, Judge of Bareilly, 2 Sept 1870. Mazhur Ally & Others, plaintiffs vs. Mussumat Ranee Ganesh Koour, widow of Chowdhree Nowbut Ram and Others. Judl. (Criml.) Progs.—for NWP for 1871, index no. 22, prog. no. 41, Appendix J.

34. [Anonymous] Report of the Muslims at the Disturbance at Bareilly. IOR, Judl. (Criml.) Progs. for NWP for 1871, index no. 37, prog. no. 54; and Report of F. O. Mayne, Officer on Special Duty, to Officiating Secretary to Government NWP, Bareilly, 27 Apr. 1871. IOR, Judl. (Criml.) Progs. for NWP for 1871, index no. 43, prog. no. 60, par. 10.

In this context, the coincidence of Muharram and *Rāmnaumī* the following year prompted elaborate arrangements by the authorities. They expected Hindus to be the aggressors, and they were not surprised that many Hindus submitted petitions to take out a greatly expanded number of *Rāmnaumī* processions. These were routinely denied. After much preliminary maneuvering and endless meetings, "influential men" of both religions chose a single *Rāmnaumī* route that seemed satisfactory to all concerned.

"Very large crowds of Hindus attended the procession and lined the road," reported one officer. "The whole of the Hindu male population seemed to have turned out and to have brought their children in arms with them."[35] After performing the rites at the garden tank of the sponsoring Rani, the Tibri Mahunt who had conducted the service left for his own house. He was murdered on the way home, at least thirty minutes before rioting broke out.

The riot itself occurred as the procession was returning to town from the garden and seems to have been deliberately provoked—not by Hindus, but by two Muslim policemen who first tried to lead the processionists up a forbidden road and then upset the crowd by breaking an *ʿalam* and shoving its bearer. As indignant cries rose from the processionists, crowds of Muslims swarmed out of a nearby *imāmbārā* and into the procession. Even when this general melee broke up and small groups of Hindus tried to return to their homes, "bands of Muslims" set on them. A gang of "Muslim ruffians" killed the priest Siva Byragee and then plundered his temple. Attacks continued sporadically in the Muslim *muhalla*s and on Hindu temples, but the combination of patrolling by the cavalry and a stringent curfew restored order by noon the following day.[36]

Indignant British officials insisted the riots had been prearranged by Muslims, who used the two policemen as agents. The district officer made it emphatically clear that any future unrest would be laid firmly at the door of the "leading Muslims." It is worth noting, therefore, that the next year most of these leaders precipitously left town prior to the Muharram observance. To what extent had the officials accurately characterized the nature of urban structures and the leaders who repre-

35. Report of F. O. Mayne, Judl. (Criml.) Progs. for NWP for 1871, par. 10.
36 Riots also occurred in nearby Pilibhit and Fureedpore, and there is some discussion about the connections between the riots in the three cities. The evidence is too inconclusive to allow us to speculate, but a similar pattern held in the 1816 house tax protest.

sented them? To answer this question we must analyze, in turn, the physical and political structures of the *qaṣba,* as well as the local forms of social affinities that mobilized the putative "Muslim" and "Hindu" communities.

Political Economy as Community "Structure"

The changing physical layout of the city of Bareilly in itself provides important evidence for the changing urban structures of community in the late nineteenth century. The two main areas of Bareilly, designated Old Town and New City, suggest by their very names and condition the shift in centers of power and affluence.[37] The history of Old Town could be traced to the end of the sixteenth century, shortly after the founding of the city itself. A garrison, the Mirzai Masjid, and the Mirzai Bagh had all been built by Ain-ul-Mulk in this area. Occupied almost exclusively by Muslims in the late nineteenth century, Old Town was a "squalid, decayed suburb" of old, mud-built houses. It was "full of open spaces, graveyards and ruined or ruinous mosques and houses" clustered around the fort of the reputed founder of the city.[38] Constituting one-third of the urban population, the Muslims who lived there had once represented a substantial force in the city. For instance, Pathans— who, from the days of Rohilla rule, retained control of almost half of the Muslim-owned land—resided primarily in Old Town. Its "squalid" condition reflected the decline in fortunes suffered by these Muslim landlords and their allies, the Mughalized service groups.

By the late nineteenth century New City, built a century after Old Town, functioned as the center of urban life: here were located the newer fort, the tomb of Shahdana, and the Sunni Jamĕᶜ Masjid. By this time the main street boasted a "continuous line of neat masonry shops, for the most part of two storeys and uniformly built of brick covered with white plaster"—one solid indication of the wealth of Bareilly's *Baniyā*s (Hindu traders and moneylenders). The city functioned as an important collection and distribution center, especially for grain, sugar, and cotton. The *Baniyā*s figured prominently in the grain and cotton trades. They also benefited from British-imposed alterations in the

---

37. The same process of urban development is described in Richard G. Fox, *From Zamindar to Ballot Box* (Ithaca: Cornell University Press, 1969), p. 27.

38. Nevill, *Bareilly Gazetteer,* p. 210. But see references, below, to its reclamation in the decades following the 1870s.

revenue collection system, becoming substantial landholders in an area essentially without any great estates.[39]

Thus, the physical layout of Bareilly juxtaposed the two elite groups (and their respective cultural styles) that had evolved by the late nineteenth century. The urban styles of both Hindu merchants and Indo-Persian service gentry encouraged those claiming leadership status to express it through religious patronage—particularly the construction and maintenance of sacred buildings—and the public processions associated with ceremonial occasions such as *Rāmnaumī* and Muharram. Moreover, the spatial arrangements aligned areas with one or the other style, for clustered around and between these two pivotal points of Old Town and New City were many of the other *muḥallas*, from which came most of the participants in religious processions. The efforts to unite spatially such disparate areas represented one of the most important functions of public festivals.

The initial impact of British rule on the Mughalized political structures of urban rule bore great similarities to the developments in Banaras. One factor that contributed to the 1816 riot, for instance, had been the installation of an "unpopular Hindu" as kotwal in Bareilly. The increasing cultural and social dominance in the city of Hindu merchants and their Brahmin allies will also look familiar to us. This led, again, to important schisms among Hindu residents. As noted, those merchants brought by the Rohilla town builders essentially identified with and supported an Indo-Persian urban cultural style. But these men had been joined by an influx of new merchant-moneylenders, who operated without the ties to the Rohilla elite or Mughal service gentry that their predecessors had possessed. As moneylenders, particularly, new arrivals had profited greatly from British-induced land transactions and changing policies over revenue collection. Inherent, then, in the political economy of this Rohilkhand *qaṣba* lay potential conflict among those staking claim to leadership of Hindus.

As we have seen, the Brahmin family of *chaudharī* Basant Rai had exercised leadership in the organization and observance of Bareilly's Hindu festivals for several decades. Undisputed leader of the *Rāmlīlā* festival, he also had played a large part in the sponsorship of the *Rāmnaumī* procession, though he shared that role with the Tibri Ma-

39. All claims to landownership postdated the cession of Rohilkhand to the East India Company in 1801; 11.29 percent of the acreage was acquired by *Baniyā* castes through moneylending activities. See *Bareilly Gazetteer*, pp. 211, 70, 88, 100.

hunt.[40] Primarily under his influence "Hindus" signed the covenant that guaranteed peace in 1837 and 1838. His assassination enabled Hindus with competing claims to leadership to refuse to honor that agreement; Basant's son Naubut had great difficulty renegotiating the agreement in 1852.[41] Yet in the face of this clamorous competition in the 1870s, Naubut's widow (the Mussamut Rani Ganesh Koour) continued the tradition of festival sponsorship. Though the family's hold had become increasingly tenuous, British support enabled them to continue to claim primacy. For instance, the Rani, designated by the British administration as "the Hindu representative," was the first to be consulted by the British administration in 1871. Through her agent Momajee she made her requests known: she willingly followed the route laid down the previous year by the police (a route not used then because the Hindus had refused to celebrate) but requested a return route as well. As the return route lay outside the city and did not go near the *chauk* or main city road, the administration had no objections.[42]

Challenges to the Rani's attempts to speak for the Hindus of Bareilly had become increasingly vociferous by 1871. One of the few British officers to note this, Judge Vansittart, put the argument forcefully:

> Chouwdhry Nowbut Ram had relatively no control over the
> Ramnowmi procession which is general to the Hindus. He had
> by usage a certain control over the Ramleela and did in good
> faith make certain concessions in those years of 1852 and 1853,
> mindful perhaps of his father's murder. But he was not spiritual
> chief or lord that he should bind all Hindus in matters of
> Ramnowmee or other religious processions.[43]

The announcement by Hindus in 1870 that they were no longer bound by the agreement, and the petitions by many Hindus to sponsor additional *Rāmnaumī* processions the following year, constitute convincing evidence in support of Vansittart's contentions. Festival sponsorship provided a particularly important means of expression for competing claims to leadership, as the prestige of religious sponsorship reaffirmed established status or buttressed claims for status by the upwardly

40. Judgment of Mr. H. Vansittart, Judl. (Criml.) Progs. for NWP for 1871.
41. Report of F. O. Mayne, Judl. (Criml.) Progs. for NWP for 1871, pars. 5–7.
42. Ibid., par. 16.
43. Judgment of Mr. H. Vansittart, Judl. (Criml.) Progs. for NWP for 1871.

mobile. It is not surprising, then, that a large number of petitions should have been submitted in 1871 for new processions to be taken out.

Given the propensity of the British to freeze in place leaders who had previously been recognized as influential and to deny recognition to new claimants to power, the names of most of those petitioning to take out *Rāmnaumī* processions are understandably unfamiliar. Still largely indiscernible through the records, the range of their actions may be suggested by a brief description of one such applicant, Buldeo Pershad. A Brahmin immigrant,[44] he not only requested permission to take out a procession during the 1870 *Rāmnaumī,* but he also was sufficiently active in the 1871 celebration to be listed as a plaintiff in the Muslim suit to enforce the 1853 agreements. No doubt other newcomers behaved as he had. Competition among those laying claim to leadership and status among Hindus thus echoes the pattern in Banaras, except that the new claimants had greater success in wresting control of public life from the old order.[45]

One reason for this success lay in the major differences between the western *qaṣba* pattern and the eastern U.P. urban pattern: the existence of a prominent and substantial Muslim upper class. Indeed, the *qaṣba* social structure encompassed a basic bifurcation among Muslims (largely missing from the urban population of Banaras) that followed what were primarily class distinctions. North Indian Muslim society could be divided into two main groupings: the ashraf and lower-"caste" Muslim occupational groups (often designated the *ajlāf*). The ashraf constituted the Muslim elite. Their members enjoying superior status based on being well born, these constituent groups shared the Indo-Persian culture fostered first by the Mughal court and then exported to the *qaṣba* urban centers.[46] Despite the nineteenth-century decline in the fortunes of those espousing sharif status, this culture continued to thrive in *qaṣba* centers, emphasizing education, literary and other artistic accomplishments, the holding of administrative positions in Muslim states, study of Islamic law, and Muslim reformist activities. Although long shared by non-Muslims (particularly Kayasths and Khattris), Mus-

44. It is likely he was an immigrant, since his court opponents could not specify his parentage, as they did for others.
45. Not least among the reasons for this success was the inability of the Indo-Persian elite to create a new form of leadership, as did the Raja of Banaras, to fit within the new structure being shaped by the British administration.
46. For a sustained discussion of the ashraf and their culture, see David Lelyveld, *Aligarh's First Generation: Muslim Solidarity in British India* (Princeton: Princeton University Press, 1978), chapter 2.

lims who embraced it perceived this elite way of life as "Islamic." This identification would prove a significant bridge to the concerns held by Muslims of lower status.

Alongside the ashraf elite group, there existed a cluster of lower-class groups defined by the traditional occupations of their members, such as butchers and weavers. Strong corporate identities (often measured by the presence of effective group panchayats, or caste councils), capable of enforcing appropriate codes of behavior and, when needed, of mobilizing for collective action, characterized many of these lower-"caste" groups.[47] Although not always punctilious in observing the injunctions of shari'a (Islamic law), by the late nineteenth century these groups had begun to place great emphasis on the maintenance of certain Islamic activities, particularly those occurring in public spaces, such as the parading of tazias during Muharram, the sacrifice of cattle on the *ʿīd*, or the prevention of music-playing in front of mosques. Indeed, administrative documents of this period measured this emphasis by consistently characterizing the foremost group—Julāhās, or weavers—as "bigoted" or "fanatics," volatile in their defense of Islamic practices. In Bareilly these lower-"caste" values received support, indirectly, from two external influences: the reformist impulse brought to the city by competing groups of ulama, particularly the Deobandis and Barelwis, and the upturn in economic well-being experienced by many of the Muslim artisans in the last quarter of the nineteenth century. In 1871, for instance, a Bareilly official noted that there was a "great deal of preaching going on, and the Moulvees are buzzing about like wasps."[48] The following year the Barelwis established a school there. Though competing Deobandis soon took over the site, the Barelwis did eventually found schools in both Bareilly and Pilibhit.[49] While the two groups of ulama differed sharply in their interpretation of legitimate Islam—the Deobandis urged reforms to return to the pristine Islam they perceived in the Prophet's time, and Barelwis were protective of custom—the important point for the atmosphere in Bareilly was the presence of the debate, which heightened the awareness of all Muslims of their identity

47. See Imtiaz Ahamad, "Caste and Kinship in a Muslim Village of Eastern Uttar Pradesh," in Imtiaz Ahamad, ed., *Family, Kinship, and Marriage Among Muslims in India* (Delhi: Manohar, 1976), pp. 319–46.

48. Letter from R. Drummond to Officiating Secretary, Government of Bengal, 6 Oct. 1871, Mayo Papers, Bundle Wahabbis 1, no. 28. Quoted in Peter Hardy, *The Muslims of British India* (Cambridge: Cambridge University Press, 1972), p. 90.

49. B. Metcalf, *Islamic Revival,* chapter 2.

within the Islamic fold and of the way that their religious practices labeled them as adherents of one or the other sect.[50]

The negotiations around kine sacrifice are an example of how Muslims had acted collectively in various negotiations with the government and "Hindus" regarding administrative control of kine sacrifice on the *ʿīd* and the overlap of public ceremonials.[51] So long as the negotiations proved successful, Muslim participants spoke with one voice. But once the court had ruled against their 1870 legal claim to enforce the 1837 agreement, at least two different contingents of Muslims become discernible in the records. Prominent men, so readily identified by the British as "natural leaders," continued to cooperate with the administration and with Hindu processionists. Despite the court setback they approved a route and patrolled the streets during the processions. But another group of Muslims (including Badr-ud-din, prime mover in the riotous attack on *Rāmnaumī* participants in the following year) launched a second court case—this one to prevent erection of the Hindu temple in a butchers' quarter. The court case against the temple constituted a statement of the centrality of the use of neighborhood public spaces to civic protection of community interests. Meanwhile, lower-class taziadars presented their own petition of protest to the British.

Thus, ashraf-style leaders could not always pursue their own power relationships with the British administration in the face of lower-class Muslim concerns. It is likely, too, that Muslim ashraf aspiring to community leadership, but out of favor with the British, would use occasions of conflict to rally lower-class support. In Bareilly in the 1870s, for instance, Badr-ud-din, the apparent architect of the attack on the *Rāmnaumī* processionists, had been stripped of the position of kotwal by the British, who had installed an "unpopular Hindu" replacement. Under Badr-ud-din's leadership lower-class activists took their protest to the public arena. Staging their own collective action the following year, large crowds of lower-class Muslims gathered in the mosque compound and waited to attack the Hindu crowd celebrating *Rāmnaumī*. To ensure that Hindu processionists came close enough to be attacked, two Muslim policemen had tried to lead the procession

50. For the debate among Barelwis and Deobandis, see ibid.
51. For the kine sacrifice issue, see A & B Genl. Progs. for August 1895 (vol. 4700) and the appendix to Bishan Narayan Dar, *An Appeal to the English Public . . .* (Lucknow: G. P. Varma, 1893), p. 42. Neither of these sources makes any reference to the other timetable, though they overlap. That is, procession events occurred in 1837, 1841, 1852, and 1870; kine sacrifice problems erupted in 1858, 1868, 1892, and 1895.

along a forbidden route and, failing that, had provoked indignation by mistreating the procession's ʿalams. They had then rushed to report their success to Badr-ud-din.[52]

Lower-class and ashraf activity overlapped increasingly during the last three decades of the nineteenth century. Indeed, in the 1870s the viewpoint among Bareilly's Muslims coalesced. Encouraged by reformism as well as opportunities presented by upward mobility, they expressed a shared concern for the status of Indian Islam. These overlapping activities of ashraf and *ajlāf* touched many of the symbolic foci of community. For instance, changes in Bareilly's Old Town reflected first decline and then new economic well-being; described in 1870 as "squalid and decayed," by 1911 the Old Town boasted "good roads and pavements," along which "substantial dwellings of brick" replaced the old mud houses. Most significant, Bareilly's Sunni Muslims had restored the Jameʿ Masjid, and Shi'as had repaired their Gudri-ka Masjid.[53] We have noted how ulama activity in the area, particularly by the Barelwis, accompanied this increasing prosperity. Preaching and exhortation, by competing groups of ulama, quickened by the end of the century. Their success both sensitized Muslims to issues of personal practice and created ties to support future public activities. Indeed, the vernacular newspaper *Nizam-ul Mulk* noted in 1890 of nearby Moradabad that *maulawī* (learned men) frequently made speeches in the public streets of the city, impressing on all classes of Muslims the importance of regularly offering daily prayers, and that "their preaching has had the desired effect. The Muslim tobacco-sellers, weavers, butchers and other lower classes of Muslims, who were not accustomed to offer daily prayers, have already begun to do so."[54]

There were, then, important divisions and lines of competition within the putative communities of "Hindus" and "Muslims" that, depending on the circumstances, could sometimes be overcome by participation in collective expressions of a larger community. Beyond even these more obvious social divisions, lay other affinities as well. Often used by leaders to mobilize supporters and to express their standing in competi-

52. Although the circumvented "natural leaders" left town in the 1870s, they did not fail to learn the lesson of these events. Significantly, by 1895 ashraf organizations championed causes dear to the lower classes. That year, for instance, a petition submitted by individual Muslims on behalf of kine sacrifice received support from another petition, this one submitted by the Anjuman Islamiyya.

53. Nevill, *Bareilly Gazetteer*, pp. 210, 213, 214.

54. *Nizam-ul Mulk*, 10 January 1890, in *SVN, 1890*, p. 24.

tion, these affinities constitute important elements of the "structure" half of communitas.

Community Mobilization Through Local Structures

Urban north Indians belonged to a series of overlapping local collectivities organized variously around ties of kinship, neighborhood, caste, occupational group, place of origin, or leisure activities. Beyond the most obvious lines of mobilization—through occupational *chaudharīs* (headmen) or the elders chosen to head caste panchayats—lay other ways of organizing the smaller units that constituted urban society. Although these do not exhaust the possibilities that could be cited, we will examine three different expressions of local community—*muhalla*s (neighborhoods), ritual organizations, and *akhāṛā*s—to indicate the avenues through which urban residents might be mobilized for collective action. In each of these three examples, of course, other kinds of identities also operated to attract members initially.

Although the evidence strongly suggests that *muhalla*s may prove to be a critical element of urban north Indian social organization, not enough work has been done to delineate their characteristics in detail. Key to our understanding, however, may be the work of Stephen Blake, which traces an eighteenth-century shift in the organization of residential space in Shahjahan's capital city at Delhi. The neighborhood pattern began as an outgrowth of the Emperor's camp organization, in which neighborhoods were centered around *hawelī*s (great houses, or palaces) of courtiers or great merchants. To be near their patrons, service and other client groups lived in domestic configurations clustered around such *hawelī*s.[55] Blake argues, however, that in the eighteenth century, as the Mughal Empire declined, this pattern began to shift to one in which caste and craft groups drew together in residence units that constituted specific *muhalla*s. The boundaries of such *muhalla*s at first coincided with a single, coterminous building extending the length of a street, but crowding and haphazard settlement soon rendered the functional boundaries of a *muhalla* more perceptual than physical.[56] This shift may have been more a matter of degree than of kind. Maps of seventeenth-

55. For a description of such a *hawelī* structure in Banaras, see chapter 1 and the more detailed discussion cited there by Bayly, "Indian Merchants in a 'Traditional' Setting," in Dewey and Hopkins, *Imperial Impact*.

56. Stephen P. Blake, "Dar-ul-Khilafat-i-Shahjahanabad: The Padshahi Shahar in Mughal India, 1556–1739," Ph.D. diss., University of Chicago, 1974.

century Agra, for instance, show that neighborhood patterns based on *haweli*s and occupations already existed in the same urban site.[57]

In any case, by the late nineteenth century, although the residential patterns of the oldest sections in the city might still have echoed the Mughalized *haweli* style, most of the *muhalla*s of Bareilly (particularly of artisan and service castes) tended to be coterminous with occupation. In elite neighborhoods, caste or class affinities served as a basis for shared residence. Migration practices also affected *muhalla* residence patterns, so that neighborhoods often, if not entirely, coincided with extended kinship patterns, regional/linguistic and even natal village origins. Shared religious beliefs often followed from these other affinities.

Though public perceptions, rather than physical constraints, often defined the boundaries of *muhalla*s, and they did not necessarily coincide with other, official units (such as wards), nevertheless *muhalla*s did play a formal role in self-government. Headmen spoke for their neighborhoods in matters of taxation and organized them for such collective action as processions and local religious activities (including maintenance of the shrines, temples, and mosques of the *muhalla*).[58] In 1816, for instance, *muhalladar*s provided the leadership in Bareilly's house tax revolt; these leaders—predominantly Rohilla chiefs and Hindu *Baniyā* raises—headed the protest structure. In 1871, too, *muhalla*s organized many of the components of the Bareilly *Rāmnaumī* procession. Organizers who lived nearby coordinated local efforts to decorate the streets along the processional route and to provide refreshments and other offerings to the paraded deity. Indeed, identification with *muhalla* could be so strong that competition among *muhalla*s located next to each other, or composed of groups with similar social standing, often countered the appeal of occupational allegiances.[59] Again, participation in *Rāmnaumī* observances frequently pitted *muhalla*s against each other, though seldom with the inter-*muhalla* violence observed in cities such as Bombay.

57. Ishwar Prakash Gupta, *Urban Glimpses of Mughal India: Agra, the Imperial Capital, 16th and 17th Centuries* (Delhi: Discovery, 1986).

58. Banaras provides the most celebrated example of *muhalla*-based taxation; see discussion of phatakbandi in chapter 1.

59. For examples, see Nita Kumar on Banaras ("Popular Culture in Urban India," Ph.D. diss., University of Pennsylvania, 1951) and Jim Masselos on Bombay ("Change and Custom in the Format of the Bombay Mohurram," *South Asia*, n.s., 5, no. 2 [1982]: 47–67).

The few analyses that have been made of lower-class and lower-caste leisure-time activities illuminate the importance to *muḥalla* (male) residents of the streetcorners and open spaces of a neighborhood. Tea and liquor shops served as social centers. As Raj Chandavarkar notes, "Street life imparted its momentum to leisure and politics as well; the working classes actively organized on the street. . . . Thus, street entertainers or the more 'organized' tamasha players constituted the working man's theatre." Indeed, both Chandavakar and Nita Kumar have demonstrated that recreation for lower-class males frequently consisted simply of "roaming" the streets of the *muḥalla*.[60]

Ceremonial committees or organizations provided another form of local affinity. Although neighborhood identity overlapped to a considerable extent with certain aspects of ritual activity, participation in such rituals must be seen as a separate form of associational activity shaped by individual decisions. Ritual organization affected a wide variety of local religious activity. Voluntary contributions in money and manpower proved essential in supporting such local activities as temple and shrine *shringārs* (annual renewal ceremonies). Indeed, most popular culture activities were very local in appeal, drawing support in small donations (one or two anna) from residents in the immediate environs.[61] These activities, organized by the unstinting, but volunteer, efforts of individuals (frequently lower-class men) provided evidence of their organizers' great "shauq" (inclination or passionate commitment).[62] Prominent among the examples of such volunteer activities from Bareilly are the taziadars who protested in the early 1870s. Responsible for raising the funds and seeing to the construction of tazias (tomb replicas), the taziadars possessed great influence by virtue of their important local, civic positions in the Muharram ceremonial. The delegation who waited on the Magistrate was composed of "the very lowest orders" of the city; yet when they did not give their approval, no tazias were prepared to be paraded during the 1872 Muharram observances. Once they "professed themselves satisfied," however, tazias began appearing throughout the city and surrounding villages, and the observances themselves took

60. See especially N. Kumar, "Popular Culture," and Raj Chandavarkar, "Workers' Politics and the Mill Districts in Bombay Between the Wars," *Modern Asian Studies* 15, no. 3 (1981):603–47. The quotation is from Chandavarkar, "Workers' Politics," pp. 606–7.

61. See Diane Coccari, "Protection and Identity: Banaras Bir Babas as Neighborhood Guardian Deities," in Freitag, ed., *Culture and Power in Banaras*; N. Kumar, "Popular Culture"; and Norman Hein, *The Miracle Plays of Mathura* (Delhi: Oxford University Press, 1971).

62. See a discussion of this aspect in N. Kumar, "Popular Culture."

place without "a single theft, or quarrel, or offence of any kind against rules or law."

Among the local forms of voluntary associational activities, *akhāṛās* may emerge, after further study, as the most important and pervasive. No systematic analysis of the structure or functioning of *akhāṛās* (or *gharana*s, the term applied particularly to Muslim musicians) has yet been made, although discussions specific to music and medicine point the way.[63] The *akhāṛā* form of organization has been identified not only for physical fitness gymnasiums—the most prevalent type—but also for mendicants, courtesans, medical practitioners, and troupes presenting various performance genres, including classical and folk music (e.g., *birahā*), as well as street theater.[64] Two disparate pieces of evidence may suggest the importance of *akhāṛās* in organizing local society. First, battles between two wrestling *akhāṛās* figure as two of the thirteen most significant events identified in a history of an eastern U.P. *qaṣba* written by a local member of the ashraf. Second, the kotwal of Agra used attendance at wrestling *akhāṛās* to calculate the size of the city's population:

> Malik Aly the *kotwal,* on the basis of counting the individuals assembled in the different *maarekahs* or theatres for athletes or pugilists, reported that in none of these places, were there fewer than 3,000 persons assembled, although it was neither the first day of the New Year nor any of those days of public rejoicing on which it was usual for people to gather for amusement. From this an estimate can be formed of the enormous multitude which thronged the city in every quarter.[65]

Based on individual recruitment, *akhāṛās* nevertheless expressed connections between members in fictive kinship/familial terms. Such familial terminology expressed the strength of ties to fellow members—ties that could be activated in a variety of circumstances. Moreover, the *akhāṛās*, organized around a teacher-student (*ustad-shaggird* or *guru-chela*) relationship, thus could enforce highly disciplined behavior

---

63. See Daniel Neuman, *The Life of Music in North India: The Organization of an Artistic Tradition* (New Delhi: Manohar Books, 1980), and Barbara Daly Metcalf, "Hakim Ajmal Khan: *Rais* of Delhi and Muslim Leader," in Robert Frykenberg, ed., *Delhi Through the Ages: Essays in Urban History, Culture, and Society* (Delhi: Oxford University Press, 1986).

64. Freitag, ed., *Culture and Power in Banaras.*

65. I. P. Gupta, *Urban Glimpses of Mughal India*, pp. 30–31. Wrestling *akhāṛā* battles listed in Gyanendra Pandey, " 'Encounters and Calamities' . . ." in Guha, ed., *Subaltern Studies*, vol. 3, pp. 231–70.

through a cultural model that cast the student in a role embodying learning, servitude, and discipleship. Perhaps most significant, the *akhāṛā* form of organization provided an alternative way to manage resources (and even to transfer them from one generation to another) for such disparate groups as soldier-mendicants (the gosains of Banaras) and courtesans (of Lucknow).[66] Thus, like neighborhood, *akhāṛā* organization provided one of the basic units for mobilizing participants in collective activities. Physical culture clubs, particularly, participated regularly in ceremonial processions, staging demonstrations of sword and stick "play" as the processions moved along their chosen routes. Riot reports suggest that they also could form the basis for goonda organization, which provided the marauding gangs that consistently emerged during communal clashes after the turn of the century.[67]

The pervasiveness of the *akhāṛā* in structuring popular culture activities suggests that its organizational characteristics should be taken very seriously; it is significant that this form seems to have been adopted to organize a wide variety of activities in the second half of the nineteenth century. Barbara Metcalf suggests a likely explanation for this development: "The great scholars and artists, particularly those of Delhi, had depended on patronage from the royal court and from nobles associated with it. With the end of this patronage they adopted new strategies to sustain themselves. . . . At exactly the same time and for the same reasons that the *gharana*s of musicians became important, physicians focused more centrally on their origins and their past."[68] That is, the innovative adaptation of this organizational form substituted popular patronage for aristocratic support and forged strong connections between practitioners and their supporters. Such striking innovation thus helped various groups adapt and survive. To confer legitimacy on such innovation, however, these forms were clothed in familiar terminologies and structures—those of fictive kinship and the teacher-disciple relationship.

---

66. For gosains, see Bernard Cohn, "The Role of the Gosains in the Economy of Eighteenth and Nineteenth Century Upper India," in *Indian Economic and Social History Review* 1, no. 4 (1964): 175–82; for courtesans, see Veena Talwar Oldenburg, "Lifestyle as Resistance: The Case of the Courtesans of Lucknow," paper presented at the American Historical Association meetings, December 1987.

67. See, for instance, the reports for Kanpur on goonda involvement (chapters 6 and 7), and Dilip Basu, "Mallabir: Life History of a Calcutta Killer" and "Mallabir: A Calcutta Killer in Action, 1946–50," unpublished papers. Nita Kumar has contrasted the British preoccupation with goondas and their connection to *akhāṛā*s with the perceptions of her Banarsi informants, who insisted that such people were not goondas but "heroes" because of their athletic prowess (comments during workshop on Banaras, March 1987).

68. B. Metcalf, "Hakim Ajmal Khan," p. 301.

To a certain extent, those prominent in the political economy worked through these kinds of affinities. Depending on the constitution of the group, then, these local structures of *muḥalla,* ritual activity, and *akhāṛā* could either provide modes of organization specific to lower-caste/class culture or serve to integrate urban residents hierarchically. In either case, however, participants' perceptions constructed the collectivity using very localized referents. Nevertheless, as these groups participated in larger arenas, their localized identities became subsumed within broader ones. Chapter 4 examines how communitas worked to create this result; here we conclude by examining the structural aspects of the process.

Structure in Public Arenas

The narrative of events in late nineteenth-century Bareilly highlights a process by which participants moved back and forth between exercises expressing localized forms of community and those referring to a larger community constructed on shared ideological bases. This process can be discerned even in the multiple uses to which the social and political structures were put. That is, multiple meanings of symbolic behavior expressing community become possible. Meanings and purposes became compounded; special political interests become amalgamated with abstract values. Even the sites used for other kinds of interactions and transactions were pulled into public arenas and thus acquired community-related meanings.

A number of examples drawn from the conflict of the early 1870s demonstrate this process. That merchants protested in 1870 by closing down their shops, thus affecting the business of the city's bazaars, not only protected their goods and brought pressure to bear on the British administrators responsible for keeping an urban center functional; it also provided a dramatic statement of the centrality to the urban enterprise of the Hindu merchants of Bareilly, and therefore of the power they possessed. At the same time, such a dramatic gesture suggested that these merchants served as spokesmen for Bareilly's larger "Hindu" community.

Similarly, the refusal of Hindus to take out any *Rāmnaumī* procession in 1870 struck important cultural chords. On the one hand, it represented a form of self-denial to convince opponents—a time-honored strategy, practiced particularly by merchants in the form of "sitting dharna." On the other hand, the very act reflected awareness by those practicing self-abnegation of the presence of a larger community, in whose interest individuals sacrificed their own immediate satisfaction. This effective combination of political strategem and expression of larger community explains why cancellation by a group of its own celebration numbered among the techniques used most frequently to redress a collective grievance. But the British misunderstood the power behind it, for the Magistrate remarked almost indignantly in 1871 that he had been expecting an outburst from Hindus rather than Muslims. He had assumed that Hindus had "lost" the contest the previous year by calling off their *Rāmnaumī* celebration. Muslims, in contrast, had perceived this as a Hindu victory and thus had organized the attack from the *imāmbārā*.

The conflation of larger and smaller community constructions worked in other ways, too. Specific, collective acts against particular groups could carry symbolic meaning against a larger "Other," defined by religion. Most noteworthy was the boycott staged by Hindus against Bareilly Muslims, in which refusals to deal with certain Muslim occupational groups became joined to a general boycott of those in the community of Islam. Thus, they refused to employ Muslim servants or musicians or to eat animals slaughtered by Muslim butchers; at the same time, Hindu merchants were not to buy from, or sell to, Muslims or to lend them money, and Hindu lawyers were not to take up Muslim legal causes.

Participants realized that these symbolic structures of the ceremonial world were embedded within the larger urban world. Protests surrounding ceremony thus often expanded to allied activities, expressing community through other urban structures shaped by the imperial order. In 1870 and 1871 an increased number of applications by Hindus for processions shows the connection between public arena competition and the administrative structure of the city. With these applications came appeals from Muslims to the British courts both to enforce the earlier ceremonial agreement and to deny construction of a temple.

Other urban structures, particularly those related to architecture, space, and time (all characteristics of the world of communitas), came into these negotiations, as well. Within its parameters the Bareilly conflict of the early 1870s encompassed not only ceremonies and boycotts but also the building (and subsequent destruction) of a temple. The debate about the temple related, in turn, to the space to which its builders laid claim—a space judged doubly inappropriate by Bareilly Muslims, as it impinged on an old mosque site, and its locale put it in proximity to butchers, whose slaughter of cattle would doubtless become the object of protest by Hindus. That the killing of kine should loom so large in a Mughalized urban space not only suggests the increasing importance of Hindu raises in the *qaṣba* but also calls our attention to north Indian perceptions of appropriate activities related to the ordering of time in public spaces. It may be remembered that the original compromise of the 1830s linked together the Hindu agreement not to take out *Rāmnaumī* processions during Muharram with the Muslim agreement not to slaughter cattle publicly (i.e., in the bazaar) on festival days.

Conclusion

The "community" invoked by the structures of urban life, often based on more narrowly construed and locally-focused forms of affinities, nevertheless resulted in a shared sense of a larger community that could be expressed in symbolic and ideological terms. In late nineteenth-century Bareilly, we have traced a number of occasions on which participants moved from the localized, relational "community" to the broader one, and back again. Moreover, in the process of intermittently invoking first the narrower and then the broader notions of "community," urban participants implicitly posited a connection between the two.

Connecting relational to ideological community had socioeconomic implications, as well. By the turn of the century, such successful efforts began to bridge the gap in Bareilly between ashraf issues and lower-class occupational groupings of Muslims. Similarly, efforts to act on behalf of all Hindus sometimes overcame the increasingly strong division between *Baniyā*s and Brahmins, on the one hand, and Kayasths and Khatris, on the other.[69] Moreover, as we have seen, attempts to renegotiate the changed status of these respective groups through influence on ceremonial expressions had been sharpened by British denial of legitimacy to new claimants. Indeed, the government's insistence on maintaining in power those they recognized as "natural leaders" carried within it the seeds of its own destruction, for it increased the emphasis Bareilly residents would place, instead, on activities in public arenas.

69. On the persistence of this division, see Lance Brennan, "Local Face of Nationalism," p. 15, for the 1920s, and A. S. Burger, *Opposition in a Dominant-Party System* (Berkeley and Los Angeles: University of California Press, 1969), p. 242, for the postindependence period.

These activities among Muslims found bases particularly in *qaṣba*s since these "medieval country towns" were, "increasingly, the centers for preserving Muslim cultural and religious life."[70] Indeed, one of the characteristics that can be traced in patterns of Muslim collective activity is the way such activity concentrated first in the *qaṣba* centers of Rohilkhand and the Doab and then moved down to the plains by the turn of the century. In contrast, the civic style associated with Hindu merchant *ganj*s moved westward, following *Baniyā* migration along the trade and rail routes that stabilized in the latter half of the nineteenth century.

It is important to keep this evolution of urban cultural styles in mind when discussing Bareilly. It explains why despite the ashraf's economic decline and related loss of political influence to *Baniyā*s and Brahmins in the city, they continued to fight for Muslim community interests. The activities of the Muslim elite occurred in a context in which notions of community for Hindus, too, moved intermittently between localized structures and abstracted ideological constructions. Implied in this movement between relational and ideological communities were invocations of broader, ideological definitions of community. Debates about what constituted "Muslim" and "Hindu" between competing members of each group, and disagreements between them about the extent to which these definitions of "Muslim" and "Hindu" identities had to be defended, sharpened the participants' perceptions of the importance of the ideological identity. Moreover, as groups of Hindus expanded their ceremonial claims to Bareilly's public spaces and civic attention, their acts carried implications far beyond the boundaries of the putative "Hindu" community. Escalation of Hindu demands—for more time devoted to ceremonials like *Rāmnaumī* and *Rāmlīlā*, for protection of Hindu values such as the sacredness of the cow—appeared to Muslims not only as a threat to their previous hegemony in the *qaṣba*'s political economy but also as a diminution of civic life available for their own community rituals. "There never was such a Ramnowmee as there was this year. Such crowds, such music, such rites!"[71] protested Badr-ud-din, the deposed kotwal.

Thus, changes in the structures of community were an important cause of the riots of late-nineteenth century U.P. These structures served

70. B. Metcalf, *Islamic Revival,* chapter 2.
71. Statement of Sheikh Badr-ud-din, 11 Apr. 1872; Judl. Progs. for 1872, index no. 35, progs. no. 52.

as focal points for intracommunity conflict and competition, channeling claims to status and exercises of power along certain social schisms within the respective "Hindu" and "Muslim" communities. As a consequence of these expanded and competing claims, however, the world of Hindu public arenas began to impinge on, and were seen to imperil, the Muslim world. Symbolic activities of the localized, relational structures of urban life were translated into ideological statements with larger referents. Hindu-Muslim riots resulted.

CHAPTER 4

Agra in the 1880s:
Communitas and Public Arenas

Analyzing conflict through the *structures* of community tells only half the story. In this chapter we examine the other half of Turner's model, that of the role of *communitas*. For illustration we turn to events in the city of Agra during the 1880s. Located in the western Gangetic Doab,[1] Agra had functioned as an urban center of some prominence at least since the 1500s.[2] Redeveloped by the Mughal Emperor Akbar as an imperial capital city, Agra "typifies the Mughal city in India," notes one scholar of the city.[3] The urban nature of Agra differed to some extent from that of the Muslim-dominated *qaṣba*s and Hindu-dominated *ganj*s. More complex in organization, this urban nature reflected a cultural balance between the two styles—perhaps the result of its experience not only of Muslim rule under the Lodi Sultanate and the Mughals but also of Hindu hegemony under Jat and Maratha rulers in the eighteenth century. Agra's place at the center of Mughal trade routes had also been important in fostering its particular urban culture. Although its population declined when the trading center shifted to the

---

1. Doab: the land between two rivers.
2. First references to its prominence relate to its use as a capital by Sultan Iskandar Lodi beginning in 1504, after which it shared the status of capital with Delhi.
3. "Akbar . . . was not only aware of the significance of towns and cities but seems to have been quite ahead of his times [sic] in giving impetus to the process of urbanisation." Gupta quotes the *Ain-i Akbari* (history of Akbar's reign) as observing that "without [towns] there will be no progress" (*Ain*, vol. 1, p. 232); quoted in Ishwar Prakash Gupta, *Urban Glimpses of Mughal India: Agra, the Imperial Capital, 16th and 17th Centuries* (Delhi: Discovery, 1986), pp. 3–4.

area around Banaras, Mirzapur, and Ghazipur in the late eighteenth century, the balance of influence in the city's culture remained. The political economy of the city reflected this balance: its Muslim third of the population included both descendants of Muslim courtiers and the artisans who produced goods for courtly consumption, and its Hindu two-thirds included a substantial number of service castes as well as Brahmins and *Baniyā*s. Gupta notes that "soon a class of brokers emerged who helped the traders and merchants in procuring manufactured goods on a commission basis. Through them orders were booked with the weavers and commission paid when the orders were executed. These brokers were also engaged by foreign merchants and foreign trading companies." The activities of these groups contributed significantly to the creation of a money market, enjoying, through the bankers, "connections with all the important cities of India and abroad."[4] As in other urban centers, these *Baniyā*s constituted a strong merchant corporation tracing its roots back to the eighteenth century, which functioned as "a kind of trades council," boasting "formal rules and recorded membership" as early as 1860.[5]

Agra's apparent social stability exhibited signs of disintegration rather suddenly during the 1880s. Beginning in 1882, collective activity led to a series of strikes, refusals to celebrate customary festivals, and continuous protests that in 1884 and 1889 led to riots. Various explanations have been proffered for the sudden emergence of conflict. Several administrators on the spot attributed it to the "needlessly aggressive and irritating" nature of Agra Hindus and the "obstinate and impractical views of the Muslims." The District Magistrate, H. B. Finlay, first suggested that it was due to economic self-interest: "The two vakils who lead the Hindus make a comfortable income by it so long as the agitation lasts, so their share needs no explanation." Then, in a last-ditch effort to defend himself to his superiors, he raised the spectre of nascent nationalist agitation: "Nearly all the Hindus . . . prominently named in the foregoing paragraphs are the ringleaders of what is called the Congress party in Agra, and a good many of them were named as delegates from here to the meeting last Christmas at Allahabad."[6] In a

4. I. P. Gupta, *Urban Glimpses of Mughal India*, pp. 42–43.
5. C. A. Bayly, *Rulers, Townsmen and Bazaars* (Cambridge: Cambridge University Press, 1983), pp. 372, 452.
6. For the first view, see A. Cadell, Report, Proceedings of the General Department for 1890, June, progs. no. 19, serial no. 10. Report by H. B. Finlay to Commissioner . . . dated 29 Oct. 1889, Genl. Progs. for 1890, progs. no. 10, serial no. 5. Report by H. B. Finlay to Commissioner . . . dated 12 Sept. 1889, Genl. Progs. for 1890, progs. no. 21, serial no. 10, par. 19.

similar vein, scholar Francis Robinson attributes the increased activity to the introduction of politics connected with passage of the Municipalities Act.[7]

It is certainly true that almost all of the Hindus visible in these actions were Municipal Commissioners and members of Congress, whether vakils (lawyers) or members of the traditional landed elite.[8] But the only official action taken by the Municipal Commission in regard to festivals concerned the granting of licenses (primarily to Muslims) for construction of *sabīl*s (refreshment stands erected along procession routes). Finlay noted in this connection that the Municipal Secretary "kept himself apart as much as was possible from all this embroglio."[9] Indeed, the only complaint (and this lodged by administrators—none by "Hindus" or "Muslims") insisted that too many new permits had been issued. Though the creation of municipal boards eventually provided a new route of expression for community conflict, then, the significance attributed to them by Robinson should not be imputed to these early years.

No doubt part of the responsibility for fostering conflict must be laid at the door of the local administration itself; District Magistrate Finlay was notoriously pro-Muslim.[10] And contradictory decisions made by Agra administrators year after year during this decade greatly exacerbated the situation. Finlay's hard line of 1882 for Hindu celebrations was reversed in his absence in 1884; a new policy introduced in 1888 was negated in 1889.[11] Although significant, this imperial interference

7. "In Agra, for example, as soon as the 1883 Municipalities Act was passed, greatly increasing the powers of the Hindu majority on the municipal board, Hindus began to refurbish and celebrate with vigor festivals that clashed with Mohurram" (F. C. R. Robinson, *Separatism Among Indian Muslims* [Cambridge: Cambridge University Press, 1974], pp. 79–80).

8. Examples include Jamna Das Biswas, vakil and editor of the newspaper *Nasim-i-Agra;* Nand Kishore, longtime resident of the town and a landowner; and Din Dayal, a bania (cloth seller). See fn. 6, Genl. Progs. for 1890.

9. Reply by H. B. Finlay to Commissioner . . . dated 10 May 1890, Genl. Progs. for 1890, progs. no. 10, par. 7.

10. Finlay contradicted himself in different letters to the Commissioner on the subject of Agra Hindus. On 29 October 1888 he wrote, "The Hindus—or rather a numerous and important section of them . . . have done their very utmost to insult the Mussalmans of the City" (Genl. Progs. for 1890, progs. no. 10, serial no. 5). On 10 May 1890 he wrote, "I admit at once that I have a very strong animus against the group of insignificant, unscrupulous and hypocritical agitators, who, under the pretext of zeal to perform a religious festival, do their utmost to bring themselves into prominence, to destroy the peace of a great city, and to exasperate and insult the followers of another creed" (Genl. Progs. for 1890, progs. no. 22, serial no. 10). See also various Muslim vernacular press observations about their "friend," Magistrate Finlay (*SVN, 1883–88*).

11. Report of A. Cadell, Genl. Progs. for June 1890, progs. no. 19, serial no. 10; par. 2, and progs. no. 22, serial no. 10.

does not explain what happened in Agra during the decade. To find that explanation, we must delve more deeply into the public arenas of Agra and analyze the nature of ceremonial life as it fostered communitas among Hindus and Muslims, respectively.

Festival as Metaphor

We have noted that participation in public rites and festivals provided an important experience and statement of group solidarity. Of special interest here are those festivals in which processions played significant roles, such as *Rāmlīlā* and Muharram.[12] Such processions—as cultural performances—provided unique occasions for participants and observers alike.[13] The experience of involvement in the acting out of major events in the lives of the deities blended momentarily with the more abstract lessons the events symbolized. This convergence of the "dispositional" and the "conceptual" aspects of religious life[14] played a particularly important part in South Asian experience, for it built on cultural assumptions that exemplary behavior gained one merit even as it trained one for future meritorious actions.[15] The processional festival thus served as a kind of metaphor for the process of group identification.

For festivals to serve as metaphors of community, they had to perform several crucial functions in an urban environment. Preeminent among these was the juxtaposition of participants in a single location, for religious processions provided an important integrative link by bringing together, in a public expression of solidarity, the neighborhood- or patron-based parties to form a whole. In the case of the

12. Chapter 1 discusses some of the more political implications of *Rāmlīlā*. As noted there, it is an autumnal festival during which events in the life of Rām are presented in dramatic form. The duration varies with locale, but the performances "employ an unusual stage technique which combines recitation of the sacred text with simultaneous acting and dialogue" (Norvin Hein, "The Ram Lila," *Journal of American Folklore* 71, no. 281 [July–Sept. 1958]: 279). See also H. R. Roe, *Guide to Muhammadan and Hindu Festivals and Fasts in the U.P.* (Allahabad: U.P. Government Press, 1934), p. 26.

13. The term "cultural performance" was introduced by Milton Singer in "Cultural Patterns of Indian Civilization," *Far Eastern Quarterly* 15 (1955): 23–26, and used by Clifford Geertz in "Religion as a Cultural System," in *The Interpretation of Culture* (New York: Basic Books, 1973), p. 113.

14. Geertz has also referred to this blending of experiences as the "model for" what is believed and the "model of " what is believed (ibid.).

15. See, for instance, a discussion of this for South Asian Muslims in Barbara Daly Metcalf, ed., *Moral Conduct and Authority: The Place of Adab in South Asian Islam* (Berkeley and Los Angeles: University of California Press, 1983). Peter Brown's article in this volume, "Late Antiquity and Islam: Parallels and Contrasts," suggests, through an analysis of the late-antiquity concept of paideia, that such assumptions about behavior may be common to a number of societies.

Juljhulni festival, for example, leaders began in each neighborhood to organize their own, smaller processions. The leaders listed for Agra's 1890 Juljhulni included:

1. *Rawatpura [muḥalla] procession*
    Piare, Chaudhuri
    Ram Baksh, Chaudhuri
    Radhe Lal, Chaudhuri

2. *Namak-ki-Mandi [an area incorporating several muḥallas] procession*
    Babu Lal, Bania
    Jaggan Nath, Brahman

3. *Phulatti [bazaar] procession*
    Gokal Chand, Pujari
    Kundho Mal, Seth
    Ram Pershad, Chaudhuri[16]

Through the work of these leaders within their smaller communities, the process of uniting Rawatpura, Namak-ki-Mandi, and Phulatti bazaar parades connected each urban area to a larger entity. For participants the linkages were expressed in graphic terms, as the various groups came together at the riverbank. At the same time, the constituent groups remained distinct within the crowd, bringing honor to those who had organized them. We know from a study of earlier Agra that the metaphorical integration brought together neighborhoods of service groups clustered around the *hawelīs* of great men built along the riverbank, middle-class neighborhoods populated by merchants and traders, and the burgeoning lower-class neighborhoods grouped by specialization that pushed Agra's urban growth to the north and west of the central city.[17]

Theoretically these religious exercises could have operated without reference to any civic boundaries. But as they involved extra-*muḥalla* concerns, they inevitably had reference to the larger administrative system: to operate, they required British government recognition of their legitimacy. As we have seen, they needed British approval of the routes, the timing, and the size and nature of the observance. This wider

16. "Orders for the Juljhulni," Magistrate of Agra, Genl. Progs. for June 1890, progs. no. 19, serial no. 10.
17. See I. P. Gupta, *Urban Glimpses of Mughal India*, pp. 20, 77, 79.

frame of reference linked people together and provided a connection between the *muhalla* and a larger entity. But how did this work?

It did not seem to link them together in an objective sense. The Indian procession functioned much less as a coherent production from start to finish than as a congeries of discrete elements almost accidentally arrayed one after another. Each group, with different sponsors, assembled at its own patron's behest and paraded with flags or floats constructed at his request, thus making a statement about the size of the patron's network and influence. Based on neighborhood, livelihood, or other affinity (such as *akhārā*), most groups traced their organizational ties back to something quite different from the occasioned religious purpose. In such processions these small groups were arranged in an imprecise formation, moving slowly through city streets along the route previously approved. This discreteness applied to the crowd, as well. Though the number of watchers might be overwhelming, they still formed small kinship groups that participated as discrete units, buying goods and dispensing them to either the deity being paraded or the processionists.

But observations on this objective level do not tell the whole story. There was, working on the psychological level, much to knit both onlookers and processionists into a meaningful whole. This integration worked in spatial, temporal, and cognitive terms. A description written in Agra in the 1880s conveys how powerful the effect was, even for an outside observer:

> And in India the crowd forms so important a part of the specta-
> cle, that the selection [of the main street] is more justified than
> elsewhere. The Singhasan pursuing its way through squalid sub-
> urbs, or over country roads, does not greatly impress the on-
> looker; but when the chief street is reached all is changed: the
> aspect of the houses with roofs, windows, and balconies crowded
> with spectators, animates the worshippers, the throng in the
> streets becomes denser, the enthusiasm increases, the shouts of
> the multitude round the car are answered by the crowds on the
> houses, and as amidst the triumphant clamour of voices the great
> mass of human beings passes up the street, the organizers of the
> festival feel that their god has been honored, and that their
> management has been a success.[18]

18. Report of A. Cadell, Officiating Commissioner, Agra Division, to Chief Secretary to Government, NWP & O, dated 4 Oct. 1888, Genl. Progs. for June 1890, progs. no. 3, serial no. 2, par. 23.

Thanks to the impact of the crowd, the enthusiasm and shouting, what began as discrete elements were welded into an interlinking whole. As we have seen in the discussion of Bareilly, structure provided an important ingredient in this integration, as reflected in that intriguing last line of the description—"the organizers feel that their god has been honored, and that their management has been a success." Beyond this structural component, however, lay the development of a sense of community, fostered by the liminal elements of the experience.

The use of urban space proved especially important in expressing community. The administrator's description of the spectacle explained why all procession sponsors wanted to go through the central *chauk* (market) and down the main street. Use of the main thoroughfare ensured the maximum audience, always an important consideration for the public exercises of religion. More significantly, it established community claims to the center of an urban locale, implying the centrality of the group to city life. It was the 1870 decision in Bareilly to forbid these areas to processionists that finally forced Muslims there to take action.

But the processions also explicitly integrated the center of town and the periphery, as well as important areas in between. This integration had important civic implications. Each procession began in the center of town, wended its way through the *chauk* and past the kotwalee (police station), and continued to the edge of town, with its final goal a tank, the river, a temple, or an *imāmbāra*. These routes served several integrative purposes. In Bareilly in 1871 the Rani requested such a route in order to show the god's image to the women and old people confined in the intervening neighborhoods, for only males and children crowded the streets to observe the procession. Beyond this purpose, a processional route made a physical statement that recognized the importance to the group of the areas through which the god's procession passed: no one was peripheral to the god.

Onlookers had much time to observe and participate, to be incorporated into the process, since these processions generally constituted very slow and dramatic productions. A Muharram procession, for instance, might take fourteen hours to go but three miles. Innumerable stops would be made along the way, perhaps at *sabīl*s (refreshment stands)[19]

19. "A sabil to the outward eye is nothing but a refreshment board, a plank with a few earthen cups and an earthen vessel on it, but esoterically it is an offering to the Prophet, a commemoration of the thirst and privations of Hassan and Hussain at Karbala, and those who drink ought to utter a certain prayer (if they know it) while the vessels themselves are held sacred from ordinary profane use. Any person may set up a sabil." Report from W. E. Neale, Commissioner, Agra Division, to Secretary to Government NWP & O, dated 15 May 1890, Genl. Progs. for 1890, progs. no. 17, serial no. 10, par. 9.

erected not only by pious Muslims (including, despite official indignation, a prostitute) but also by cooperative Hindus. Similarly, during the *Bhārat Milāp* procession of *Rāmlīlā,* shopkeepers would interrupt the leisurely procession to "invite the impersonators of the deities into their shops and offer refreshments and small gifts of money."[20]

The interplay of sacred and profane space deserves special attention. The very mobility of the sacred space surrounding a procession, while providing an element essential to fostering community, posed some crucial problems. These occurred primarily when one group's sacred space overlapped another's, and these circumstances often prompted riots. The shouting and music of a Hindu procession within a certain distance, for instance, would violate the sacredness of a mosque. To prevent this, all revelry, music, and shouting had to stop within a specified zone around a mosque. The delimitation of just which space should be defined as sacred expanded continually, however. One administrator regretfully noted that at the end of the divisive decade in Agra, temporary tazia stands and *sabīl*s had come to be treated as spaces similar in stature to mosques. Moreover, such space could be vertical as well as horizontal, as attested by the recurring contests between the heights of the tazias and the lowest branches of the sacred pipal tree. In these circumstances, then, space could be divisive as well as integrative and did serve to define participants against an "Other" considered outside the community involved in the observance.

Sacredness operated in temporal, as well as spatial, terms. For Hinduism and Indian Islam, as for most religions, ceremonials to some extent ordered time. They did this in two ways. First, they measured the time between events by "creating intervals in social life."[21] In this respect, the two religions exhibit striking differences in their sacred calendars.[22] Virtually every lunar month contained a festive event for Hinduism, with a regular mix throughout the year of processions, fairs, and related occasions. Clusters of events in the fall balanced out those in the spring; each cluster built to a crescendo, culminating in large festivals (Dasehra/*Rāmlīlā* and Divali in the fall; Holi in the spring). Equally important, an overwhelming publicness characterized the Hindu festival calendar: virtually all of these events came to be signified through public ceremonies or had major public components. The style

20. Hein, "The Ram Lila," p. 293.
21. Edmund R. Leach, "Time and False Noses," in *Rethinking Anthropology* (London: Athlone Press, University of London, 1961), pp. 124–36.
22. Plotted from Roe, *Guide.*

of Hinduism most characteristic of revivalist and merchant-dominated cities quite consciously aimed at public time and public space.

In contrast, the Muslim calendar of the nineteenth century, like that of the Christian West, divided the year into passive and active halves; the latter could be said to begin with the month-long fasting of Ramazan. It was punctuated by the two *ʿīds*: *ʿīd ul-fiṭr* to break the Ramazan fast, and *Baqar ʿīd* to observe the sacrifice of Ishmael by Ibrahim. The first third of the month of Muharram marked the high point, during which observances of the martyrdom of Husain claimed the attention of both Sunnis and Shi'as in the late nineteenth century. The next two months each contained an observance, but then five months passed without an important celebration. Moreover, with the exception of the tazia-parading portions of Muharram, these events took predominantly private forms.[23] The nonpublic nature of Muslim observances became increasingly important as reformers concentrated on altering their characteristics.

Just how far should temporal perceptions be pressed in exploring this metaphor?[24] To the extent that the popular culture of public arenas consisted of shared ceremonials, in which putative "Hindus" and "Muslims" moved easily between observances ostensibly targeted at only one of the Great Tradition religions, temporal perceptions conditioned by the metaphor may mean little. To explore the implications of reformist efforts to contain fellow believers within one tradition, it may suffice for the moment to show that the Hindu and Muslim calendars, punctuated very differently, fostered different cognitive senses of time. That is, the perceptual calendars, perhaps even the mental process of measuring time, differed in Hinduism and Islam. Moreover, the nature of Hindu festivals, predominantly joyous celebrations tied to the season, contrasted dramatically with Islamic ones, movable occasions predominantly of self-denial or mourning. These characteristics may have had a subtle, but profound, impact. In an urban setting in which members of other communities ostensibly joined in the observance of a particular religious group, it may be that they actually infused a quite different

23. This pattern may have begun to change in the twentieth century with the emphasis among reformists on public observances of the Prophet's birthday. See Muhomad Ali, *My Life: A Fragment,* ed. Afzal Iqbal (Lahore: Sh. M. Ashraf, 1946).

24. For implications more complex than those treated here, see Charles Phythian-Adams, "Ceremony and the Citizen: The Communal Year at Coventry 1450–1550," in Peter Clark and Paul Slack, eds., *Crisis and Order in English Towns 1500–1700* (London: Routledge and Kegan Paul, 1972), and Carol Appadurai Breckenridge, "Risking Incorporation and Worship in a South Indian Temple," paper presented to the SSRC/ACLS Workshop on Risk and Uncertainty, Philadelphia, 1977.

meaning into the same activity. Certainly, once reformist impulses quickened in the communities examined here, these subtle differences became accentuated. This is not to argue that Hindus and Muslims inevitably differed. Rather, it is to suggest that although their public *actions* may not have differed substantively from that of their neighbors, the *sense* of the occasion among Hindu and Muslim participants may have possessed the potential to separate them in significant ways. Given a heightened awareness in a time of conflict, these fundamental differences of pacing and tenor of religious time could begin to separate effectively the believer participants from an "Other."

The second way in which time was ordered juxtaposes what in Durkheimian terms would be called Normal-Profane and Abnormal-Sacred time. It is not just the two diametrically opposed periods of sacred and profane that have importance: the periods of transition are equally significant in the experiences of the participants.[25] In processions, as in pilgrimages, cultural performances moved the participant and even the onlooker from one type of time to another: "He was no longer involved in that combination of historical and social structural time which constitutes the social process in his . . . urban home community, but [he] kinetically re-enacted the temporal sequences made sacred and permanent by the succession of events in the lives of incarnate gods, saints, gurus, prophets and martyrs."[26] Participation thus became a way of transposing one's self to the sacred time in question. By enacting the events alongside the religious figure, one fused the "models of " and "models for" appropriate behavior. This identification seems particularly significant for events around the stories of *Rām* and of Muharram, for in both cases the enactments involved embattled groups fighting evil forces to preserve right and their moral community. Public participation created perceptions of community identity more effectively than could any other experience.

Looking back at Bareilly's *Rāmnaumī* procession, we can see that festival as providing the very paradigm for processionists moving through the transitional stage to sacred time, as participants followed the image of *Rām*, surrounded with fluttering flags and accompanied by exuberant music, through the city to the sponsoring Rani's garden. After an appropriate ceremony marking the sacred nature of the occasion, the procession returned to town. Even bystanders could enter

25. See Leach, "Time and False Noses."
26. Victor Turner, "Pilgrimage as Social Process," *Dramas, Fields, and Metaphors: Symbolic Action in Human Society* (Ithaca: Cornell University Press, 1974), p. 207.

sacred time by watching the procession or by providing refreshments, flowers, or other offerings to the deity. Though each group of participants might remain distinct from its neighbors, they shared involvement in the same observance for the same ostensible object. Community connections must have been felt at their most tangible and concrete, fostered by these very specific physical, psychological, spatial, and temporal influences. As long as the impact of all of these influences still operated, the overarching nature of group identification based on religious community appeared utterly convincing. Threats to community values during these occasions of integrative collective activities could prompt immediate and vehement responses.

Equally important, the urban environment carried with it the sense that sacred time and sacred space had to be reckoned as limited commodities.[27] Any move by one group to expand its share of them constituted an effort to subtract from the share of another group. In this way, intragroup rivalries affected intergroup relationships, as well. Thus, in the very process of fostering a sense of shared identity lay the potential for conflict. Given certain circumstances, the integrative nature of public ceremonials could work, instead, to exclude those considered outsiders. Any definition of community stressed shared characteristics and values and drew boundaries that were simultaneously inclusive and exclusive. The emotional and psychological state of communitas could not help but emphasize differences as well as similarities, exaggerating the importance of each.

Festival as Competing Definitions of Community

Two types of competition, creating the circumstances in which festivals worked to pose groups against each other, can be illustrated by U.P. examples drawn from festivals before 1890. On the one hand, new claimants to status attempting to sponsor such events could suddenly emerge, demanding the opportunity for involvement: we saw examples of this process in Bareilly in the 1870s. On the other hand, the festivals themselves could become weapons in the struggle for dominance between groups with very different definitions of religious observance; it is this phenomenon that shaped the events of Agra during the 1880s.

Perhaps surprisingly, given the historical explanations previously offered, this shape had little to do with Hindu lawyers, Muslims, or

27. See the classic essay on the concept of "limited good," George M. Foster, "Peasant Society and the Image of Limited Good," *American Anthropologist* 67, no. 2 (April 1965).

British administrators. Rather, the evidence points repeatedly to a connection between Hindu participants and an organization called the Sanatan Dharm Sabha. The founding of the Agra branch of the Sanatan Dharam in turn occurred shortly after the arrival in Agra of the Hindu reformist organization, the Arya Samaj.[28] Arya Samaj founder Swami Dayanand Saraswati gave a series of lectures in Agra in 1880, and residents founded an Arya Samaj lodge in Agra the following year. In the early 1890s the number of Aryas in the district remained under one thousand, but in the following decade the number almost trebled. The Samaj preached a reformist version of Hinduism that denied status to Brahmins, recognized only the Vedas as scriptural authority, and downplayed the significance of caste. In short, the impact of Dayanand's preaching and the organization's activity in Agra constituted an attack on customary Hindu practices.

In response, the Sanatan Dharm Sabha's membership, which in the 1880s "greatly outnumbered the Aryas," defended the "old faith and practices." But Sabha actions constituted proselytization as much as defense.[29] The antagonists fixed their focus firmly on festivals, for the activities of Agra's public arenas provided the ideal battleground for the competing definitions of Hinduism pursued by the Arya Samaj and the Sanatan Dharm. As noted by Hein, though ideally there should be only one celebration of an occasion in a locality, it was true that "any group of malcontents or enthusiasts [was] conceded the right to organize an independent performance in their ward of a town and to compete for preeminence. If they prove[d] clever in assembling talent and funds they [might] eventually win" citywide recognition for their observance.[30] The British desire to capture on paper customary practice through definitive description that became the "norm" (thereby freezing it indefinitely) complicated this dynamic process. But public arena activities still provided the most accessible battleground for defining through practice what Hinduism meant and, in the process, enabling those defending ostensible "custom" to respond to the challenges issued by reformers such as the Arya Samaj.

Part of the Sanatan Dharm Sabha's strategy involved mounting a concerted effort to revive old religious observances and to infuse reli-

28. H. R. Nevill, *District Gazetteers of the United Provinces of Agra and Oudh,* vol. 8, *Agra* (Allahabad: U.P. Government Press, 1901–1911), p. 72.
29. See Kenneth Jones, "Sanatan Dharm: Hindu Orthodoxy in Defense of Tradition," a paper presented to the Midwestern Conference on Asian Affairs, October 1978.
30. Hein, "The Ram Lila," p. 292.

gious symbolism into hitherto secular festivals. The renewed attention paid to the Krishna festival of Juljhulni in 1888 is a case in point. Two processions with idols from different parts of town passed through the bazaar, before the kotwalee, to the bank of the river, where they joined a third procession from a temple. In returning, two of the processions carried the god back through the center of town to their respective temples. Because the celebration at the temples could "only" boast a pedigree of twenty-two or twenty-three years, British administrators indignantly discounted it as a "second-rate" festival.[31] Jamna Das Biswas, of the Sanatan Dharm, on the other hand, insisted in 1890 that "there was no Ramlila this year because Krishna's festival which is first in rank, had not been observed, that year[,] that is Juljhulni."[32]

An even more obvious example of Sanatan Dharm strategy is provided by the *Pairākī,* or swimming fair. Revivalist attention to this fair prompted the unrest of 1888. "A festival which had its origin in the respect paid to a Muhammedan teacher of the art of swimming"[33] may not seem an obvious candidate for a refurbished religious festival and a rallying point for traditionalist Hinduism, but it suggests how *akhāṛā* ties could be extrapolated to express the ties of a larger community. Organizers expanded the basic ceremony for boys—"wearing jewels and beating sticks, assembled from each mohulla," and marching in procession through the various bazaars—to include a stop at the Balkaisar temple. Here the observance began with a religious ceremony to the god Mahadev, followed by nautches (dances) and then a swim to the Jumna's Chhota Ghat, from "whence each band passed to its mohulla[,] . . . the boys dancing and beating sticks to midnight." A similar format was followed two days later in a procession to yet another location. "Grand preparations" were made for the ceremonies: "caps and dresses of all kinds and of various colors [were] prepared. Sweetmeats of all descriptions and eatables of all kinds [were] prepared

31. List of important religious festivals that occur during the year in Agra, Genl. Progs. for 1890, progs. no. 12, serial no. 5, item (13); Note on the Juljhulni File, by A. Cadell, Commissioner of Agra Division, dated 14 Apr. 1890, Genl. Progs. for 1890, progs. no. 29, serial no. 10. Another source called it "fourth rate"; see Neale, in cover note to Abstract of a Statement of Representative Men of Agra, dated 6 May 1890, Genl. Progs. for 1890, progs. no. 18, serial no. 10, statements dated 30 Apr. 1890. Finlay outdid them all (as usual), calling it "not even tenth rate" (Report by Finlay, dated 10 May 1890, par. 10).

32. Abstract of a Statement. In fact, *Rāmlīlā* had not been celebrated from 1885 to 1889. List of important religious festivals, item (14). We might speculate that this is also an attempt by the Sanatan Dharm to influence the reverence of Krishna over *Rām.*

33. Report of A. Cadell, Genl. Progs. for June 1890, progs. no. 19, serial no. 10, par. 5.

from days before."[34] Clearly, revivalist Hindus used this occasion to graft religious observances onto a festival already popular with the residents of Agra. In this case, we can see how such an operation served to exclude some urban residents as well, and to force them to make active choices about their own definitions of Hinduism. Thus, two observances of *Pairākī* occurred in 1888. The traditional observance appealed to Muslims and Hindus who did not share the goals of the Sanatan Dharm. The second fair attracted the revivalists organized by the Sanatan Dharm. Those who wished to participate in the swimming festival had to choose between these two versions of it—versions that also implied certain values, modes of appropriate behavior, and affiliations opposed to an "Other."

The Ga'ocharan festival provides a final example of altered public festivals in Agra. In this celebration, a "procession of cows richly ornamented in various ways," accompanied by music from temples, moved through the main bazaars. This festival emerged for a sudden and short-lived popularity in 1884. No doubt part of that popularity was due to the possibilities it offered for irritating Muslims involved with Muharram. But the timing also coincided with the surge of enthusiasm for Cow Protection that swept U.P. in this decade. The festival afforded an opportunity, for those defending what were perceived as traditional Hindu values, to involve large numbers of people in an entertainment that also functioned as a statement of community solidarity.

Beyond these efforts to revive old religious observances and to infuse religious meaning into previously secular festivals, the Sabha also took up the task of defending the "ancient rights" of Hinduism. This organizational role became most apparent when the Commissioner of Agra Division summoned six of the Hindu signatories to the 1890 protest petition. "When asked to produce the orders they complained of, and to state what were the points of which they complained, [Amir Singh, Nand Kishore, and Shib Narayan] said the orders would be produced tomorrow by Mathura Dass, Secretary of the Dharm Sabha." Indeed, the latter two "old inhabitants and [owners] of land" insisted, in letters to the Magistrate, that they had been "cajoled into signing the petition by being told that it merely asked for the usual mela (fair) to continue

---

34. Copy of the order of the Officiating Commissioner, Agra Division, dated 12 Sept. 1888, Genl. Progs. for 1890, progs. no. 6, serial no. 20; petition of Hindu residents of Agra to Commissioner, dated 11 Sept. 1888, Genl. Progs. for 1890, progs. no. 6, serial no. 20, pars. 3, 4.

and contained no complaint of anybody."[35] The two had nothing concrete to say about Hindu dissatisfactions when queried.

More knowledgeable—though he was dismissed impatiently by Magistrate Finlay as a "cat's paw"—was Gokal Chand, Chaudhari.[36] His role as the leader responsible for organizing the Phulatti (bazaar) procession indicates the part played in the Dharm Sabha by neighborhood leaders. Gokal Chand delineated precisely the details to which he objected.[37] More important, when the decision had to be made whether to have the procession, he played a foremost role in dealing with the Magistrate. He "spoke out plainly and stated that unless they were allowed to raise the jaikara [cries] and have music where they pleased . . . they would have no procession."[38]

Thus, the Sanatan Dharm functioned in several ways to heighten the awareness of Hindu residents in Agra of the importance of their role in expressing community ties through public ceremonies. The example of Gokul Chand demonstrates how Sanatan Dharmis crystallized the issues on which Hindu activists should take stands. By singling out certain ceremonials, they also pointed the way for patronage by wealthier urbanites. In a period in which Hindu merchants increasingly prospered, this ability to align appropriate charitable objects with community activism proved a particularly important refinement of urban practices;[39] this refinement grew directly from the competition between the Sanatan Dharm and the Arya Samaj.

Finally, the Sanatan Dharm demonstrated that during festivals the leadership could participate selectively to shape collective expressions of community:

> On the occasion [of the 1888 celebration of the Juljhulni] the leaders of the Hindus deserved commendation. Men who had hidden themselves away on the 13th [during the earlier *Pairākī*

35. Abstract of a Statement, statements dated 29 April 1890.
36. Report by Finlay, dated 10 May 1890, par. 6.
37. Abstract of a Statement, last statement dated 30 April 1890.
38. Report of H. B. Finlay, dated 12 Sept. 1889, Genl. Progs. for June 1890, progs. no. 21, serial 10.
39. For a discussion of Hindu-merchant charitable practices and religious piety, see especially Bayly, *Rulers, Townsmen and Bazaars,* chapter 10. For Agra's merchants particularly, Gupta has noted that the city's "Hindu *banias* (merchants) . . . were affluent but lived frugally. The wealth which they amassed was spent on the construction of houses, gold ornaments, dowry, presents in marriages, festivals, birth of a male child and other rituals, specially funeral ceremonies. They also spent lavishly on the construction of charity wells, temples, gardens, hospitals, and on providing free food and fresh cool drinking water to passers-by. The latter was considered a very pious act. A lot of money was spent on pilgrimages and other religious and social functions" (Gupta, *Urban Glimpses of Mughal India,* p. 78).

festival], and had during the intervening days been late at every meeting, came into the streets on the 17th, superintended and controlled the procession, seconded the efforts of the police, and ensured the absolute punctuality that under the circumstances was so necessary. If they had taken the same trouble on the 13th, the authorities might have had fewer difficulties to contend with, and the city of Agra might have been spared much of the excitement and alarm which it experienced.[40]

From Intracommunity Competition to Intercommunity Conflict

As the more traditionalist members of Agra's Hindu population tried in a variety of ways to define Hinduism, and as they competed with the Arya Samaj for leadership over public ceremonials, their disputes made an impact on Muslims as well. No doubt the aggressive proclamation of Hindu "rights" and the defense of the group's psychic boundaries against Muslims served as another way to enhance the Sanatan Dharm's claim to leadership. Although it seems clear that these actions had arisen originally not from an increased awareness of Hindu-ness vis-à-vis Muslim-ness but as an emphatic avowal of traditionalist Hinduism against the revisionist Arya Samaj, these disputes nevertheless had another outcome as well. In an urban environment perceived by its inhabitants to have only limited quantities of sacred time, space, and "rights," the competition-driven expansion within one community was seen as subtracting from the rights of the other.

Protests of the developments in Agra during the 1880s suggest the nature of these perceptions of "limited good" available to competing communities. In 1883, for instance, a memorial to the government noted that, in response to a protest filed by Agra Muslims, the Magistrate "directed that the procession should not pass through the usual route but should pass and repass only through an unfrequented and dirty lane, through which orthodox Hindus do not generally go even for ordinary business and which is too narrow for any procession of this kind." It continued by bemoaning the fact that

> in practice [Hindus] do not enjoy equal liberty with their
> Muhammedan fellow subjects in the observance of their religious
> and social observances. Muhammedans were allowed to go in
> procession through the streets with tom toms beating, naked

40. Note on the Juljhulni File, by A. Cadell, Genl. Progs. for 1890, progs. no. 29, serial no. 10.

swords playing, and with burning sticks and Zulfikar, that is to say a large number of swords arranged in line on a piece of wood, to the great annoyance of the public; whereas the quiet and unobjectionable Gaocharan ceremony of the Hindus was prohibited. Moreover, the Muhammedans are always allowed during their Muharram festival to mourn near Hindu temples and Hindu dwelling houses where marriage rites and ceremonies connected with child birth etc. are being performed. On such auspicious occasions the Hindus regard the mourning as an omen of evil, yet the Muhammedans are not prevented from annoying the Hindus in this matter.[41]

As a framework of perceptions became established that linked developments in one city with those in another, both the image of "limited good" and the evocation of precedents extended to this larger world. The above memorial, quoted in the *Tribune,* spoke to other interested Hindus, as well, when it concluded, "your memorialists beg to observe that in other places, such as Allahabad, Muttra and Mainpuri, Hindu religious processions were allowed to pass through the public streets during the last Muhurram." Thus, local precedent became available to argue for community rights in an expanded context.

Moreover, although conflict in Agra really revolved around competition between Aryas and Sanatan Dharmists, the intercommunity implications of the conflict heightened Muslim awareness of the significance of public arena activity. Indeed, the conflict meant that Muslims had to act in collective ways, and they used the Hindu interaction in public arenas as a pattern for their own activities. For instance, in 1881 Hindus had postponed their festival (*Bharat Milāp*) for several days in order to honor the death of a local Hindu notable.[42] On the basis of this precedent, Muslims requested in 1882 that the Hindu Kine Fair (Ga'ocharan) also be postponed until after Muharram concluded. Hindus refused, and persisted in planning to hold the fair; in protest, Muslims ceased observing Muharram midway through the ten-day cycle.

The concurrence of Muharram and Ga'ocharan in 1883 produced a stalemate. Perhaps heartened by the Magistrate's argument that the fair should be returned to its original site outside the city, "the lower classes of Muslims began to taunt and insult Hindus in the streets and thor-

41. Quoted in *The Tribune* (Lahore), 10 February 1883, p. 9.
42. *Agra Akhbar,* 14 Nov. 1883, in *SVN, 1883,* pp. 947–48.

oughfares" and then paraded tazias "this time even in those parts of the city to which they were never taken before." The press even accused Muslims of having "submitted a petition praying that [sacred] pipal trees situated in the premises of Hindu temples should be cut down." In reaction, "all classes of Hindu traders" in the city and its suburbs closed their shops for a week. This strategy by Hindus for gaining a moral victory through collective self-denial was much emphasized in the Hindu press: "The immense loss involved to the mercantile community . . . may be easily imagined, and the poorer classes of people . . . are starving. Hindus, overwhelmed with grief and sorrow, sit silently in their houses, while Muslims loudly proclaim their Muharram cries in the streets."[43]

Muslims also organized. Several merchants and butchers made special arrangements for the collection and sale of grain to fill the void created by the Hindu shopkeepers' strike.[44] Their success may be measured by the Hindu threat to escalate the conflict by stopping all dealings with Muslim traders and artisans.[45] Although isolated incidents continued to be reported in the press, and a warning came in the form of a Muslim refusal to celebrate the *Chamāhī* (a ceremony normally observed six months after Muharram),[46] no other overt incidents of collective violence occurred until observances overlapped again the following year.

Given the fact that conflict had spread from the particular issue to general relations between occupational groups within each community, it is perhaps surprising that when the clash erupted, it should have been so mild. Although "upper class Muslims" professed satisfaction with a magisterial compromise, a large crowd of "lower classes" carried a petition protesting the decision to share the streets between a Muharram tazia and a Hindu procession. When the decision was not changed, "they held a panchayat then and there just outside [the] compound, and . . . passed a resolution that all sabils should be taken in before night, and not a single tazia be brought out, in fact that the Muharram should be brought to a close."[47] Indeed, Muslims refused to parade

43. *Nazim-i-Agra,* 11 Nov. 1883, in *SVN, 1883,* p. 947. There is no evidence that the accusation was based on anything but rumor.
44. *Mufid-i-Am,* 20 Nov. 1883, in *SVN, 1883,* p. 965.
45. *Agra Akhbar,* 21 Nov. 1883, in *SVN, 1883,* pp. 965–66.
46. *Anis-i-Hind,* 15 May 1884, in *SVN, 1884,* p. 379.
47. Genl. Progs. for June 1890. IOR, L/P&J/6, vol. P3596, progs. no. 3, serial no. 2, p. 13; see also p. 5.

during the first five days of Muharram. On the night prior to the kine procession, some Muslims attained a symbolic moral victory when they took their tazias along a traditional route, which happened to follow the street down which the Hindu procession had been directed.[48] Although no violence broke out at that site, attacks occurred the next day on Hindus moving to and from the procession through neighborhoods that included Muslims.

This pattern marked the remainder of the decade: segments of one or the other community refused to hold an observance, or observances were marred by small street fights around the processions. Nevertheless, indications are that—lacking a long history of conflict—this uneasy decade still did not establish such ongoing ruptures between communities as were experienced in centers like Bareilly and Mau (see chapter 5). Indeed, as early as 1890, a vernacular newspaper noted that Agra's Hindus and Muslims had joined together again in observing Muharram.[49]

Conclusion

From expansion of the ceremonial world of public arenas would come self-conscious efforts to define and protect community boundaries against those perceived to be outside. Despite this encompassing dynamic, community identity during the late nineteenth century still functioned generally as a notion constructed from localized, group loyalties. Only when it became necessary for participants to define themselves against an "Other" did the definition of community expand. In the process, the language and self-consciousness developed in opposition to a narrowly defined "Other" (such as the Sanatan Dharmis' perceptions of the Aryas) could then be turned against a more broadly defined "Other." In this dynamic, the larger constructions of "Hindu" and "Muslim"—rather than the smaller ones of "Arya" and "Sanatan Dharmi"—ultimately triumphed. Just as the structural component of community identity contributed, ultimately, to a sense of a larger community, so too did the communitas component of that identity.

Thus, as the events of Agra and Bareilly suggest, public ceremonials provided the raw materials for creating community identity. From the communitas fostered by festivals came an ideology and symbols to

48. *Nazim-i-Agra*, 7 Nov. 1884, in *SVN, 1884*, p. 770.
49. *Murfid-i-Am*, 1 Sept. 1890, in *SVN, 1890*, p. 585.

express common values; from the inherent structure, and from those aspiring to leadership positions, came collective activities to further the educational, social reform and political goals of the emerging communities. Public arenas, encouraging as they did both competition and conflict, provided the crucible in which these raw materials were refined.

The sense of community, however, continued in the late nineteenth century to be very limited in nature, tied to a particular central place, often restricted even to specific *muhalla*s within a city. We will examine in Part III the early twentieth-century events that led to the creation of larger identities capable of uniting urban residents throughout U.P. Even when these requisite conditions emerged, however, they remained preeminently urban in nature. Only once did a movement expressing community identity move beyond the cities to the countryside. We turn now to an examination of that movement, for the history of Cow Protection suggests both the potential and the limitations of elements of communitas and its attendant structures to link an ideological movement with local relational communities.

CHAPTER 5

The Cow Protection Riots of 1893: Community in Public Arenas and Political Movements

Sacred and sustaining, the cow served as a central symbol of Hindu life in north India. "The Panchagavya, or five products of the cow—milk, curds, butter, urine, and dung—are efficacious as scarers of demons, are used as remedies in disease, and play a very important part in domestic ritual."[1]

> Though cow worship was little known in the Vedic period, by the time of the compilation of the Institutes of Manu it had become part of the popular belief. He classes the slaughter of a cow or bull among the deadly sins; "the preserver of a cow or Brahman atones for the crime of killing a priest;" and we find constant references in the mediaeval folk-lore to the impiety of the Savaras and other Dravidian races who killed and ate the sacred animal. Saktideva one day, "as he was standing on the roof of his palace, saw a Chandala coming along with a load of cow's flesh, and said to his beloved Vindumati: 'Look, slender one! How can the

---

1. This description, and the quotation that follows, is drawn from a "folk-lore" study completed by a British administrator in the same decade as the Cow Protection movement took hold. Some sections reveal administrative concern with the potential violence related to the relatively "modern" reverence for the cow (see vol. 2, p. 235), but most of the material included in this study reflects the two key sources available to scholars at the time: the actual "folk-lore" gleaned from native informants, and scholarly discussions published in such sources as *North Indian Notes and Queries* and *Memoirs of the Anthropological Society of London*. Although the discussions fed the pseudoscientific theories of such armchair anthropologists as Sir James Frazer, they would also have been available to educated Indians who participated in the urban Cow Protection movement. William Crooke, *The Popular Religion and Folklore of Northern India* [1894], 2 vols. (New Delhi: Munshiram Manoharlal, 1978), vol. 2, pp. 228, 230–31.

evil-doer eat the flesh of cows, that are the object of veneration to the three worlds?' Then Vindumati, hearing that, said to her husband: 'The wickedness of this act is inconceivable; what can we say in palliation of it? I have been born in this race of fishermen for a very small offence owing to the might of cows. But what can atone for this man's sin?' "

A powerfully evocative symbol, not only was the cow sacred in itself, but its byproducts played essential roles in most Hindu rituals.[2] Moreover, evocation of the cow allowed more Westernized Hindus to defend an important facet of Indian life in terms deemed legitimate by the Western world, for the cow occupied a vital position in the agrarian economy.

Urban Cow Protection

In the late 1880s and early 1890s the movement to protect the sacred cow demonstrated both the potential for, and the limitations on, the expansion of localized community to larger groups over a broader territory. A widespread movement, it galvanized the province through a symbolic language that referred to values shared by most of the area's inhabitants. Although the symbol of the cow could unite a wide range of people, the meaning behind the shared symbol varied. The movement spread through existing local structures and fed into existing local social schisms: hence, it meant different things to different people. Nevertheless, the late nineteenth-century movement did succeed in linking together disparate local Sabhas. In that respect the Cow Protection movement represents the first phase in a development that quickened in the early twentieth century, by which "community" conveyed to its partisans a broad, encompassing, ideological identity. As the concept of community evolved from one based on face-to-face relationships in the locality to one based on broader ideological ties, community identity acquired the potential for politicization.

As befit a movement that fostered a more broadly based notion of community, Cow Protection garnered support throughout much of the subcontinent.[3] The movement's history in U.P. must be divided into two phases. These phases were quite distinct from each other. The first phase

2. See, for instance, the discussion of the cow as sacred symbol in Anand A. Yang, "Sacred Symbol and Sacred Space," *Comparative Studies in Society and History* 22, no. 4, (Oct. 1980): 576–96.
3. See reports on the 1893 riots in Rangoon (Burma) and in numerous Indian cities, in *British Parliamentary Papers*, Command Paper No. 63 for 1893–1894.

in U.P. shared characteristics with the movement's development in much of the rest of India: during this period, the movement was urban (based in smaller towns as well as large cities), with the message linking these centers being carried by stump orators and in printed materials. In this communication the urban elite played a special role, particularly as the translators of collective symbolic behavior into the printed texts of newspaper, pamphlet, placard, and organizational rules.[4]

Beginning, like many religiously focused movements, in the Punjab, the Cow Protection movement spread to U.P. through urban networks that ultimately reached most of the towns and cities scattered throughout U.P. Dayananda Saraswati formed the first Ga'orakshini Sabha in 1882, and soon after published a book on the subject.[5] The movement intensified dramatically when, in 1888, the North-Western Provincial High Court decreed that a cow was not a sacred object. This meant that cows were not covered by section 295 of the Indian Penal Code, which stipulated:

> Whoever destroys, damages or defiles any place of worship, or any object held sacred by a class of persons, with the intention thereby of insulting the religion of any class of persons, or with the knowledge that any class of persons is likely to consider such destruction, damage or defilement as an insult to their religion, shall be punished with imprisonment.[6]

This denial of sanctity was so contrary to the shared values of north Indian Hindus that a variety of Hindu groups united to resist this government intrusion through judicial fiat. The nature of their unity, and elements of the actual organizational structures developed, will be discussed in more detail below. Here we concentrate on the ideological component of the movement.

The ideology is suggested by the persons against whom the movement defined itself. In the cities, those seen as the opposition symbolized alien ideological systems. It is therefore no surprise that attacks were made not only on Muslims but also on other groups:

---

4. The similarities among Cow Protection movements during this first phase (and the differences that emerged in U.P. in the second phase) are suggested in S. Krishnaswamy, "A Riot in Bombay, August 11, 1893: A Study in Hindu-Muslim Relations in Western India During the Late Nineteenth Century," Ph.D. diss., University of Chicago, 1966.

5. John Nicol Farquhar, *Modern Religious Movements in India* (New York: Macmillan, 1918), p. 111.

6. IOR, L/P&J/6/376, file 298 for 1894, "Note on Agitation Against Cow Killing," p. 4, footnote. Although there was an earlier judgment, this is the one that seems to have galvanized the movement.

Pandit Mathura Prasad, a preacher in the service of the Cow
Protection Society of Lucknow and Babu Lalta Prasad, the President of the Society . . . were charged with having exhibited on the
10th of May before a crowd of people, among whom there were
native Christians, an image of Jesus Christ suspended by the
neck, and with having told the people that the image was that of
the God of Christians who was struck with shoes and who was
the son of an unchaste woman.[7]

Not all of those active in the Ga'orakshini Sabhas, even in the cities,
agreed on the exact nature of the ideological component. Political
activists certainly tried to use the movement for their own purposes.
Indeed, the British administration's Special Branch made much of the
connections between the Ga'orakshini Sabha and the Indian National
Congress.[8] And there is some evidence that Congress members attempted to connect support of Congress and adherence to the Cow
Protection movement. The Swami Alaram, for instance, addressed two
meetings in Mirzapur in late 1890. At the second he "referred to the
advantages of union, and supported the aims and objects of the Indian
National Congress."[9]

More to the point, we can see in such Sabha rules as those adopted in
Gorakhpur substantial evidence of efforts by social reformers. Sabha
organizers showed a list of rules adopted by other Sabhas to those
attending a meeting in Gorakhpur. The Gorakhpuris deleted one rule,
adopted the others, then added eight more of their own. The new list
reflected reformist concerns, for instance, in the admonitions against
"foolish expenditure on marriages" and in stipulations concerning the
maximum number of persons in a *barāt* (wedding procession) and the
number of rupees to be expended in the ceremony of tilak (spot of color
placed on the forehead).[10]

Still, traditionalists accomplished their purposes in the Gorakhpur
rules, as well. Naturally, the bulk of the rules exhorted certain basic
agrarian practices for the care and protection of kine (rules 1, 2, 3, 7, 8,

---

7. *Dinkar Prakash*, June 1888, in *SVN, 1888*, pp. 419–20.

8. Following the Congress session of 1891, several Congress delegations addressed
the Sabha, which met in the Congress pavilion. See "Note on Agitation," p. 8.

9. *Khichri Samachar*, 22 Nov. 1890, in *SVN, 1890*, p. 813. See also "Note on
Agitation," p. 7, and Oday Pertap Singh (Raja of Bhinga), "The Cow Agitation, or
Mutiny-Plasm in India," *Nineteenth Century*, April 1894, pp. 667–72. When we have
discounted for the obvious paranoia of the Special Branch, and the self-serving nature of
the Raja's argument, it is doubtful that these efforts were particularly successful.

10. IOR, L/P&J/365, file 84 for 1894, "Note [by Hoey] on the Cow Protection
Agitation in the Gorakhpur District," p. 3 (henceforth "Note on . . . Gorakhpur").

9, 19, 23). But several of them aimed at personal religious practices and at the observation of proper Hindu ritual—such as rule 14, which reiterated that "on all dwija castes (i.e., brahmins, kshatriyas, and vaisyas) it shall be obligatory to recite the gayitri at the three divisions of the day . . . and he who fails in this shall be expelled from the brotherhood;" and rule 16, which stated that "women shall be instructed as to the contribution of *chuṭkī* [the handful of rice set aside daily for Sabha support] in proper fashion with due regard to pardah [seclusion of women]."[11] Cow Protection supporters pursued a variety of goals through such Sabha rules, and traditionalists selectively emphasized certain aspects of Hindu religious life. Those aspects appealed to upwardly mobile reformists, concerned as they were with incorporating into the lifestyles of their constituents certain appropriate, higher-caste practices.

For all these reasons the Cow Protection movement proved highly successful, and organizing efforts swept the urban centers of U.P. between 1888 and 1890. In the first year reports focused on collective activities on behalf of the cow in cities such as Kanpur, Lucknow, Ghazipur, Banaras, Aligarh, Partabgarh and, preeminently, Allahabad.[12] At these meetings, organizers coupled reminders about the sanctity of the cow with recommendations of actions to be taken, both collectively and individually, by those in the crowd. These references to the cow became linked, in turn, with the creation of a local organizational apparatus.

An example drawn from Azamgarh district indicates the organizational procedures involved.[13] A large meeting would be called by someone with local influence. At Azmatgarh, five thousand to six thousand people attended a meeting organized by Karria Misra, a highly influential zamindar and the family priest of the government treasurer. Though the treasurer was absent, his household supplied "earthen vessels and other necessaries" to those attending the meeting. Organizers circulated a picture of a cow, representing the residence of all the Hindu gods.

11. Ibid.
12. This roster of sites is culled from "Note on Agitation Against Cow Killing" and *SVN, 1887–1893*. Conspicuously absent are the towns of the region of Rohilkhund, in the far north of the province; the only cities of that area in which Cow Protection Sabhas were founded were Bareilly, Hardwar (as a pilgrimage site, it was one of the organizing centers for the Cow Protection movement), and nearby Dehra Dun.
13. The following details are based, except as noted, on the description for Azamgarh in "Report on Azamgarh" by H.E.L.P. Dupernex, Officiating Magistrate of Azamgarh, to Commissioner, Gorakhpur Division, IOR, L/P&J/6/365, file 55 for 1894 (henceforth Dupernex, "Report").

Placing it on a stool before the platform, the speaker exhorted participants to protect the cow: they were only to milk her after her calf had
been satisfied. Since every man drank cow's milk, the cow served as
"universal mother"; therefore, it was matricide to kill a cow.[14] Depicting the cow as standing next to a Muslim with a drawn sword, the
illustrations conveyed the necessary subliminal messages even to the
most illiterate viewer. To prevent this "matricide," the participants
agreed to establish a Sabha, adopt rules, and choose officers. The local
sponsors also spoke, the most prestigious of them presiding to indicate
his support and enthusiasm.[15]

The feeling of shared cause and values fostered by such a meeting led
directly into an organizational framework. A local agent, or *sabhāsad*
(evidently at least one was assigned to each village or urban *muhalla*),
would collect *chuṭkī*, or household contributions of grain, and convert
them to cash.[16] In Azmatgarh the stamp vendor Bairon Pershad, Agar-
wala had this responsibility. While in some areas these collections were
retained locally, in others the money worked its way up a chain of
command to central figures in the larger cities. Gorakhpur designed a
sabhāpati for every forty or fifty villages; each of them reported to a
divisional representative. Whether retained or forwarded, the money
bought cows otherwise destined for slaughter, established and maintained *ga'oshālā*s (cattle pounds or refuges), and paid traveling preachers to hold follow-up meetings throughout the surrounding area.[17]

Responsibility for enforcement rested with these same local agents.
To Muslims they applied a combination of incentive and coercion. The
Rani of Majhauli, for instance, deputed an agent to buy eighty head of
cattle being taken by butchers through Salempur.[18] She also promised to
give local butchers rent-free land if they would give up their trade in
cattle. To prevent cow sacrifice at the important Islamic festival of
Baqar ᶜĪd, activists boycotted Muslims and, in several places, gathered

14. "Note on . . . Gorakhpur," p. 1.
15. See, for instance, descriptions of meetings in Pratabgarh and Darbhanga in *Bharat Jiwan*, 28 May 1888 and 10 Sept. 1888, in *SVN, 1888*, pp. 346, 614. The Darbhanga meeting was organized by the local Marwaris and presided over by the Maharaja; Pandit Jagat Narayan of Banaras spoke.
16. Gorakhpur rules specified that each household was to put aside a *chutki* of rice equal to one paisa per member. For lists of agents, see Dupernex, "Report," pp. 14–18.
17. The Nagpur Society even organized classes to instruct these lecturers ("Note on Agitation Against Cow Killing," p. 10).
18. Evidently the Rani did not pay full price and managed to compel the sale, for the difference had to be made up by local butchers ("Note on . . . Gorakhpur," p. 5). The cattle were then distributed free to Ahirs and others on her estates.

in large crowds to compel agreements, or *igrārnāma*s, in which the Muslim signatories promised not to sacrifice.[19] Enforcement procedures against recalcitrant Hindus proved equally emphatic. One such Hindu, Lachhman Paure, described what happened to him:

> Five days ago I sold a bullock to Waris Khan. No one interfered at the time of the sale. Two days after Gurbin Sahu, Niranjan Sahu, [and] Maharaj Sahu came up to me and asked why I had sold a bullock to a Muhammedan. I said it was nothing unusual. They then said I should be cut off from water and from my food vessels. Debidial Sahu and Bechu Sahu and others assembled together and said that all my work should be stopped. They pulled down the tiles of my roof and smashed my earthen vessels. Gurbin Sahu and Maharaj then slapped me, and he and others stopped the Kahars who were carrying sweetmeats for my daughter's entry into her father-in-law's house. All these people threatened that if I did not get the bullock back they would loot my house and kill me.[20]

Sometimes the trials conducted by Sabhas applied coercion more formally. The trial of "Ga'o Mahdrain (Cow Empress) vs. Sita Ram Ahir of Haider" serves as an example. For impounding a cow which was then sold to a butcher, Sita Ram Ahir had to buy back the cow and then "stand trial." Because he refused to pay the fine determined by the "court," he faced a sentence of twenty-four days' outcasting, as well as various religious penalties.[21]

Clearly, such a complex apparatus of resource redistribution and collective public enforcement could not be created and superimposed overnight. During the urban phase of the movement, the most successful and long-lived Sabhas elaborated their structures on existing organizational frameworks such as those provided by, or at least utilizing personnel from, the local Arya Samajes and Sanatan Dharm Sabhas.

19. See, for instance, the boycott in Aligarh as discussed in various vernacular newspapers during 1890. The agreements also are treated in "Sir Charles Crosthwaite's Speech in Azamgarh," reprinted in full in an appendix to Pandit Bishan Narayan Dar, "An Appeal to the English Public on Behalf of the Hindus of the North-Western Provinces and Oudh" (Lucknow, 1893), p. 10. Included in IOR, L/P&J/6, vol. 368 for 1894, file 328, and in Dupernex, "Report," p. 9.

20. Dupernex, "Report," p. 10. Dupernex used the fact that Azamgarh Cow Protectionists did not distinguish between cows and bullocks as proof that the movement had ulterior motives.

21. Confidential letter to Advocate General, from D. J. Lyall, Secretary to Government of India, Home Department, IOR, L/P&J/6, vol. 376 for 1894, file 298. As noted in chapter 2, evidence of this kind of self-sufficiency among clandestine organizations was viewed as especially threatening by the British administration.

Much of the preaching took place in public arenas, for cultural and social gatherings proved ideal occasions. Activists frequented the various bathing fairs and melas. Allahabad's Magh Mela, for instance, provided Cow Protection preachers ideal access to large and receptive crowds. But even everyday life in the city created opportunities. In Kanpur, "Hindu speakers" in 1888 delivered lectures along the main thoroughfares of the city, appealing for help in the agitation against cow slaughter. They even mounted the Kanpur stage, for "during the performance of the Laila Majnun at the theatre on the 21st of March, a calf and some Muslim boys were brought on the stage, and the latter, addressing the calf, highly praised kine."[22]

The list of *sabhāsad*s from the town of Azamgarh indicates that Sabha organizers also worked through the existing urban social networks, calling on *muḥalla* leaders, occupational *chaudharī*s, and caste leaders.[23] Supporters in certain occupations could turn their professions to the service of the movement: moneylenders, traders, and liquor vendors prominently displayed collection boxes; pleaders directed appeals to their rich clients. Often the economic functions of supporters made it especially easy to organize support. Many bankers, traders, and others subject to the Pandri tax, for instance, paid 20 percent of their assessments as a contribution.[24] This public support, however, easily identified them. Disgruntled Muslims in Aligarh attacked certain Hindu shopkeepers and Kayasths in 1890, holding them responsible for the communal tensions in that city.[25]

Publicists and their presses prominently supported the movement, as attested by the wealth of printed materials distributed at meetings by Cow Protectionists (placards, pamphlets, pictures, and lists of rules). On occasion they assumed even more direct leadership. Madho Prasad, editor of the vernacular newspaper *Khichri Samechar* and secretary to the Hitkarni Sabha, moved beyond printing stories that detailed Muslim mistreatment of cows on the streets of Mirzapur.[26] He led a group in seizing a cow they claimed was being beaten and then, as representative of the crowd, fired off a telegram to the District Magistrate. Ultimately Madho also facilitated a compromise by bringing together his much

22. *Alam-i Taswir,* 6 Apr. 1888, in *SVN, 1888,* pp. 250–51.
23. See list in Dupernex, "Report," p. 5.
24. "Note on Agitation Against Cow Killing," p. 10.
25. *Hindustan,* 17 and 19 Oct. 1890, *SVN, 1890,* p. 680.
26. See, for example, *Khichri Samachar,* 5 July and 8 Nov. 1890, *SVN, 1890,* pp. 459, 744–45.

revered teacher, Babu Benimadho Das (another reference to the importance of *akhāṛā* ties) and Muslim leader Farzand Ali.[27]

The Sabha's initial success depended in part on support from prominent leaders. Officials often played key roles in organizing and garnering support for the Sabhas during this urban phase. The large public meeting held in Partabgarh during 1888, for instance, featured the British Deputy Commissioner (who chaired the meeting) and the District Engineer.[28] The Indian officials who participated included a subordinate judge, a *munsif* (the lowest-ranking civil judge), and the vice president of the district and municipal boards. Two talukdars also took part.[29] Those labeled "natural leaders" by the British proved very active in the Cow Protection movement: larger meetings and subscription lists boasted several Awadh talukdars (including Raja Rampal Singh of Kalakankar, who was another active supporter), as well as the Maharajas of Banaras, Darbhanga, Hatwa, and Bettiah.[30]

This description of the organizational and ideological aspects of the urban phase of Cow Protection suggests the extent to which the movement successfully linked the ideology and local structures of public arenas with the more overtly political activities of a literate elite accustomed to operating within the imperial government's institutional framework. Indeed, in this respect the first phase of Cow Protection was, to a large extent, one of a series of experiments aimed at organizing an urban public around issues identified as important to a putative "Hindu" community. To understand the implications of this phase, we must place Cow Protection into this larger framework of civic institutions.

Other Organizational Experiments in the Cities

The organizational structure created to espouse and protect an ideology centered on the cow related to the general process by which articulation of Hindu community sharpened. Events in Bareilly and Agra illustrated the variety of messages available to define and delineate—in other words, to construct—the putative community of "Hindus." We have

27. *Public Service Gazette*, 8 and 16 Nov. 1890, and *Khichri Samachar*, 8 and 15 Nov. 1890, in *SVN, 1890*, pp. 744–45, 765–67.
28. "Note on Agitation Against Cow Killing" reports that three Deputy Commissioners in Awadh presided over Cow Protection meetings during 1888.
29. *Bharat Jiwan*, 28 May 1888, *SVN, 1888*, p. 346.
30. "Note on Agitation Against Cow Killing," pp. 4–5. In November 1888, however, the Raja of Banares cut off support to the cattle pound.

noted that as articulation of these definitions became increasingly coherent, so did the competition among those who espoused them; such competition worked at first to separate rather than to unify. Important to this process was the evolution in the late nineteenth century of a variety of Hindu organizational experiments to channel the expressions and resulting competition among definitions of "Hindu" community.

This development related, of course, to the widespread adoption of Western forms of organization and protest.[31] Characteristic forms appropriated by Indian activists included "monster" protest meetings and new public associations on the Western model, with elected officers, rules for the membership, fundraising drives, and printed records of the meetings. The employment of publicists or propagandists to circularize causes (through the new vernacular presses and in broadsheets) proved to be the most significant development of this kind. Many organizations also worked to connect the urban areas of north India through personal appeals by stump orators. Increasing sensitivity among Hindus to Muslim efforts at community organization—though these were internally focused and not principally designed to intimidate Hindus—gave an impetus to those efforts. As we have seen, introduction of the Arya Samaj into U.P. towns also gave an impetus, for the Samaj polarized many Hindus, forcing them to define and identify their "community." This polarization, in turn, made such Hindus more self-conscious about their religious identity.

Although it proved to be the most influential "Hindu" organization of the period, Cow Protection was both preceded and accompanied by other organizational efforts among Hindus. The most prominent of these, though not the most influential in U.P., was the Arya Samaj.[32] Supported in the main by professionals educated in English attempting to reformulate their indigenous traditions, the Arya Samaj had first taken root in 1877 in the Punjab, where it initially proved more popular. When exported to the cities of U.P., its adherents remained small in number and moderate in tone until after the turn of the century. Yet its impact in U.P. was doubtless felt beyond its numbers, for it abrasively put forth a radical vision of Hinduism, one that emphasized monothe-

31. See John R. McLane, *Indian Nationalism and the Early Congress* (Princeton: Princeton University Press, 1977), for a discussion of this connection, though it overemphasizes the early political role of religious identity.
32. See Farquhar, *Modern Religious Movements in India,* and Kenneth W. Jones, *Arya Dharm* (Berkeley and Los Angeles: University of California Press, 1976), for detailed discussions of the Arya Samaj.

ism and the Vedas, and condemned idolatry and the intercessional role of Brahmins.

Such ideas prompted reactions from a wide range of Hindus with very different visions of their religion and community. The program of Agra's Sanatan Dharm demonstrated one such reaction. We noted earlier that although the Sabha saw itself as defending the "old faith and practices," it also proselytized—reviving existing religious observances (and infusing new religious symbolism into hitherto secular festivals) and defending the "ancient rights" of Hinduism by agitating to preserve aspects of existing festivals. At least in some areas it also produced didactic literature and later established its own schools.[33]

A dividing line implicitly separated Sanatan Dharmis from less conservative Hindus, as a speech by Pandit Shraddha Ram suggests:

> But only those people can provide protection [of Hinduism] who are themselves firm Hindus. Even though all of us think we are firm Hindus only a person who accepts the teachings of Shruti and Smriti can be a firm Hindu and if he thinks that the Vedas and Dharm Shastras are the products of Brahmans and accepts this as Hinduism he cannot be a true Hindu.

Thus anyone

> who was against Shruti and Smriti and who [did] not keep a knot on his head and [did] not wear the sacred thread which is essential for a vaishya and who hate[d] to have cow dung paint in the kitchen and who use[d] a dining table and called Bhojan as Khanna and [thought] all the caste system is useless then how [could] Hinduism be spread or prosper through his efforts, [that] is impossible.[34]

Although traditionalist in tenor, the Sanatan Dharm Sabha campaigned against many practices that educated and upwardly mobile Hindus also wanted to delete. It was possible, therefore, for Hindus both more and less traditionalist to arrive at a certain level of agreement about festival and ritual practices.

By the late 1880s Hindus had founded other organizations of a similar nature, some with specific goals, such as gaining control of a

33. For the literature produced in the Punjab, see Kenneth W. Jones, "Sanatan Dharm: Hindu Orthodoxy in Defense of Tradition," paper presented to the Midwestern Conference on Asian Affairs, October 1978. Regarding education, there were two Sanatan Dharm colleges in Kanpur in the thirties. IOR, L/P&J/7/75 for 1931, Commission of Inquiry Report on the Cawnpore Riot of 1931, Evidence, p. 10.

34. Jones, "Sanatan Dharm," pp. 11–12.

mela or local temple endowment, others designed to serve as umbrella organizations uniting all Hindus.[35] These groups exhibited a wide variety of supporters, organizational formats,[36] and definitions of Hinduism. We might posit a continuum of Hindu organizations, bounded at one end by the reformist Arya Samaj and at the other by the traditionalist Sanatan Dharm Sabha. Hindus arrayed between the two ends of the spectrum shared a concern for the role of religion but supported differing definitions of that religion and—as Shraddha Ram's list suggested—demanded differing styles of behavior to express those definitions. These new-style organizations represented more than just new organizational forms and, frequently, Western-influenced styles of operation—although it is for this reason that they have been studied previously. Equally important was their effort to link elite political organizations to values with a wider mass appeal. Connections between these organizations and public arena activity remained intermittent, but their espousal of popular values represented the first, more permanent, step in this direction.

If measured by its ability to link elite political organizations and popularly held values, the Bharat Dharm Mahamandal must be numbered among the more effective of such organizations, for it joined together campaigns for Western-style education, publication programs, and modern publicity techniques with the reinvigoration of what was defined as traditional Hinduism. At its 1890 meeting, for instance, participants passed resolutions urging "the due performance of fixed religious ceremonies," protesting the Age of Consent Bill (which raised the marriage age) and condemning "extravagant marriage expenses." Other speakers encouraged the study of Hindi and Sanskrit, and organized a subscription program for a Sanskrit college at Delhi.[37] The "wealthy" and "influential" members of the Mahamandal looked to the Raja of Darbhanga (a powerful landholder of Bihar) for substantial financial support, and to Pandit Madan Malaviya (a religiously educated member of the new urban leadership of Allahabad and Banaras) for guidance.[38] Before the turn of the century, the Mahamandal re-

35. See the excellent section in C. A. Bayly, *Local Roots of Indian Politics: Allahabad, 1880–1920* (Oxford: Clarendon Press, 1975), pp. 104–17, which analyzes the place of several of these organizations in the late nineteenth-century urban context.

36. Bayly, *Local Roots,* p. 115. Bayly argues that neither the Sanatan Dharm Sabha nor the Bharat Dharm Mahamandal became ascriptive organizations, like the Arya Samaj.

37. See the report of the [second?] annual meeting held at Delhi in 1890, in *Bharat Jiwan,* 24 Nov. 1890, in *SVN, 1890,* p. 794.

38. Farquhar, *Modern Religious Movements in India,* p. 320, quoting the *Indian Social Reformer,* vol. 22, p. 121. Farquhar's dates for the Mahamandal, as for the Sanatan Dharm Sabha, clearly are incorrect.

mained loosely organized, depending—as did most such organizations at the time—on local, often ad hoc arrangements for recruitment and for implementation of its program.[39] Thus, the Mahamandal would be located somewhere near the middle of our continuum. It pursued both traditionalist goals—for example, protection of the ceremonial aspects of religion—and those more often considered reformist, such as limitation of marriage expenses. It also utilized some modern tactics to forward its program, as its subscription drive and publication lists attest.

Despite the fact that these organizations often worked against each other, their very existence—and the organizing and propagandizing efforts they mounted—contributed to the increased activity on behalf of "community." In turn, these public activities fostered a consciousness among Hindus that they counted as members of an identifiable group. As noted, there were issues, too, on which these various organizations could unite—issues that came to be identified as important to "Hindus." The Allahabad-based Prayag Hindu Samaj provided an early example of this initial unity of effort, drawing on the energies of both traditionalist Hindus and reformist members of the Arya Samaj. Active in a wide variety of "Hindu" causes, the Hindu Samaj became involved in the Hindi vs. Urdu language controversy, produced Hindi school texts, worked for control of the largest fair (the Magh Mela), and even represented " 'Hindu' interests in a minor commercial dispute."[40]

Among these Hindu organizational efforts, Cow Protection made the most widespread and dramatic impact. Its unparalleled success in north India can be attributed to at least two important characteristics. First, as we have seen, its ideological platform appealed alike to orthodox, traditionalist, and reformist Hindus. Second, its organizational structure united urban centers and their rural surroundings. This latter characteristic distinguished Cow Protection—at least in degree—from its predecessor political movements, and thus closer analysis is warranted.

When Cow Protection moved to the countryside beginning in 1890, a number of connections proved influential in initially establishing the movement in villages. These connections related primarily to organization and communication networks. We have noted that as the Sabhas became established throughout U.P., supporters instituted a multitiered hierarchy of officers. When effective, this hierarchy established important links between town and village, directing the flow of money from

---

39. See Farquhar, *Modern Religious Movements in India,* for the story of the re-founding of the Mahamandal in 1902 with a stronger organizational structure.
40. For further details, see Bayly, *Local Roots,* pp. 107–8.

locality to urban center, and the flow of information (primarily in printed form or carried by itinerant preachers) from center to locality. In Azamgarh district, for instance, the collection of *chuṭkī* generally followed the lines of British administrative units: the *sabhāsad*s for each village in Nizamabad pargana passed on the subscriptions to *sabhāpati*s Setu Ram and Antu Singh. They in turn gave the money to faqir Naga Babu, "the leading spirit in fanning the agitation" in Azamgarh city, who was to buy cows and look after them.[41] Similarly, *sabhāsad*s in each village of Nathupur division of Sagri pargana handed over their collections to *sabhāpati* Ram Saran Rai, who then gave them to Sabha president Ghansiam Narain Misra, a man who linked neighboring districts as he traveled between his landholdings in Ballia and Azamgarh.[42]

The direction of the flow reversed with the preachers of Cow Protection. Such preachers seem to have been drawn from two very different groups. Some were local holy men, often already established in the countryside, who simply incorporated the movement into their usual wanderings. Others, urban activists, had previously been employed by the elite connected with the politicized movements of the towns. Most prominent among the latter was Sriman Swami, who remained active throughout the movement.[43] On behalf of the Allahabad Sabha (with Hardwar, Allahabad served as a pivotal center of the movement in its urban phase), he traveled throughout India, preaching Cow Protection from Calcutta to Lahore, from Bombay to Bihar. During 1888 alone the Swami held forty to fifty meetings across U.P. Other lecturers cut smaller swathes but similarly linked town and countryside. Gopalanand Tewari, a member of the Banaras Arya Samaj, was connected with a near riot in Ghazipur,[44] as well as with several meetings held at various locations in Gorakhpur.[45] Khaki Baba, also known as Khaki Das, acted as Gopalanand's counterpart in Azamgarh. Principal speaker and often chief organizer of these meetings, this holy man confidently requested financial support for the movement and for his pilgrimage from the Muslim tahsildar (revenue officer) of Deogaon.[46]

41. Dupernex, "Report," pp. 12, 14.
42. Ibid., pp. 2, 9, 11–12, 15–16.
43. A Madrassi previously known as Desika Chari, Sriman Swami had a checkered background. The British made much of the fact that he was an ex-convict. He briefly dropped out of sight in 1891, prompting disgruntled questions from the vernacular press, but reemerged in 1892 ("Note on Agitation Against Cow Killing," pp. 8–10, and *SVN, 1888–93*, passim).
44. "Note on Agitation Against Cow Killing," p. 4.
45. "Note on . . . Gorakhpur," pp. 1, 5.
46. Dupernex, "Report," pp. 9, 12.

Zamindar Jagdeo Narain Singh worked with Khaki Baba. Jagdeo personifies for us yet another pattern in this rural-urban connection. The "soul of the movement" in Azamgarh, Jagdeo also served as President of the Ballia Sabha, and he traveled continually between the two districts. Capitalizing on the location of his Ballia estate, he evidently developed an escape route along which captured cattle were spirited away from protesting butchers. Though he avoided direct involvement in the riots, Jagdeo proved highly visible both in Sabha activities and in the mobilization of men on the ʿĪd. Moreover, he often traveled "to Allahabad to transact legal business in the High Court for those dupes who have at his instigation involved themselves by rioting and cattlelifting in criminal proceedings."[47] Notices sent by Jagdeo (and leaders like him) proved the method most successful in mobilizing men to attend meetings, capture cows, or prevent sacrifices. "The method . . . is simplicity itself. A leading fakir or pandit sends a letter to a friend adorned with a picture of a cow, informing him that a Sabha will be held on a certain date at a certain place. The recipient of the letter is enjoined to communicate its contents to five villages." Alternatively, activists might prepare printed notices, then post and circulate them throughout the affected area.[48]

Thus, the flow of resources—money and other material support from the countryside, ideology espoused through placards and by orators from the city—created the ties between city and countryside in the Cow Protection movement. But the characteristics of the movement in its second, rural phase changed in important respects, including the rural content behind the symbolism of the cow, the way in which the movement became linked with other kinds of rural social schisms, and the devolution of leadership made necessary by the provincial government's attempts at suppression. The rural phase of Cow Protection provides an important example of the adjustment of the *content* of symbolic collective behavior to fit very different local *contexts*.

The Rural Phase

The Cow Protection movement entered its second phase by 1891–1892, when the center of support shifted quite noticeably to the eastern rural districts bordering Bihar—the districts of Ghazipur, Ballia, Azamgarh, and Gorakhpur. Indeed, most of the U.P. areas in which riots occurred

47. Ibid., p. 12.
48. Ibid., p. 11, and "Note on . . . Gorakhpur," p. 5. Access to printing presses suggests urban-based assistance in these organizational efforts.

during 1893 had not organized Sabhas until that very year. This shift in Sabha activity, when plotted on a map, shows first a dramatic contraction from Sabhas blanketing urban U.P. to Sabha activities concentrated in the east, and then a further shift in 1893 to an almost exclusively rural area in the eastern districts. Together with contiguous districts in Bihar, these districts were the center of Bhojpuri language and culture. That is, starting as an urban, broad-based movement, Cow Protection in U.P. became instead a rural, Bhojpuri phenomenon.

The "rurban" centers of eastern U.P. doubtless played an important role in this shift to the countryside. They were ideal for this purpose, since they performed important cultural hinge functions for the area and thus could serve as the point at which Cow Protection ideology came to be reinterpreted in terms that would appeal to villagers. Rurban central places emulated higher-level urban centers in their economic, political, and ritual functions, in the process connecting their resident lineage elites with the movements of U.P. cities. Nevertheless, they remained closely linked to the countryside, not only because the "rural peasantry more regularly came into contact" with these urban places, but also because "the nature of these links to the rural fringe was more directly interactional, and more heavily based on ascriptive social institutions such as caste and kinship which duplicated closely the organizational bases of the rural areas."[49] Indeed, because they were "relevant to territories of limited extent," and because their urban natures "were defined and behaviorally executed within the multiple little tradition regions," these rurban centers shared much with the rural hinterland.[50] In this way they provided the sites at which both the movement's organizational structures and its ideological messages could make an initial impact on the hinterland.

In the movement's shift from city to countryside, the ideology remained centered on the cow. Only the sacred cow could have bridged the gap so easily between urban searches for community identity and rural values. The importance of Brahmins in the eastern districts doubtless facilitated this transition, as did the participation by rurban lineage elites. Nevertheless, the rural ideological appeals on behalf of Cow Protection in 1893 looked rather different from the urban appeals

---

49. Richard G. Fox, "Rurban Settlements and Rajput 'Clans' in Northern India," in Fox, ed., *Urban India: Society, Space, and Image,* Program in Comparative Studies on Southern Asia, Monograph and Occasional Papers Series, no. 10 (Durham, N.C.: Duke University Press, 1970), p. 180.

50. Ibid., p. 169.

crafted earlier. In the countryside of the eastern districts, such ideology followed local rural social organization and drew on established social schisms for targets and for patterns of behavior to be emulated.[51] Thus, a much more parochial ideology emerged in the second phase of the movement, with ascendant but generally low-caste groups as the targets for discontent. Given Cow Protection's emphasis on purity and concerns of ritual (i.e., Brahminical) status, such groups (butchers, itinerant packers, leather workers) represented the rural "Other," or "outsiders," alien to the Brahminized high-caste culture espoused by rural activists.

The threatened ascendancy of low-caste groups proved an important aspect of the altered ideology. Significantly, cow-focused agitation, such as waylaying herds driven by butchers, occurred within a general complex of rural social unrest in which figures for agrarian riots, dacoities (organized banditry involving five or more participants), and religious riots dramatically escalated in 1893.[52] Thus, any explanation for rural espousal of Cow Protection must move beyond the sudden, if partial, introduction of an urban movement into the countryside. Certainly a series of factors external to the Bhojpuri region had given rise to the movement initially. A climate had been created by the judiciary for a Hindu ideological movement focused on the cow. Urban organizational experiments, including a broad range of "Hindu" activists, had pioneered successful tactics and materials and suggested methods to link town and countryside. But the question still remains: why did this particular urban-based movement result in riots only in the eastern region of rural U.P.?

The answer seems to lie in the particular socioeconomic conditions of the period. Perhaps perversely, it was not a matter of an economic downturn, for there had been a good harvest and low food prices.[53] Indeed, the standard of living seems to have risen substantially in the last decade of the century, though this "marked improvement" was maintained only through a variety of strategies, for these areas included some

51. For rural social organization, see Anand A. Yang, "The Agrarian Origins of Crime: A Study of Riots in Saran District, India, 1866–1920," *Journal of Social History* 13 (Winter 1979): 289–305. See also chap. 4 of Sandria B. Freitag, "Religious Rites and Riots," Ph.D. diss., University of California, Berkeley, 1980, for a more detailed discussion of the implications of rural social organization for Cow Protection.

52. *Report* of the Administration of the North-Western Provinces for the Year Ending 31 March 1894, vol. 21, p. 18.

53. Even the more sophisticated explanation of the "J-curve" (indicating a sharp reversal after a general upturn of economic conditions) does not seem to apply. See James C. Davies, "Toward a Theory of Revolution," in Ivo K. Feierabend et al., eds., *Anger, Violence, and Politics: Theories and Research* (Englewood Cliffs, N.J.: Prentice-Hall, 1972), pp. 67–84.

of the highest population densities in the province. Moreover, the area could not utilize artificial irrigation to foster commercial agriculture, as did western U.P. But a good climate guaranteed subsistence farming, and the value of agricultural produce had risen reassuringly.[54]

Relative prosperity, however, had profoundly affected local social relationships. The social structure of the eastern districts proved to be more sharply hierarchical, thus distinguishing them from other areas of U.P. Although few large landholders existed, a separation between cultivator and proprietor had evolved, with proprietors holding land generally through zamindari or "imperfect pattidari" tenures.[55] Even tenants were divided between "high" and "low" cultivators, the former doing as little direct cultivation as possible while receiving special rent concessions. Though caste identity was not the determining factor, high-caste status did coincide generally with noncultivation; thus, the important proprietary and tenant castes were the Rajputs, Muslims, Bhumihars, and Brahmins. Landlord status historically had proven profitable in this area, for landlords lived on a combination of proceeds from cultivation of *sīr* (home) land, moneylending, and rental returns.[56] Significantly, however, in the last quarter of the nineteenth century these proprietors struggled increasingly to retain landlord status even as they were being "driven closer" to the soil. Indeed, it is clear that, as in Ballia, in the eastern districts in general

> the value of the tenant right is very much greater than that of the proprietary right in most instances. The proprietary right is a multiple of rent less the revenue, generally 16 times. The tenant right is a much greater multiple of the rent, 20 or 30 or 40 times. . . . [It is insignificant for his profit] whether a given individual is a zamindar of a fixed-rent tenant or an occupancy tenant. The material point is whether he holds his land at favorable or unfavorable rates, and whether he has got enough of it.[57]

54. One successful strategy for economic growth was emigration, for between 1891 and 1900 thirteen million rupees were remitted annually by emigrants to their families still in eastern U.P. (H. R. Nevill, ed., *District Gazetteers of the United Provinces of Agra and Oudh*, vol. 33, *Azamgarh* [Allahabad: U.P. Government Press, 1911], p. 118 [henceforth *Azamgarh Gazetteer*]).

55. See Eric Stokes, *The Peasant and the Raj* (Cambridge: Cambridge University Press 1978). In papers 3 and especially 10 he uses this distinction to explain why in this area the "institutional descent from landlord status failed to generate an answering entrepreneurial drive in the newer role of farmer" (pp. 241–42).

56. *Azamgarh Gazetteer*, p. 115. For struggles to retain landlord status, see Stokes, *The Peasant and the Raj*, pp. 79, 238–39.

57. D. T. Roberts, Settlement Officer in Ballia, divisional report, in Report to the Board of Revenue on the Revenue Administration of the North-Western Provinces, 1882–83, p. 26, cited in *Azamgarh Gazetteer*, p. 219.

Residents made pronounced efforts to get more land. Most of the Bhumihar and Rajput land losses had been picked up by Ahirs and members of the "religious orders."[58] There may also have been some material gains by lesser men in lineage structures at the expense of those in higher positions. Studies seem to indicate that those tenants or lineage mates who enjoyed favorable terms generally garnered increased profits from cultivation,[59] and that landlords foisted economic pressures onto tenants at will.[60] When we speak of peasants growing wealthier, we refer only to those peasants who were higher in status and holdings—that is, those able to profit by fixed rates and favorable tenures.

We have, then, two parts of a process, either of which would provide greater receptivity to an ideology espousing agrarian cultural values and centering the cow. On the one hand, richer peasants enjoyed increased prosperity and, in the process of securing legitimacy for their claims to higher social status, proved willing and able to support cow-related values. On the other hand, an embattled landholding elite attempted to maintain its previously dominant status. Both groups could, of course, be served by support of Cow Protection, but it must have been particularly convenient for lineage elites and zamindari landlords to find a cause to which their peasants would readily rally, the very response of the peasants sounding a reassurance of landlord status and control.

This context of social unrest and ideological receptivity required only a catalyst to prompt collective violence. The young Acting Magistrate (with the all too appropriate name of H. E. L. P. Dupernex) provided such a catalyst in 1893 in Azamgarh by his overzealous preparations for the Muslim celebration of Baqar ʿĪd. He began by requesting that all thanadars (subordinate police officers) send in lists of villages likely to riot if Muslims sacrificed cows for the observance. By return he directed that Muslims of those troubled villages should be asked to register, by

58. Ahirs gained 42 percent more land (*Azamgarh Gazetteer,* pp. 106–7). As Stokes suggests, patterns of land change were largely established by 1857. However, the early gains by *Baniyās* and Khatris (up to 70 percent) quickly tapered off. Service castes, such as Kayasths, had lost much of their land (down 20 percent).

59. Fox notes that "at all levels lineage brethren and elite held superior proprietary rights over the actual cultivators. Sometimes members of the kin body were also cultivators—such was particularly the case in highly ramified land-poor lineages—in which case, they usually held at preferential revenue rates lower than cultivators of the kin group." He adds that "the relationship between the lineage elite and their kin brethren was not often genial." The more "republican lineages" were located at least in Ballia and Ghazipur (Fox, "Rurban Settlements," p. 175).

60. Elizabeth Whitcomb, *Agrarian Conditions in Northern India,* vol. 1, *The U.P. Under British Rule, 1860–1900* (Berkeley and Los Angeles: University of California Press, 1972), p. 150.

June 15, their intention to sacrifice. Dupernex evidently intended by this to pinpoint the possible areas of trouble, as the orders designated only disturbed villages and applied only to Muslims who, by established custom, had been sacrificing for years. But the order went out to *all* villages and did not contain within its wording any warning about customary usage. Hindus protested that many of the numerous Muslims who registered had no established right to sacrifice. The authorities discounted the protest, for they did not view the registration process as implying any authoritative sanction. They seem never to have understood that, indeed, this interpretation colored the view of rural residents.[61] Certainly, the move proved unfortunate, as Muslim claims could not be verified in the ten days that remained before the ʿĪd.

Riots and Rural Communities

Dramatic reactions followed this misunderstanding. Foremost among centers of the disturbances, Azamgarh played host to "35 cases of unlawful assembly and rioting . . . nearly all [of which] were the work of large bodies of excited Hindus who had been collected from the Ballia and Ghazipur districts to join in an attempt to prevent the Muslims [of Azamgarh] from sacrificing."[62] Men collected at several locations to protest the treatment of cows in the locality. Leaders responsible for the actual recruitment of men are already familiar to us:

> The police guard . . . at Adri, the village midway between Mau and the border where the Ballia men assembled in the early morning, state that a number of zamindars were there on elephants, etc., marshalling the people. Three of the guards agreed that two of the leaders were addressed as Jagdeo and Ghansiam Narain. Early that morning . . . an Amin on the Ballia border had reported . . . that Jagdeo was on his way to Mau with a large body of men.

Moreover,

> One of the first three prisoners captured in Ghazipur stated to me [Dupernex] that he had come to our district on the 25th to attend a sabha of Jagdeo by order of his zamindar.[63]

61. Ibid., pp. 12–18.
62. "Government Resolution on the Cow Disturbances in the Azamgarh District," dated Naini Tal, 29 Aug. 1893, par. 5. Printed in full in an appendix to Dar, "An Appeal to the English Public," p. 16, par. 11.
63. Dupernex, "Report," pp. 11, 1.

Hundreds of men gathered first at Jianpur, some three miles away. When driven off, they moved to the village of the treasurer's priest, Karria Misra (familiar to them from the described Sabha meeting), and then went on to Azmatgarh, determined to prevent the Muslim zamindar Muhammad Asgari from celebrating *qurbānī* (kine sacrifice). The presence throughout the day and into the evening of some two thousand men prevented the zamindar from observing ʿĪd in the customary manner.[64]

Perhaps most serious was the action at Mau, which tapped historically deep schisms between the putative Hindu and Muslim communities. In addition, the story at Mau presents a stark contrast to the general lack of reaction of rural Muslims as a collectivity to Cow Protection, particularly in the Gangetic plain. Isolated Muslim zamindars in the countryside seldom did more than appeal to the administration for protection: a large crowd would gather outside a zamindari compound, and public pressure would prove sufficient to dissuade Muslim zamindars from sacrificing on the ʿĪd. Incidental acts of defiance or revenge did sometimes occur, such as the false charges levied at various times by Muslims against Hindus for "cattle rescue."[65] Occasionally, although relatively infrequently, these Muslims even assumed leadership roles. In Lar (Gorakhpur) the Rankis (wealthy Muslim traders and dealers in produce, hides, and leather goods) gathered in an idgah and chose resistance in response to a Ga'orakshini meeting. When leading Muslims in other parts of Gorakhpur received threatening demands to pay Cow Protection contributions, the Rankis of Lar designated an alternate Islamic charity for Muslim donations. Nevertheless, this coherence and self-consciousness proved unusual, and there was an implicit limit—perhaps related to class interests—in the actions Lar's Muslims were willing to take. They refused, for instance, to help a deputation of Salempur butchers, declaring at the mosque that the "butchers' quarrel was not an essential part of the Islamic faith."[66]

Against this background of limited and intermittent cooperation, the events in Mau reveal a very different set of local relationships. As early as 1806 there had been a riot in Mau, during which several people were killed or wounded. In response, the Nizamat Adawlat passed an order (no. 102 of 1808) declaring that "the sacrifice of cows, calves and bullocks by Muslims was not permitted under [the previous] Govern-

---

64. Ibid., pp. 5–7.
65. Ibid., p. 2.
66. "Note on . . . Gorakhpur," pp. 1, 4–5, 7.

ment of the [Muslim] Nawab Wazeer, in consequence of the religious abhorrence of the Hindu inhabitants to such sacrifices."[67] This prohibition remained in effect until 1863, when some Muslims applied for permission to sacrifice. Unaware of the earlier decision, the Magistrate granted permission, only to have indignant Hindus produce copies of the Nizamat Adawlat's ruling. The Magistrate changed his order, but his very vacillation fueled the unrest. Several other appeals followed in 1863 and 1864, as did a case of assault by Hindus on Muslims who had killed a wild cow outside town. Four additional cases followed in rapid succession, in which the Magistrate persisted in asserting that Muslims were at liberty to slaughter, and the Judge invariably held that the practice had been forbidden. Not surprisingly, it became impossible for the Magistrate to maintain order in the town. He imposed a punitive police force—maintained at the expense of "the Hindus"—and authorized construction of a slaughterhouse, inside which the killing of cows for utilitarian purposes could be accomplished without offense. Prohibition of ritual sacrifice remained in effect.

Drawing on this past history, Cow Protection rekindled Hindu dissatisfaction in Mau. In 1886 Hindus again petitioned the government, objecting to any slaughter of kine there. After painstakingly reviewing the evidence, the District Commissioner of Banaras supported the distinction made twenty years earlier between sacrifice and ordinary slaughter. No one in town could deny that the slaughterhouse had been in use for twenty years, although the current location had proved far from ideal. The commissioner spent several days reviewing other possible sites with the "leading" Hindus and Muslims of Mau, but could not effect a compromise agreement. Into this impasse rushed the roving crowds from Ghazipur during the Cow Protection riots of June 1893. Saying they had come to support local Hindus who were "agitated," they intended "to ask the Muslims not to do kurbani and to prevent them if they did so."[68] Despite a driving rain and firing by the armed police, the crowd attacked 150 local Muslims in the Muslim quarter of the town, then broke into Muslim houses and murdered seven residents. Mau experienced the highest level of violence committed in U.P. during

67. Orders of the Nizamat Adawlat, no. 102, to J. Ahmutty, Magistrate of the Zillah of Gorakhpur, dated Benares, 25 June 1808, and signed by J. H. Harington. Published in an appendix to Dar, "An Appeal to the English Public," pp. 21–22.

68. The Deputy Collector had tried to "talk matters over" with "the leading Hindus and Muslims of Mau" on June 24. Report of E. L. L. Garstin, District Superintendent of Police, Azamgarh, to District Magistrate, Azamgarh, dated 26 June 1893, L/P&J/6, vol. 365 for 1894, file 55.

the riots; the violence only abated after Mau Muslims were coerced into signing an agreement that they would not kill cows. They were forced, as well, to release the cows they had collected for the ʿĪd sacrifice.

These events at Kopagung, Azmatgarh, and Mau point up several important characteristics of this rural phase. The first is the source of leadership in the countryside. We might have expected, from the nature of the movement's urban supporters, that talukdars and zamindars would be prominent. This was not the case.[69] Early in the government's campaign to discourage support of the movement, it had targeted these high-ranking supporters and officials. The cases of three tahsildars (subdivisional revenue officials), though late, were no doubt representative. The three were transferred or demoted, one for soliciting subscriptions from talukdars, another for holding a Cow Protection meeting at his own residence and "inducing" subscriptions, and the third for using his official position to aid the agitation.[70]

Instead, leadership passed to those at lower social levels: to zamindari landowners, to lineage elites, to rural-based raises, and to "lower subordinate officials." In Kopagunj, for instance, "Brahman village schoolmasters" provided the movement's most active leadership; sub-postmasters and kanungos proved active, as well. The Magistrate lamented that he had "found it impossible to obtain information of any sort concerning the [Cow Protection] league from any minor official of this type. They either wilfully ignore what is going on around them or else they deliberately set themselves to misrepresent the true state of affairs."[71]

Returning to Jagdeo Narain Bahadur for a moment enables us to see how this devolution of leadership worked in the countryside. Despite the fact that his once-impressive estate had been reduced in size, Jagdeo still commanded substantial influence in both Ballia and Azamgarh districts, as the first prisoner attested. This traditional influence was reinforced when Jagdeo gained an administrative position as judicial *muḥarrir* (clerk) for a time. Beyond these claims to status and hence support, Jagdeo exercised indirect influence, doubtless based on a com-

---

69. The one exception is the Rani of Majhauli. Her continued participation seems to have been possible because, as a woman, she worked through intermediaries and hence was shielded from direct British pressure.

70. "Minute" in response to Wedderburn question in Parliament, IOR, L/P&J/6/370, file 557 for 1894.

71. Dupernex, "Report," p. 11. The few visible exceptions to this—the Rani of Majhauli and the "elephant-riding" leaders noted above—may have been special cases. As for the latter, they seem to have been leaders of large, joint zamindari lineages and thus operated much as their fellow zamindars would have done.

bination of zamindari power, high social status, and effectiveness in leading his caste fellows.[72] Thus, a letter from him caused Ghazipur zamindars to mobilize their men and caused others of his caste living near Chiriakot to mass there to prevent sacrifices.

The same pattern can be traced among the rurban lineage elite, the Babus of Surajpur—Bhumihars with estates in Azamgarh, Chapra (Bihar), and Ghazipur. Active Cow Protectionists, the Babus called on their lineage and caste fellows to assist in the Kopagunj cattlelifting and built a cattle pound of their own that effectively circumscribed the operation of a government pound.[73] Among the Bisens, similar lineage elite—the Babus of Lar—exercised leadership. Largely responsible for introducing the Sabha into Gorakhpur district and figuring prominently among the two thousand zamindars who attended the large meeting held at Majhauli, the Babus came to the meeting "with elephants, horses and palkis in great state." Indeed, Magistrate Hocy of Gorakhpur ennumerated in great detail the extent of the Bisen connection and influence through the Majhauli family and the villages that had been granted by their estate. In villages largely populated by Bisen Thakurs, the caste connection provided the necessary climate in which the movement could take hold. It then spread among "the rest of the Thakurs and Brahmans of a vast number of villages" bound to the estate by grants "held from former Majhauli Rajas," until "all Hindus are now in it, from the chaudhri Ahirs of Mail to the Tewaris of Ukina, and Dubes of Barkagaon."[74]

Beyond leadership, the riot narratives suggest the extent to which the countryside reshaped Cow Protection ideology. We noted earlier the differences between the urban and rural targets of the movement. In the cities, representatives of different ideologies generally provided the "Other" against whom the movement was articulated. In the countryside, more parochial considerations pinpointed certain caste or religious groups: the significant fact is that the definition of "Other" varied with the locality. In Azamgarh, for instance, Ga'orakshini Sabha members

> practically preach[ed] a crusade against Muhammedans, and particularly against butchers. If reference is made to the list of cases . . . showing the ill-feeling between Hindus and Muhammedans, it will be seen that they refer mostly to quarrels about

72. Ibid., pp. 11–12.
73. Ibid., pp. 1, 5–6.
74. "Note on . . . Gorakhpur," pp. 5–6; see especially the tables of villages held by Majhauli estate and other Bisens.

buffaloes and not cows. In the disturbance that occurred on the Bakr Id the Hindus made no distinctions between buffaloes and cows, and where there were no officials present to keep them in check they would hardly tolerate the slaughter of goats and sheep. The Azamgarh butchers have several times informed me during the past month that they have been stopped on the roads and threatened by villagers while leading along goats.

The demands for Muslims to cease sacrificing were

backed up by threats of boycotting and loot. Where the Muhammedans are weavers the threat of boycotting appears to be usually employed, the idea being that no cloth should be bought by Hindus from weavers and no grain sold to weavers by Hindu baniyas. The tall talk about loot is indulged in when a land-owning Muhammedan community is dealt with. In two cases the Muhammedan villagers have informed me that the threat of plunder was qualified by a message that they would be left alone if they contributed a certain sum in money and a certain quantity of rasad for the purposes of the League.[75]

In much of Azamgarh district, then, a long-standing antagonism toward Muslims was the predominant focus of Cow Protection, though the strength of this antagonism obviously varied with the locality.

The movement could have taken a different form. In Gorakhpur, Sabha rules warned against wounding the feelings of Muslims of high status and directed that actions even against butchers masquerading as Brahmins or holy men be limited to petitioning the authorities. Instead, agitation focused on lower-caste *Naṭs*, *Banjārā*s, and Chamars, for they bought cows and sold them to butchers, and the agitators therefore held them directly responsible for cow slaughter. Moreover, rule 20 noted:

As a Chamar is a cow-killer it is most reprehensible that he should be employed to attend cows, or that cows, bullocks and so on should be left to his mercy: and therefore no Chamar shall, as far as is possible, be employed as a cowherd, and whether a ploughman be a Chamar or not, the employer shall first make sure, and if he be sure the ploughman will not be cruel to the bullocks, he shall employ him.[76]

The rule demonstrates the process by which local Cow Protection supporters reshaped a general ideological framework to accommodate

75. Dupernex, "Report," p. 9.
76. "Note on . . . Gorakhpur," rules 6 and 20, pp. 2, 4.

local antipathies. The coherent pattern throughout these rural eastern tracts applied the ideology against existing parochial fissures, working through local Sabha rules to separate from upper-caste culture these lower-caste "outsiders." Chamars, often cultivators for upper-caste tenants or landholders as well as tanners of hides, obviously were outside the twice-born Hindu matrix, as were Muslim butchers and weavers. The wandering "tribe" of *Naṭs*, like the peripatetic *Banjārās*, could not fully participate in local Hindu culture. Moreover, it may be that anti-Chamar activity emerged in part as a reaction to Arya Samaj appeals to convert and incorporate the lower castes.

Reinterpreted ideology in the countryside thus accommodated parochial concerns. Those perceived as outside the twice-born Hindu value system became targets. Most important, by emphasizing common symbols and targets, the movement shored up deteriorating relationships within the twice-born level of local society. Rural Cow Protection briefly united landlords and wealthier peasants—groups whose diverging interests ultimately resulted in the rural peasant protest movements (Kisan Sabhas) of the 1920s. Indeed, several scholars have noted that the groups active in the 1890s emerged again in the 1920s and 1930s. The fissures that were papered over by Cow Protection in 1893 continued to widen until, in the 1920s, a "survey . . . of Congress leaders and organizers in Agra, Allahabad, Azamgarh and Rae Barelli districts revealed heavy representation of small zamindars and patidars and, especially in Agra, relatively affluent merchants and moneylenders, apart from the independent professionals."[77]

Conclusion

The collective violence of the rural phase of Cow Protection in 1893 characterized the movement's ability to mobilize sometime competitors against a common "Other" of Muslims and *Naṭs*. Devolution of leadership, and a changed meaning behind the ideology of the cow, contributed greatly to the changes in the movement between the first and second phases. These two characteristics were accompanied by a third essential aspect of rural mobilization: the very different nature of collective violence in the countryside from that in the cities. In part this reflected the difference in spatial organization of populations—concen-

---

77. Gyanendra Pandey, "A Rural Base for Congress: The United Provinces, 1920–40," in D. A. Low, ed. *Congress and the Raj* (Columbia, Mo.: South Asia Books, 1977), p. 214. Pandey also cites conclusions by C. A. Bayly and Lance Brennan.

tration in urban *muḥalla*s in contrast to dispersion in villages. But it also reflected a difference in the relations between people in the countryside, where victims generally recognized assailants, and where psychological pressure often sufficed to accomplish the desired ends. Indeed, attackers and victims tended to be acquainted in a peasant society organized around common marketing structures.[78] This difference, of course, is more a matter of degree than of kind. Still, it remains a significant indicator of the differences in mobilization in the two phases of the Cow Protection movement, for the rural practice mobilized supporters from one area to march on another. Thus, the large crowds from Ballia overwhelmed Muslim ʿĪd sacrificers in Mau and Azmatgarh, whereas previous urban skirmishes—in 1890 in Aligarh, for instance—involved only relatively small local groups attacking a nearby *muḥalla* or other local target. In contrast, the ratio of physical to psychological violence tended to be in inverse proportion to the size of the crowd. In much of Azamgarh district, for instance, attacks on persons or property proved unnecessary; the protesting crowd achieved its aims simply by assembling in large number near the places of sacrifice.

The differences in the two phases of the Cow Protection movement ultimately proved more significant than the similarities of symbol that seemingly united them. By 1893 very few connections remained between the movement that began in the cities and the one that emerged in the countryside. To some extent British repression may be held responsible for severing these ties. Of more significance, however, were the actions of its own adherents. So thoroughly had they reinterpreted "community" that its meaning had become limited to very localized relationships. In the process, the rural proponents of Cow Protection ultimately had denied the movement's ability to serve as a broader, more encompassing political statement.

---

78. See Yang, "Sacred Symbol and Sacred Space," for a well-documented discussion of the connection.

PART III

From Community to Communalism

The Politicization of Community

Central to the writing of recent European social history has been its illumination of the process by which popular identification with local "community" became transmuted into identification with a larger entity. The timing and character of this shift differed significantly in early modern England and France, but the underlying components of the process were strikingly similar. Of particular interest for us was the role played in this process by collective ceremonies and protests, for collective rituals provided an enlarging ideological frame of reference and a vocabulary of values and standards that informed the connection between nation-state and individual. Public participation in such collective activities resulted ultimately in the creation of an important corollary to the nation-state: the "public sphere," in which individuals participated in the shaping of their states through the exercise of public opinion.

Approaching the subject through collective cultural exercises is particularly helpful for analysts looking at world areas to which the western European concept of "the nation" was imported. That is, this concept was used in very different ways in imperialized areas. Although the concept of nation became embedded in the modern states formed from previous colonies, it necessarily had to connect to, and build on, the local social fabric. This fabric differed in important ways from that of western Europe, and herein lay the crucial, but nuanced, difference in developments in north India and western Europe. Given limitations of space and intent, we can make no definitive statement here about the general development of "nation" or its connections to modern citizens.

Instead, the discussion focuses on the ideological relationship between "community" and "nation" during the transitional period leading to the emergence of the nation-state. Since Part III examines the ways in which collective and symbolic activities have played a central role in transmuting "community" into other, larger meanings in north India, we begin, in this introduction, with a brief comparative sketch of how the process worked in England and France during the eighteenth and nineteenth centuries.

From "Community" to "Nation" in England and France

At least two elements proved important in the European shift of popular identification from local community to that of the nation-state: (1) participation in collective rituals informed by an ideological framework that came to equate "community" and "nation"; and (2) creation of a "public sphere" in which citizens of the nation helped shape it through the exercise of informed public opinion. A relatively smooth transition marked the emergence of these aspects of collective life from an earlier English society structured around a series of local communities. By contrast, the transition in France seems to have been more intermittent, characterized by a series of abrupt changes through the eighteenth and nineteenth centuries that only resulted, in the late nineteenth century, in the creation of a nation-state with public participation. Although the timing differed in each country, similar political and economic developments—particularly civil unrest and the impact of industrialization—led to new state structures, simultaneously sensitizing inhabitants to the fact that they participated together in a new order and ensuring that some broader alternative to the local community would emerge.

The translation of community to larger referents in England can be traced at least to the eighteenth century, and scholars have identified the rise of the "middling sort" as the key theme of developments in the seventeenth century. Certain characteristics of the activity of this middling sort have significance for us:

> The middling sort [were] the 30 per cent, or perhaps 40 per cent of the nation's population who were relatively comfortably off, ranging from yeoman and prosperous tradesmen to husbandmen and craftsmen. . . . They took advantage of the socially selective "educational revolution," and improved their literacy. They made up the expanding electorate, perhaps up to 40 per cent of the adult male population. . . . They joined the sects and the

radical movements of the 1640s and 1650s. They petitioned, demonstrated and agitated in London in 1640–42, forcing the pace of the English Revolution. Appropriately, then, the middling sort have a high profile in this volume [on popular culture in the seventeenth century]: as the consumers of popular print, as the organizing core of charivaris, as participants in the legal process, as guild members, and as those who committed their religious, political and social beliefs to the historical record.[1]

The eighteenth century witnessed a consolidation of power by new local elites and members of this middling sort. The work of both Underdown and Bohstedt documents the efforts of many of the middling sort to suppress local community rituals, such as church ales, and to replace them with ones that explicitly connected the individual participant to the larger ideological community, the state.[2]

An increased politicization accompanied this broadened frame of reference. Bohstedt tells us that during the English civil war years the process of "nationalization of political conflicts" led to "an unprecedented widening of the organized political public on both sides." This phenomenon provided "what was genuinely new" in the period: "The significant transition was mobilization, the emergence of perceptions and organizations having regional and national, not merely local, horizons."[3] As we know from Underdown's study, the popular support or resistance taken by a locality in this period had been shaped by the area's previous receptivity to definitions of community organized around the individual and the state. That is, to the extent that an area had persisted in protecting localized expressions of collective culture, it supported "Church and King"; where it had embraced the state's new values and rituals, it supported Parliament's Roundheads. What signifies here is that areas rallied not only to different visions of shared values shaped by differing forms of the state but also, and more

1. Barry Reay, "Introduction," in Barry Reay, ed., *Popular Culture in Seventeenth Century England* (New York: St. Martin's, 1985), p. 1.

2. As noted in Part I, Golby and Purdue dissent from this general emphasis on suppression of so-called popular culture activities by an alliance of state and bourgeoisie in *The Civilization of the Crowd*. More to the point would be the insistence that an oppositional relationship, and particularly lower-class "resistance" to this ostensible suppression, may not be a sufficient characterization, and that we must also look to examples in which the different levels of society simply interpreted the signs of public discourse in different ways (see Thomas E. Crow, *Painters and Public Life in Eighteenth-Century Paris* [New Haven: Yale University Press, 1985]).

3. John Bohstedt, *Riots and Community Politics in England and Wales, 1790–1810* (Cambridge, Mass.: Harvard University Press, 1983), pp. 219, 223.

especially, to the process behind such collective decisions: popular support did emerge for each side of this national issue, and supporters of one or the other side of the conflict in particular localities shared similar, consistent cultural and socioeconomic configurations.[4] Historiography has thus traced a pattern for eighteenth-century England that links changes in localized collective or popular culture activities with politicization and an increased awareness of national referents.

Although the timing may have been more protracted, and the players may have differed somewhat, similar developments seem to characterize the pattern in France. And although the turbulence of historical developments makes the direction less clear, and the scholarship linking popular activities and historical developments is less developed, we can discern certain significant moments in the transition process. Lynn Hunt details the self-conscious efforts made during the Revolutionary period to create a new political language in rhetoric and collective action. These efforts may have made little difference at the time, but, as the events after the Revolution reveal, ultimately they had a profound impact: "By the end of the decade of revolution, French people (and Westerners more generally) had learned a new political repertoire: ideology appeared as a concept, and competing ideologies challenged the traditional European cosmology of order and harmony; propaganda became associated with political purposes; the Jacobin clubs demonstrated the potential of mass political parties; and Napoleon established the first secular police state with his claim to stand above parties."[5] Ritual constituted the heart of this new political language: "The ritual forms were as important as the specific political content. Political symbols and rituals were not metaphors of power; they were the means and ends of power itself." As a consequence, the invented ritual forms drew heavily from the repertoire of popular cultural activities. At the same time, however, Revolutionary publicists made conscious efforts to circumscribe popular participation: "The people's enthusiasm had invested

4. "Popular royalism was most widespread in areas where the old festive culture had successfully resisted Puritan attack in the forty years before the civil war." Referring to the later Monmouth rebellion to demonstrate the effect of the increased politicization of the populace after the civil war, Underdown notes that "the most striking aspect of the rebellion is the speed with which thousands of people, without gentry leadership, took up arms in what was essentially a dispute over national, not local issues" (David Underdown, *Revel, Riot and Rebellion: Popular Politics and Culture in England, 1603–1660* [Oxford: Clarendon Press, 1985], pp. 206, 290).

5. Lynn Hunt, *Politics, Culture, and Class in the French Revolution* (Berkeley and Los Angeles: University of California Press, 1984), p. 2. Hunt draws on Mona Ozouf, *La fête révolutionnaire, 1789–1799* (Paris, 1976).

those symbols with meaning in the first place; now official ceremonies regularized them. In this fashion, the popular contribution was at once recognized and partially defused. . . . Just as the Counter-Reformation church of the late seventeenth century had tried to discipline popular religious festivity, so too the officials of the revolutionary regime tried to discipline popular political festivity."[6]

The creation of a language to express the Revolutionary and republican tradition was the most important contribution of this period. But other work suggests that symbolic incorporation of the styles and values of popular culture did not develop in the political realm alone. In cities, particularly Paris, we may look for wider referents. Perhaps most intriguing for us is Thomas Crow's analysis of the creation of an art "public" in eighteenth-century Paris—a first stage in the process that led to popular participation in "the nation":

> The year 1789 . . . brings to an end this first stage in the formation of the modern public space for art. After this date, the connection between advanced painting and the demands of public life rapidly ceased to be a matter of resistance to cultural hierarchies, becoming rather one of expected and even legislated identity between the new, egalitarian political order and the practice of art.[7]

Not coincidentally, Jacques-Louis David, identified by Crow as the eighteenth-century artist most successful in catering to emerging public taste, left behind with the Revolution "the confines of canvas and studio, however large, for the orchestration of mass symbolic behavior in the streets: the famous Revolutionary festivals that David planned and supervised."[8] Rituals of state, with their larger ideological frames of reference, thus began to substitute, particularly in urban areas (and especially in Paris) for collective symbolic activities tied to local community. Indeed, as Hunt has noted, "The preference for large, open spaces, for circular arrangements, and for huge monuments all bespoke the desire to submerge individuality and particularity in the new collectivity. . . . As presented by Ozouf, therefore, the festivals exemplify the leveling, standardizing, and rationalizing process that in Toqueville's opinion served the further extension of absolute state power."[9]

6. Hunt, *Politics, Culture, and Class*, pp. 54, 60–61.
7. Crow, *Painters and Public Life*, p. 255.
8. Ibid., p. 258.
9. Hunt, *Politics, Culture, and Class*, pp. 205–6.

Thus Crow and Hunt can point ahead to notions of "the nation" that drew on evocations of mass pre-Revolutionary symbolic behavior. Accompanying the shift from society organized around local community to one in which individuals identified with "the nation" was the creation of a "public sphere" that ultimately mediated collective participation in the emerging nation-state. With roots in the eighteenth century, the "public sphere" became fully elaborated by the late nineteenth century.

The term "public sphere," originally coined by Jürgen Habermas,[10] refers to a mode of public participation with a complex relationship to the state, for—as Crow demonstrates convincingly—it was born of state efforts, and yet, when first formulated, it articulated "public opinion" in opposition to the state. A further stage may be reached, Habermas argues, "only when the exercise of political control is effectively subordinated to the democratic demand that information be accessible to the public," for then "the political public sphere wins an institutionalized influence over the government through the instrument of law-making bodies."[11] The most salient point for us (whether the "public sphere" existed in counterpoise to, or aligned with, the state), is that state and "public sphere" drew on the same collective values and behavioral models in their frame of reference.

Although limited to the ostensibly elite realm of painting, Crow's study nevertheless provides extraordinary documentation of the first phase in the emergence of a "public sphere" so essential to the western European nation-state. On the one hand, certain actions taken by the state—represented by the ministers of the king—fostered its development. Not only had these ministers been responsible for establishing the monopolistic Academy of Painting and Sculpture, but also they had insisted on initiating (under Minister Mansart until his death in 1708) regular Salon exhibitions of the recent work of Academy artists, which were open to the public. Again in 1737 it was agents of the king who revived these exhibitions. On the other hand, the 1737 revival of Salons resulted from state fears of the development of a healthy alternative to officially approved art—namely, *amateur* exhibitions organized outdoors. Thus the revival of public exhibitions of art officially approved by the Academy had been prompted by its antithesis.[12]

10. "Although state authority is so to speak the executor of the political public sphere, it is not a part of it" (Jürgen Habermas, "The Public Sphere: An Encyclopedia Article [1964]," trans. Sara Lennox and Frank Lennox, reprinted in *The New German Critique* 3 [Fall 1974]: 49–55).

11. Habermas, "Public Sphere," p. 49.

12. "It may not be coincidental that the re-establishment of the Salon followed a particularly healthy run of exhibitions at Corpus Christi, events which never failed to

Ironically, in shielding the state's monopoly on cultural production, Orry, the new Protector, contributed to the creation of a new structure, the public sphere, which provided an alternative to the state. This structure drew not only on the previous state-supported Salons as a model but also on the public venues of entertainment created for Parisians by the *parades* offered urban dwellers. These participatory processions were staged during the fairs that extended for several months at St. Germain and St. Laurent. It is in the interaction between these forms of popular culture and the art fostered by state monopoly that Crow's study has significance for us. Not least important among the cultural activities staged at these urban fairs was an alternative type of theater that owes its form to attempts to avoid theatrical monopolies supported by the state:

> This public space paralleled the one developing in the realm of
> the visual arts to the extent that it emerged from a conflict over
> legitimacy. It is not to be identified with either the official
> cultural institutions of the modernizing state or with the older,
> festive forms of "popular" collective life embodied in the fairs: it
> was rather the very process by which the former was resisted and
> modified by the latter. As it proceeded, that resistance, though
> perhaps atavistic in origin, took on a good measure of the
> intellectual resources and self-consciousness of its official an-
> tagonist. Something new had been born.[13]

Something new: an informed public opinion, shaped by an arena born in opposition to the state—this is the development of greatest significance for us. The evolution of public opinion, first as the underpinning of the Salon exhibitions and ultimately as a counterpoise to the state, provides a singularly apposite example for comparative history. Crow posits a very direct relationship between the state, mass symbolic behavior, public opinion, and cultural producers. He points the way for more general discussions of developments in western Europe as he delineates the creation of this "something new"—this public sphere that came to

---

produce invidious comparisons to the dereliction of the Academy. Orry, the new Protector, appears to have been relatively insensitive, if not indifferent to artistic practicalities and consequently was more attentive to the letter of the company's mandate and the needs of the state. The lifeblood of the evolved cultural structure of the Old Regime was monopoly. In that intermeshed system of exclusive corporate bodies, there were not supposed to be spaces for alternative and rival cultural practices" (Crow, *Painters and Public Life,* p. 86).

13. Ibid., p. 55. See also Robert M. Isherwood's studies of these evolving forms of theater, *Farce and Fantasy: Popular Entertainment in Eighteenth Century Paris* (New York: Oxford University Press, 1986).

express public opinion in opposition to (and finally subsuming) the emerging nation-state. His study demonstrates the ability even of an elitist cultural form, as painting was at the time, to build on more popular forms and their (public) spaces of interaction. Taken together, the Crow and Hunt studies illustrate that roughly contemporaneous developments in cultural and political arenas could lead to public participation in the nation-state.

Such studies provide evidence to substantiate the theories of Jürgen Habermas and Benedict Anderson. If Habermas focused on the process whereby "a portion of the public sphere comes into being in every conversation in which private individuals assemble to form a public body" and thus forms "something approaching public opinion,"[14] Anderson is concerned with the nation constructed by that public opinion. The result, he argues, is an "imagined political community"—imagined both as inherently limited (and thus likely to define some individuals as within, and others as outside, its boundaries) and as sovereign (in which legitimacy attaches to the participatory state rather than to a "divinely-ordained, hierarchical dynastic realm").[15]

Both Habermas and Anderson see as central to the development of public opinion and its imaginings what Anderson calls "print capitalism." Habermas considers the printing industry essential to ensuring the accessibility of the public sphere and sees the press as "an institution of the public itself, effective in the manner of a mediator and intensifier of public discussion."[16] According to Anderson, print capitalism is significant not only because it made participation accessible for the many literate in vernacular languages (particularly merchants and women). However, it also limited accessibility, since a particular item could appeal only to those in whose (now standardized) tongue it was cast.

There is no question that print capitalism played a profound role in the development of the European public sphere in terms of both accessibility and boundary establishment. Certainly it is not coincidental that the largest source of evidence available to Crow is the series of independently produced pamphlets that served as guides and critiques of the Salon's exhibitions. Hunt notes that French "clubs, newspapers, pamphlets, posters, songs, dances . . . developed rapidly between 1789 and 1794," thus contributing to the proliferation of politics "out of

14. Habermas, "Public Sphere," p. 49.
15. Benedict Anderson, *Imagined Communities: Reflections on the Origin and Spread of Nationalism,* (London: Verso, 1983), pp. 15–16.
16. Habermas, "Public Sphere," p. 53.

doors." The result was "the politicization of the everyday."[17] Similar developments occurred in England, where their impact was even more sustained. In his various studies of eighteenth-century English political culture, John Brewer has traced the establishment of the public sphere: "While institutionalized politics stagnated, other means of political expression and new sources of political information became available to a public eager for the chance to express its (admittedly fairly unsophisticated) political views. . . . Theatre, press and club, all provided an indigenous popular political culture that flourished in the metropolis even while the forces of political constraint were at their height."[18]

Lest we think that this technological revolution limited participation in the public sphere only to those who were literate, we must heed the reminders of Roger Chartier, who argues convincingly that pre-Revolutionary chapbooks (*bibliothèque bleue*) provided reading matter for "different social groups, each approaching it in ways ranging from a basic deciphering of signs to fluent reading." Chartier argues as well against "a too simplistic opposition between oral culture and scribal or print culture":

> Between literacy and illiteracy there exists a wide range of reading abilities . . . [and] between private, individual reading and passive listening to spoken words there exists a wide range of attitudes toward print culture, collective and utilitarian, rooted in the basic social experience of the popular urban classes, developed in the workshops, the festive confraternities, and the Protestant conventicles. . . . Between learned books and simple images there exists a wide range of printed materials that merge texts and pictures. Their deciphering necessarily involves decoding the imagery and reading the texts that comment on or explain it.[19]

Thus, even in the western European countries in which literacy expanded rapidly, the smaller communities organized by work and leisure mediated the participation of semiliterate and illiterate members of the nation. Primarily, this mediation continued to take the form of collective rituals.

17. Hunt, *Politics, Culture, and Class*, p. 56.
18. John Brewer, *Party Ideology and Popular Politics at the Accession of George III* (Cambridge: Cambridge University Press, 1976), pp. 6–7; see also Neil McKendrick, John Brewer, and J. H. Plumb, *The Birth of a Consumer Society: The Commercialization of Eighteenth-Century England* (London: Europa Publications, 1982).
19. Roger Chartier, "Culture as Appropriation: Popular Cultural Uses in Early Modern France," in Steven L. Kaplan, ed., *Understanding Popular Culture: Europe from the Middle Ages to the Nineteenth Century* (New York: Mouton, 1984), pp. 231, 236–37.

In England, for instance, political agitation used during the career of John Wilkes profoundly altered the nature of popular participation in eighteenth-century politics.[20] "Legitimation and the expression of political belief do not have to assume the form of the printed or even the spoken word. Ritualised conduct, the employment of symbols, or engagement in symbolic action can all be used to convey a political creed"—and all were so used by Wilkes and his supporters. Indeed, "the conception of politics that Wilkes sought to project" involved a new scale of "skilled marketing techniques, the advocacy of political participation, and the highly effective use of wit and humour. . . . [These] all demonstrate[d] how Wilkes commercialised politics and developed, as a consequence, the notion of politics as a form of entertainment." This notion should not suggest the trivialization of political activity. On the contrary, Wilkes's "defence of the printers and publishers of parliamentary proceedings . . . exemplified an anti-aristocratic, anti-oligarchical conception of politics which emphasized the importance of the accountability of the people's representatives to their public, and underlined the necessity for open political discussion. . . . This recruitment of popular support was deliberate and self-conscious; it sought to mobilise opinion as a counterweight to the powerful forces of administration." In this way the middling sort—the "newspaper proprietor, the printer of cartoons, the producer of artifacts, the brewer, the tavern proprietor, and the city merchant"—all came into their own. The eighteenth century, then, should be seen as the period in England in which "the scope and scale of this alternative political nation" evolved and increased its impact. For the most part, eighteenth-century developments provided links between the local world and larger events through elaborations of collective ritual behavior.

Collective ritual continued to play a central role in the nineteenth century, but with important differences in the manner and impetus of its creation. It interpreted on a broader stage the signs communicated through print, and it played a crucial role in shaping public opinion in the public sphere. Particularly by allying itself with the past, such collective ritual could finesse the connections between new "nation" and old "community." Eric Hobsbawm has written at some length on the processes by which "tradition" was "invented" to serve this purpose. As he notes, invented traditions are "responses to novel situations which take the form of reference to old situations, or which establish

20. Brewer, *Party Ideology and Popular Politics*. The following quotations come, respectively, from pp. 22, 21, 165–66, 268.

their own past by quasi-obligatory repetition." Indeed, "we should expect [such invention] to occur more frequently when a rapid transformation of society weakens or destroys the social patterns for which 'old' traditions had been designed." The result is a striking "contrast between the constant change and innovation of the modern world and the attempt to structure at least some parts of social life within it as unchanging and variant." Looking particularly at the "invented traditions of the period since the industrial revolution," Hobsbawm identifies three overlapping types of activities in which the efforts to establish or legitimize institutions and socialize individuals grew out of "those [efforts] establishing or symbolizing social cohesion or the membership of groups, real or artificial communities." Implicitly, through their participation in invented traditions, such communities became transmuted into a "nation."[21]

Invented traditions relied particularly on the interplay of public sphere and ritual. In this way, collective behavior meshed with political behavior in the sense of overt popular participation in institutions of government. Building on developments of the eighteenth century, this new alignment was very much a product of the nineteenth, taking explicit political form especially toward the end of the century. It is to that time that we can trace the emergence of political participation predicated on establishment of a relationship between the individual and the state.

Once again, we can understand the process best by analyzing it through developments related to collective activities. In England studies of the efforts to substitute "rational recreations" for street football in the early nineteenth century and of the evolution of working men's clubs and music halls in the late nineteenth century point the way.[22] Shrove Tuesday and Ash Wednesday marked more than religious holidays in Derby at the beginning of the nineteenth century. "Highly popular, rowdy and controversial" street football events were staged there each year, on the Tuesday by men and on the Wednesday by boys. Much more a "popular festival" than a game, street football brought out the

21. Eric Hobsbawm, "Introduction: Inventing Traditions," in Eric Hobsbawm and Terence Ranger, eds., *The Invention of Tradition* (Cambridge: Cambridge University Press, 1983), pp. 2, 4, 9.
22. See Anthony Delves, "Popular Recreation and Social Conflict in Derby, 1800–1850"; Penelope Summerfield, "The Effingham Arms and the Empire: Deliberate Selection in the Evolution of Music Hall in London"; and T. G. Ashplant, "London Working Men's Clubs, 1875–1914"; in Eileen Yeo and Stephen Yeo, *Popular Culture and Class Conflict, 1590–1914* (Atlantic Highlands, N.J.: Humanities Press, 1981).

denizens of two parishes, All Saints and St. Peters, to compete: hordes from each parish would run after a ball thrown out in the marketplace, fighting in a "rough melee" for some six hours through the streets of the town, aiming to get the ball into their respective goals at the opposite ends of town. In this form a popular recreation represented both competition between neighboring local communities and, Anthony Delves argues convincingly, a public statement of lower-class control over the streets and central market of Derby. By 1847 the annual observances had been suppressed, although only after very pronounced struggles between the city government (allied with "rational recreationists") and lower-class footballers. Efforts to suppress succeeded not only through the imposition of force by the state (both local peacekeepers and military troops were called in) but also through the substitution of other forms of popular recreation. Various public facilities were provided—parks, museums, libraries (in Derby an arboretum was founded in 1840)—and an alternative collective activity, albeit one in which the lower classes were observers, not participants, was introduced: horse racing.[23] The implications behind the substitution of observer sports for participant popular festivals is suggested by Hobsbawm's analysis of the potential of lower-class sports enthusiasm—particularly as it came to be expressed in organized football—to forge a national identity for the lower classes. The "Other," previously identified as the neighboring parish, came to be seen as (teams from) other countries. Observer sports reinforced a larger view of the world, in which

> the state was the framework of the citizens' collective actions. . . . To influence or change the government of the state, or its policy, was plainly the main objective of domestic politics, and the common man was increasingly entitled to take part in it. . . . It was thus natural that the classes within society, and in particular the working class, should tend to identify themselves through nation-wide political movements or organizations ("parties"), and equally natural that de facto these should operate essentially within the confines of the nation.[24]

23. As Delves makes clear, these two alternatives—socially and morally improving leisure activities such as libraries and museums, and observer activities, such as horse racing—split the coalition that had united against street football. Evangelical Christians dominated the group opposed equally to football and to racing. Those from the "liberal" school of rational recreationists included the town's mayor and "those elusive middle-class traditionalists." The debate, Delves notes, was an "intra-class dispute, at least in so far as the most active parties came wholly from the middle class" (pp. 101, 110).

24. Eric Hobsbawm, "Mass-Producing Traditions: Europe, 1870–1914," in Hobsbawm and Ranger, eds., *The Invention of Tradition*, pp. 264–65.

Key in this shifting definition of home community and "Other" was the process by which the dynamics of working-class cultural expressions shifted from "confrontational" to "consolational."[25] As leisure became commercialized in the late nineteenth century, the cultural forms that had previously shaped and expressed class conflict were "tamed" in significant ways; the "Other" defined by class antipathies was subsumed, to a large extent, within a framework in which an "Other" came to be defined for the lower classes by the nation-state. The working men's clubs and music halls that evolved in this period illustrate the process well. Clubs moved in these decades from self-reliant collections of members who instructed, informed, and entertained each other (and thus, in the process, perpetuated perceptions of class conflict) to commercialized collections of spectators attracted to the clubs by professional entertainment of broad-based and depoliticized appeal. That is, competition among clubs led to expanded offerings of leisure facilities, since "one way for the clubs to secure their existence was to adapt to the business mode, by providing expensive entertainment in comfortable surroundings. But operating as a business involved accepting the consequent commercial priorities. . . . The clubs had paid the price usually extracted from a working-class organization for long-term survival—adaptation in large part to the dominant culture."[26]

The shift in styles of entertainment in what became music halls was even more pronounced, perhaps because of the overt role played in the process by government regulation and reformation. Government action affected not only the content of the entertainment but even the structural layout of the public spaces and the relationship of performer to audience. The point can be made by comparing lyrics from the beginning and end of the period. In a song from the 1850s a man condemned to the gallows for theft laments: "I procured for the widow and orphan their bread, / The naked I clothed and the hungry I fed; / But still I am sentenced, you must understand / Because I had broken the laws of the land." Contrast the ironic social and political criticism of that lyric with a Kipling song of 1899 designed to raise money for the troops in South Africa: "Cook's son—Duke's son—son of a belted Earl— / Son of a Lambeth publican—it's all the same today! / Each of 'em doing his

25. The terms, drawn from G. Stedman Jones ("Working-Class Culture and Working-Class Politics in London, 1870–1900: Notes on the Remaking of a Working Class," *Journal of Social History* 7 [1974]), have been elaborated and refined by Penelope Summerfield.
26. Ashplant, "London Working Men's Clubs," p. 265.

country's work / (and who's to look after the girl?) / Pass your hat for your credit's sake / and pay—pay—pay."

Even the "selection" of themes emphasized at the turn of the century "had to be made from the cultural stock generated by the working class" itself. Nevertheless, only a very narrow range of items from that cultural stock were deemed acceptable: "The 'audience,' once taking it in turns to do an act, came to be 'sedated' in fixed seating and more of a spectatorate. The performer . . . came to be a syndicated artist for a limited liability company, and a worker. . . . The reinforcing interaction of the government's concern to create orderly places of popular entertainment and the proprietor's need to protect the investment of capital" led to a form of entertainment that differed greatly from that enjoyed even fifty years earlier.[27]

Similar changes affected the frames of reference held by rural inhabitants in France during the late nineteenth century. Examining the conscript army, schools, churches, expanded markets, and popular culture as agents and evidence of change, Eugen Weber establishes that "material conditions, mentalities, political awareness, all underwent massive alterations."[28] For us these changes may be signified most aptly by alterations in civic rituals. Rural festivals attracted the disapprobation of the local bourgeoisie; they "were sources of disorder, of moral laxity, indulging superstition and heathenish debauchery; they disrupted production, encouraging people to waste their time drinking and dancing when they should be at work." Even as the local bourgeoisie withdrew from these occasions, festivals also presented threats to "government and police officials," for "manifestations of almost every kind incorporated a traditional ritual (rough music or the farandole), and this could easily be made to serve for, or turn into, a political demonstration." In a pattern familiar to us, Weber does not argue that this potential was completely smothered, only that "there had been transference, that serious clashes continued to occur, but within the structure of modern institutions—in political rivalry or conscript drafts." And in the process there had been "very serious efforts to *create* feasts where there had been none before," for "since the Revolution, festivals had been recognized as useful didactic instruments to create desirable attitudes." The heyday of civic ceremonial came in the 1880s, which can serve as a marker of the period in which massive transformations took place.[29]

27. Summerfield, "The Effingham Arms," pp. 236–37.
28. Eugen Weber, *Peasants into Frenchmen: The Modernization of Rural France, 1870–1914* (Stanford: Stanford University Press, 1976), p. xi.
29. Ibid., pp. 379, 385, 387, 389.

The interplay of public sphere and ritual; the meshing of collective activity and political behavior; overt popular participation in the institutions of the state: taken together, these characteristics of the emerging nation-state of modern Europe in turn provided an important model for Third World nationalism. But to what extent were these processes replicated in colonized parts of the world? The answer to that question is complicated because it was often assumed—by participants as well as scholars—that the cultural meaning behind the European model remained the same in the Third World. Distinguishing between the *uses* to which this model was put and the cultural *meaning* imputed to the model is the task of Part III. Once again, we begin by delineating the regional cultural meaning of "community" and "nation."

"Community" and "Nation" in North India

The very nature of the imperial "intruding state" of British India carried implications, embedded in its ritual relationship to the general populace, that differed dramatically from the pattern of state intrusions in England and France. The ideological structure from which ritual and rule stemmed offered no significant place for a direct relationship between individual and state. Rather, the imperial state emphasized "a representational mode of government based sociologically on communities and interests[,] with [particular] individuals representing those entities."[30] At the end of the nineteenth century in north India the provincial government still designated "natural leaders" as community representatives, even while slowly elaborating a second representational structure of political institutions, in which selected (and even elected) individuals represented specific communities.

Particularly in the case of state-level rituals, this representational mode, as expressed in an imperial setting, functioned in a very different way from the evolving collective activities of eighteenth-century western Europe. Whereas national rituals in Europe emphasized the common values and "tradition" or history that defined participants as alike (that is, in the same relationship to the state), imperial rituals in British India stressed "diversity as a statement of the need for British imperial rule. . . . [Viceroy Lord] Lytton proclaimed that if one wanted to know the meaning of the imperial title, all they [*sic*] had to do was 'to look around' and see an empire 'multitudinous in its traditions, as well as in

---

30. Bernard S. Cohn, "Representing Authority in Victorian India," in Hobsbawm and Ranger, eds., *The Invention of Tradition*, p. 166.

its inhabitants, almost infinite in the variety of races which populate it, and of the creeds which have shaped their character.' "[31]

Thus, when searching for integrative rituals in north India, we must look not to those rituals created by the state but to those that occupied the public arenas of U.P. These activities, as they had been elaborated over much of the nineteenth century, had but little reference to the activities of the state. This isolation created two legacies for the early twentieth century. First, an environment had been created in which the individual did perceive, through his participation in symbolic ritual behavior, his connections to larger ideologies (these ideologies themselves were not embraced by the state). Second, through imperial connections with Europe a new model of "community"—"the nation"— became accessible through importation. A political narrative of early twentieth-century Indian history is the story of attempts to fuse these two legacies.

Public arenas figured prominently in these attempts. Their role in facilitating popular participation in ritual enactments of the polity provided an important impetus to integration. By serving as a conduit for the expression of symbolic statements of collective values, they performed a role very similar to that of public opinion in Europe expressed through the public sphere. Part III documents the reinterpretation of the vocabulary and styles of behavior connected to this borrowed model (a reinterpretation utilizing phenomena that often appeared to be very similar to their European precedents). Particularly important in this respect was the late nineteenth-century development of communications networks, from the railways to the burgeoning vernacular press. Nevertheless, despite superficial similarities that suggested that the European models of "the nation" and its public sphere could be borrowed directly, very substantive differences prevented an easy translation to British India. We can identify the differences in these north Indian developments most clearly by looking at the two key areas in which "community" became transmuted into "nation" in western Europe: collective symbolic ritual, and the creation of the equivalent of a public sphere, founded on an accessible public opinion.

Most studies of the nationalist period have dealt with the creation of South Asian public opinion only obliquely; especially noteworthy have been Rosalind O'Hanlon's monograph on Phule (which looks at an intellectual's efforts to create a lower-class public opinion by reformulating the views and historical interpretations of his constituents' experi-

31. Ibid., pp. 193–94.

ences) and Majid Siddiqi's article linking folksongs, as evidence of popular opinion, to a number of political and social changes.[32] The subject has been dealt with directly only in a study of Delhi by Narayani Gupta. Pertinent chapters are revealingly titled "Public Opinion: Education and Elections (1877–85)" and "Confrontations: Citizens and Government (1883–1908)."[33] Gupta's sophisticated treatment of public opinion in Delhi identifies certain key components, which to some extent parallel the characteristics of the western European public sphere. She discusses the membership and activities of the "debating societies and literary institutions" (as one journal put it), the character of English and Urdu newspapers and journals, the agenda of the few reform associations, and, preeminently, the agitations over educational institutions in the city. Most important in this discussion is the interrelationship among these various activities. Referring to education, for instance, she notes that "the Delhi College controversy had demonstrated that there was in the city a body of public opinion which straddled the older generation of loyalists and their sons (most of whom had received a more formal education than their fathers) and linked them to the literati, the Muslim aristocrats and the numerous alumni of the College." Similarly, in tracing the debate over elected versus appointed members of the Municipality, she sketches the relationship among the influential elite of Delhi whose activities constituted public opinion: "In short, the principle of election was welcomed by Muslim and Hindu intellectuals and professionals and some merchants, and nomination was favoured by Europeans, by some loyalists and those mercantile groups who were dependent on British trade." This was not, however, a public opinion shaped by, or accessible to, those outside this favored group, as she demonstrates in discussing the "dread" felt by municipal committee members for the lower classes.[34]

Protest activity, whenever possible, also remained within the rather narrow confines of this elitist public opinion. Campaigns over educa-

32. Rosalind O'Hanlon, *Caste, Conflict and Ideology: Mahatma Jotirao Phule and Low Caste Protest in Nineteenth-Century Western India* (Cambridge: Cambridge University Press, 1985); Majid Hayat Siddiqi, "History and Society in a Popular Rebellion: Mewat, 1920–1933," *Comparative Studies in Society and History* 28 (1986): 442–67.

33. Narayani Gupta, *Delhi Between Two Empires, 1803–1931: Society, Government and Urban Growth* (Delhi: Oxford University Press, 1981).

34. Ibid., pp. 115, 117, 118. This point, that Muslim and Hindu intellectuals agreed on election, is an important one; Gupta makes clear that this agreement flew in the face of the British administrative position that nomination was necessary to protect minority "Muslim" interests. Indeed, immediate history contradicted the British attempt to create separate identities, for "voting was on occupational and not communal lines" (p. 120).

tion, for instance, moved from petitioning government to fundraising among elite agitators and their peers. But on some occasions, notably relating to antiplague measures (1898), imposition of a house tax (1902), and even municipal reform (1906), these influential denizens made common cause with the lower classes of the city. Indeed, the elite-style agitations through press and petition provided a model later used by smaller groups, including lower-class ones: "Once the tactics of protest had been used by a heterogeneous group with a common grievance, it was copied by sectional groups, by Muslim butchers protesting Municipal bye-laws, and then by upper-class Hindus against a tax on cows." The impulse remained, however, an elite one, focused primarily on local issues: "That year [1906] there were three associations in Delhi with overlapping membership, and drawn chiefly from members of the legal profession and from St. Stephen's College. . . . These Associations sought to build up public opinion. . . . [A spokesman, Syed Haidar Raza,] gave publicity to the butchers' protest in Delhi, seeing it not as a victory of Muslims over Hindus but of public opinion against the Municipality. He quoted its example when he urged that 'Hindus and Muslims should unite and refuse to pay' the house-tax."[35] There was, then, a "vocal public opinion" in early twentieth-century Delhi that commented, particularly through the press, on a wide range of issues of local import.

What is less obvious is the process by which connections were forged between elite public opinion and mass collective activity, especially given the dread many of the influential felt for the process of soliciting support from the lower classes. Indeed, most historical accounts present an abrupt shift from discussions of elite petitions in the late nineteenth century to descriptions of collective action in the streets by the 1920s. Such histories establish no real connection between the two except through juxtaposition of these narratives. The implication is that this shift was very sudden; often it is attributed to Gandhi (with preliminary bows to B. G. Tilak).

In fact, the shift was more prolonged and subtle, and the connecting points between the two types of expression of public opinion grew out of public arena experiences. Tracing this shift or transitional period, chapters 6 and 7 discuss the changing meaning behind public arena symbolic behavior—especially the ability of ceremonial processions and sacred spaces to carry the new messages that created and shaped

35. Ibid., pp. 145, 149.

collective public opinion (chapter 6); and the attempt through reformist-style processions and other public activities to make these messages applicable to the ordinary person as well as to members of the elite (chapter 7).

This new emphasis on the political significance of individual action struck important chords in terms of the borrowed European model of "the nation," which was predicated on the relationship of the individual to the state. But attempts to establish such a relationship in north India were fostered primarily by reformists. This fact exacted a high price on public arena activities. For reformism constituted not only an effort to connect the acts of the individual to the larger community but also an attempt by the elite to impose on the populace certain (purified) modes of behavior. It could take the form of efforts to improve adherents' practices so that they could live self-sufficiently without reference to the imperial state (the Deobandis), or it could demonstrate the ability of Indians to be self-disciplined and hence capable of ruling themselves (Congress). The effort to connect elite public opinion and mass action difference in the north Indian experience, however, is that given the presence of the imperial state, the north Indian elite could not rely on the backing of a bourgeois-dominated state, but was forced by the very structure of government to work against the imperial state.

In the guise of anti-imperialism the reformulated collective activity of public arenas thus reflected a larger process whereby north Indians tried to reclaim the legitimacy of rule from the imperial government. By invoking the European rulers' own history against them, Indians made of the borrowed European model a potent force. To be convincing, however, such agitations had to effect an amalgamation of public arenas and state institutions. This goal appeared potentially achievable because so many aspects of the model had been duplicated in India: an active public opinion was shaped and informed by rapidly expanding print capitalism; collective symbolic rituals were reworked to reflect new needs and to reclaim legitimacy from an alien imperial state.

Ultimately the goal could not be achieved, in large part because too many definitions of community-as-nation competed for primacy. That is, the process hinged on determining which constellation of "community" should be viewed as the equivalent of the European concept of "nation." By relying on public arenas to function as the public opinion became, in the 1920s and 1930s, a process parallel to that traced for nineteenth-century Europe, whereby many members of the elite attempted to change the nature of collective ceremony. The significant of Europe's public spheres, anti-imperial agitators unwittingly created an environment whose reference points were drawn not from the European model but from definitions of "community" established in north India in the late nineteenth century. As we have seen, for a variety of rhetorical and symbolic reasons most of these north Indian definitions revolved around religious identity. As a consequence, politicized religious identity—that is, communalism—emerged as an equivalent, and viable, alternative to nationalism. Indeed, this plethora of definitions of primary "community" constituted the most troublesome legacy of the imperial connection. It has carried with it to the present day important implications for the process by which individuals define the basis of the "nation" with which they identify. The current separatist movements in independent India and Pakistan measure the potency of that legacy.

CHAPTER 6

The Rani of Jhansi, Cows, and Mosques: Public Opinion Beyond the Locality

Two clusters of events in the early decades of the twentieth century suggest that the meaning and function of collective symbolic rituals in north India had begun to change in important ways. Events connected to *Rāmlīlā* and Cow Protection in 1911 and 1912, and those related to the Kanpur Mosque Affair of 1913, together demonstrate that new definitions of community were being forged that would link putative fellows beyond the locality. They also sketch the ways in which collective action both fostered and expressed a new and expanded public opinion. For the impact of the Kanpur Mosque Affair paralleled that of the Bengal Partition (1906) in arousing, among Muslims, the perceptions and expressions of a community in danger.[1] Although the *Rāmlīlā* and Cow Protection activities cannot claim that scale of significance, they do provide a revealing counterpoint among Hindu activists to the process described for Muslims.

Consequently, the expansion of public arena activity in these decades must also be seen as an essential building block of communalism—that ideology of community organized around religion, combined with the structures through which collective activity could be mobilized. The events also make clear why religion provided the most compelling basis for community. Drawing on the symbolic behavior and rhetoric that

---

1. Even U.P. Lieutenant Governor James Meston noted the importance of the affair, in correspondence at the time. See Letter to J. Ramsay MacDonald, 11 September 1913, Meston Correspondence, IOR, Eur. Mss. Col., F 136/3, pp. 72–73.

had developed around religion in nineteenth-century public arenas, communalism gained popular support more easily than did the other available ideological alternatives.

A mass movement quickened by a politicized religious identity, communalism emerged in U.P. as competing ideological definitions of community that mobilized supporters for collective action. In ways strikingly similar to eighteenth-century developments in western Europe, communalism built on two important processes. First, the symbols of community became integrated into a coherent ideology of collective identity. We have already examined, in Part II, the process by which a symbolic vocabulary was created through intragroup competition over definitions of community. The next step abstracted the emerging rhetoric from the different meanings attached to it by specific groups. Then, repetition of these symbols in various public arena activities ensured the evolution of a shared understanding of their meaning (one that frequently differed substantially from the original usage). The emphasis on specific personal practices lessened; the original actors—particularly the ulama and religious activist groups like the Arya Samaj or the Sanatan Dharm—played less central roles. Definitions of community became less divisive within the large overarching rubrics of "Hindu" and "Muslim." Moreover, the emerging ideologies proved sufficiently effective to be used against the state as well as against an "Other," and this development invited participation by a very different roster of erstwhile leaders. Although the occasions described here illustrate the dramatic differences between the emerging Hindu and Muslim ideologies, their significance rests in the similarity of process in forging, within each putative community, a shared ideology, and the similar impulses out of which the two very different ideologies grew.

Second, these symbols became the common property of people in a number of different urban locales. A kind of public opinion was created, one that recognized as legitimate certain shared values and styles of behavior, which were expressed symbolically. As we shall see in the discussion of *Rāmlīlā*, these symbols included historical events (not surprisingly, these were frequently battles to defend strongly held values) as well as personages, both gods and humans. They might also include sacred places: the Cow Protection riots in 1911 and 1912 in Muttra and Ajodhya, for instance, took on added significance because cow sacrifice was being performed in places auspicious in the life stories of *Rām* and Krishna. And, as the events in Ajodhya and Kanpur make clear, they focused on sacred spaces and objects, such as mosques and cows. Unified in their perceptions of shared values and activities, those advocating collective action on behalf of community could mount appeals that proved effective throughout north India.

The significance of these decades, then, was in the elaboration in this period of a sustained ideology of community that united "Hindus," and another that united "Muslims," residing in north Indian urban areas. At the same time, mobilizing on behalf of this ideology—in opposition to both the state and the "Other"—imbued actions by individuals with political significance. Communalism emerged as an extralocal unity of self-conscious political activity by newly defined collectivities. Chapters 6 and 7 chronicle the events that contributed to this emergence. Chapter 7 discusses the events that can accurately be characterized by the term "communalism," tracing the politicization of community ideology. First, however, we must examine the process by which symbolic rhetoric was forged into a coherent ideology, or public opinion, that motivated people in widely dispersed urban locales and created the preconditions for communalism.

Incorporating Symbols into the Army of Rām

In 1911 the provincial administration became alarmed at the unusual number of "innovations" introduced into the staging of *Rāmlīlā*, that ubiquitous north Indian reenactment of the Hindu epic, the *Rāmāyan*. This was the most widely celebrated observance in all the province; gazetteers of the period list more than three hundred towns in which it was performed every year. Indeed, "there must have been few North India villagers in the first half of the twentieth century who did not live within an evening's walking distance of a Ramlila during the dasahra season."[2] The number of viewers was extraordinarily high. The crowds attending the indoor staged dramas could number twenty-five hundred; the outdoor pageants attracted twenty thousand to one hundred thousand people in Muttra, and three hundred thousand in Banaras. For

2. Norvin Hein, *The Miracle Plays of Mathura* (Delhi: Oxford University Press, 1971), p. 102. Hein's study, drawn from research conducted in the 1940s, provides a useful bridge between contemporary studies of performance and the historical documentation we have for the early twentieth century. Judging from the work done on the Ramnagar *Rāmlīlā* (see Richard Schechner and Linda Hess, "The Ramlila of Ramnagar," *The Drama Review* 21, no. 3 [1977]; other essays by Hess; Poonam Mathur, "Observations on the Enactment of the Ramlila During October 1977," *N. K. Bose Memorial Foundation Newsletter* 1, no. 1 [1978], and "Notes on Banaras 'Ramlila,' " *Bose Newsletter* 2, no. 1 [1979]), these 1940s descriptions appear to accurately reflect early twentieth-century activities as well.

instance, a production in the late 1940s in Muttra was described as a "spectacle . . . massively and crudely presented under the open sky . . . before a crowd equal in number to the entire population of the city. The arena was a sunken field at the edge of town, surrounded by banks and hillocks from which a hundred thousand people looked on."[3]

Messages conveyed through "innovations" in *Rāmlīlā*, then, could influence very large numbers of people. Worried administrators collected information on the observance in key urban areas, concluding that a significant collection of new figures and tableaux not previously part of the staged story of *Rām* had begun to be included. British alarm no doubt stemmed at least in part from an awareness of the expansion of the urban public attracted to these public ceremonials. More people lived in urban centers, and they brought more resources to devote to the community. Besides the administrative class, which became more prominent in community interest organizations,[4] new trading groups had developed. In Allahabad, for example, "the years 1902–12 also saw the emergence of thirteen registered general trading companies, as the town pulled out of the depression of the late 1890s. Nine of these appear to have been located in the new residential areas which indicates the swing of commercial activity away from the central marketing area."[5] Moreover, rising prices and easier access to credit sources (such as Post Office savings facilities) had benefited the growing number of middle-class residents of U.P. towns and cities.

Community-focused activism appealed to leaders as well as potential audiences. The emergence of new men anxious to operate in public arenas led to competition for increased influence. Bayly documents for Allahabad the fact that such men initially had not succeeded in dislodging dominant "natural leaders" from district politics and so turned to the arena of community activism to demonstrate their effectiveness. They found that they could more easily influence appeals mounted for collective action (such as Cow Protection) or broadcast during public performances (such as *Rāmlīlā*). Thus, the period was marked by an increase in public campaigning for a wide variety of causes; taken

3. Hein, *Miracle Plays*, p. 76.
4. The Banaras Sabha membership was typically drawn from the ranks of "the subordinate civil servant, district and municipal board schoolmaster, or village pandit"; the Allahabad branch included headmasters, an accountant, a journalist, a subordinate judge, and a senior auditor, among others (C. F. Bayly, *Local Roots of Indian Politics: Allahabad, 1880–1920* [Oxford: Clarendon Press, 1975], p. 218).
5. Ibid., pp. 230–31.

together, the successes of these experiences formed a universe of aggressive, but optimistic, activism.

Public opinion began to be mobilized during the early twentieth century, and performances of *Rāmlīlā* provide the historian with an especially appropriate means of gauging it. Particularly useful is the fact that the Dasehra *Rāmlīlā* "is produced both by and for local people. It is organized, financed and staged in each town under the supervision of a committee selected for this duty in a roughly democratic manner by the local Hindu community."[6] The values personified in *Rāmlīlā* performances, then, give uniquely reliable insights into the collective value system of Hindus. Based on the *Rāmāyan* as interpreted by Tulsi Das, *Rāmlīlā* "grips its audience of thousands because the community as a whole is its producer and to some extent its playwright; it is the mirror of traditional folk interests and ideals."[7] The powerful potential of *Rāmlīlā* to express popular interests and ideals is suggested in this description from 1911:

> The *Ramlila* is a crude form of dramatic representation, introduced for the purpose of conveying moral lessons in an agreeable manner. Old Hindu writers on rhetoric have declared that . . . the dramatic representation of the life of Ram is made to bring home . . . to the people, the lesson that one should behave like Ram and not like Ravan. . . .
>
> As there has never been much painted scenery in Hindu drama for purposes of scenic display, the only occasion that was found was the military display in connection with Ram's final onslaught, and the idea that all the gods and goddesses gave their help to Ram afforded the incentive to the various representations that figure in the 'army' of Ram (*Ramdal*).[8]

Thus, processional activities proved particularly appropriate venues for incorporating new expressions of popular values. Even beyond *Rām*'s "final onslaught," such processions were numerous: the gods went in procession to plead for help from Brahma; *Rām* and the demoness Taraka led their forces through the streets before battling each other; the wedding procession of *Rām* and *Sītā* mirrored secular ceremonies;

6. Hein, *Miracle Plays*, p. 71.
7. Ibid., p. 98.
8. Thus begins the opinion requested by the provincial government from Jagat Nath Prasad Mehta, B.A., Deputy Superintendent of Police, Criminal Investigation Department (IOR, P/8649, Genl. Admin. Progs. for July 1911, Confl. progs. nos. 5–7, serial nos. 1, 2, pp. 10, 5 [henceforth listed as P/8649]).

Rām led a triumphal procession to visit his brother after slaying *Rāvan;* and "the great pageant of the slaying of Ram's demon enemy" provided the "last and greatest of these vast open-air spectacles."[9]

The processional army of *Rām* newly mobilized a wide array of figures possessing symbolic importance in 1911. The most widely invoked historical figure, the Rani of Jhansi, represented "an Indian heroine as well as an Indian hero" by virtue of her resistance against the British during the Mutiny/Revolt of 1857. Indeed, rumors, of the type frequently created about revered figures, circulated in Bundelkhand that only the Rani's attendant had been captured and that the Rani was still alive and in the protection of some Raja. The Rani not only marched in the *Rāmlīlā* processions in Allahabad but also commonly figured in other city processions there. She also marched in the *Ramdal* in Banda, Aligarh, Banaras, and Kanpur. The Banda apparition particularly disconcerted the British, as the figure rode "on horseback with a British soldier transfixed on her spear."[10] Other historical figures included Aurobindo Ghose and B. G. Tilak; pictures of Lajput Rai show the continued activity of the Arya Samajists as well. Representations of ideals, particularly "Bharat Mata," figured as people in these processions. Auspiciousness accrued to these members of *Rām's* army, viewed by the audience as larger than life: "According to a prime doctrinal assumption of the Vaishnava stage, they were thronging to welcome the god-king himself, incarnated temporarily in the body of an actor."[11]

The symbols incorporated into these religious processions in 1911 proved conspicuously historical, relating to a variety of events having more to do with political and state structures than with religion. Moreover, they represented ideals and issues of significance in different parts of the subcontinent and among different groups. Perhaps the most striking effort at incorporation was that attempted in Agra, where the local community of Bengalis tried to amalgamate the *Rāmlīlā* and the *Kālī* Puja. When the administration refused permission for *Rām* to "join Kali in her temples" because "this had no warrant in religious customs, nor precedent in the history of Ramlila,"[12] a figure of *Kālī* instead posed on a platform with attendants, who stabbed a man assumed to be

---

9. Hein, *Miracle Plays*, p. 76.
10. IOR, P/8649, pp. 8, 9, 7, 5.
11. Hein, *Miracle Plays*, p. 100.
12. IOR, P/8649, p. 8. However, Jagat Nath points out that it was not totally unprecedented: "Ram is described as having had to perform, before he got his final victory, the worship of the female divinity, but . . . it was Durga whom he worshipped. In

Rāvan. Bengalis figured in other tableaux as well, most of which presented violent scenes.

The roster of participants also suggests an effort to incorporate a broad range of social groups. Hein noted for 1940 that "the actors are recruited from the community in which they perform. The minor parts in the plays are open to all boys and men who belong to one of the four castes and whose age is regarded as proper for a particular role. Opportunities to act in the Ramlila tend to be sought after particularly by certain families who provide a disproportionate number of the community's performers."[13] The 1911 innovations may have given the men personating the historical figures an unprecedented opportunity for ceremonial involvement. These participants were drawn from the semiliterate urban lower middle classes, which benefited in this period from rising prices and a general growth in economic well-being during the early twentieth century,[14] and which so often expressed their values in street performances.[15] The Rani and her attendant in Allahabad, for instance, were played by compositors for the *Pioneer* Press. A trains head clerk and a vakil's clerical employee had created two *chaukī*s (platforms) bearing symbols of *Bhārat Mātā*. One of the Bengalis participating in the *Kālī* Puja worked at a railway stall where stonework was sold.[16]

Wealthier and higher-status urbanites participated as well: a number of goldsmiths headed the rosters compiled for other cities, and rais, zamindari, and merchant families figured prominently. The values of the influential local men were also reflected by their participation in the managing committees, elected by an annual meeting of previous subscribers. These committees, writes Hein, "raise and spend the budget, marshall the public processions, and exercise a power of final decision in every matter connected with the observances." Although committee members actively recruited actors, they did not take direct responsibility

---

Bengal, however, where the female divinity is mostly worshipped, the ordinary man does make any distinctions between the several forms . . . such as Kali, Tara, Durga, etc. etc." (p. 10).

13. Hein, *Miracle Plays*, p. 72; see also Anuradha Kapur, "Actors, Pilgrims, Kings and Gods: The Ramlila at Ramnagar," *Contributions to Indian Sociology*, n.s., 19, no. 1 (1985): 57–74.

14. Bayly, *Local Roots*, chapter 8.

15. See the work by Kathryn Hansen on the values and subject matter expressed in popular street plays, "*Sultana the Dacoit* and *Harishchandra:* Two Popular Dramas of the Nautanki Tradition of North India," *Modern Asian Studies* 17, no. 2 (1983): 313–31.

16. IOR, P/8649, pp. 7–10; Bayly, *Local Roots*, p. 263.

for rehearsals or stage management, which was left to those who had acquired practical skills through their previous performances.[17]

Rāmlīlā reflected views beyond those of the performers or management, however, since it was funded through subscriptions. The managing committee owed ultimate responsibility to the subscribers, predominantly small contributors, who pledged one rupee each when the committee members canvased for the month preceding the observance.[18] Another portion of the budget was raised through offerings made on ritual occasions connected with the performances themselves. Thus, in terms of both direct monetary gifts and contributions of time and energy (for example, boy volunteers maintained order and directed the crowds), the *Rāmlīlā* possessed broad-based support: "It would be hard to find any activity which expresses more directly the ideals and tastes of the entire Hindu public of a North Indian town."[19]

The desire to please subscribers by putting on a good show led the organizers to include figures who would impute stature as well as relevance to the display. The integration in 1911 of historical figures with mythical ones, of Bengali and other regional cultures with the local one, of all-India events with local occurrences naturally increased the relevance and implied importance of a local observance. Indeed, the very arrangements for physically presenting *Rāmlīlā* reinforced the connections between the locality and the outside world. In Agra in 1911, for example, the activities moved among five different locales over the ten days, including the *barādarī* of Chunna Mal near a major temple, the banks of the Jumna, the bazaar, and the specially constructed *Rāmlīlā* enclosure; each of these locations represented different places featured in the narrative, such as Janakpur, Ajodhya, Prayag, Sri Lanka, and so forth.[20]

Incorporation lay, too, in the catholicity of the ideals represented. At this level of popular symbolism, the sharp debates of preceding years between Aryas and Sanatan Dharmis, or ones then emerging between

17. Hein, *Miracle Plays*, pp. 93, 97; see also references to festival and fair management throughout Bayly, *Local Roots*.

18. Hein, *Miracle Plays*, pp. 94–95. For instance, Hein's examination of the Brindaban *Rāmlīlā* in the mid-1940s found that of the Rs. 891 raised, Rs. 727 came from 613 contributors, and the largest contribution was Rs. 40 from the municipal government. Of the donors, 183 names were clearly Brahmin; 164 were "recognizable" as merchants; 3 were Muslim.

19. Ibid., p. 96.

20. See program from Agra *Rāmlīlā* appended to IOR, P/8649; Hein describes a similar layout for Muttra (*Miracle Plays,* p. 89). The Ramnagar *Rāmlīlā* stands out for having the most permanent installations built in the city to represent other parts of the world.

nationalist Extremists and Moderates, had been smoothed over to result in a parade that simply praised activism. *Rāmlīlā* provided a particularly appropriate venue for universalism. As Hein notes, "in the region . . . it is the most universally accepted and the most widely attended of Hindu festivals, having an appeal as non-sectarian as that of the Ramayana."[21]

Nor was it insignificant that a number of the scenarios emphasized violence as a legitimate means of community defense. Even Tulsi Das's version displays an "earnest moral idealism of the Ramlila's ingenuous tale of a clear-cut struggle between good and evil."[22] The most important characteristic of these violent encounters was their aura of success and aggressive optimism. In addition to the battles waged by and for *Rām* that trace back to Tulsi Das's version, however, the 1911 observance included scenes connected to *Kālī* and the Rani of Jhansi. These historical figures successfully defended popular values, nationalistic and religious at the same time: all joined a parade that presented itself as a triumphant army defending basic Hindu values. The ease with which activists could alternate between an emphasis on a nationalistic message and on one more overtly Hindu in its values is equally significant.

Administrators naturally grew concerned about these innovations in 1911. But they might well have been worried about their proliferation as well. They did note that performance of the *Rāmlīlā* throughout the year had become more frequent, as troupes or companies of players traveled throughout north India, gaining in popularity with all classes.[23] In addition to these casual, year-round performances based on the *Rāmāyan*, other opportunities arose for incorporating these symbols, ranging from Holi to marriage processions to a clay toys festival in Kanpur. As the number of occasions expanded on which such symbols could be paraded, so did the message they carried.

This message of successful community defense turned, in these same years, to focus on protection of the preeminent Hindu symbol, the cow. Although the cow may have played a bit part in *Rāmlīlā* performances, it reoccupied center stage again after 1910.[24] As in the 1880s, a court decision made cows a central issue: the Allahabad High Court issued a

---

21. Hein, *Miracle Plays*, p. 100.
22. Ibid., p. 98.
23. See, for instance, the autobiography of an actor in a troupe from Ajodhya that traveled through the Punjab and NWFP (North-West Frontier Provinces) in 1910, cited in Hein, *Miracle Plays*, p. 71.
24. Early in the *Rāmlīlā* cycle at Agra in 1911 "Demeter or Mother Earth" went "in the guise of a cow with the saints to the presence of demi-gods, who in their turn approach[ed] the omnipotent Vishnu at the sea of Milk (Shir Sagar) and pray[ed] to him" (IOR, P/8649, Appendix: Program of *Rāmlīlā* in Agra).

new ruling delineating a basic Muslim "right" to sacrifice cows, whether or not they customarily had exercised this "right" in a particular locality:

> Under certain limitations the slaughter of kine by Muhamma-
> dans is not illegal. It is the legal right of every person to make
> such use of his own property as he may think fit, provided that in
> doing so he does not cause real injury to others or offend against
> the law, even though he may thereby hurt the susceptibilities of
> others. . . . The right claimed is one to which [Muslims] are
> legally entitled irrespective of custom, and it is only when they
> abuse the right that its exercise can be interfered with.[25]

Emboldened by this enunciation of community "rights," Muslims in the Ajodhya-Fyzabad area challenged a general prohibition on *qurbānī*, or kine sacrifice, issued by the Deputy Commissioner in 1911. Although the administration attempted to prosecute a Muslim for sacrificing in the face of these orders, the Lieutenant Governor vetoed the action and, responding to Muslim appeals, launched a full-scale inquiry.

The Ajodhya-Fyzabad area proved an apt one for staging the clash of community symbols. In this period only four miles separated Ajodhya, an ancient city with great religious significance for Hindus, from Fyza-bad, a city that had served intermittently as capital for the Nawabs of Awadh. In Ajodhya cow sacrifice apparently had never taken place openly before 1910, although it probably had occurred "surrepti-tiously." Protesters did not link slaughtering kine for meat, which apparently occurred without notice in Ajodhya, with sacrifice.

General attention having been focused on the issue by the 1911 dispute, each side staked out its territory. Hindus refused to counte-nance cow sacrifice in the sacred confines of Ajodhya. Muslims, in turn, insisted on their "rights." Faced with the High Court decision, the local administrator gave permission to six Muslims to sacrifice, the result of which was "very serious rioting."[26] Since this broke out almost simulta-neously "all over Ajodhya" on the morning fixed for sacrifice, it was "undoubtedly . . . organized beforehand. . . . Considerable dam-

25. Allahabad High Court Ruling in Shahbaz Khan v. Umrao Puri, pp. 181–88 of vol. 30, Indian Law Reports, Allahabad series; quoted in IOR, P/9419, Genl. Admin. Progs. for June 1914, file no. 297 of 1913, Strictly Confidential Letter from Chief Secretary to Government, U.P., to All Commissioners of Divisions and District Officers, dated Naini Tal, 2 June 1914, p. 2.
26. This general outline is provided in IOR, Genl. Admin. Dept. of the Govt. of U.P. Confl. Progs. II, for November 1915, progs. nos. 1, 2, serial nos. 1, 2, file no. 413/1915 (henceforth Confl. Progs. II).

age was done. One Muhammedan was killed by a Hindu who has not yet been arrested; another Muhammedan either fell or was pushed into a well; mosques were violated and a number of Muhammedan shops were looted." The violence moved to Fyzabad the following day, where "blustering" by some Muslims "led to retaliation by a Hindu crowd. The chief result was that a perfectly inoffensive Maulvi, who was crossing one of the streets near the scene of the altercation, was set upon by a number of Hindus, pursued down a lane and battered to death."[27]

On the face of it, the administration grappled with a real dilemma. The High Court had removed considerations of "custom," long the touchstone in rationalizing administrative policy, from the array of possible solutions. Instead, provincial authorities had to find other grounds on which to base their policy.[28] On the one hand, they would have liked to argue that the very sacredness of Ajodhya was grounds for preventing *qurbānī*. Yet there were "many other sacred spots in Hindustan" and— as had been demonstrated when debate arose over the same issue in Muttra, where cow sacrifice had customarily occurred despite the prominence of the area in the Krishna stories—the lines could not easily be drawn even when using this guidepost. On the other hand, they could fall back on the issue of "danger to the public peace."[29] But deciding not to enforce a civil decree "purely through fear of a riot" would be "an intolerable confession of weakness on the part of the executive."[30]

Although, in the end, the Lieutenant Governor's staff urged this latter guideline on district officers, a much more basic consideration colored their decision. As Meston and his chief secretary forcefully put it, "The Muhammedan population of Ajodhya is extremely small and comprises practically nobody of any importance. The Hindu population is large, influential, and swollen to gigantic numbers from time to time by the influx of pious pilgrims. For a mere handful of ignorant Musalmans to flout the strongest sentiments of the Hindus in such circumstances is sheer provocation."[31] Doubtless this decision made sense politically.

27. Comments by Meston in a letter to Sir Reginald Craddock, Member of the Council in Delhi, dated 2 February 1914, Eur. Mss. Col., F 136/3, pp. 114–16.
28. As was suggested in chapter 2, the High Court ruling did not prevent administrators from describing customary practices in loving detail in district notebooks. But district officials were directed to use this information not to decide the merits of competing claims but to pinpoint likely trouble spots. See the elaborate instructions issued in IOR, P/9419, Genl. Admin. Progs. for June 1914, progs. no. 1, serial no. 1, Strictly Confidential Instructions from Chief Secretary to Government, U.P., to All Commissioners of Divisions and District Officers, dated Naini Tal, 2 June 1914, pp. 1–17.
29. IOR, Confl. Progs. II, pp. 3–4.
30. IOR, P/9419, p. 4.
31. IOR, Confl. Progs. II, p. 4; echoed in Meston's own correspondence.

But its logic posed a fundamental question of increasing importance in this period: did the population and status of the community numerically dominant guarantee protection for its values and inevitably imperil those of the minority? If answered in the affirmative, the issue presented a central dilemma for a pluralistic society as it struggled to define "nation" through "community" referents.

Moreover, the government's brutally frank assessment proves particularly interesting when placed next to the different patterns of symbolic ideology developed by Muslims and Hindus in this period. It certainly was not true everywhere in U.P. that the Muslim population was small and unimportant. But various groups of Hindus among the majority population had successfully supported shared values through collective activities; against this backdrop, the flouting of "Hindu" values did, indeed, appear to be "sheer provocation." In this context, it is significant that little distinction was made between issues of importance to nationalists and those of significance to the Hindu community. Studies of Congress mobilization at the local level[32] make it clear that the same leaders moved back and forth between nationalist activities and those protective of more overtly Hindu values.

The histories of two such Hindu populist leaders, Bishan Narayan Dar and Madan Mohan Maulaviya, demonstrate the interrelationship they each perceived between nationalist and Hindu causes. Dar had first become prominent in U.P. agitations as a result of the 1893 Cow Protection riots. He "occasionally used violent language" in the intervening years, yet he became President of the Congress in 1911 and received Lieutenant Governor Meston's nomination to represent "advanced Hindu thought" on the proposed Lieutenant Governor's Council. Meston rebutted the Government of India's disapproval of Dar as an agitator with the argument that he "carries more weight in his party, and is more generally respected and widely consulted, than any other resident in the province, excepting perhaps Pandit Madan Mohan Malaviya. . . . if we persuade or refute him, we have persuaded or refuted his party."[33] Malaviya, in his turn, "was personally president, office holder, founder, or celebrity of almost every organization which could become involved with Congress." He, too, had been President of

32. Bayly argues this point directly in *Local Roots,* and it is substantiated indirectly in Gyanendra Pandey, *The Ascendancy of the Congress in Uttar Pradesh, 1926–34: A Study in Imperfect Mobilization* (Delhi: Oxford University Press, 1978).

33. Confidential letter to H. Wheeler, Secretary to GOI, dated Lucknow, 1 January 1913, in Meston Correspondence, IOR, Eur. Mss. Col., F 136/15.

a Congress session, this one held in 1919. "Between 1907 and 1917, borne aloft on new contacts made through the Benares Hindu University movement and in the Viceroy's council, Malaviya and the [journal] *Abhyudaya* group gave the Hindu wing of the Allahabad Congress a new energy and depth."[34]

Despite their efforts on behalf of Hindu causes, neither Dar nor Malaviya would have regarded himself as a communalist. In this decade there was no need to distinguish between activism on behalf of nationalist activities and that on behalf of such causes as Hindu education. Bayly has aptly designated the combination a kind of Hindu populism, stressing vernacular education, village work, and land reform to benefit smallholders, who could cooperate easily with leaders (like Malaviya) interested in "the regeneration of Hindu society for its own sake." Such populism reached deeply into popular culture through "increased vernacular literacy, primary education, . . . the expansion of the Hindi press,"[35] and, as we have seen, public arena activities like *Rāmlīlā*. In its efforts to forge connections with a large portion of the populace, such populism bore a close relationship to the development in western Europe of a public sphere and its reliance on print capitalism. Yet the developments in north India remained distinctive, for the society so affected consisted not of the general public, all members of which had equal access to the public sphere, but solely of those who identified themselves as "Hindus."

The self-confidence generated by this populism proved well founded, as the outcome of the Ajodhya agitation attested. In 1915 cow sacrifice was permanently banned in Ajodhya. Instead, a special walled enclosure for sacrifices was constructed in the four-mile area between Ajodhya and Fyzabad, thus redirecting Muslim activities outside the sacred city's borders. The success in Ajodhya suggests the symbolic success enjoyed generally by Hindu/nationalist agitators. Hindus emerged from this decade with an "army" of activists espousing an aggressive ideology compounding nationalist and Hindu sentiment. After the expanded *Rāmlīlā* and the successful Cow Protection campaigns of the 1910s, British administrators and adversary Muslims had discovered what throngs of Hindus knew from marching in the army of *Rām:* "Hindus" could now be unified, patriotic, and victorious.

34. Bayly, *Local Roots*, pp. 215–17.
35. Ibid., pp. 214–15.

Mosques and Martyrdom Among Muslims

The emerging rhetoric of Muslim community activism contrasted sharply with this victorious Hindu populism. The most ubiquitous of the sacred spaces of U.P. Muslims, the mosque, provided the central symbol of this differing rhetoric. Among such spaces, the "small, plain building" of the Macchli Bazaar mosque seemed an implausible object for the sudden notoriety it acquired in the middle of 1913.[36] Yet from an inconsequential mosque for *Bisātīs* (peddlers) in a congested part of Kanpur, it became likened to the "hundreds of mosques . . . destroyed in Macedonia" and "the tombs of Imam Raza . . . desecrated in Meshed."[37] Indeed, as a result first of the Kanpur Mosque Affair of 1913 and then of the fierce communal riots of 1931 in the same urban spaces, the Macchli Bazaar mosque came to invoke a symbolism for South Asian Muslims outside Kanpur as well as within that city. To an astonishing degree the Affair demonstrated how members of a small neighborhood mosque symbolically shared with Muslims from other parts of India a set of values and interests. The elaboration of symbolic vocabulary not only provided a means for linking Muslims throughout India but also established a style of rhetoric that differed dramatically from the nationalist/Hindu one that emerged from *Rāmlīlā* and similar public observances in these years.

By 1913 the area near the Macchli Bazaar mosque, built before the Mutiny/Revolt, had become one of the most congested parts of Kanpur.[38] The peddlers whose shops surrounded the mosque served as its principal worshipers. They chose informally from among themselves the manager of the mosque; the last decision, made in 1906, had designated two such mutawalli. Not long afterward, the municipality developed an improvements scheme that included running a new road through the mosque site. In large part because the route endangered two temples and three mosques, the plan was amended in 1909 so that only a bathing place (*dālān*), which had been added sometime after the mosque was built, had to be relocated. A final amendment to the plan—made by splaying the road—avoided harming a nearby temple used by Telis (oil

---

36. "Minute by the Lt. Governor [James S. Meston] on the Cawnpore Mosque and Riot," 21 Aug. 1913, IOR L/P&J/6, vol. 1256, file 3374 for 1913, p. 11 (also located in IOR, Eur. Mss. Collection, F 136/15) [henceforth Meston, "Minute"].

37. *Muslim Gazette,* 2 June 1913, in *SVN, 1913.*

38. The following narrative is based on Meston, "Minute." The account is corroborated (except as noted) by stories in the vernacular press in 1912 and 1913, in *SVN* for those years. See also chapter 2 for more details about the event.

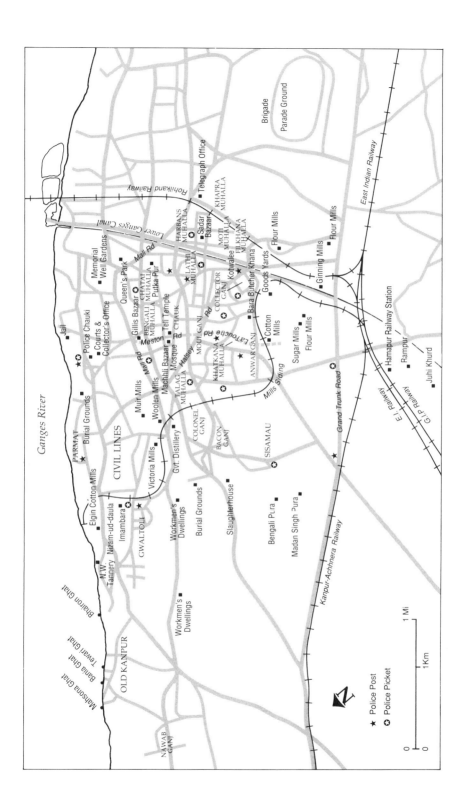

Ganges River

Bhairon Ghat
Mahsona Ghat
Bania Ghat
Tewari Ghat

OLD KANPUR

NAWAB GANJ

Workmen's Dwellings

Burial Grounds

Slaughterhouse

Bengali Pura

Madan Singh Pura

SISAMAU

BACON GANJ

COLONEL GANJ

Victoria Mills

Govt. Distillery

GWALTOLI

Imambara

Nizam-ud-daula

N.W. Tannery

Elgin Cotton Mills

PARMAT

Burial Grounds

CIVIL LINES

Muir Mills

Woolen Mills

Machhli Bazaar

TALAQ MUHALLA

Meston Rd

Mall Rd

Mall Rd

Gillis Bazaar

BENGALI MUHALLA

CHATAI MUHALLA

Queen's Park

Memorial Well Gardens

Police Chauki

Courts & Collector's Office

Jail

Teli Temple

Halsey Rd

CHAUK

Talaq Mosque

KHATKANA MUHALLA

MOUL GANJ Rd

ANWAR GANJ

LaTouche Rd

COLLECTOR GANJ

Putka Pur

LATHI MUHALLA

Kotwalee

Bara Butcher Khana

Goods Yards

Cotton Mills

Sugar Mills

Flour Mills

Mills Siding

Grand Trunk Road

MOTI MUHALLA

FILKHANA MUHALLA

Sadar Bazaar

HARRANS MUHALLA

KHAPRA MUHALLA

Telegraph Office

Rohilkand Railway

Lower Ganges Canal

Flour Mills

Ginning Mills

Flour Mills

Hamapur Railway Station

Rampur

Juhi Khurd

E. I. Railway

G. I. P. Railway

East Indian Railway

Brigade Parade Ground

Kanpur-Achhnera Railway

★ Police Post
✪ Police Picket

1 Mi

1 Km

0

0

pressers). All inhabitants were left undisturbed until 1913, when other work on the road was completed. The European chairman of the Municipal Board made a last visit to the mosque, accompanied by several Muslims—all of whom walked, without incident, through the *dālān* in their shoes. This action, of little moment at the time, acquired greater significance for both sides as the dispute developed.

Kanpur's Magistrate called the dispute a "fractious grievance," ignoring the pleas of a deputation that the bathing place be left intact. However, to get a resolution in favor of the route, the Municipal Committee Chairman had to outmaneuver the Indian members. As chapter 2 suggested, the administration was confident in its stance, for "trustworthy and good Muhammedans" had unanimously assured the Lieutenant Governor that a bathing place need not be an integral part of a mosque and had provided him with examples of exceptions.[39] Moreover, the wearing of shoes in the *dālān* was taken by the administration as evidence that the area was viewed as "less sacred."

In spite of these arguments, protests became widespread by mid-May. Lieutenant Governor Meston argued down the Raja of Mahmudabad, the indefatigable talukdar of Awadh, who possessed all the appropriate attributes of a "natural leader."[40] Meston also put his arguments in correspondence with Muslim activist Mohamad Ali, who published it in his journal, the *Comrade*. Although Meston received a memorial from the Raja on 28 June, the washing place was removed swiftly and without fanfare on 1 July. No violent reactions occurred immediately, but "as soon as news reached the mills, large crowds of julahas left their work and went to the spot . . . and [then] went off to see their moulvis."[41] The three thousand people who attended a meeting that night decided to send a telegram to the Viceroy and, while awaiting his reply, to seek legal remedy, as it was argued that the official notices had never properly been served to the mutawalli, who had refused to act as legal representatives for the mosque. The protestors sent copies of the telegram to U.P. and local officials, as well as to Mahmudabad, the "natural leader," and to publicist Mohamad Ali.

This refusal of the mutawalli to act as legal representatives and the recourse of the crowd to (unnamed) *maulawi* suggest that the *Bisātīs'* community leadership did not extend to mosque management and,

---

39. Meston, "Minute," p. 12.
40. For other activities by the Raja, particularly as regards Conciliation Committee work on Ajodhya and other sources of communal tension, see Meston, "Minute."
41. Ibid., pp. 9–10.

therefore, that a certain vacuum in leadership existed in the Macchli Bazaar mosque. Other Muslims, however, soon moved to act in ways the original mutawalli would not. On 16 July a small meeting, attended by about 125 Muslims from all quarters of the city, chose eleven new mutawalli for the mosque. Though the two original managers were included among the eleven, this election marked a radical departure from custom. Despite Meston's protests, this move constituted more than a political ploy by out-of-towners. Instead, this citywide election of the managing committee suggested that every Muslim of Kanpur could have a potential stake in any mosque, regardless of location. The move meant, too, that when the demand arose, traditional positions of leadership could be infused with new purpose, for the new mutawalli immediately began to act as the corporate representatives of the mosque. As their first act, they asked the Municipal Board Chairman for the names of those Muslims who had worn shoes in the bathing place.[42] They then published a rejoinder to a press communiqué issued by Meston and called two public meetings to discuss Muslim reaction to the demolition.

The second meeting took place at the idgah on 3 August, six days before Meston was scheduled to meet with a delegation organized by the Raja of Mahmudabad. Elaborately planned, this general meeting invoked motifs of martyrdom and mourning. Placards urged "all Mohammedan gentlemen whose hearts [were] upset and agitated by the martyrdom of part of the mosque" to "postpone their urgent duties and take part in the assemblage."[43] Muslim neighborhoods were canvased door-to-door. The mourning symbolism commonly observed during Muharram was invoked: "Large groups of Muslims from every quarter of the city were seen proceeding towards the 'Idgah barefooted and carrying black flags. . . . Some of the groups used to halt at intervals during their march . . . and at every halt a man recited an elegy on the demolished portion."[44] Though early speeches related more to Persian poetry than to aggrieved Muslim sensibilities, the rhetoric became increasingly heated. Yet even when the crowd of ten to twelve thousand left the idgah, it did not seem bent on violence.[45] It headed for the

42. Although this information was refused to them, they must have discovered at least some of the "culprits." One told Meston that "he dared hardly stir out of his house on account of the fury of his co-religionists" (Meston, "Minute," p. 13).

43. Ibid., p. 22.

44. *Muslim Gazette*, 6 Aug. 1913, in *SVN, 1913*. The editor of the *Advocate* (11 Aug.), perhaps reflecting Sunni-Shi'a tension (see chapter 8), insisted that Sunnis seldom marched barefooted carrying black flags. The symbolism may suggest the widespread influence of this important public ceremony among both Sunnis and Shi'as of the area.

45. Meston, "Minute," p. 24.

mosque, ostensibly to pray there. Instead, men tried to symbolically rebuild the washing place by piling the bricks back up. When the kotwal attempted to intervene, the crowd began showering police (and then the nearby Teli temple) with debris from demolished houses nearby. After some ineffectual efforts to control the crowd, armed police fired into the crowd and finally dispersed the rioters.

For some time before this incident, Muslim opinion had been coalescing against the government. Heavy press coverage stated the case plainly. The *dālān* had been demolished because "Muslims are loyal and they obey all the just as well as the unjust orders of the authorities"—another in a long line of newspaper laments over the reunification of Bengal. Moreover, "when hundreds of mosques have been destroyed in Macedonia, when the tomb of Imam Raza has been desecrated in Meshed, it is no wonder that a mosque is being demolished in India": a reflection of the anguish felt by Indian Muslims for the international condition of Islam.[46] Newspaper editors and prominent Muslims from other areas of India had come to Kanpur to see the site for themselves, passionately urging local Muslims to express their concern. "Every day," admitted Meston, "brought news of meetings and telegrams in different parts of India."[47]

The form taken by these protests suggests the shape of the symbolic rhetoric. The treatment of Islam in Kanpur, Bengal, and elsewhere in the world—and hence of the Muslim community in those places—was perceived as a measure of its decline. Once powerful in the world, the community seemed helpless to stave off these assorted blows; the fate of the mosque in Macchli Bazaar was symptomatic of the "martyrdom" of Muslims in general. The invocation of this idiom, involving mourning, martyrdom, and defeat, would powerfully shape the demand for action in the coming decades.

A revealing indication of the wide range of Muslims affected by the Kanpur Mosque Affair was the juxtaposition, on the one hand, of the roster of rioting millhands and other lower-class Muslims and, on the other hand, of the delegation to Meston led by the Raja of Mahmudabad six days later. The prominent Muslims of this delegation were joined by other signatories to a memorial they presented to Meston at the meeting. All fourteen were from outside Kanpur (generally Delhi- or Lucknow-based) and had been active in province- or India-wide Muslim

46. *Muslim Gazette,* 2 June 1913, in *SVN, 1913.*
47. Meston, "Minute," p. 20.

public organizations, ranging from the anti-Nagari campaigns and the Turkish Relief and South African Committees to the Muslim Defence Association, the Muslim League, and the Board of Trustees for Aligarh University. They included lawyers and judges, landholders and pirs, Legislative Council and Municipal Board members, Sunnis and Shi'as, "young" and "old" party members.[48] Signatories included both factions of several strong rivalries. They certainly provided living proof of their memorial's first contention that "the feelings of our community on this question as a whole are neither individual, local nor manufactured." Indeed, by this time they could also speak for the rioting Pathan and *Julāhā* weavers when they insisted that "these feelings are genuine, real, and founded upon the bedrock of religious faith."[49]

Thus, a new rhetoric of communalism for north Indian Muslims had emerged. That it departed from previous perceptions made it especially difficult for the administration to grasp the significance of the situation. It seems clear that although local practice had tolerated the wearing of shoes in the *dālān*, once this practice became common knowledge it proved an embarrassment to the Muslim community in general; for this reason the new mutawalli made it their first act to try to find the culprits. Similarly, an agreement to relocate part of the mosque might be possible to arrange quietly when confined within a local context; but once the cause received publicity, particularly in an atmosphere already laden with despair about the position of Islam, such an arrangement became impossible. Indeed, there is a special irony here. Though the government had previously pointed to the cooperation of Lucknow's Muslims in a similar case, Meston now had to admit that as a result of the Kanpur agitation, the mutawalli of the Lucknow mosque had suddenly told the government that they could not move a similar bathing place.[50]

Development of this communal rhetoric brought into play a number of important symbols and Islamic paradigms. The invocation of a shared literary heritage, the concept of martyrdom, and the replication of Muharram mourning practices applied now to a mosque, the preeminent sacred space. A reshaped institution of mosque management fulfilled new purposes. Face-to-face contact (through neighborhood canvasing to publicize the protest meeting) reinforced and personalized

48. List of signatories for "Address by Muhammaden Delegation and Lt. Governor's Reply" (n.d.), appendix 11 to Meston, "Minute," p. 4. Biographical information on signatories from appendix to F. C. R. Robinson, *Separatism Among Indian Muslims* (Cambridge: Cambridge University Press, 1974).
49. "Address by Muhammaden Deputation," in Meston, "Minute," p. 3.
50. Meston, "Minute," p. 15.

the sense of shared community among Muslims. An unprecedented scale of protest against the government's actions resulted. Besides collective agitation, a less tangible result of this clash was a compelling vision of community with symbols and vocabulary capable of transcending local boundaries. In the rhetoric invoked at the mass meeting, the success of the Kanpur Mosque Affair could be measured by the amount of "zeal" exhibited by Muslims. Speakers had lamented that in the past Muslims had passively accepted their treatment at the hands of the government. No more. "There are 47,000 Muslims in the city [of Kanpur] and only women are left in our houses; cannot our zeal now be called real? . . . Can Government have any objection to recognizing our zeal now?"[51]

The triumphant tone was well taken, as the agitation set a new pattern for the future. A more sustained effort for a larger cause—the Khilafat Movement—would be required to pull a broad spectrum and substantial number of Muslims into collective protest activities. But a vision of a declining community had been articulated that connected Muslims throughout India and outside it. A later observer likened the Islamic world to "a gigantic drum, the reverberations from one end being felt at the other."[52] In this way the fate of the mosque in Macchli Bazaar could be seen as symptomatic of the "martyrdom" of Muslims in general. The fate of the caliph provided the most obvious example, but other issues soon loomed as proof of martyrdom, including, in Kanpur, limitations on employment and access to patronage.

Conclusion: The Ideology of Community

In the end the administration pardoned the rioters from both Ajodhya and Kanpur. Lieutenant Governor Meston carefully calibrated the Ajodhya pardons. Among the thirty prisoners convicted for rioting, "four men . . . were clearly guilty of collecting gangs of men to break the law and of inciting them to wholly needless violence[;] three men . . . were clearly guilty of deliberate looting. . . . The other 23 men were mainly tools in the hands of the ringleaders." Having postponed his decision until a quiet ᶜId had been observed in Ajodhya in 1913, Meston then released the twenty-three and reduced by half the sentences of the others. He let stand the convictions of the Fyzabad mob

51. Ibid., p. 23.
52. Marshal Lyautey (1854–1934), cited in Peter Hardy, *The Muslims of British India* (Cambridge: Cambridge University Press, 1972), p. 176.

who murdered the "inoffensive maulvi," arguing that "the change of venue, the lapse of time and the unprovoked brutality of the murder deprive the prisoners of all claim to consideration."[53]

Although pleased that this action "completes a general amnesty for offences due to religious fervour up to the date of the Cawnpore settlement,"[54] Meston was less eager to pardon the Kanpur rioters. He wanted to delay until the Sessions trial had "vindicated" the action of the government in the courts. But the Government of India forced the provincial hand; suddenly summoned to Simla, Meston's Chief Secretary was told that the Governor General wanted to avoid a trial "in which there would be charges and recriminations of all sorts which, however baseless themselves, would be accepted by credulous people, and that he understood there was a likelihood of a civil suit to set aside the acquisition proceedings [of mosque land] as irregular." Having all along argued that the Macchli Bazaar imbroglio was a local affair gratuitously exaggerated out of all proportion by out-of-town extremists, the provincial government tried unsuccessfully to point out "that though this arrangement was being undertaken on imperial considerations, His Excellency was dealing throughout with local people and that the local feeling in Kanpur was at present not dangerous and in fact that throughout the provinces the keen feeling on the subject was subsiding." Nevertheless, the central government insisted on announcing a general pardon during a visit by the Governor General to Kanpur; Meston's substitute noted indignantly that "it was with considerable trouble that I got even the mild acknowledgement of [Muslim] wrong doings which [the pardon] contains inserted in it."[55]

The differing provincial reactions to the Ajodhya and Kanpur events were no doubt due in part to the fact that in Ajodhya rioters had struck against other Indians, whereas in Kanpur protest had been directed against the government. Even more than anti-imperial agitation was at stake, however. Meston himself, comparing parallel agitations in Bengal and Kanpur, commented with thinly veiled exasperation on the difference between the approaches of Hindu and Muslim agitators: "The Hindus were striving after a larger share of political power; they are now getting it by degrees. The Muhammedans make no such claim. It seems to me that they feel that they are being gradually ousted by the

53. Meston Correspondence, IOR, Eur. Mss. Col., F 136/3.
54. Ibid.
55. "Note for Sir James Meston" by D. C. Baillie, dated 15 Nov. 1913, in Meston Correspondence.

Hindus, and that their resentment against their own impotence and ineffectiveness is at the root of most of the irritation."[56] In fact, however, it is unlikely that the two approaches appeared significantly dissimilar to participants. That is, Meston's expectations regarding nationalist-motivated political aspirations, prompted by the western European model with which he was familiar, did not operate in north India in ways dissimilar from communal aspirations. The underlying impulse to resistance—whether aimed against a dominant community or against the imperial state—was uncomfortably similar. Action against both targets could be expressed through evocation of a larger community. In one case, the invocation of community ideology took the shape of nationalism, in the other, of communalism. The historical implications of these developments had much significance. By politicizing an expanded definition of community (particularly as it came to be expressed against an alien imperial state), activists reshaped the symbolic behavior of public arenas. They implied a functional similarity between the public opinion of western Europe, expressed through the press and electoral politics, and the expressions of collective activity in public arenas. In the process they brought collective action closer to the implications of the similar role played in western Europe by the public sphere. These developments heartened—but also misled—the elite interested in replicating in India the circumstances of western Europe.

Coincident with the emergence of nationalism, public arena activity resulted by the 1920s in the creation of symbolic ideologies that defined two different communities, and that would serve as the basis of communalism. Although emerging from the same process, the two communal ideologies differed in dramatic ways. Hindus embraced an optimistic, expansive rhetoric that made little distinction between Hindu and nationalist symbols. Repeated success in nationalist campaigns eased the divorce of symbols from their religious, even sectarian, significance. In contrast, Muslims developed a much more defensive posture, due in part to the fact that they had neither the numbers nor the influence for optimistic symbolism. This martyr motif also resulted from the Islamic paradigms on which Muslims drew, including the notion of decline from the Prophet's era and literary conventions elaborated in Urdu poetry. Most important, it related to the sense of community witnessed and experienced through collective activities in public arenas, such as

56. Letter to J. Ramsay MacDonald, dated 11 Sept. 1913, Meston Correspondence, p. 73.

Muharram. Once again these north Indian Muslims were likened to a drum, this time by the oft-sardonic poet Akbar Illahabadi (1846–1921):

> The Englishman is happy, he owns the aeroplane,
> The Hindu's gratified that he controls all trade,
> 'Tis we who're empty drums, subsisting on God's Grace,
> A heap of biscuit crumbs, the froth of lemonade.[57]

57. Translated in M. Mujeeb, *The Indian Muslims* (Montreal: McGill University Press, 1967), p. 477.

CHAPTER 7

Communalism Emerges:
Public Arenas Versus
State Structures

By the 1920s activists in U.P. had successfully mobilized public support for ideological appeals that defined and united communities beyond the locality. Significantly, such appeals could be aimed both against the imperial state and an Indian "Other." Although these activities could only have emerged in the particular context of the early twentieth century, they represented the culmination of a long process. We must not lose sight of that process: the constructions of community had very special characteristics *because* they developed in the north Indian public arena—a world that had been kept distinctly separate from the institutional structures of the imperial state.

Yet the very acts of community agitation made this separation between public and state structures appear increasingly artificial in the twentieth century. The devolution of responsibility for local administration brought Indians into the center of state structures. To establish their legitimate claims to that center, however, those operating in institutional politics were obliged to demonstrate their appeal in public forums. This led to a popular expectation that the disjuncture between public arenas and state institutions, previously introduced by a state ruled by imperial outsiders, would disappear. The point was not only, as previous historiography would have it, that nationalists began clamoring for a larger say in state institutions. It was also that this clamor led many to expect that the values informing successful collective action could be transferred to the state itself, even that the legitimacy of the state rested on this conjuncture. In large part these expectations arose from reference to the European model that nationalists wished to emulate and even to use against the European ruler. Public arena activity, evolving to meet twentieth-century needs for political activism and a greater sense of community, seemed to resemble the public spheres of modern European nation-states. Since in that model the legitimacy of such states was rationalized by reconciling state actions with public opinion (the collective values of the public sphere), north Indians looked for a closer alignment between their own public arena activity and state institutions.

But implementing symbolic rhetoric in the concrete infrastructure of rule proved more problematic than it seemed. Because they had been treated as mutually exclusive in the British imperial system, the public and state structures had developed in very different directions. As we have seen, larger ideological communities had been defined in public arenas around identities such as religion; when sufficiently abstracted in form, community identity could transcend locality. State structures, however, operated through connections more difficult to abstract and in ways rooted in their localities. Participation in local institutions and organizations was directed through smaller networks based on very personal and localized patron-client considerations. (In past studies these have been referred to as "factions." Heeding David Hardiman's quite valid criticisms of the term, we might characterize these networks as a modern, politicized form of face-to-face "relational" ties.)[1]

The lack of fit in north India—between the extralocal ideological constructs of community that had evolved in public arenas and the local relational networks developed for participation in state structures—pinpoints in the starkest terms the differences between the north Indian public arena and the western European public sphere. The latter had provided Europeans an ideal locale for integrating relational ties and larger ideology. Indeed, the very operation of public opinion served to knit the two together. But under an imperial structure such integration was impossible for U.P. Despite their superficial similarities, then, public arenas and public spheres operated in very different ways in their respective societies. The implications of this difference began to emerge in the 1920s.

When north Indian community activists attempted to transfer the successes enjoyed in public arenas to the state infrastructure, they

---

1. David Hardiman, "The Indian 'Faction': A Political Theory Examined," in Rana-jit Guha, ed., *Subaltern Studies,* vol. 1, pp. 198–232 (Delhi: Oxford University Press, 1982). Hardiman does not, unfortunately, supply a convincing alternative to "faction."

discovered that this process required more than the development of an ideology applicable to the state. Instead, programs and ideological rhetoric had to be linked together. Events of the 1920s and 1930s represent efforts to integrate the two realms: the measure of their success became, implicitly, the degree of concrete state protection extended to important community issues. Attempts to reunify public and state structures fall into three relatively distinct phases—dated roughly 1916 to 1922, 1923 to 1929, and 1930 to 1947.[2] Although the emphasis in each phase was distinctive, our focus on public participation makes clear the significant continuity of experiences from one phase to the next. It would be a mistake to see the evolution of communalism as, for instance, the "breakdown" of India-wide programs like Khilafat[3] or the result of machinations of actors not involved in the nationalist movement.[4] Instead, communalism emerged when a variety of efforts resulted in an inability to integrate successfully public and state realms.

The Evolution of State Structures: Kanpur, Congress, and Khilafat, 1916–1922

In the first phase, those claiming leadership positions attempted both to exercise power within state institutions and to expand their activities in public arenas. To be effective, these activities had to turn community ideologies against the state, connecting their local expressions to a national-level ideology of anti-imperialism. Such attempts dominated activities from 1916 to 1922. Changing circumstances shaped these experiments. If concepts of extralocal community had crystallized after 1913, they were accompanied by changes in the very process by which leadership in urban north India was legitimized. Previously, leaders—as embodiments of their communities—had received informal recognition in conjunction with their public arena activities, but many had also received official recognition and legitimation by playing roles in the

2. For a similar periodization, see C. A. Bayly, *Local Roots of Indian Politics: Allahabad, 1880–1920* (Oxford: Clarendon Press, 1975), and Gyanendra Pandey, *The Ascendancy of the Congress in Uttar Pradesh, 1926–34: A Study in Imperfect Mobilization* (Delhi: Oxford University Press, 1978).

3. See Gail Minault, *The Khilafat Movement: Religious Symbolism and Political Mobilization in India* (New York: Columbia University Press, 1982).

4. In this I disagree fundamentally with the interpretations of Mushirul Hasan, who sees the ulama as designers of communal activity, in contrast to the actions of the politicians in the nationalist movement. See Mushirul Hasan, "Religion and Politics in India," in Hasan, ed., *Communal and Pan-Islamic Trends in Colonial India* (New Delhi: Manohar, 1981).

Raj's institutions. After the turn of the century, however, the expansion of the franchise and increasing reliance on collective activity meant that recognition of leadership status was validated increasingly through popular support.

At the same time, to gain sufficient leverage in state institutions, Indian leaders formed coalitions with spokesmen for other interest groups. Only in this way could they wield power effectively, dispensing the patronage available to them. Of necessity, these local relational alliances bore little similarity to the ideological constructs of religion or class; instead, they had to cut across these constructs as well as the other community constellations of neighborhood, caste, and occupation. The appeal of these concepts did not lessen, but leaders could not use them as their sole inspiration for actions if they wished to operate at a practical level in the structures of the state. Another process exacerbated the difficulties of responding in these two very different modes: the introduction of new opportunities enabled professional men to erode or augment the influence of "natural leaders." In large part this process resulted from efforts made to expand the political base among the masses. New people were pulled into the political process, including government servants, students, schoolteachers, and small absentee landlords, all of whom became politically active in the 1920 Khilafat/ Congress NonCooperation movement.[5] Significantly, the Muslim politicians dominating Khilafat possessed frames of reference and power bases not rooted in the locality. These politicians included many who were attracted by the ideological issue "Islam in danger."

Efforts to move between public and state structures marked the frenetic organizational activity of 1919 and 1920. Though the Rowlatt Satyagraha of 1919 was not a locally-based program, it demonstrated the effectiveness of organized mass protest. Congress capitalized on this notion of mass support in its 1920 reorganization, recruiting for the first time from urban *muḥalla*s for its "four anna" members. Units of Congress, newly organized around linguistic affinities, more effectively incorporated the rural areas. Khilafat preachers canvased the country-side. The Montague-Chelmsford reforms, implemented in the Government of India Act of 1919, both extended the franchise by lowering the property qualifications and increased the opportunities for political

5. These broadened appeals could capitalize on the impact of a four-year economic crisis resulting from the war, which reversed the previously good economic position of salaried middle-class wage earners and those on a fixed income. Bayly, *Local Roots*, p. 245.

patronage by giving Indians charge of "transferred" subjects.[6] By 1920, then, important changes had been effected both in state institutions characterized by relational, pragmatic politics and in the public arenas in which ideological appeals were made. While the experiments of this phase did succeed in raising public expectations and in creating an ideology of nationalism to compete with communalism, they did not prove successful in integrating popular ideological concerns with the techniques necessary to operate effectively in state institutions. As a consequence, the public opinion expressed in collective activities could have little direct reference to those institutions.[7]

The tactics used in Kanpur during this phase provide useful examples of the difficulty of integrating the different operational strategies required, respectively, by the institutional and the ideological arenas. As befitted the premier industrial center of the province, commercial men dominated Kanpur's state structures of local government and politics. A resident noted in 1931 that "Cawnpore is neither a cultural nor a historical place. It is an industrial town with shifting population. Most of the residents are either middle class people engaged in independent professions or labourers of the mills living in rented houses without much regard for their neighbours."[8] By the mid-1920s traders aspiring to city leadership roles had joined the barristers and honorary magistrates as municipal commissioners and as members of the District Board, the Kanpur Improvement Trust, and the Provincial Legislative Council.[9] They also had enlisted in Congress, working to outmaneuver newcomers or challengers; in this way they rendered the nationalist movement a mere extension of existing local power configurations.

Through the Kanpur Congress organization these same leaders then ran a variety of programs, not all fostered by the provincial or all-India Congress committees. These included *muhalla*-level Congress committees but also *prabhāt pherīs* (nationalist processions taken out each

---

6. See Jim Masselos, *Nationalism on the Indian Subcontinent* (Melbourne: Thomas Nelson, 1972), for a general outline of the events of this period.

7. The Rowlatt Satyagraha was an agitation, not a concrete program; Congress, reorganized, and Khilafat functioned as institutions, but they remained outside the state structures. Moreover, to be successful in recruiting the largest possible number of people, these mass organizations tended to gloss over local factional divisions whenever possible. Indian efforts to implement the Montague-Chelmsford reforms made little reference to ideology.

8. Statement of Azizuddin, son of Nihalchand, in the Court of the Additional Sessions Judge, Cawnpore, no. 10 of 1931, "King-Emperor vs. Amjad Hussain." Included in Commission of Inquiry Report on the Cawnpore Riot of 1931, Evidence, located in IOR, L/P&J/7/75 for 1931 [henceforth "Evidence"], pp. 300–301.

9. "Evidence" lists the variety of positions held by those testifying.

morning) and the *shuddhi* (Hindu reconversion) and *Sangaṭhan* (community defense) movements. The Municipal Board, moreover, seems to have used its funds to start *akhāṛās* to "teach the art of warfare."[10] The use of *prabhāt pherīs* and Congress *akhāṛās* reveals both the strategies and the limitations of maneuvers by relational leaders within state political structures. To the extent that they proved successful, these two forays into public arena activity reflected the ability of local relational networks to connect with some forms of community structure. *Prabhāt pherīs* became the local Congress equivalent of religious processions, appropriating to the nationalist cause the symbolic behavior of song and prayer. Physical-fitness *akhāṛās* not only permitted political figures to establish additional political alliances through the guru-chela relationship but also harnessed the martial impulse of community defense to local forms of nationalism. As we saw in Part II, however, *akhāṛās* and processions formed the most localized, least ideologically rationalized level of community. Implicit problems were embedded in such a strategy. Given the context of the 1920s and 1930s, localized identities invoked in this way nevertheless had to operate within a larger world in which being identified with "Congress" carried certain implications.

Combined with local power configurations, these implications translated in Kanpur into communal competition. In addition to their natural objections to *Sangaṭhan* and *shuddhi,* Muslims considered the municipally sponsored *akhāṛās* to be "Hindu-only." However, the evidence suggests that those in positions of power were not acting in a communal manner. That is, they were not motivated by a concern for Hinduism or Hindu community interests. They moved, instead, to control each new arena of public participation as it emerged, and in the process they successfully shut out all those without preexisting power bases in the city. Since those shut out were consistently, though not entirely, Muslim, this process was perceived by affected Muslims as communally inspired.

The history of the labor movement in Kanpur makes clear the acommunal motivations of local powerholders. Because popular support for the labor movement had proved strong, the same men who controlled the other institutions of the city also worked to control the labor unions. Once successful, they responded to the demands of practical accommodation within the state structure, which were stronger than

10. For *prabhāt pherīs,* see "Evidence," testimony of Sabu Narain Prasad Nigam on 22 Apr. 1931, pp. 89–93; for *shuddhi* and *sangaṭhan,* testimony of L. Diwan Chand, p. 254; for *akhāṛās,* testimony of Khaliluddin, p. 105.

the ideological appeals of labor organization. As a result, labor leaders had to cooperate at the municipal level with mill owners and others supposedly opposed to this cause. They subsumed the ideological appeals of class interests within these localized relational considerations— labor conditions being only one issue in a welter of competing special interests. That is, institutional day-to-day maneuvering depended on alliances between representatives of the entire range of special or group interests.

When it began, the labor movement in Kanpur figured as the strongest in India. The textile mills of the city spawned a sense of class identity powerful enough to counteract communal and other divisions among its workers. G. S. Vidyarthi, leader of the local Congress committee, had organized an impressive union, the Kanpur Mazdur Sabha, in 1928. The extent of his popular appeal may be measured by the fact that his murder in 1931 signified the complete breakdown of control over the civil disobedience hartal, or strike; it was only a short time later that the hartal turned into a communal riot. Continuing without its first leader, the union reached its peak of industrial action in 1937 and 1938, when it allied itself with the Communists in a crippling strike. Though effective, the union was co-opted: shortly after the strike, the predominant city political network counted among its members both the industrialist who had been struck and the labor leaders who had worked against him.[11]

Almost of necessity, each of the resulting alliances, though shifting, tended to contain the full spectrum of interests in the city—and, when necessary, to encompass new claimants to leadership. Thus, a deep but distinctly personal pattern of local alliances prompted this scramble for control of Congress, labor unions, and other institutional and ideological avenues.[12] This competition for control centered on personal animosities, rather than on ideological or class differences, meant that the very real issues of Kanpuri life were neither reflected in, nor provided an outlet through, the political structures of the city. One casualty of this fluctuating system was the working relationship that had been established earlier between the commercial men and their British rulers. As

11. For details of the history of the labor movement in Kanpur, see Paul R. Brass, *Factional Politics in an Indian State* (Berkeley and Los Angeles: University of California Press, 1965), pp. 195–202.

12. For a detailed discussion of these small group alignments, which dictated power relationships in Kanpur for at least forty years, see ibid., chapter 8. Both of the alliance leaders discussed by Brass were politically active in 1931; see discussions of Municipal Board and other activities in "Evidence."

competition escalated between the "natural leaders" and others claiming leadership roles, control by the elite over their ostensible constituencies weakened. This weakening disillusioned British administrators, who saw their carefully constructed methods of social control disintegrate measurably from year to year. The implications became painfully apparent in Kanpur during the 1931 riot, when there was no communication, coordination, or cooperation between self-styled Indian leaders and the administrators who still possessed formal responsibility for maintaining order.

Against this background of changing conditions, the agitations of the 1920s attempted to forge local-national connections while demonstrating that public ideals could be given concrete protection by the state. Working the Municipalities Act of 1916, staging the Rowlatt Satyagraha in 1919 and 1920, and implementing the Montague-Chelmsford reforms were all experiments in accomplishing these two goals. But the most successful of these efforts was the combined Khilafat/NonCooperation movement of 1920 and 1921. Its symbolic importance as a joint campaign is obvious; one of its most important contributions was its casting of anti-imperial ideology in a rhetoric that not only appealed to Hindus and Muslims but also underscored shared goals. In addition, the movement addressed directly the key issue of forging connections between the public arena and state institutions.

Khilafat established connections in several ways. To begin with, it created the first effective organizations built on a broad membership base. Capitalizing on discontent prompted by the economic dislocation of the period, local cells pulled in large numbers of new supporters, not only in the professional and literate classes, but among the urban and rural masses as well. As an economic base, the support of commercial groups proved crucial.[13] At the same time, Khilafat agitation extended the cultural connections between elite-styled Urdu poetry readings (*mushāᶜaras*) and the popular tradition of singing devotional poetry at religious festivals and pilgrimage sites. Not only did the Khilafat cause foster development of a suitable oral tradition to express both Islamic values and anti-British sentiment. It did more: just as the new schools like Deoband provided lessons in "ashrafization," these new forums both nurtured Muslim high culture and gave the lower classes access to it. Expression of a shared culture through newspapers and public meetings underscored for large numbers of participants the Islamic

13. Pandey, *Ascendancy*, pp. 57ff.

values of Khilafat and other "Muslim" causes. In the process the political message, presented in high culture form, reinforced connections between ashraf and *ajlāf* based on community values and identity. Indeed, in these activities we can trace the impact of the Indian equivalent of print capitalism. A variety of public arena performances, linked by similar messages with press and educational institutions, developed a common set of motifs with ideological appeals that bridged social and economic divisions. This shared value system was then abstracted to work on a national level.[14]

The local recruitment of volunteers proved to be a crucial innovation in the integration of public arenas and state structures. Many of these new volunteers were women: even in Khilafat, whether observing pardah or not, women (particularly those connected to male principals, such as the mother of the Ali brothers and Mohamed Ali's wife) took leadership roles. This leadership proved especially useful while the males were interned; these women also competently raised funds for a variety of Muslim causes throughout the period. Women attended, and responded to, political meetings in large numbers and enrolled as volunteers for demonstrations and processions.[15] Moreover, these female audiences had immediate access to contributions of jewelry and cash, as well as to the foreign cloth that fed Swadeshi protest bonfires.

This local form of recruitment gave nationally focused movements the ability to establish personal, face-to-face relations with their supporters and with potential recruits. It is not coincidental that all of these groups sent their volunteers parading through the neighborhoods each day "preaching Swadeshi and singing effective poems about Swaraj and the arrest of beloved leaders."[16] Indeed, we may measure the extent to which Khilafat successfully linked its all-India framework with the localities by the fact that "calls for nonviolence and self-discipline . . . were drowned out by a welter of appeals based on *local* economic grievances and sectarian religious sentiments," or even by the "disturbing slide toward violence" that the movement took in late 1921.[17] The style of leadership exercised by Khilafatists proved equally

---

14. Minault, *Khilafat*, pp. 151, 155; Barbara Daly Metcalf, "Conflict Among Muslims: New Sects, New Strategies, Old Paradigms," paper presented to the American Historical Association, 1978.

15. Participation by women may have varied with the region; it was most noticeable in the Punjab. See Minault, *Khilafat*, pp. 150–51, as well as the later example of Lucknow Shi'a women, chapter 8 below.

16. From a newspaper account, quoted in Minault, *Khilafat*, p. 164.

17. Minault, *Khilafat*, pp. 113, 165 (emphasis added).

significant. Most of the movement's leaders played prominent roles in regional or all-India politics, though they possessed less effective local political bases. Thus, the movement permitted people like the Nehrus to "project their provincial status back into the localities."[18]

Yet for all its success in linking the localities and regional or all-India politics, the ability of the Khilafat movement to develop a mass base remained limited by the uneasy integration of the different behaviors and values appropriate to public and state structures. For instance, many of the Congress district organizations had evolved out of Hindu Seva Samiti-type activities at religious fairs and festivals.[19] To these people the connection between communal ideologies and public activism must have appeared more obvious than would that between anti-imperialism and activism. It therefore proved very difficult to prevent public arena rhetoric from shifting its primary focus from anti-imperialism to communalism, from seeing the enemy as the "Other" Indian community rather than as the foreign ruler. Indeed, although Congress and Khilafat activities joined together rhetorically, they actually depended on separate volunteer structures, which existed side by side but developed independently. A similar distinction marked the differences between sources of support for Congress and Khilafat organizations: for the former, support came from Hindu commercial groups, and for the latter, from those active in Indo-Persian cultural centers. Institutional development proved just as uneven; in 1920 in U.P., for instance, only seven of twenty-six districts with volunteer organizations boasted Khilafatists.[20] Not surprisingly, the activities of the next phase, from 1922 to 1930, were not so much a measure of the disintegration of this first

18. Bayly, *Local Roots,* p. 273; see also supporting evidence in Pandey, *Ascendancy,* pp. 48–49. The way this worked is indicative of the general process by which local relational alliances were pulled into larger public arenas. Minault's study of Khilafat, for instance, traces the connection between the so-called "factionalism" inherent in the administration of Muslim educational institutions and the efforts of Muslim leaders to appeal to a wider audience. Looking at Aligarh, Deoband, and Farangi Mahal, she points out that in each case one alliance was successful in establishing control over the institution. The dissident minority, obliged to solicit support from outside, tended to make its appeals more popular and outspoken. Both groups then turned to broad-based methods of mobilization, in the process expanding these internal rivalries into competition for community leadership. Because this conflict between relational alliances inevitably involved the British as well, the fact that one group received British support allowed the other to justify its stance as "anti-British" (see Minault, *Khilafat,* p. 13). A similar rivalry between the Malaviya and Nehru families can be traced through many of the nationalist and communal issues played out in Allahabad and environs during this period (see Bayly, *Local Roots,* and Pandey, *Ascendancy*).

19. Pandey, *Ascendancy,* p. 36.

20. Minault, *Khilafat,* p. 163.

broad-based national effort as the logical outcome of constant publicity and agitation emphasizing community. In creating a South Asian equivalent of the nation-state's public sphere, then, anti-imperialism could not provide the same base as nationalism would have: the second phase looked to community as the base instead.

Personal Practices in Public Arenas: Prabhāt Pherīs
and Tanzīm, *1923–1929*

Developments outside India short-circuited the efforts of Khilafat, and a renewed emphasis on communal issues emerged between 1923 and 1929. In this second phase the most prominent communal projects were efforts aimed not at the state structure but at individuals, enjoining them to observe the proper practice of religion. These programs achieved far-reaching results. To begin with, by interpreting broader movements in personal terms, these efforts accomplished on an extraordinarily broad scale a feat hinted at earlier: they imbued personal religious commitment with political significance. Moreover, they provided a new forum for collective action—action that was primarily communal, rather than nationalist, in emphasis. Of these collective activities, the most important were *Shuddhi/Tablīgh* (conversion, purification) and the *Sangaṭhan/Tanzīm* (community defense) movements. For the first time the political energies of reformism were harnessed to create public opinion. In the process these activities on behalf of religious community posed communalism as a distinct, alternative ideology to nationalism and, by implication, suggested another basis for participation in the South Asian equivalent of the public sphere.

A brief comparison of religious festivals in Allahabad in 1919 and 1924 graphically portrays the difference between the first and second phases of this period. Dasehra and Muharram coincided in 1919. The Khilafat movement in that year prompted a level of cooperation and good will that led to publicized mutual embraces of Hindu and Muslim "city fathers" as they patrolled the streets. Muslim butchers, long unpopular, now exchanged betel nut and cigarettes with passing Hindus.[21] In contrast, five years later an observer noted that "the religious processions . . . had in recent years . . . been devoted largely to the display of weapons and physical force by both Mohammedans and Hindus. . . . Weapons and ammunition were purchased in large

21. *The Leader*, 18 Sept. 1919, cited in Bayly, *Local Roots*, p. 252.

quantities by the inhabitants in September [1924]." Though a committee of nonofficials had been appointed by "the leading men" of the town to accompany the Muslims' *Chehlum* and Hindus' *Rāmlīlā* processions, "most of its members were away from Allahabad at the time of the Ramlila, and those who were present were not in evidence."[22] At no time were the efforts of "influential men" of any assistance: "A few of the leading men, e.g. Mr. Zahur Ahmad, Barrister, and B. Parshotam Dass, member and ex-chairman of the Municipal Board, attempted to exert their influence in the direction of peace, but they were subjected to much abuse, and could effect nothing in the way of reconciliation."[23] Moreover, Jawaharlal Nehru noted to Gandhi in 1924 that an increase in participation by villagers in the city's public arenas and the incorporation of the city's lower classes in the communal clashes had created a ceremonial world very different from that of five years earlier:

> Ordinarily great crowds come from the rural areas to see the Ram Lila. In times of tension, every big banker or *rais* engages some of these professional fighters [village lathiwalas or budmashes] to defend his house. In the result a considerable number of such persons must have been in Allahabad. I do not think the Hindu Sabha as such invited such people. But the Hindu Sabha might have expected that the lower classes—*chamars, pasis,* etc. would be useful in a conflict with the Muslims. These classes, for the last few years, have been asked to take part in the Ram Lila processions.[24]

We may see this change of tone as the logical outcome of local reinterpretations of the emphases of Khilafat and NonCooperation. Community-specific efforts—to sensitize individuals to proper religious practice and to train participants to protect community interests—had originally been introduced as national-level movements. Branches of these organizations had been established in many major urban centers. By the mid-1920s, however, any overt coordination among them had atrophied, and very localized interests predominated. This resulted from efforts in the neighborhoods to express sentiments in locally meaningful

22. IOR, L/P&J/6, vol. 1889, file 4034 for 1924, The Allahabad Disturbances of 1924, pp. 1, 5. *Chehlum* is the last day of a forty-day mourning period, in this case, the fortieth day after 10 Muharram.

23. Ibid. On the third day the Commissioner had appointed some one hundred "special constables" who assisted in patrolling, but no indication is given in the records regarding who these men were or how they were selected

24. *Selected Works of Jawaharlal Nehru,* vol. 2 (Bombay: Orient Longman, 1972), p. 189.

terms, as well as from the reemergence of locally based leaders uninterested in pursuing extralocal connections and issues. As J. Nehru observed of Allahabad from his national viewpoint: "The local Hindu Sabha consists of a number of very narrow-minded persons with little ability or power even to organise the Hindus but able enough to increase the dislike of the Musalmans." At the same time, the "Musalmans are very poor in their leaders. There are hardly any with whom one can discuss such matters on an intellectual level."[25]

Kanpur once again provides useful evidence of the developments of this phase. In the late 1920s the city experienced a spate of overtly religious, mass-oriented programs. As one witness put it:

> There is not much of real religious animosity among the people here, but mutual rivalry and jealousy between Hindus and Muslims have always been in existence here. Both communities have been vying with each other in Muharram and Dasehra celebrations, and Ryabbi Sharif and Arya Samaj processions. The Shuddhi and Sangathan and Tabliqh movements touched Kanpur too. . . . For some time almost daily [*Tanzīm*] processions were organized, and the weekly Sunday procession, in which the mill hands could also join, were much more elaborate and attracted a bigger crowd.[26]

Local interest in these movements had ebbed and flowed. At the end of the 1920s neighborhood or other local groups took up the movements once more.[27] In this as in any public activity, the same leaders prominent in state institutional politics maintained their control. Power relationships fragmented, even in these organizations, thereby reflecting the factionalism among them. Among Muslims, too, the population remained fragmented, unable to accomplish much for themselves as "Muslims" in the midst of network alliances. Although Kanpuri Muslims often united in public arena activity, their connections to institutional politics still suffered from sharp organizational and spatial divisions between lower-class Muslims and wealthy Muslim merchants or zamindars. Those few Muslims who found places in the local alliances

---

25. Ibid., p. 188.
26. Written statement of Daya Narain Niyam, 25 April; "Evidence," p. 242.
27. On *shuddhi* see Kenneth W. Jones, *Arya Dharm* (Berkeley and Los Angeles: University of California Press, 1976); there are short sections on all four of these movements in Pandey, *Ascendancy; Tablīgh* and *Tanzīm* have received very little study, but see short sections in Y. B. Mathur, *Growth of Muslim Politics in India* (Delhi: Pragati, 1979).

were not there as "Muslim" voices. This lack of "Muslim" representation would have been less significant had there not been as well an escalating commercial competition between wealthy Muslims and Hindus with municipal connections.

Many Muslim merchants dealt in foreign goods; the most successful of them had moved late in the decade to large shops located prominently on one of the main roads.[28] Such a central road became a major locale for enforcing Congress' Civil Disobedience hartals in 1930, but by this time few Muslims sympathized with Congress, which they perceived to be a Hindu organization. Moreover, the late 1920s witnessed Muslim merchants being forced out of certain professions and locations by successful entrepreneurs who were also Hindus. Forced ejection of a group of Muslim dyers from their traditional market area became the first celebrated issue.[29] Prolonged litigation against wealthy and influential timber merchants continued for three years and then turned against vegetable and fruit sellers. Internal evidence suggests that these actions were not directed against Muslims per se;[30] rather, the Muslim merchants in question, like others in the city, fell prey to those who could manipulate municipal connections for their own economic advantage.

In a similar way the patronage distributed by Municipal Commissioners found its way to few Muslims, as they seldom served in positions deemed useful to the competing alliances on the Board. Figures show only six Muslims hired to fill fifty-three municipal clerical positions between 1926 and 1929.[31] The statements presented to the Riot Inquiry Commission of 1931 make it clear that all Muslims testified to these "slights" and perceived them as a sign of Muslim powerlessness and systematic subjection to discrimination. Though few witnesses put together as integrated an interpretation as the advocate Syed Zakir Ali—who linked "an organized legal attack on the mosques in Kanpur district" with the calculated harassment and impoverishment of Muslim merchants and the psychological pressure exerted by the "non-violent" persuasion of Congress[32]—all Muslim witnesses saw their exclusion from power as deliberate and communally inspired. In fact, many

28. This was the road disputed in 1913; see chapter 6. In a touch no doubt more ironic than its perpetrators realized, the road had been named after Lieutenant Governor James S. Meston.

29. See, for instance, testimony by Syed Zakir Ali, 4 May 1930, in "Evidence," p. 427.

30. See machinations among Municipal Board members, "Proceedings of the 37th meeting of the Cawnpore Municipal Board, 5 March 1930," in "Evidence," pp. 303–13.

31. "Evidence," p. 592.

32. Ibid., pp. 422–36.

Hindus suffered similar slights and found it impossible to penetrate the relational alliances that dominated in the municipality.

Denied outlets in state structures, community activists returned to public arenas, pushing reformism. By this time reformism constituted a style that could be adapted to different contents. Whether practiced by Deobandis, Arya Samajists, or Congress-wallahs, it encompassed efforts to purify the lifestyles of its participants. In the case of Congress, such purification focused particularly on prohibition of alcoholic consumption and on self-discipline, linking them with consumer boycotts of foreign goods and resistance to the imperial government's monopolies. Whereas the latter two strategies were conceived as political acts, by combining them with attributes more typical of reformism and urging them on adherents through public arena processions, prayers, and singing, Congress turned anti-imperialism into a popular movement aimed at the personal practices of its supporters. In the process Congress implied that every person had access to the collective world that passed for imperial India's public sphere.

This new collective emphasis on reforming personal practices led, first, to the formation of *prabhāt pherīs*. Introduced in 1929 by the local Congress committee, these were designed to appeal to youthful supporters—"a sort of morning prayer in which young men and students [made] a round in [the] city . . . singing national songs on the way."[33] Composed of "small parties of people, about 10 to 12," these processions "used to go to the Ganges for their morning bath and in returning, they used to form themselves into groups, one leading singing and the others following. . . . They were singing Congress songs." Adorned with flags and nationalist rhetoric, such *prabhāt pherīs* soon became incorporated into Congress's special "Sunday Programmes," thus providing the youthful activists with special recognition throughout the city.[34] All of these Congress activities attempted simultaneously to propagandize the nationalist message and to effect a social cum religious reform. The Congress program included picketing of toddy shops, whose clientele was estimated to be about 60 percent lower-class Hindus and 40 percent Muslim. Numerous Congress-run *akhāṛās* paid their teachers from municipal funds to teach "the art of warfare."[35] Whether

33. Statement of Sabu Narain, Prasad Nigam, in "Evidence," p. 92.
34. Testimony of R. B. Pundit Baldev Ram Dave, in "Evidence," p. 258; Pandey, *Ascendancy*, p. 81.
35. Statement of Sabu Narain, and testimony of Khaliluddin, Honorary Assistant Magistrate, in "Evidence," pp. 92, 105.

adherents perceived these activities as "nationalist" or as "communal" is debatable. Without doubt, those viewing them from outside saw their communal implications.[36]

Among Kanpuri Muslims the *Tanzīm* movement enjoyed a resurgence in direct response to the organization of the *prabhāt pherīs*. Neighborhood groups exhorted the Muslim lower classes to reform religious and social practices. One witness described "youngsters coming both morning and evening and persuading people to offer prayers and observe Ramazan etc. In honor of the death of Maulana Mohamad Ali these youngsters used to recite 'mersias.' " Another said that "the slogans shouted by the processionists were 'say your prayers regularly' and during the last Divali 'do not gamble.' "[37] These neighborhood activists fostered feelings of group identity and solidarity, as had the *prabhāt pherīs*, by giving processionists green flags and banners and as much of a special uniform as they could afford. One observer submitted this translation of *Tanzīm* verses recited by processionists:

Wake up now, sleeping Muslims: get ready to support Islam.
Time is coming for you to sacrifice yourself (when time comes). Losing
   your life (getting beheaded) become the Leader (sardar) of your
   community.
Even the sceptics (denyers) acknowledge your sensitiveness and cour-
   age. It is a mere trifle for you to get ready for fighting.
Those who ridicule your shariat and worship, such unpious persons
   should be consigned to flames.
We shall wake up the world; we shall shake up the world when, united,
   we shall raise the monotheistic cry. With the light (splendour) of
   Monotheism, we shall light a fire and shall obliterate, O Infidelity,
   thy existence out of the world.
We shall place our throats on swords, on spear heads. Where religion is
   involved, we shall get beheaded.[38]

Though the verses support the testimony of Hindus that many of the actions of the *Tanzīm* committees were aimed against them, it is clear that the perception of Islam as endangered, and of Muslims as an abused

---

36. For the impact on public arena activities of nationalist reformism in Banaras, see Nita Kumar, "Popular Culture in Urban India: The Artisans of Banaras, c. 1884–1984" Ph.D. diss., University of Chicago, 1984; and Sandria B. Freitag, ed., *Culture and Power in Banaras: Community, Performance, and Environment, 1800–1980* (Berkeley and Los Angeles: University of California Press, 1989).

37. Testimony of Islam Nabi Khan, and testimony of S. G. Chatterji, in "Evidence," pp. 76, 116.

38. Statement of L. Diwan Chand, in "Evidence," p. 249.

minority, is central to the resurgence of *Tanzīm* in Kanpur. Seen in this light, the efforts by some branches of the *Tanzīm* movement to teach the "use of lathi, ballam and sword, pharik gadka and wrestling" may be construed as defensive, not offensive.[39]

No apparent ties bound *Tanzīm* and the few prominent Muslim leaders of Kanpur. Instead, the assorted *Tanzīm* committees remained firmly rooted in their various *muḥalla*s. No citywide network united them, nor did ongoing connections tie them to similar organizations, such as the one in Allahabad. Optimistic Muslims did try to use the movement to establish connections between groups of Kanpuri Muslims, but more than one observer bemoaned the fact that the *muḥalla anjuman*s

> instead of concentrating their attention to the main work before them drifted into rivalry one against the other: who had the largest number of members, who had the largest number of volunteers, whose flag was highest; who looked smarter, who resembled this high personage or that high functionary, were some of the matters that riveted the attention in the spirit of rivalry.[40]

That is, they continued to operate in a manner long associated with public arena activities. Certainly, organization within the *anjuman*s remained a very local affair:

> There was a Tanzim-ul-Salat in Ghoolwali Gali [*muḥalla*]. I was its vice-chairman. Now the Anjuman is closed. The Anjuman is closed since the riots. Hafiz Qadrutulla was the president of the Anjuman. This Anjuman had twelve members. . . . There were 35 volunteers. . . . A rough register used to be kept which was kept in the custody of the President. Its president is absconding these days. He is involved in a case of murder and other offences. The volunteers had uniforms. . . . The Anjuman of Tanzim was started ten or eleven months ago. It was started by all the Mohulla people. It was started to keep up Som and Salahat. These people used to induce those who did not say prayers, to say prayers, give charity and do good deeds. They used to request people. They also used to boycott them socially and did not join

39. Statement of Azizuddin, in court of Additional Sessions Judge, in "Evidence," pp. 300–301.

40. Statement of H. H. Hosain, MLC, representative to the first Round Table Conference, in "Evidence," pp. 589–95.

their funerals. . . . The meetings were held in the evening on Sundays. No record was kept of the proceedings. There were no written rules in connection with these Anjumans. No servants were engaged for the work of the Anjuman. . . . Subscriptions used to be paid by office bearers and members. Volunteers paid no subscriptions and even if they did pay it was nominal. . . . Hafiz Qadrutulla used to preside [over] the meetings of the Anjumans and used to take part in the processions. He used to give larger subscriptions and nothing was done in the Anjuman without his consent.[41]

Following the standard public arena pattern, these localized exercises acquired a wider frame of reference when *muḥalla* committees amalgamated in Sunday processions, "which the millhands could also join" and which were "more elaborate and attracted bigger crowds."[42] Occasionally speakers with all-India stature, such as Shaukat Ali, came to Kanpur; on these occasions the various *muḥalla Tanzīm* organizations marched together to the mass meetings.

This renewed emphasis on collective activity dramatically increased the number of riots that occurred during this second phase. Particularly between 1923 and 1925, there was a substantial increase in the incidence of small-scale riots in most of the province's urban centers. Significantly, a large number of cities with no previous tradition of communal unrest now joined the roster; incidents occurred in places like Saharanpur and Agra in 1923; Meerut, Delhi, Lucknow, Shajahanpur, and Allahabad in 1924; and Delhi and Aligarh in 1925. None of these riots was as severe or important as those we have previously examined. Nevertheless, the number of communally oriented incidents was unprecedented.[43]

The role of leading men in these riots and other public arena activities of the period has been regarded as suspect, and their actions have been seen as calculating appeals by "secular" Congressmen "to overtly religious sentiments for the sake of immediate electoral gains." Perhaps that

41. This evidence was tendered not to the Riot Commission but in a court case prosecuted earlier (Statement of Azizuddin, in Court of Additional Sessions Judge, reprinted in "Evidence," p. 300).

42. Statement of Daya Narain Nigam, in "Evidence," p. 241.

43. Riots evidently occurred also in Meerut and Shahjahanpur in 1923, though no riot reports have been stored in London (IOR, Genl. Admin. Confl. Progs., July 1926, prog. no. 3(a), serial no. 3, par. 12, p. 10). Small incidents also took place in several other U.P. towns in 1925 (Bombay Confl. Progs., vol. 271).

characterization applies to some participants, but to many the situation must have been more complex.[44] Especially in this decade it is difficult to define "secular" in functional terms. Do scholars use the term to mean local politics? Or elite politics rather than mass participation? Certainly Muslim witnesses seldom perceived Congress activities as "secular" by the mid-1920s. Still, while we may begin to distinguish analytically between "secular" nationalism and communalism in this phase, to many leaders the distinctions had not yet become so apparent. They still felt it necessary to move back and forth between them as the context demanded. Nevertheless, in this decade their flexibility began to be constrained. Of great significance was the fact that the linkage of local behavior to larger ideologies decreased the ability of local leaders to move between ideological and relational appeals. Equally important was the reified division between communities that had resulted from repeated experiences of conflict and riots. These antagonisms made it difficult to act without being labeled "national" or "communal," depending on the symbols one's actions invoked.

Indeed, previous events, even those which had had little communal significance when they occurred, were reinterpreted in this period in communal terms. Thus, in Kanpur the targets for the first attacks in the 1931 riot gained significance in retrospect. Though in 1913 the Teli temple, for instance, had commanded very little attention, by 1931 there was a tradition that cast the temple, rather than the government, as the antagonist in the 1913 Kanpur Mosque Affair. What had been an antigovernment protest in 1913 became, in retrospect, a Hindu-Muslim riot.[45] Similarly, Kanpuris considered a particular cap merchant aggressively competitive, dating his activities from a 1927 riot. His shop became one of the first objects of attack in 1931.[46] The administration as well as popular opinion fostered these retrospective emphases.

Perversely, this use of communal symbolism can be taken as a measure of success in interpreting national-level movements in locally meaningful terms. But the problems inherent in the process also emerged in this phase. Most dramatically these problems took the form of a weakening of control over those involved in collective action. Given

44. See Pandey, *Ascendancy,* p. 117, for a discussion of "secular" Congressmen using religion. For a more complex discussion of their motivations and the context in which they operated, see Richard Gordon, "The Hindu Mahasabha and the Indian National Congress, 1915–26," *Modern Asian Studies* 9, no. 2 (1975).
45. *Report of the Commission of Inquiry and Resolution of the Government of U.P.,* vol. 12, United Kingdom, Parliament, Cmd. 3891 (1930–1931), p. 12.
46. Written statement of Syed Zakir Ali, in "Evidence," p. 422.

the increase in the sheer number of persons participating, this decline in control is hardly surprising. But more than numbers contributed to the lack of control: it became apparent that leaders' techniques, based on working through small, relational groups in the state political structures, were irrelevant when judged by mass expectations that community concerns should be protected by state programs. We have seen how, in Kanpur's reinvigorated *Tanzīm* movement of 1929, Muslims within the various *muhalla*s organized themselves without reliance on, or public support from, the prominent Muslims of the city. In 1931 the inflexibility and insensitivity of the youth group in Congress, the Venar Sena, alienated many Muslims and non-Congress Hindus in the city. Despite great effort, older Congressmen could do little to contain the Venar Sena's enthusiastic enforcement of hartals. Similarly, when the riots broke out, even the most important *muhalla* leaders found it difficult to control emotions within their own neighborhoods. Roving mill workers and budmashes, in the best of times only tenuously connected to the usual networks of social control, were, in the chaotic conditions of the riot, beyond the reach of civic leaders.

Thus, the immediate outcome of the localizing tendencies of this second phase was increased activity in public arenas. There were longer-term results and implications as well. The increase in violence, for instance, may be seen as an indication that regardless of their leaders' political concerns, participants in public arenas were determined to pursue community interests. This communal potential profoundly affected events in the third phase and indicated the direction in which public arena activity was becoming set: the base for public participation, even in the nascent nation-state, would be religious community identity.

Communalism in U.P.: Irreconcilable Structures and the Kanpur Riot of 1931

After an unusually quiet period at the end of the 1920s, mass mobilization of public arena activities finally became symbolically integrated with issues relevant to state institutions. This integration was accomplished on an all-India level through the symbolism of the Salt March. Equally important, however, the second NonCooperation movement successfully reinterpreted all-India issues in terms that carried local significance. The activities ushered in by these events built on the legacies of the two preceding phases. From the first phase came the ability to mobilize on behalf of an ideology that transcended locality; although this ideology was rooted, especially at an elite level, in anti-imperialism, popular predilections infused it with communal implications as well. From the second phase came a reformist emphasis on personal practice as an expression of community membership, which became, simultaneously, a political act for the ordinary person. Both phases had aimed at integrating public and state structures, although the first phase had concentrated on activities relevant to state institutions, whereas the second emphasized public arena activities.

In the third phase, however, the logical extension of these earlier experiences made clear the basic dilemma beyond symbolism that underlay the discontinuities between public and state structures. A state sensitive to popular values faced two increasingly divergent sets of such values, those labeled "Hindu" and those labeled "Muslim." Moreover, a state faced with community demands had either to ignore them or accede to them. If it acceded to the demands of the majority community, the minority would perceive the state as denying it a place in society—a place previously validated in the public arena. When the state was perceived as ignoring community demands, public attention turned to collective actions, often violent, to achieve recognition of these demands.

The developments of the 1930s, then, extended the phases that had preceded them. While the aim continued to be the integration of public and state structures, they resulted, instead, in a territorial division. This redrawing of geographical boundaries sidestepped the central issue by allowing each community to become the majority in its respective locale. In this way majority needs could, under most circumstances, be accommodated indirectly by a state that continued to operate through relational networks. In practical terms this accommodation stemmed from the fact that although the interests of no community were dealt with directly in the state structure that emerged from the nationalist struggle, the sense of frustration was strongest for those who perceived themselves part of a minority.

Thus, if we look for the central dynamic of the 1930s and 1940s, we must seek a process by which many participants chose communalism over nationalism as the ideology of public spaces, and by which they acted out in violent ways their frustration with the inability of the changing state to accommodate this ideology. Such developments carried profound implications for the shape of the South Asian equivalent of the public sphere. In particular, they pointed to the growing influence of Hindu merchants and the religious values they espoused through patronage. Such values, however, left no room in public arenas for minority groups, and hence they shaped public arenas in ways quite different from the model provided by the public sphere of the European nation-state.

We can discern in the Kanpur riot of 1931 the emergence of this new pattern, which would continue through independence/partition.[47] The pattern evolved from the all-encompassing practices, characteristic of Kanpur, that by the 1930s provided for overlapping memberships in such political organizations as Congress and the Hindu Mahasabha. As a result of this tactic, government support from Congress was implied for Hindu community activities like *shuddhi,* self-defense *akhāṛās,* and reformist pursuits such as *prabhāt pherī*s. This Congress program reflected an important amalgam of the popular culture of public arenas and the values and worldviews of the Hindu merchants who increasingly dominated the urban political scene.

Indeed, as a measure of the increased influence of Hindu merchants, we may discern as well another critical characteristic in Kanpur. In a negative way the presence of budmashes represented the connection between the relational politics of state institutions and the ideological values of public arenas. A fact of Kanpuri life, the intervention of budmashes in communal activities had become increasingly prominent. Their relationship to civic powerholders thus proved an important issue. One witness speculated that "there might be about 100 or 150 of these ringleaders," many of whom "had great influence and control." They were supported financially by cocaine smuggling and gambling dens; they also lived on retainer fees from Kanpur business firms and election

47. The riot is extraordinarily well documented. Yet none of the published discussions of the riots conveys the complexity of Kanpur as reflected in more than six hundred pages of richly detailed evidence that was collected by the government-appointed Commission of Inquiry. The commission was ordered on 13 April 1931; its findings are available in "Evidence." The official report of the commission—which in fact does not adequately reflect the insights provided by its own evidence—was published as *Report of the Commission of Inquiry and Resolution of the Government of U.P.,* vol. 12, pp. 3–66, Cmd. 3891 (1930–1931) [henceforth Cmd. 3891]. Congress conducted its own investigation and then issued a massive report that attempted to put the riot in a general historical context. This report has been published as *Roots of Communal Politics,* ed. N. G. Barrier (Columbia, Mo.: South Asia Books, n.d.). Because Congress did not give the names or identities of any of its witnesses, generally I have used the testimony to the commission. These witnesses, identified by name and local significance, express the same general complaints encountered by the Congress committee.

candidates. For "once such a practice is taken up by a merchant, his competitors in trade do not consider their position safe without having recourse to the same means."[48]

Large bands in this underworld mirrored the strife of the political world to which they lent their lathis, and city life was punctuated with their factional vendettas. The budmash element contributed measurably to the general lawlessness once the riot broke out. "The badmashes after looting . . . made away with their loot [to their villages] and after safe deposit have come back to Kanpur to look after their patrons' interests; . . . if they are arrested their patrons come to their rescue by standing sureties to the extent of Rs. 50,000."[49] But budmashes also possessed special significance in the general urban context in which the riot occurred. That is, the prominence of commercial men in the state structure was in part demonstrated by the control they exercised through the budmashes and by their imprint on the city. Thus, budmash participation in the 1931 riot was rightfully seen as an extension of the power held by Kanpuri leaders—who were also, for the most part, Hindu merchants.

The conundrum presented by discrete values and strategies separating public and state activities centered by 1930 in the potential for any mass mobilization to turn to communalism. Even national-level Congress leaders perceived this danger. In their own report on the Kanpur Riot of 1931 they noted that "the pre-occupations of the political leaders left them little time or inclination to fight this rising tide [of communalism]. The programme of Council entry made them susceptible to the influences of popular mood." Indeed, a footnote goes on to urge that "not one of the galaxy of the great Hindu leaders of the Congress came forward to combat the re-actionaries of the Hindu Community or such co-workers who had seceded from the Congress, or were openly abusing it and carrying a stormy propaganda against its accredited leaders." Worse, in the eyes of the report writers, was the strategy of Kanpur Congress leaders in joining the local Hindu Sabha. Although they claimed that they joined "with the object of capturing it," the Congress analysts argued that this "not only created misunderstand-

48. For numbers of ringleaders, see translation of statement by Hafiz Mohummad Siddiq, in "Evidence," p. 84. Another witness, Sabu Narain, Prasad Nigam, thought there were forty such leaders (ibid., p. 97). For financial support, see ibid., pp. 92, 97, 191; connections with business are detailed on p. 474, and examples are given on p. 191.
49. Written statement of Syed Zakir Ali, in "Evidence," p. 427.

ing in the minds of the public, both Hindu and Musalman; but, what was worse, most of the Congressmen . . . could not escape its baneful influence." Thus, Hindus and nationalists were perceived as acting in concert for community defense; these actions led, in turn, to reactions by the opposing community. As a result, "a vicious circle is established from which there is no way out."[50]

Exacerbating this development was the fact that, simultaneously, the alienation of many Muslims from majority-style nationalism meant that they perceived activities aimed against the British to be anti-Muslim as well. For many Muslims, then, the choice of a public arena ideology narrowed. But for those Muslims who rejected continued British rule, the choice of an alternative presented a serious predicament. Despite their success in creating a community ideology for public arenas, Muslims in the early 1930s had no alternative to offer to a state structure that embodied Hindu populist ideology. Sensing this difference, the principal of Dayanand Anglo-Vedic College argued that

the recent [1931] riots at Cawnpore were, strictly speaking, not communal in character. They were not due to religious fanaticism, intolerance or bigotry. . . . The all-absorbing passion of the Hindu intelligentsia had been Politics, and politicians of all schools have been speaking against bigotry and intolerance, and stressing Hindu-Muslim Unity as a necessary means to political advance. . . . High aspirations were roused by the Congress [in 1929]. The steady, silent work, in a spirit of absolute nonviolence that was demanded by the Leaders of the organisation, was beyond the capacity of a large number of the followers. In their case, a state of tension was produced. . . . The movement of 1930 was in theory nondenominational and non-communal, but in actual fact it was mainly supported by the Hindus. . . . [The *Tanzīm* movement, in contrast,] was meant as a vehicle of self-expression and a means of self-affirmation. It was not political in the sense of being directed against the authority of the Government, as at present constituted. It was directed against non-Muslims, I should say, Hindus. . . . Thus the two dominant ideas in the collective life of Cawnpore in 1929 were *Civil Disobedience* and *Tanzeem*. They were not exactly antagonistic—one was anti-Government and the other was anti-Hindu.[51]

50. Reprinted in Barrier, ed., *Roots of Communal Politics,* pp. 222, 245–46.
51. Testimony to the Commission of Inquiry, in an appendix to Barrier, ed., *Roots of Communal Politics,* pp. 481–82.

The implications of these "two dominant ideas" proved to be quite different. Hindu populism continued to link antigovernment and Hindu community interests so that, ostensibly, community interests could be protected by the imposition of an independent Indian state informed by Hindu majority values. In contrast, Muslim interests could not be protected by either the British Raj or by a majority-dominated independent state. That such a large contingent of the body politic should not have access to influence on the state, through public opinion expressed in public arenas, precluded the development of a public sphere like that represented by the western European model.

These diverging perceptions shaped the 1931 riot in Kanpur. Although the immediate provocation for this riot was the hartal called by Congress to protest the execution in Lahore of the bomb-throwing revolutionary Bhagat Singh, it did not long remain the central issue. This was but one in a long list of hartals called by Congress, and few Muslims willingly observed these Congress-initiated protests. As a consequence, in order to achieve strict observance of the hartal, youthful Congress volunteers had to coerce Muslim (as well as British and some Hindu) travelers to get down from their conveyances and walk. They constantly patrolled the commercial areas to induce Muslim merchants to close their shops; they even forced Muslim women to walk on the main thoroughfare, Halsey Road. Congress officers proved unable to contain this enthusiasm: in early afternoon the Venar Sena volunteers rushed down Halsey Road smashing windows, especially those of Muslim shopkeepers. Soon thereafter, a similar attack was made by a crowd on a Muslim shop in Meston Road, Kanpur's other major artery.[52] The crowd moved down the road to attack the *Bisātīs*' now-famous Macchli Bazaar mosque and a bookstore located within it. This action was followed by retaliatory attacks on the nearby Teli temple. Violence continued for several days, moving from commercial to residential areas. Crowds used hit-and-run tactics, attacking people hiding in houses and then looting and sometimes firing the houses. Though evidence shows that neither of the most turbulent elements of Kanpur—

---

52. Cmd. 3891, pp. 15–16. The Congress report, in Barrier, ed., *Roots of Communal Politics,* suggests that the riot was fomented by a CID agent provocateur dressed as a Congress volunteer. There is no indication, however, that this story was reported to the authorities at the time it was supposed to have happened, although there was an ideal opportunity to do so (pp. 271–74).

the mill workers and the large budmash population—initiated the riot, its scale worsened significantly when they became involved.[53] The duration of the riot, and perhaps the level of violence as well, can be attributed to official incompetence. Severely understaffed and confused about tactics, the few available policemen stood watching the attacks on shops and homes.[54] The beleaguered District Magistrate, a man whose unsympathetic temperament emerges clearly from the records, disdained the assistance of prominent Indian civic leaders. Even when forced to call for military support, he did not request sufficient aid to quell the disturbance. When compared with earlier riot reports, official ignorance of city conditions seems unprecedented: administrators proved to be completely unaware of the extent of the trouble. In part this ignorance was due to their insistence on staying at a "control center," a site near a telephone but away from the center of the city and from the worst of the rioting once it had moved to the *muhallas*.

Not until the third day did administrators tour the city. They found more than three hundred people killed, numerous houses burned and looted, and at least forty-two mosques and eighteen temples desecrated or destroyed.[55] The unprecedented scale of damages and deaths signified a heightened scale of physical violence that would remain the norm through 1947. Though in large part this scale can be attributed to the criminal level of official ineptitude, the underlying factors that turned an ostensible civil disobedience strike into a widespread communal riot cannot be explained so simply.

Instead, there is evidence to support the contention that the riot stemmed from the vague hope, fostered by the preceding decades of agitation, that creation of an indigenous state structure would protect community interests. As the discussions of local politics and the *Tanzīm* movement have suggested, these expectations were prompted for the majority community by Congress support of Hindu communal activities, such as *Sangathan* and exclusively Hindu *akhārās*. The Congress

53. In the case of the mill workers, this only happened late in the morning of the second day of the riot (Cmd. 3891, p. 17).
54. Even when it became apparent that the event had changed from political protest to communal riot, the police continued to follow the policy of "beech bachao," or "go slow," that it had adopted in connection with nationalist activities.
55. That is the official death count. Even the government report admits that probably at least two thousand more people were killed (Cmd. 3891, p. 4; see also Barrier, ed., *Roots of Communal Politics*).

version of state structures, then, came to be perceived by both Hindus and Muslims as capable of pursuing Hindu interests and values. In contrast, the Muslim experience of *Tanzīm* prompted a very different perception. Even when Congress activities took on a nationalist, rather than a communalist, tone, their impact on Muslims was negative. As Syed Zakir Ali argued, "the so-called non-violent picketing is a contradiction in terms[:] there can be no picketing without doing violence at least to the ideal of the person being picketed."[56] Muslims, turned once more to public arenas. Because they had "no accepted leaders," the same witness suggested, "congregations resorting to each mosque at least five times a day formed into small groups . . . to create unity among themselves if possible." Thus, in the 1930s Muslims, not yet thinking in terms of separate state structures to protect their interests, saw their primary goal as protection against the predatory nature of the majority-run state structure; they sought this protection in local, public arena activity. This solution replicated the pattern pursued earlier by Hindu populists. In another decade Muslims, too, would demand their own state structure in order to protect their community values.

This demand would, in some respects, be prompted by the fact that even public arenas had become fraught with disaster for minority communities. Our Muslim witness surveyed the whole range of public activities, dividing them into "religious," "economic," and "political" causes of the riot. Citing a series of court cases dating from 1927 "when Shudhi and Sangathan had accomplished all what [*sic*] they could," this witness gave as part of the "religious" cause "an organized attack launched on mosques in general in Cawnpore district." Under "economic" causes, he traced the history of attacks on Muslim merchants. Looking at "political" issues, he noted, "Muslims began to realize" that Swaraj would work against their interests: "in every institution they found their language, their culture was being trampled down. . . . The word nationalism was used as a synonym for Hinduism. The Congress and the Mahasabha[,] the two aspects of the Hindu ideals[,] are practically swamping the whole field[,] pushing aside all other ideals."[57]

Both Hindu communalists and Congress nationalists, then, could concentrate on state structures to achieve their goals. Their collective activities made public arenas into a fairly close approximation of the

---

56. Written statement of Syed Zakir Ali, in "Evidence," p. 430.
57. Ibid., pp. 427–30.

European public sphere, with their participants at least enjoying equal access to the state and the consequent ability to influence it. Moreover, neither group's purposes were necessarily undermined if the mass mobilization supporting their state-focused activities acquired a communal emphasis. For Muslims, however, the disjuncture between mass (public arena) values and factional (state structure) strategies proved acute. Not least of the casualties of this disjuncture was the perception by Muslims of their inability to act as full participants in the state. That is, the access that should have been provided to them through the equivalent of the public sphere instead separated them from the state by its very definition of community. The implications of this disjuncture were played out in the next two decades, leading ultimately to territorial division.

Conclusion

The Kanpur riot of 1931 brought out clearly the depth of popular support for communalism. The riot, both Hindus and Muslims argued, demonstrated the unbridgeable gulf between the contending communities. Ironically, the riot had resulted from the very processes of creating a national ideology. Intent on connecting local issues to all-India issues, activists had infused local community significance into the national-level ideology. Because this provided an ideological system incapable of being translated into the smaller group (relational) interests that ran local institutions, it prevented institutional implementation of ideological constructs. By definition, then, the public arenas created in an imperial state could not function as equivalents of the public spheres of western European nation-states since they denied equal access to influence on the state. At least in the short run, however, these differences in function, as well as the distinction between nationalism and communalism, proved to be insignificant to members of the majority community. Even those favoring a so-called secular state thought that public and state structures could be brought together to accommodate popular values once the imperial ruler was removed.

But minority community members faced another order of political choices entirely. Riots in this third phase expressed popular reactions to the sharp boundary lines drawn around each community. This reaction measured the loss of control by minorities in both public arenas and state structures. In searching for a new strategy, two choices emerged. First, returning to the pattern developed in the late nineteenth century, minority groups could re-create public arena activities as a substitute for a state structure. This was the solution chosen, for instance, by the Shi'a of Lucknow. But as the changing composition of Kanpur's neighborhoods suggests, a second alternative, territorial in nature, emerged as well. In the wake of the 1931 riot, the Congress report noted that "whole masses of population had shifted their quarters, and Hindu and Muslim areas had become well-demarcated, and well-defined from each side. The mixed areas had suffered the most and had practically ceased to exist."[58] This might well have been a prediction for 1947, when territorial separation became tacitly recognized as the only way to reintegrate, in appearance at least, the public and state structures. Hoping to achieve this amalgam in the 1940s, many Muslims insisted on erecting their own state structure on territory physically located outside the boundaries of a Hindu community.

58. Barrier, ed., *Roots of Communal Politics,* p. 367.

CHAPTER 8

Alternate Definitions of Community: Lucknow's Sunnis and Shi'as

Neither in other regions of the subcontinent nor even in U.P. itself was the formation of community identity limited to those who defined themselves as "Hindus" or "Muslims." We conclude this study by looking at an alternative pattern in the process of community formation for two reasons. First, tracing the history of developments in Lucknow demonstrates that the dynamics of the process did not depend on the particular content of the community ideology or identity that the process fostered. Second, the strategy followed by Shi'as in Lucknow provides a case study of a group that, although it encountered circumstances very similar to that experienced by Muslims in the rest of the province, chose a different political solution from territorial division.

Sectarian competition closely resembled the community conflict we have examined. In the Shi'a-dominated cultural center of Lucknow, those defined as outsiders—Hindus and others—were pulled in as allies of either Sunnis or Shi'as. Not surprisingly, the process structuring sectarian conflict paralleled that of Hindu-Muslim friction in other U.P. urban centers, in part because Lakhnawi Sunnis and Shi'as could draw on the reservoir of experiences and models developed in the subcontinent in this period. That is, the India-wide impetus to define one's community provided material that could be used by both groups of Lakhnawi Muslims. Virtually all of the Muslim reformist groups, for instance, agreed in excluding Shi'as from their Islamic universe. Further, Lucknow's Muslims could tap the range of organizations and ideological appeals that had been created for the political expression of Hindu-

Muslim competition. In Lucknow community identity impinged on an age-old conflict in Islam, sharpening a recurring ideological tension between the two groups. In addition, the Muslim population of Lucknow exhibited stark economic and social differences that coincided to a large degree with this sectarian division. It may even be that the sectarian division, in moments of conflict, took on added significance precisely because the city had witnessed the accession to state power of a group that usually functioned as a minority community. The reworking of these artifacts to fit the specific sectarian needs of Lucknow's public arenas is discussed in some detail in this chapter. We begin, however, by tracing the antecedents of this process back to the Nawabi period in Awadh.[1]

The Shi'a State and Public Arena Activity

Although at certain key moments Lucknow became the focus of intra-Muslim conflict, perhaps the most striking fact about the city's last two centuries is the relatively integrated character of its political and cultural life. In the regional kingdom of Awadh the Shi'ism of its rulers provided both a liminal cultural glue and a set of structural lines of schism along which conflict could be routed. As a result, at moments when political and social relationships shifted, Shi'ism became the cultural conduit for expressing competition, as well as the dominant symbolic rhetorical device for expressing and effecting social adaptation or change.

In certain symbolic ways the successor state in Awadh resembled the regional kingdom established in nearby Banaras.[2] Both concentrated on creating an alternative state culture to that fostered by the Mughals and thus patronized a popular devotional religion as state policy. By conflating civic ritual and collective devotional activities, the Nawabi state could draw implied popular support through popular participation in devotional religious activities. This symbolic sleight of hand (or, to

1. A significant cluster of works now exists for Awadh. For the Nawabi period these include Richard B. Barnett, *North India Between Empires: Awadh, the Mughals, and the British, 1720–1801* (Berkeley and Los Angeles: University of California Press, 1980), and Juan Cole, *Roots of North Indian Shi'ism in Iran and Iraq: Religion and State in Awadh, 1722–1859* (Berkeley and Los Angeles: University of California Press, 1988). Michael Fisher, *Clash Between Cultures* (Riverdale, Md.: Riverdale Co., 1987), became available too late to be used here. For British Lucknow, see especially Rosie Llewellyn-Jones, *A Fatal Friendship: The Nawabs, the British and the City of Lucknow* (Delhi: Oxford University Press, 1985), and Veena Talwar Oldenburg, *The Making of Colonial Lucknow, 1856–77* (Princeton: Princeton University Press, 1984).

2. For the sake of simplicity I have ignored in both this chapter and chapter 1 the political interaction between the two regional kingdoms.

use a more positive image, political "translation") proved to be an important component in Awadh's efforts to forge a close relationship between the state and its constituent communities. In essence, the strategy involved elaboration of a collective civic identity around the ideological core of the counterculture within Islam.

The split between Sunnis and Shi'as reflected more than the dispute surrounding the successors to Muhammad.[3] Although reciting verses that defended their respective positions on the succession issue became the key symbolic act for both Sunnis and Shi'as, the underlying differences in attitudes toward authority mattered more. Muharram figured prominently in the Shi'as' worldview precisely because it glorified a rejection of state authority. It attempted, one scholar has argued, to achieve "the alignment of individuals with the subjective qualities" of the martyred Imam Husain. This alignment was "not mediated by doctrines, laws or objective representations of Kerbala. There [were] no doctrines or rules of conduct that govern[ed] these expressions." That is, Muharram turned the usual attitudes and values upside down. "As a martyr, the position of Husain define[d] spiritual strength and authority as a condition of weakness in the world of men, and 'nearness to God' as a distance from overt authority."[4] Connected with this distrust of official authority was the Shi'i emphasis on taqlid (the delegation of authority) and the personalized reliance on religious leaders for guidance (before reliance on *shari^c a* and Hadith).

These characteristics did more than facilitate the survival of Shi'as in hostile environments. They also provided an underlying philosophy that, when combined with a popular devotional form of religion, could also appeal to non-Muslims. Taken together, these characteristics may go far toward explaining how, in the course of the eighteenth and nineteenth centuries in many parts of urban, Muslim India, Muharram became *the* popular expression of Indian "Islam." In Lucknow, however, Muharram had to fulfill additional functions. The situation in Lucknow was shaped by the paradoxical fact that in that city Shi'as had become the paramount power. Indeed, Keith Hjortshoj speculates that the inversion of the usual Shi'i relationship with secular authority may have been responsible for the significantly more elaborate ritual structures developed for Muharram there. This very paradox thus led to an

---

3. Shi'as argued that Ali should have immediately followed Muhammad as first caliph; Sunnis recognized the intervening three caliphs as legitimate successors to the Prophet.

4. Keith Hjortshoj, "Kerbala in Context: A Study of Muharram in Lucknow, India," Ph.D. diss., Cornell University, 1978, pp. 108, 114, 137, 144.

increasing reliance on Muharram as a collective expression of shared civic culture.

Like Banaras, then, the successor state of Awadh created new symbolic structures to express its relationship with those it ruled.[5] These structures performed a critical function in Awadh, as they linked a disparate population whose constituent communities—predominantly Hindu and containing a substantial number of Sunni lower-class artisanal groups—were well removed from the Shi'i rulers. A shared ceremonial culture, to the extent that the Nawabs proved successful in creating one, was based in the cities, most notably Lucknow.[6] For the cities possessed the requisite relational structures of *muḥalla*s, occupational networks, *akhāṛā*s, and the like to enable the Nawabs to link the popular culture centered on shrines with a devotional-style state religion. Expressed through literary forms (particularly vernacular elegiac poetry for Muharram known as *marsiya*s) and public architecture (especially the building of *imāmbāṛā*s), the resulting civic culture proved almost as accessible to the ordinary person of Lucknow as to the courtier—though doubtless it was interpreted differently by each.

Focused on "mourning for the wronged family of the Prophet," this culture united Hindus, Sunnis, and Shi'as, for the latter constituted a very small portion of the urban population. The exact population attributed to each constituency, particularly in the Nawabi period, may be of little moment. It always has been difficult to count Shi'a, in part because they often practiced dissimulation (although doctrinally this practice should have been abandoned once the Nawabi had been declared *dar ash-Shi'a*). When census takers found the population unwilling to use the labels "Sunni" and "Shi'a" to identify themselves, British administrators attempted to make the distinction on the basis of style of prayer:

> For the less instructed of Muhammadans and especially amongst the Sunnis, the difference between the two sects is little understood, and the enumerator had in general to ascertain the sect by a question as to how the hands were placed in prayer. Sunnis

---

5. This discussion of the Nawabi state is not, of course, a detailed analysis of its political history. What is intended here is to present a rather stylized model, in which the key elements are highlighted for comparison with Banaras, and to indicate their significance for the general analysis presented in this study. For a detailed political history, see Barnett, *North India Between Empires*.

6. Thomas R. Metcalf notes the utterly separate worlds of talukdar and courtier, which indicates the limited appeal of Nawabi courtly culture in the countryside (*Land, Landlords, and the British Raj* [Berkeley and Los Angeles: University of California Press, 1979], p. 38).

pray with one hand placed over the other in front of the body, Shias with both hands depressed by the sides.

But, as Cole has suggested, for the "many laboring-class Muslims who did not say their daily prayers, such criteria would have been meaningless."[7] Moreover, the distinctions—even assuming they could be drawn in a more meaningful way—though important in certain contexts, generally paled beside the shared popular culture of devotional religion.

Upper-class culture may have retained more distinctive differences among Hindus, Sunnis, and Shi'as. Even here, however, the predominant upper-class style was shaped particularly by courtly values and styles. The court, not surprisingly, fostered a variety of symbolically Shi'i styles, even the design of a five-cornered hat to signify the Prophet's family.[8] Courtesans, as cultural repositories, often served as valuable mediators between the culture of the court and that of the wealthier urban dwellers. Mirza Ruswa's *The Courtesan of Lucknow: Umrao Jan Ada,* despite its limitations as historical evidence, accurately details the careful training of young girls in the cultural activities prized by courtier-patrons, including singing, dancing, and, especially, the composition and recitation of Urdu poetry.[9] Beyond their cultural pursuits, such courtesans also provided important indicators of status, often accepting or rejecting patrons on the basis of their power and influence at court as well as of their wealth. Given that rural landlords had few other ties to the Shi'i court, the links with them fashioned by courtesans may have served a particularly significant function.[10] Indeed, as Sharar noted in 1913:

> In Lucknow, association with courtesans started during the reign of Shuja ud Daula. It became fashionable for noblemen to associate with some bazaar beauty, either for pleasure or for social distinction. A cultivated man like Hakim Mahdi, who later became Vazir, owed his initial success to a courtesan named Piyaro, who had advanced her own money to enable him to make an offering to the ruler on his first appointment as Governor of a Province of Avadh. These absurdities went so far that it was said

7. Cole, *Roots of North Indian Shi'ism,* p. 86. Census procedures are described in D. C. Baillie, *Census of India, 1891,* vols. 26–28, *The North-Western Provinces and Oudh,* 26:177; quoted in Cole, p. 85.

8. Abdul Halim Sharar, *Lucknow: The Last Phase of an Oriental Culture,* trans. and ed. E. S. Harcourt and Fakhir Hussain (London: Paul Elek, 1975), p. 172.

9. Mirza Ruswa, *The Courtesan of Lucknow: Umrao Jan Ada,* trans. Khushwant Singh and M. A. Husaini (New Delhi: Orient Paperbacks, 1961).

10. See Cole's reference to zamindars assigning lands to Muslim dancing girls and prostitutes, in *Roots of North Indian Shi'ism,* p. 88.

that until a person had association with courtesans he was not a polished man. . . . At the present time there are still some courtesans with whom it is not considered reprehensible to associate, and whose houses one can enter openly and unabashed. Although these practices may have had a deteriorating effect on morals, at the same time manners and social finesse improved.[11]

In this context it is important to note that Shi'ism in Lucknow may well have served as the basis of a particular subculture for women, one fashioned under the Nawabi but continued long after its demise. In 1904, for instance, some two-thirds of those who identified themselves as Shi'as were women.[12] Despite rulings by the Lucknow *mujtahids* against Sunni-Shi'a marriages, they remained common;[13] and the devotional culture of the women's quarter of a household could plausibly have perpetuated Shi'ism with relatively little interference from men.[14] Shi'ism was particularly popular among courtesans. In part this popularity may have stemmed from the legal protection Shi'ism provided for courtesans by its recognition of temporary marriage (*mut͏ᶜah*).[15] But it may also have related to the nature of an alternative culture developed by these women, characterized recently by Veena Oldenburg as "a style of non-confrontational resistance and packaged . . . not as a sporadic activity, but as a way of life."[16] If so, it was a way of life in which

11. Sharar, *Lucknow*, p. 192.

12. H. R. Nevill, *District Gazetteers of the U.P.*, vol. 37, *Lucknow* (Allahabad: U.P. Govt. Press, 1911), p. 69.

13. Cole, *Roots of North Indian Shi'ism*, p. 232.

14. Mrs. Mir Hasan Ali, for instance, noted that "in commemorating this remarkable event [Muharram] . . . the expressions of grief, manifested by the ladies, are far greater, and appear to me more lasting than with the other sex; indeed, I never could have given credit to the extent of their bewailings, without witnessing, as I have done for many years, the season for tears and profound grief return with the month of Mahurrum. In sorrowing for the martyred Emaums, *they seem to forget their private griefs*. . . . They tell me, 'We must not indulge selfish sorrows of our own, whilst the Prophet's family alone have a right to our tears.' " She goes on to describe the role of educated women, "chiefly daughters of poor Syaads, who have not been married for the lack of a dowry; they live devoutly in the service of God, according to their faith" in teaching "the Khoraun to the young ladies" and in reading, during Muharram, the texts used in the daily *majālis* (Mrs. Meer Hassan [Mir Hasan] Ali, *Observations on the Mussulmauns of India* [1832], revised and edited by William Crooke [1917; reprint, Delhi: Deep Publications, 1975], pp. 24, 29, emphasis added).

15. Cole, *Roots of North Indian Shi'ism*, p. 88.

16. Veena Talwar Oldenburg, "Lifestyle as Resistance: The Case of the Courtesans of Lucknow," paper presented to the December 1987 meeting of the American Historical Association, p. 2. Oldenburg goes on to draw a parallel for courtesans of the thesis developed by Romila Thapar for ascetics that their lifestyle, based on a rejection of the householder phase, is an act of rebellion that constitutes a "counterculture" (Romila Thapar, *Ancient Indian Social History* [New Delhi: Orient Longman, 1978], pp. 63–104). Oldenburg's strongest evidence of this alternative culture for courtesans is the "vivid

economic independence was buttressed by a specific and personalized form of religious devotionalism that provided outlets for ostentatious display and patronage.[17]

Three types of physical structures provided representations of devotional, collective activity that served to anchor the shared culture of Shi'ism in Lucknow.[18] Preeminent among Lucknow's shrines, the *dargāh* of Hazrat Abbas in Rustumnagar played a central role in devotional life in the city and particularly in the observance of Muharram.[19] Popular history credited Asaf ud-Daula with erecting the Rustumnagar shrine to hold a crest of Abbas Ali discovered by a hajji to Karbala. Mrs. Mir Hasan Ali comments on the "great repute" the shrine enjoyed "amongst the general classes of the Mussulmaun population":

> Here the public were permitted to offer their sacrifices and oblations to God, on occasions of importance to themselves; as after the performance of the rite of circumcision in particular, grand processions were formed conveying the youthful Mussulmaun, richly attired, attended by music, &c. and offering presents of money and sweetmeats at the shrine. . . . Recovery from sickness, preservation from any grievous calamity, danger, or other event which excites grateful feelings, are the usual inducements to visiting the Durgah, with both males and females, amongst the Mussulmaun population of Lucknow.[20]

Because the shrine figured in such moments of personal importance, it provided a key structure through which to signify state ideology. It therefore played a central role as well in the elaboration of Muharram, the observance that united the state and its constituent communities. As though to tie the locality to a worldwide observance, the banners to be

---

reversals of social perception" in courtesan "secret" speech and song: "Affinal kin, particularly fathers and brothers-in-law, are caricatured in countless risqué episodes enacted regularly and privately among women. They mock the repressive relationships and male sexuality in the conjugal home, even as they amuse, educate, and edify the denizens of the *kotah*. These routines, studded with subversive and irreverent jokes and obscene gestures, are performed like secret rites, which have been carefully distilled and historically transmitted from generation to generation, to form the core of their private oral heritage and consciousness" (Oldenburg, "Lifestyle as Resistance," pp. 32–33).

17. V. Oldenburg provides evidence of the economic activity of these women both in the Mutiny period and in contemporary times.

18. These structures came to perform so central a function in Lakhnawi life that after the British destroyed the Jame͞c Masjid in the Mutiny, no new structure was built to function as a central mosque for Friday prayers (Oldenburg, *The Making of Colonial Lucknow,* pp. 36–37).

19. See Llewellyn-Jones, *A Fatal Friendship,* p. 207; and Letter 3 in Mrs. Meer Hassan Ali, *Observations.*

20. Mrs. Meer Hassan Ali, *Observations,* pp. 34–35.

used in tazia processions on the tenth of Muharram first were taken to the shrine to be consecrated. It is an important comment on the state's effort to ally itself with its subjects that in this procession on the fifth of Muharram "no material difference" could be observed in the countless multitude who touched their banners to the crest for consecration: "The most wealthy and the meanest subjects of the province make displays commensurate with their ability."[21] Mrs. Ali goes on to note, after describing the elaborate procession of a wealthy denizen of Lucknow, that the processions "all partake of one style—some more splendid than others; and the very poor people parade their banners with, perhaps, no other accompaniment than a single drum and fife, and the owner supporting his own banner." Thus, Rustumnagar, center for the popular devotional religion pursued throughout the year by the ordinary people of Lucknow, also functioned as a pivotal focal point for the Muharram ceremonial calendar.

*Imāmbārā*s and *karbalā* sites, as other central signifiers of the shared civic culture attached to Muharram, also functioned as physical structures expressing the cultural coherence of Lucknow. Both were ubiquitous throughout Lucknow and were used frequently for a variety of cultural activities. As the structures "housing" tazias and ʿalams before they are paraded through the streets to be ceremonially buried, *imāmbārā*s emerged as buildings "suitably solemn and grand." Once constructed, their patrons filled them with other awe-inspiring decorations, including "chandeliers of all shapes and sizes and the huge stands for lamps or candles, often five feet or more in height, and made from highly decorated china, coloured glass or metals."[22] The aesthetic appeal, used to heighten religious experience, fulfilled a crucial social function as well. "The development of the *imāmbārāh* as an architectural form under the patronage of the nawabi court and courtiers," Cole tells us, "provided a crucial meeting place for Shi'is."[23] As public spaces, used

---

21. Although, Mrs. Ali admits, "those persons who make the most costly exhibitions enjoy the greatest share of popular favour, as it is considered a proof of their desire to do honour to the memory of Hosein and Hasan, their venerated Emaums" (Mrs. Ali, *Observations*, p. 36).

22. Llewellyn-Jones, *A Fatal Friendship*, pp. 202–3. Mrs. Ali describes the structures thus: "An Emaum-baarah is a square building, generally erected with a cupola top, the dimensions guided by the circumstances of the founder. The floor is matted with the date-leaf mats, in common use in India, on which is spread a shutteringhie (cotton carpet), and over this is a clean white calico covering, on which the assembled party are seated, during the several periods of collecting together to remember their leaders: these meetings are termed Mudgelluss [majālis] (mourning assemblies)" (*Observations*, p. 19).

23. Cole, *Roots of North Indian Shi'ism*, p. 98.

by Shi'as and others participating in Muharram,[24] *imāmbārā*s thus served as central organizing spaces as well as physical statements uniting the populace of the city. Even for the year-round activities not open to everyone, the structures still conveyed a shared culture based on the court-patronized activities: "For the notable class, *imāmbārāh*s performed many functions. They served as places for ritual mourning and worship, as literary salons, as personal monuments, and as family cemeteries [where founders and members of their families were buried]."[25] Beyond their roles in Muharram, their function as literary sites may have been their most important, for "the elegiac poetry [*marsiya*s] that dominated the religious culture of the *imāmbārāh*s gave more public exposure to poets and reciters than to the staid ulama,"[26] and hence emphasized the aspects of Shi'ism that could unite, rather than divide, the people of Lucknow. *Marsiya*s, moreover, because they were composed in the vernacular (rather than in Persian, as were the formal texts of the *karbalā* story, read during the ten days of Muharram), proved accessible to all Lakhnawis.[27]

Karbalā grounds (the field traditionally set aside to symbolize the original battlefield in Iraq), as the "burial" destination for the tazias on the tenth of Muharram, also functioned as important physical statements. "A building which represents and commemorates the battlefield and the burial place of Hasan and Husain in Iraq," the *karbalā* site in Lucknow would figure largely in twentieth-century disputes. Llewellyn-Jones describes the main such site:

> The largest kerbala at Lucknow is the Talkatora to the southwest of the city, approached through a large gateway of European pattern. But the buildings within are entirely Islamic, consisting of a large square bordered by a series of cells, and the square

24. See Mrs. Ali: "It is creditable to the Mussulmauns, that they do not restrict any profession of people from visiting their assemblies; there is free admission granted when the Emaum-baarah is first lighted up, until the hour of performing the service." Lower classes, at least during the ten days of Muharram, have open access to the *majālis* that follow (*Observations*, p. 27 et seq.).
25. Cole, *Roots of North Indian Shi'ism*, p. 96; Llewellyn-Jones, *Fatal Friendship*, p. 204.
26. Cole, *Roots of North Indian Shi'ism*, p. 97.
27. "This ceremony [the reading during the *majlis*] terminated, the Murseeah is chanted, by several well-practised voices, with good effect. This part of the service is, perhaps, the most impressive, as the very ignorant, even, can comprehend every word,— the Murseeah being in the Hindoostanie tongue, a poetical composition of great merit, and embracing all the subjects they meet to commemorate" (Mrs. Ali, *Observations*, p. 23).

central building on a raised platform which is properly speaking, the kerbala itself. This building is topped by a gilt dome and flanked by two *minars* or towers. The ground between the kerbala and the cells in the outer wall is filled with graves, marked by plain stones. Outside the main square is a semi-ruined barahdari in a highly decorated style.[28]

These physical sites, in a city dramatically imprinted by the construction of "political architecture" to satisfy the Nawab's "building mania," played an obvious role in forging a shared culture for Lakhnawis.[29]

Other collective experiences reinforced this sense of shared values and worldview. The processions associated with Muharram filled the streets of the city on several of the first ten days of the month, particularly on the fifth, seventh, and tenth of Muharram. The *majālis* (private meetings held twice daily, during which segments of the *karbalā* story were recounted, sermons were preached, and stylized lamentations, known as *Mātam,* were enacted) had a narrower scope, because they occurred in various locations and were privately sponsored. Nevertheless, these gatherings conveyed similar messages, even as they took place in *imāmbārās,* which had been built according to a shared model and often were open to the public. Such experiences, while separating one *majlis* from another, also united the attendees within a larger ideological framework. Both processions and *majālis* thus provided significant occasions for large numbers of people to gather and enact simultaneously their parts in the collective mourning rituals led by the state for the family of the Prophet.

Because they played such a central role in perpetuating and personalizing the stories of Husain and Hasan, these occasions clearly carried the greatest meaning for the Shi'a of Lucknow. But Hindus, too, participated in great number, as attested by visitors such as the Iranian traveler

28. Llewellyn-Jones, *Fatal Friendship,* p. 206. Without giving the dates on which they were introduced, Llewellyn-Jones describes several other sites: "There are several other kerbalas of similar form in the city, the second largest being that of Malka Jahan in the Aishbagh Road, and there was an extensive group of buildings including a kerbala on the north bank of the Gomti named after Mariam Makam Sahib, as well as the kerbala in the newer part of the city to the east of the present-day Sikander Bagh road. The kerbala of the eunuch Dianutud Daula in Saadat ganj is particularly noteworthy because of its original and unusual mirror work interior. . . . This mirror work is frequently found in palace rooms . . . but this appears to be the only surviving example in the city and certainly the only use of mirror work in a religious building." Judging from the footnote for this section, Llewellyn-Jones's source appears to be a series of correspondence with Anwar Askari, who "comes from an old Lucknow family of writers."

29. The first term is Llewellyn-Jones's; the second is Abu Talib's (Llewellyn-Jones, *Fatal Friendship,* pp. vi, 197).

Shushtari and the British observer Emma Roberts.[30] Each Hindu upper-caste group allied with other groups sharing cultural and administrative affinities under the Nawabi. Shi'as and Kayasths (who had adopted the Persianized lifestyle of the Shi'i elite) predominated in the executive and financial branches of government, while Sunnis, *Baniyā*s, and others dominated the economic life of the city. Thus Kayasths had particular predilections for, and reasons to embrace, courtly culture. But lower-class Hindus, too, participated in these devotional activities. Roberts, for instance, noted that "Hindoos . . . are frequently seen to vie with the disciples of Ali in their demonstrations of grief for the slaughter of his two martyred sons: and in the splendour of the pageant displayed. . . . A very large proportion of Hindoos go into mourning during the ten days of Mohurrum, clothing themselves in green garments, and assuming the guise of fakeers."[31]

Both structural and liminal artifacts, then, ensured a cultural coherence in Nawabi Awadh, particularly in its capital city. At the same time, however, certain political pressures within the mature Nawabi state also worked against cultural integration. Central to these pressures, Cole argues, were the "rationalizing tendencies of the growing Usuli hierocracy," which ultimately targeted both Hindus and Sunnis: "Shi'i clerics exhibited intolerance of Hinduism, although the Awadh government co-opted rural Hindu elites and employed Hindus in the bureaucracy." Where many Shi'a had originally allied themselves with Sunni landholders against Hindus, ultimately Shi'i patronage of polemical literature against Sunni doctrines became "a major industry in Awadh." As "the Shi'i ulama began to influence state policy in the 1840s," they shaped a variety of state policies that provoked popular resentment, on the part of both Hindus and Sunnis, against the Nawabi.[32] However, conflict between the sects seems to have arisen after the relationship had changed, and it emerged at those moments when state policies led to explicit actions denying the shared nature of Nawabi culture. Particularly striking from our point of view are the occasions when state power was used to separate Shi'as from the population at large—as in 1828 and 1829, when the Nawab decreed that the observances for Muharram would extend for the full forty days rather than conclude in the usual

30. See Emma Roberts, *Scenes and Characteristics of Hindostan,* 3 vols. (London: Wm. H. Allen, 1835), and Sayyid Muhammad Abbas Shushtarī, *miᶜraj al-mu'minīn* (Lucknow: Matbaᶜi majmaᶜ al-ᶜulam, 1293/1876), both cited in Cole, *Roots of North Indian Shi'ism.*

31. Roberts, *Scenes,* 2:192–93, cited in Cole, *Roots of North Indian Shi'ism.*

32. Cole, *Roots of North Indian Shi'ism,* pp. 242–44.

ten,[33] or during the Mutiny/Revolt, when rival courts were created to express Sunni-Shi'a competition during the 1857 Mutiny/Revolt.[34]

The other striking characteristic of these moments of conflict relates to the palpable presence of the British Resident. Cole's narrative makes it clear that in the 1820s and 1830s the intervention of the Resident prompted the Nawab and his advisers to insist on their antagonistic policies in order to demonstrate their independence. After 1837, however, "the Awadh government, threatened with annexation by the British, sought to prevent Sunni-Shi'i violence." Thus, even when it resulted in quite opposite policies, the presence of an intruding imperial state profoundly affected the interaction between Indian ruler and his subject communities. The scale of intervention, of course, became that much greater after 1856, when the British deposed the Nawab and began to rule the area directly.

Sunnis and Shi'as Under the British Imperial State

Even a cursory comparison of the Nawabi and Banarsi regional successor states points out instructive differences that may go far to explain the different community identities and patterns of conflict that developed in each. The Nawab clearly proved less successful than the Raja of Banaras in forging a collective, public culture that could be shared between the state and its communities. In part, no doubt, this failure resulted from his more tenuous hold over his hinterland. (It is one of the great ironies of the region's history that only the British, by pressuring the talukdars to move into Lucknow and become absentee landlords, effectively tied them to the urban culture of the state.) Probably more important was the fact that the role created by the Nawab for himself did not figure at the center of the civic ritual of Muharram. That is, at no time could the Nawab present himself as a figure equal in importance to the Prophet's family, as had the Raja vis-à-vis *Rām*. Indeed, to the extent that any figure symbolically integrated the constituent communities of the realm in Lucknow, it surely was that of the saint of the Rustumnagar shrine. To these symbolic limitations, imposed by the nature of the Shi'i rituals of state, must also be added the impact of "rationalist" ulama, whose legalistic zeal apparently paralleled that of Aurangzeb's court, both in tactics and in results.

33. See Cole, *Roots of North Indian Shi'ism*, chapter 9, for detailed descriptions of these efforts to distinguish Shi'a from the rest of his subjects.
34. Sharar, *Lucknow*, pp. 66–67.

For all of these reasons, then, although both the rulers of Banaras and Awadh ultimately lost power, the cultural legacy of each has been quite different. Banaras has remained a much more culturally integrated society than Awadh (and the continued presence of the Raja doubtless facilitates the continued cultural integration). The cultural base of popular devotional religion remains at the center of collective activity in Awadh, but its ability to unify the society depends quite directly on the relationship among communities at any given time, and particularly on the relationship of the Shi'as of Lucknow and the ruling state power. Perhaps as a direct result of this last characteristic, collective expressions of Shi'ism also remain the primary conduit along which social conflict in Lucknow is directed.

This is not to say that the twentieth-century conflicts we will examine should be seen as extensions of conflict that emerged during the late days of the Nawabi. Unlike Cole, we would not imply that the precedents established during the Nawabi were important because they solidified Sunni-Shi'a antagonisms. On the contrary, as had been the case for Bareilly and Agra Hindus and Muslims, the Sunni-Shi'a disputes under the British did not begin with friction between those two groups. Instead, these disputes grew out of competition *within* the Shi'a community between advocates of differing religious practices. That is, they related to necessary adjustments made by Shi'as to a world in which they no longer exercised state power. The resulting conflict between Sunnis and Shi'as peaked in two periods: the first point of pronounced violence lasted from 1906 to 1908; the second occurred in 1939. Significantly, in both periods disputants expressed the clash through the same symbolic rhetoric, using the same ritual practices to channel the conflict. But the substantive differences underlying the two periods of dispute help us gauge both the processual meanings in symbolic behavior and the development of communal sentiment in the intervening decades.

Assorted practices designed to define the Shi'i community had been fostered by the court culture of the Nawabi. Cultural ascendancy had prompted distinctions in religious practices, social etiquette, and even costume.[35] The impact of these distinctions doubtless had been diluted by the fact that after 1857 Nawabi courtiers moved to Delhi. But much of their culture remained in Lucknow, popularized and adapted by

---

35. Ibid., pp. 172–73; see, for instance, Sharar's explanation for the court preference for five-cornered hats over four-cornered ones.

resident Muslims, both Sunni and Shi'a. Efforts to reform this shared Lakhnawi culture led to sectarian conflict. Sunnis particularly had experienced a period of reassessment and reform in the late nineteenth century. These reform efforts led to several examples of ill will between Sunnis and Shi'as, including two court cases launched in the 1880s and a campaign in the 1890s by the Ahl-i Hadith directed against the Shi'a.[36] The virulent anti-Shi'a position of the Ahl-i Hadith (which proved a significant factor in the late 1930s as well) arose in part from the fact that both groups drew from the same north Indian aristrocratic and courtly population and milieu.[37] But these acrimonious exchanges still proved the exception. Although Sunni-Shi'a relations were not always cordial, they were generally characterized by cooperation. The observance of Muharram, for instance, continued to be a citywide event, both Sunni and Hindu tazias joining in the processions. Sunnis even regularly attended Shi'a *majālis,* and Sunni numbers swelled Muharram processions, with "thousands of Hindus" joining them in chanting the dirges that accompanied the mourning observance.[38]

All this changed in 1906. The Sunnis began to take their tazias to a new *karbalā.* Though viewed as a dramatic turning point by the participants, this separation of the *karbalās* actually figured in a series of events that began earlier, in 1904. The events form a story quickened by reformist movements and the self-conscious efforts by each community to publicly define its boundaries. The outline of that story will prove a familiar one when viewed against the backdrop of Hindu-Muslim conflicts of the same period.[39] That the events are so closely connected to Muharram, and particularly to the *karbalās,* should not surprise us. The processions that formed the public portion of the observances continued to play a central role in uniting the Shi'a of Lucknow with the other Indians resident there. Public structures of Muharram, interweaving public processions and privately sponsored *majālis,* dramatically expressed the metaphor of community, and the separation of the *karbalās* in 1906 must be seen as an important alteration in that metaphor.

---

36. *Selections from the Vernacular Press, 1890.*

37. Barbara Daly Metcalf, *Islamic Revival in British India: Deoband, 1860–1900* (Princeton University Press, 1982), chapter 7.

38. IOR, P/8098, Genl. Admin. Progs., progs. no. 35, serial no. 13, "Humble Petition of Sunni Community of Lucknow," p. 46; Sharar, *Lucknow,* p. 149.

39. The following narrative is based on documents in file IOR P/8098, "Papers Collected by the Piggott Committee" [henceforth "Piggott Committee"].

The Twentieth-Century Public Arena as Metaphor of Community

Reforming tendencies among the Lakhnawi Shi'a received an important impetus with the arrival of Maqbul Ahmed in 1904. Resident of the princely state of Rampur, Maqbul toured U.P. Shi'a communities, particularly those of Lucknow, Jaunpur, and Faizabad.[40] His exhortations led to the systematic introduction of recitations designed to symbolize, through collective speech, the distinct doctrinal and historical position of the Shi'i community. Two forms of recitation were used: *tabarrā* (a stylized abuse of the intervening three caliphs) and *bilā faṣl* (an assertion of the rightfulness of Ali's immediate succession on the death of Muhammad).

Shi'i leaders also cast a critical eye at the observance of Muharram, attacking those "abuses" connected with the tenth-day tazia processions to the most popular site, Tal Katora Karbala. Beginning with the 1905 *Chehlum* (the tazia procession held forty days after Ashura, the tenth of Muharram, and usually observed only by Shi'as), leading Shi'as convinced the owners of land near Tal Katora Karbala to discontinue the booths, shops, and displays that constituted the "fair" traditionally held in conjunction with tazia processions. With the Collector's approval, they also published a list of rules to be observed by all those attending the *karbalā*. Thus, these reforms, enacted during a part of the Muharram ceremonially observed by only a fraction of Lakhnawis, did not have a serious impact on Hindus or Sunnis.

The tenth of Muharram (Ashura) observances in 1906, however, provided a very different occasion. A list was reissued for Ashura, with no official notice taken of the increased stringency of the rules. They now prohibited games (especially characteristic of Sunni tazia processions), entertainments, all shops, the chewing of pan, the smoking of tobacco, and swearing and jesting in the *karbalā* compound.[41] Though the allegation was denied by Shi'a witnesses, several Sunnis insisted that when their tazias arrived at the *karbalā*, they were told that they had to enter the compound bareheaded and without shoes, in the Shi'i manner. Sunni reactions to these reformist measures had crystallized slowly.

40. Maqbul was asked to leave Lucknow, but he was prosecuted and convicted in the other locations. For government reactions to later activities of Maqbul, see chapter 2.

41. "Piggott Committee," p. 97. There were also stringent regulations against prostitution.

Few of the wealthier and more influential Sunnis actually participated in the processions; hence they had little reason to oppose what were presented as moral reforms, particularly the removal of prostitutes from the fairgrounds. Moreover, few of the poorer Sunnis—the vast majority of Lucknow's Muslims—had been affected by the original changes introduced at Chehlum, since they only participated in that part of Muharram observed during the first ten days of the month. When the changes began to affect the 1906 Ashura, however, Sunnis reacted strongly. The night before Ashura the administration approved a Sunni petition, requesting that if the new rules could not be rescinded, then Sunnis should be permitted to bury their tazias in Kakori, a new site donated by a prominent Sunni mill owner.

That these Sunnis willingly changed to a new and barren site, one without any historically sacred associations, indicates the strength of their protest. It also suggests the significance of the *karbalā* site in the general observance of Muharram: the sacred site itself fulfilled certain basic requirements in the unfolding of the observance, and these requirements differed between Sunnis and Shi'as. Moreover, relocating to the new site gave Sunnis a chance to redefine their use of this sacred space without reference to Shi'i values. The relocation may also have been a spatial expression of the changing economic conditions of Muslims in Lucknow. The city had expanded out from the old site of Tal Katora, and Sunnis, now more prosperous than before, often lived a great distance from Tal Katora Karbala. Though aggrieved, these Sunnis may not have been entirely averse to establishing their own, more accessible sacred site, over which they could exercise complete control.

Control proved important to reformers active among Lucknow's Sunnis. It would have been too much to ask Lakhnawi Sunnis to cease observing an event that, although contrary to doctrine, possessed great popularity. The sympathy with which the martyrdom of the Prophet's family was viewed had become part of the larger fabric of popular devotional religion, represented by such institutions as the shrine in Rustumnagar. Reformers therefore sought to reconcile observance of the murder of Husain with more orthodox Islam. *Chār yārī*, as a form of collective recitation, became the reformers' most obvious technique. The recitation of verses in praise of all four caliphs encouraged additional collective action by a group and, in the process, defined the basis for shared identity among the reciters. It also provided a mirror activity of the now systematic cursing engaged in by Shi'as: "The verses are now being sung along the entire route of the tazias; they are halted every few yards while a verse is sung, and then after the refrain has been repeated they move on."[42] This recitation of verses defending mainstream Islam had once been an intermittent and private practice; it now became systematic and public—an exercise that simultaneously delineated community boundaries and educated lower-class Sunnis away from Shi'i "misinterpretation." New verses damned anyone unwilling to join in these praises, and special *jhandā*s, or poles bearing long banners with the word *chār yār,* began to be carried with the tazias. Even some of the tazias themselves were marked with the names of the four caliphs.

Thus, changes, introduced by reformers interested in reinvigorating the practices unique to each of the two Muslim sects, affected the observances of both groups. Although most of the conflict of this decade can be traced directly to these trends, it must still be asked why they had such impact at this particular time. The answers are varied and complex, but they relate directly to important changes in the composition of the groups in Lucknow, in their relationship to each other and to the state, and in the relationship between leaders and followers of the respective communities.

The intellectual changes included those influenced by the burgeoning publications industry.[43] Lucknow figured prominently among U.P. publishing centers in the early twentieth century, jockeying for the lead each year with Allahabad, Agra, and Moradabad. Religious works always comprised the bulk of the publications, and many of these attacked opposing philosophies even as they reiterated their own values. Though controversy fostered by and about the Arya Samaj or Western missionaries initially shaped this style, most contending groups soon adopted it, including Sunnis and Shi'as. As early as 1890 the publication of a collection of Shi'i verses for *majālis* had prompted a court complaint by Sunnis. In this decade publishing trends faithfully mirrored the heightened friction in Lucknow: the category "The Differences Between Sunnis and Shias" suddenly emerged as a popular topic for books published in 1904–1905, and administrators labeled the intracommunity controversy "especially virulent" in the 1908–1909 list of publications.

Even as intellectual trends reinforced group identities, economic developments began dissolving old social bonds. After suffering four years of plague (1902–1906), U.P. was buffeted by famine, followed in

42. Ibid., p. 86.
43. IOR, V/10/172, *Reports* on the Administration of the U.P. for 1903–1910 (Allahabad, those years). See pp. 46, 45, respectively, in the appropriate annual report.

the fall of 1908 by the most severe malaria epidemic in thirty years. Perhaps perversely, these natural disasters were accompanied by quite prosperous economic indicators. Though the price of grain rose steadily, wage scales more than kept pace with inflation.[44] At the same time, employment opportunities increased substantially, in part through short-term government-sponsored projects. The substitution of new manufactures for old provided new opportunities; for instance, though fine weaving was no longer produced in Lucknow, demand increased for cloth dyeing.

These quite drastic changes in economic conditions could not help but alter the social relations allied to them. The plight of Shi'i *wasīqadārs* (pensioners of the East India Company and the ex-royal family) no doubt is indicative: tied to fixed incomes, these people were the first to suffer in an inflationary period.[45] With their buying power severely reduced, they proved less able to fulfill expected charitable roles in the times of epidemic and famine that characterized this period.[46] Indeed, it seems likely that they became recipients of such private relief instead. Moreover, the changes in demand and competitive conditions related to the various Lakhnawi crafts meant that only the most flexible and adaptive of "natural leaders" could survive.

Disaster- and employment-induced changes in the population proved significant, as any increase or decrease in population had important ramifications for the interrelationships between Sunnis and Shi'as, particularly given the unbalanced class distribution between them. Whereas the Sunnis could be identified as having a "highest," a "second or middle," and a "lowest" class,[47] the Shi'as had virtually no lower-class members who would so identify themselves in this period.[48] Even the

44. Wages for most skilled and unskilled positions at least doubled, and in some cases tripled, between 1906 and 1911 (see *Wage Census Reports* for those years), whereas in famine years grain prices less than doubled (see *Resolution on Famine Relief,* [Allahabad, 1908], p. 151).

45. Over time, however, the *wasīqadars* fared better than the royal pensioners. See Veena Talwar Oldenburg, "Peril, Pestilence, and Perfidy," Ph.D. diss., University of Illinois, Champagne-Urbana (1979), p. 194; now published as *The Making of Colonial Lucknow, 1856–1877* (Princeton: Princeton University Press, 1984).

46. Private relief measures were an important feature in the 1907–1908 famine, especially in Lucknow city (*Resolution on Famine Relief,* p. 58).

47. See the remarkable description by the Sunni representative, in "Piggott Committee," p. 124.

48. For a discussion of lower-class Shi'a under the Nawabi, see Cole, *Roots of North Indian Shi'ism,* pp. 85–89.

"middle" class of Shi'a, though in a more precarious economic position than the "highest" class, still acted as a leisured class. Their influence with government and their control of positions of power and prestige remained from their privileged status under the Shi'i court of Awadh. Those Shi'a who gave testimony before the compromise-seeking Piggott Committee, for instance, included Mirza Nazir Hasan Khan Sahib, a Khan Bahadur and Honorary Magistrate for twenty-three years; Muhammad Jafar Hasan Khan, a *wasīqadār;* and Nawab Rahat Ali Khan Sahib, Secretary of the Husainabad Endowment and an Honorary Magistrate. Still, the number of those who identified themselves as Shi'a was shrinking. Though they had constituted as much as 23 percent of the Muslim population in 1881, by 1904 they represented only 14 percent, two-thirds of whom were female.[49] (The figures may also, of course, reflect some shift in population through in-migration of Sunni laborers; since the total population increase was not large—from 261,303 in 1881 to 264,049 in 1909—it is unlikely that this shift accounts for most of the change.)[50]

This shrinkage in the number of self-avowed Shi'as was accompanied by an increase in the ratio of Muslims to the total population, which by 1916 had risen from 16 to 21 percent.[51] The increase was especially noticeable among "shaikhs," the category most often claimed by up-wardly mobile Sunnis.[52] Even those who continued in traditional lower-class occupational categories had gained new assertiveness at the turn of the century. David Thomas has identified two coherent collective efforts in this period: ekka drivers protested in 1901, and butchers struck in 1908 against "unfair municipal regulations and fines." The former protest was staged "in retaliation against what they believed to have been discriminatory disciplinary action taken against them by the local Municipal Board," which was dominated at this time "by a small group of wealthy Hindu merchants and professionally-trained people." A few words may suggest the changing nature of lower-class self-perceptions, as well as changes in the relationship between the lower classes and the

49. Nevill, *Lucknow Gazetteer,* p. 69. Some of this decline may also have been related to Shi'i perceptions that this was a period in which they should practice deception about their identity.
50. Statistics cited in David A. Thomas, "Lucknow and Kanpur, 1880–1920: Stagnation and Development Under the Raj," *South Asia* 5 (December 1982): 69.
51. *Supplement* to *District Gazetteers of the U.P.* (Allahabad, 1916), p. 20.
52. John C. Nesfield, *Brief View of the Caste System of the North-Western Frontier Provinces* (1885), p. 122.

(increasingly dominant) Hindu merchants of the city. The Municipal Report of the incident asserted that

> some drivers had been rowdy and very unpleasant to private citizens of the city during their annual celebrations, which occurred at this time. As a result of their behaviour some were fined. Most of the drivers met and decided that the fines were too harsh and that they would go on strike. During the numerous public demonstrations held in the city by the ekka drivers, the majority of those present each time were not themselves ekka drivers.[53]

Thus, social mobility and lower-class assertiveness combined with dislocation in traditional employment categories to require new relationships between those who would lead and the members of the various economic and religious groups in the city. At the same time, it seems likely that upwardly mobile "shaikhs" embraced religious change as well; as Barbara Metcalf has shown, such social mobility generally included "ashrafization," the patronage of the (usually reformist) religious establishment, and a new adherence to high-culture Islam.[54] For all of these reasons the number of Sunnis embracing orthodoxy would have been increasing.

In these new circumstances two very different kinds of leaders emerged among the Muslims of Lucknow. The first type, the traditionally prestigious ulama, had begun to acquire more influence, using such new tools as publishing and mass meetings. Maulvi Muhammad Abdu'sh-Shakur, though he spoke no English, was an effective and compelling representative for the Sunnis on the Piggott Committee. His lengthy note of dissent, while concerned primarily with the doctrinal aspects of the question, evinced an impressive analysis of social considerations and an intriguing civic sense:

> Besides the Shias and Sunnis, the general public, too, had acquired a sort of civic right in connection with this Karbala celebration, and it was of long standing . . . [with] people from distant places coming to take part therein. This gathering was not only an occasion for petty trading, the values of which amounted to thousands of rupees, but contributed to the general prosperity and . . . grandeur of the city in diverse ways.[55]

53. Thomas, "Lucknow and Kanpur, 1880–1920," pp. 68–80. For strike of Ekka drivers, see especially p. 76. Butchers are discussed in n. 17.
54. B. Metcalf, *Islamic Revival,* chapter 7.
55. "Piggott Committee," p. 126.

The second type of leader had long been active in public arenas. Such innovative but traditional-style leaders demonstrated a flexibility and adaptability to the new circumstances of late nineteenth-century British rule. Munshi Ehtesham Ali, a rais and a zamindar, also was prominent as a mill owner, a member of the district board, and a participant in various Muslim political activities of the period, such as the anti-Nagari Resolution campaign of 1900 and organization of the Muslim Political Association in the following year.[56] Though his cousin regularly paraded with the tazias, Ehtesham never did, and perhaps this was the reason he approved the initial Shi'i reforms proposed for Muharram.[57] Once the Sunni protest was organized, however, he moved to the forefront, donating the site for the new *karbalā*, acting as spokesman, and proffering compromise solutions on a conciliation committee.

Both types of Muslim leaders necessarily brought with them a new style of mobilization, and this style often prompted friction with the opposing community. Weavers might still be activated by calls from their traditional middlemen, but mill workers and other Sunnis who had moved into new occupations had to be reached in new ways. These new communications networks shared public venues more broadly than their predecessors had: these networks included the posting of placards, the printing of collections of verses for recitation, the publication of "inflammatory" appeals, and even the recitation of verses stating a doctrinal position. The impact of print capitalism, especially when mediated by continuing traditions of orality, ensured the participation of an ever-larger number of people. Moreover, the public discussion and practice of religion modified, even as it expressed, religious beliefs. At the same time it defined community on the basis of these shared practices. Indeed, the new publicness of community practices figured at the heart of the controversy over the Shi'a *bilā faṣl* recitations and the Sunni *chār yārī* verses. A public opinion—albeit one confined to the respective communities as they were defined—was being formed.

Thus, similar changes affected both Sunnis and Shi'as in intellectual atmosphere, economic conditions, and the relationship between leaders and followers of the two communities. But the impact of these changes within each community differed. If upward mobility and increasing

56. Details are from "Piggott Committee" and from appendix to F. C. R. Robinson, *Separatism Among Indian Muslims* (Cambridge: Cambridge University Press, 1974).

57. Hamid Ali Khan testified before the Piggott Committee that "M. Ehtisham Ali said, 'I was at Kakari; otherwise I should have gone in the deputation [to the Deputy Commissioner]' " ("Piggott Committee," p. 73).

population provide a ready explanation for new assertiveness by Sunnis, their opposite must be seen as the motivation for action by Shi'as. Fear among Shi'as that they would be swallowed up by a successful and culturally exuberant Sunni community led them to reiterate the differences between sects. Indeed, the popularizing of Shi'i court culture in Lucknow may have succeeded too well. To Shi'i leaders it must have seemed that the very process of popularization carried with it the seeds of destruction, as the expansion of the *karbalā* fair so well illustrated. As Shi'as drew boundaries around their practices, they reverted to their older self-perception as the martyrs of Islam—a tactic that foreshadowed their strategies for survival in later decades.

Whatever the motivations of these groups, it must be emphasized that in the early twentieth century neither the new publicness of reform efforts nor the self-conscious definitions of community proved sufficiently broad to encompass political institutions or the social life of community leaders. Sunni leader M. Ehtesham Ali, for instance, counted among his friends and within his social circle at least one of the leading reformist Shi'as and several prominent Hindus, including the Congress cum Hindu populist Bishan Narayan Dar.[58] Ehtesham had also joined with the Shi'a barrister Hamid Ali Khan to help organize the Muslim Political Association and continued to work with him on Muslim political causes. Thus none of the activities of these prominent participants in the world of state institutions as yet was directly affected by the intensification of sectarian conflict.

Nevertheless, by 1906 two separated observances of Muharram had come into existence—separated both in the public aspects of the processions and in the privately organized *majālis*. The doctrinal base of this separation, as well as the metaphorical distinctions of community, found public expression through competing verse recitations: Shi'as (through *bilā faṣl* and *tabarrā*) asserted the rightfulness of Ali's immediate succession and abused the three intervening caliphs; Sunnis (through *chār yārī*) praised all four caliphs and condemned anyone refusing to recognize them all.

State Structures and Community Conflict

Over the next three decades the Piggott Committee's compromise solution—to forbid recitation of either community's verses—worked relatively well to defuse hostility in Lucknow.[59] But with this compro-

---

58. Dar was author of the Pamphlet *An Appeal to the English Public*, on Cow Protection; see discussion in chapter 6.
59. Although there was one altercation in 1912.

mise the position of Shi'as subtly changed. In contrast to their presumed superiority from the days of the Nawabi, they now had to be grateful for parity—the equality with Sunnis that the Piggott Committee declared for them. This change in state perceptions reflected the fact that although they retained their precarious claims to high status, their connections with government became increasingly tenuous. This situation was exacerbated as the state structure reoriented itself toward the concept of majority rule and its expression through public opinion.

When this reorientation led again to conflict in the late 1930s, the new clash bore superficial similarities to the earlier one. Community spokesmen tailored expressions of the conflict in public arenas along familiar lines: in 1935, and again in the following year, Sunni leaders urged their followers to recite *chār yārī* verses (now called *madḥ-i ṣŏḥbān*), and Shi'as eventually retaliated with curses through *tabarrā*. But an important difference marked the renewed recitation of these verses: they now represented acts aimed against the state. As with the collective protests staged in other cities by Hindus and Muslims, respectively, the ability had developed to turn community ideology either against an Indian "Other" community or against the alien state.

This potential inherent in community ideology led to very complex political alignments in Lucknow. For instance, agitators for the majority Sunni community began their campaign because, they argued, the provincial government continued to deny them religious freedom, despite the fact that this government was now essentially Indian, not British. Though this was a logical position for those hoping to influence a local government controlled by Congress, the complaint reveals much more than it suggests on the surface. Sunni religious freedom—defined by the situation as the right to recite *madḥ-i ṣŏḥbān*—always had been denied. Indeed, under the Nawabi government Shi'i practices had been so much the norm that the notion of Sunni public statements was unthinkable. The British profoundly altered this situation by a policy of "evenhandedness" in dealing with the communities, which gave Sunnis more so-called religious freedom than they had ever had before. But by the 1930s parity proved insufficient. Instead, the increasing success and influence of Sunnis made them feel acutely the gap between officially observed parity and their new social and economic predominance. In the politicized atmosphere of the late 1930s, then, their claim to increased religious freedom can be seen as a reflection of their new importance in Lakhnawi society.

The likelihood of their claim gaining recognition improved when Husain Ahmed, leader of the Ahrars, took up their cause. Allied with a Congress labeled by many opponents as "Hindu," the Ahrars used their

Muslim identity as a bargaining point with those in power, supplying in return important Muslim support for the nationalist movement. Their support of *madḥ-i ṣŏḥbān* thus prompted serious concern among Congress ministers.[60] Turning to tactics of mass mobilization, thousands of Sunnis gathered to court arrest by reciting *madḥ-i ṣŏḥbān* verses. The twenty-five hundred Sunnis imprisoned as a result of these recitations presented a distinct problem for the Congress government, some of whose ministers viewed the Sunni position sympathetically. Ignoring the findings of both the earlier Piggott Committee and its own advisory group (the Allsop Committee), in March the U.P. Congress government issued a communiqué allowing the Sunnis to organize a single *madḥ-i ṣŏḥbān* procession, on the Prophet's birthday only, in a location thought to be sufficiently removed from Shi'i neighborhoods to avoid objections.

Not so. Stunned by this betrayal of the evenhanded British policy they had come to accept, Shi'as immediately organized a protest. They vowed to recite *tabarrā* to court arrest until the government rescinded the communiqué. The strength of Shi'i reaction took the government by surprise, as did the degree of coordination and mass mobilization possessed by the small community. Volunteers poured into Lucknow from all over India. In all, more than fourteen thousand Shi'as were arrested during the long months of the protest.

This battle of public verses gave the conflict a familiar appearance, as the symbols of protest connected the events of 1906 and 1939. A processual analysis makes it clear, however, that this symbolic behavior had been given new meaning by the important changes that had occurred in the intervening years. The new meaning was attested to particularly by the choice of the government as target, the involvement of a large number of people drawn from all over India, and the selection of nonviolent civil disobedience tactics in courting arrest. To place these changes in greatest relief, we will look again at two areas important in the earlier conflict: first, the reformist nature of the protest, for what it tells us about the interaction of state and community to infuse new meaning into public arena activity; and second, the relationship between leaders and followers, for what that reveals of the differences between minority and majority participation in public arenas.

The rosters of participants register most clearly the new channels into which the energy and zeal of reformist impulses were now being di-

---

60. Report by Lt.-Governor H. G. Haig, on the Lucknow Madha Sahaba Controversy [henceforth Report by Haig], IOR, L/P&J/7, file 2587 for 1939, especially p. 10.

rected. The kinds of people involved expanded dramatically to include, most significantly, women.[61] Though still in pardah, ten thousand women met in Lucknow to pass resolutions in support of the Shi'i cause and to form a fundraising committee for assistance to those arrested in the *tabarrā* agitation. These Shi'i women constituted members of an old elite—"S[h]ahzadis, Nawabradis, descendants of the late King of Oudh, rai'ses of the city and ladies of the 'ulama." Nawab Qamar Jahan Begum Sahiba headed the fundraising committee; she also acted as secretary for the ladies of the Anjuman-i-Islahul Khawateen (ex-royal family and talukdars of Awadh) when they submitted a petition to the Prime Minister in July.[62]

Moreover, by 1939 participants no longer needed to be located in the focal city. Local issues often exercised an extralocal appeal by this time, and the Lucknow conflict was a celebrated case in point wherever Shi'as and Sunnis mixed. Though drawn from the majority community, Sunni arrests only totaled twenty-five hundred before the communiqué was issued; to reach fourteen thousand arrests, Lucknow's Shi'as had to attract supporters from other parts of India. "Batches" of protesters descended on Lucknow from all over U.P. and the Punjab, even from Bengal and Bombay. Protests were held in other areas as well, such as Jubbulpore, Azamgarh, and Fyzabad. Sometimes these protest meetings even led to clashes, as in Nasirabad and Rae Bareli.

How these numbers of protesters came to be arrayed across the political and religious spectrum is also of some interest, particularly in the ways these Muslim sects allied themselves with the emerging communalist and nationalist organizations. The Ahrars, although the Muslim support group for Congress, acted as spearhead for the initial Sunni antigovernment protest. Once successful, however, the Ahrars and the (predominantly Hindu) Congress government then closed ranks and together faced Shi'i organizations like the Tanzeem-ul Momineen and the All-India Shia Political Conference, which themselves were often at odds. But the Shi'as, too, had allies, perhaps the most notable being the revivalist Nagar Hindu Sabha of Lucknow.[63] In response to a Tanzeem-ul Momineen resolution passed in April 1939, the Sabha

note[d] with pleasure the determination of the Shia community of Lucknow to respect Hindu sentiments and traditions with

61. *The Leader* (Allahabad), 13 April 1939.
62. Petition of Anjumani Islahul-Khawateen of Ex-Royal Family and Taluqdars of Oudh, IOR, L/P&J/2587 for 1939.
63. *The Leader*, 12 April 1939; see also the *Leader* of 21 April for the text of a telegram sent to Jinnah, Bose, Nehru, and the Chief Minister of U.P. from "The Shias and Hindus of Murshidabad."

reference to cow sacrifice and music [played before a mosque]
. . . [and took that] opportunity to point out that the Hindu
community always [stood] for religious freedom and mutual
tolerance . . . [and gave] full support in their efforts to insist on
their right of religious recitation on a par with the Ahrars.

In contrast, the Muslim League—shut out of the provincial government,
which was controlled by Congress—feared the conflict as a political
weapon that could be wielded against itself. It had either to choose sides
and admit the fragmentation of its constituency or to ignore the controversy, and abandon its claim to leadership.[64]

The situation thus proved structurally similar to that in Kanpur in the
1930s: ideological community concerns could not be addressed through
local relational alignments. Local leaders faced difficult choices. In
1939, as in 1906, the Shi'as remained a more cohesive community than
the Sunnis. Their economic position had not improved, and their political position had certainly worsened, but they clung to their claim of
social distinction. Indeed, what alarmed the government most about the
tabarrā protest was that "Shias of the most respectable families have
been reciting the Tabarra and going to jail."[65] The newspaper daily
published lists of the members of the ex-royal family, prominent members of the All-India Shia Political Conference, barristers, M.L.A.'s
(Members of the Legislative Assembly), large landlords, and others who
were being arrested.[66] Indeed, the very strength of Shi'a protest pulled
the community even closer together, both within and outside Lucknow.
Like all effective communalist actions after the 1913 Kanpur Mosque
Affair, the agitation dramatized a symbol that reinforced ties among
community members scattered across the subcontinent.[67]

Under those circumstances few Shi'a leaders chose to remain outside
the community's publicly proclaimed boundaries. The Lucknow *mujtahid*s, leaders in most Shi'a causes, played prominent roles in the protest.[68] Even the Raja of Mahmudabad, from a family that had long been
one of the most influential among U.P. Shi'as, became involved. His
father had managed to remain relatively aloof during the earlier Sunni-

---

64. Statement to *The Pioneer* (Allahabad) by U.P. League Secretary Abdul Waheed
Khan, quoted in Mirza Sajjad Ali Khan, *Why 14,000 Shias Went to Jail?* (Lucknow,
1939?), pp. 35–37. I am grateful to Barbara Metcalf for this reference.
65. Report by Haig, p. 9.
66. See, for instance, *The Leader*, 21, 25 April 1939.
67. See *The Leader*, 8 April 1939, for Kanpuri support.
68. *The Leader*, 12 June 1939; Ali Khan, *Why 14,000 Shias*, p. 35.

Shi'a conflict, directing his energies instead to the wider issues affecting such organizations as the Muslim League, in which he was initially quite active. By 1939, however, the new Raja felt obliged to take a leading role in the protest, acting as public spokesman and representative of the community of Shi'as.

Fellow Shi'a Hamid Ali Khan found himself in a similar position. He, too, had held aloof from the earlier conflict, preferring to work on issues that united, rather than divided, Muslims—such as organization of the Muslim Political Association and the anti-Nagari resolution campaign. But by 1939 he felt forced to take a stand for the narrower construction of community, and was finally arrested for public recitation of *tabarrā*.[69] Not only a strengthened community consciousness but also the intersection of public and state structures moved these leaders to a public position. Syed Hyder Mehdi, Congressman and Chairman of the Allahabad Improvement Trust, expressed the point most poignantly. In a statement to the press, he noted that

> public recital of Tabarra is not [an article of] faith of the Shias
> and is not sanctioned. Such being my faith, it has become neces-
> sary to explain why I am prepared to court arrest. . . . The
> deliberate intention to recite tabarra is not to cause annoyance to
> any Sunni as there are few Sunnis to hear it, but *is in the nature
> of a defiance of the Governmental order.* . . . My difficulty is that
> I have not been able to find any other [way] from which Shias can
> give a fight to the government. If the right of the recitation were
> conceded to Shias I would be the first person to use all my
> influence that the Shias should voluntarily give it up out of
> respect for the Sunnis.

Thus, the situation became acute in 1939 because, although the state structures had come within the ambit of Indians, these leaders did not place a high priority on protecting minority rights in public arenas. Hyder Mehdi further argued that

> it is my duty as a Congressman to purge the Congress ministry of
> this [bigoted] mentality. . . . I have no anger or hatred against the
> Ministry. I have still the same affection for the hon. Mr. Pant and
> my friend Dr. Katju, and my sister Viyaya Lakshmi and my boss
> Sampuranandji, all of whom I have known ever since I was
> young and had the honour to work with them.[70]

69. *The Leader*, 23 April 1939.
70. Ibid., 1 May 1939 (emphasis added).

But for Sunni ulama the alignments proved more complex. The leadership of the 1939 *madḥ-i ṣöḥbān* movement had been taken up by an alim who had gained prominence in the clash of 1906. Abdu'sh-Shakur provided persistent publicity through his vernacular newspaper; he was joined by members of the Jamiat-ul 'Ulama. The Ahl-i Hadith, which had honed its characteristic combativeness in decades of campaigning against Shi'ism, used its numerical strength in the area east of Lucknow to play a prominent role in the *madḥ-i ṣöḥbān* agitation.[71] Not surprisingly, the two groups of Sunni ulama most closely associated with Congress or with the government—the Farangi Mahallis and the Nadwa ulama—did not participate. Similarly, many Sunnis with influence in state institutions remained aloof. Maulana A. K. Azad, for instance, saw his first responsibility to Congress. Rejecting a Shi'a appeal, he denied that government should be involved in what was "a conflict between two sections of Muslims" and refused to intervene unless protesters suspended all civil disobedience against the government. Though the two Sunni ministers in the U.P. Congress government, Ibrahim and Kidwai, clearly felt sympathetic to the *madḥ-i ṣöḥbān* cause, they, too, remained aloof from the issue.[72] Since leaders of the Muslim League also refused to involve themselves, few prominent Muslims were willing to provide public leadership for the protesting Sunnis. Maulana Husain Ahmad, leader of the Ahrars and Vice President of the Provincial Congress Committee, was one of the few prominent leaders arrested for *madḥ-i ṣöḥbān*.[73]

For Sunnis the issue of leadership thus became acute. Though the Ahrar and the aristocratic ulama of the Ahl-i Hadith provided leadership for the movement, they generally remained invisible, a great social gulf separating them from the mass of the movement's supporters. Indeed, in marked contrast to those Shi'as subsequently arrested for *tabarrā* recitation, "those offering themselves for arrest" in the Sunni civil disobedience "were generally the riff raff."[74] Regardless of whether the principal purpose of the agitation, as an Ahrar spokesman suggested, was to "discredit taziadari in the eyes of the ignorant Sunni masses and prevent them from being proselytized by the Shias,"[75] there emerged a gap between the lower-class Sunni participants and the

71. Ibid., 7, 13 April 1939.
72. Ibid., 10 June 1939; Report by Haig, p. 6.
73. Ali Khan, *Why 14,000 Shias*, pp. 37–38.
74. Report by Haig, p. 9.
75. Ali Khan, *Why 14,000 Shias*, p. 28.

Sunnis who ordinarily exercised leadership in Lucknow but in this instance remained aloof. For the "majority community" of the city, then, the pattern experienced in other north Indian cities, in which the elite first tried to purge public arena activity through reformism and then increasingly withdrew from collective exercises, held true.

Lack of participation in these public arena agitations by leaders concerned instead with relational influence in state structures created a number of problems similar to those identified for other urban areas. Perhaps the most dramatic example occurred in late April, when an "unruly mob" of more than one hundred Sunnis invaded the U.P. Provincial Assembly Hall and stopped the proceedings. The youthful protesters had broken away from a demonstration of some five thousand people taking place opposite the building. Though the protesters had a clear-cut demand—that either the government stop the recitation of *tabarrā* or that Sunnis also be allowed to recite without limit—the politicians were "especially irate at the leaders of the Sunnis, who were not in evidence."[76] This situation thus reflected a pattern common by the 1930s. The combination of mass mobilization and religious rhetoric and causes had proved increasingly successful in bringing pressure to bear on the state. But providing practical action to satisfy the rhetoric turned out to be beyond the abilities of the leadership, at least in part because the political realities of a locality depended on political alignments shaped by more personal and relational networks. These alliances, tying each disputant to supporters whose ideologies differed, precluded action informed by one community's ideology and values.

Thus, although boundaries around communities could be drawn quite successfully in the abstract, no concrete action could follow. To the extent that they could express collective public opinion in modes accessible to all, the public arenas of Lucknow could function as the equivalent of the European public sphere of the nation-state. But to the extent that the relational political structures of the state precluded any real interaction with political arenas, they were prevented from functioning as true equivalents. The impasse led to much frustration, and thence to endemic popular unrest. That this kind of unrest became highly ritualized in the 1930s and 1940s (as well as in the 1960s and 1970s) suggests the continuing gap between India's public arenas and the public sphere model of European society.

76. *The Leader*, 26, 29 April 1939.

Conclusion

The lesson agitators learned from these two decades included how to move from community rhetoric in public arenas to mass mobilization against the state. But minority communities saw in the events other lessons as well. Though the ideology of communalism proved to be a powerful force, it was a two-edged sword that was bound to cut against those groups without sufficient numerical strength in an indigenously ruled, postimperial nation-state. Any minority that hoped to protect its interests, then, had to pursue one of two possible strategies. Either it could insist on a separate territory in which it could be the majority, or it had to forge strong ties with others involved in local, relational politics—ties that held irrespective of ideological differences.

In this context a Shi'i Muharram innovation of the early 1940s has special significance. *Mātam on Fire* began to be held on the sixth of Muharram in Lucknow. One of few avowedly public observances, it was staged at the large and impressive Asafi *Imāmbārā*, the compound known as "the most conspicuous symbol of Shi'ism for non-Shi'as" in the city. The new event was patterned after an important component of traditional Lakhnawi Muharram observances, the *Mātam*, or mourning part of the *majlis*, that concluded the services held twice daily during the ten days of Muharram. Mrs. Mir Hasan Ali described the *Mātam* of the 1830s:

> Mortem follows, beating of breasts in unison with the voices, and uttering the names of Hasan and Hosein. . . . I have been present when the effect produced by the superior oratory and gestures of a Maulvee has almost terrified me, the profound grief, evinced in his tears and groans, being piercing and apparently sincere. I have even witnessed blood issuing from the breast of sturdy men, who beat themselves simultaneously as they ejaculated the names 'Hasan!' 'Hosein!' for ten minutes, and occasionally during a longer period, in that part of the service called Mortem.[77]

The form of *Mātam* initiated in the 1940s involved young Shi'as demonstrating their "zeal" (to use a term from Kanpuri rhetoric) by walking through fire. It was organized by a Shi'i association, which was presided over by a leading *mujtahid*, and attended by prominent "political and administrative leaders and other people of influence in the city." Printed invitations ensured attendance by non-Shi'i leaders, as well as by

---

77. Mrs. Meer Hassan Ali, *Observations*, pp. 23, 22.

"other members of the central, state and city governments."[78] Indeed, so sensitive were the Shi'a to the deliberate publicness of the event that they even provided "reaction cards" for invited guests. Some non-Shi'as doubtless still valued *Mātam on Fire* as "an expression of grief and devotion to Husain," which echoed the shared popular devotional culture of the area. Others could accept it as a miracle, for miracles of faith drew from a shared cultural system of values and beliefs that required no reference to specific ideology or community membership.[79]

The significance of the new Muharram ceremony seems particularly obvious after the problems encountered by Shi'as in the 1930s in their attempts to integrate public and state structures. Having learned well the dangers faced by a minority community in a politicized communal atmosphere, Shi'as designed a new public rite. The rite "invented" a tradition central to the worldview of Shi'as in Lucknow. In this case, however, the values emphasized in public were not those that separated the minority sect from the Indian society in which it resided. Rather, the rite stressed cultural values shared in common among Shi'as and other Indians, simultaneously placing Shi'as in the mainstream of public opinion. This tactic proved to be particularly effective, drawing heavily on the historical lessons provided by the process of community definition. Indeed, as history has shown, no other approach has successfully bridged the chasm created in the 1930s between ideology and program, between state structures and the community identity fostered in public arenas.

78. Hjortshoj, "Kerbala in Context," p. 158.
79. Ibid., p. 161.

Conclusion: Community and State in the Twentieth Century

Never was there such a Ramnaumi. Such crowds, such rites, such music!
—*Badr-ud-din of Bareilly, 1871*

The further East you go, the greater becomes the importance of a bit of bunting.
—*Viceroy Lord Lytton, 1876*[1]

Collective action, whether ceremonial or violent, served to define community symbolically. In western Europe, before the public sphere came into its own through print capitalism, collective rites formed the primary mode through which social and power relationships were communicated, negotiated, or resisted. As Lytton's snide remark suggests, the creation of the modern nation-state in Europe, and the concomitant development of a public sphere, brought with it the implication that such relationships, once rationalized, no longer stood in need of such ritualized legitimation. Despite this perception by its participants, however, ritual remained an important mode of legitimation. Indeed, as Eric Hobsbawm points out, although the rhetoric of pseudo-social science may have convinced European participants of the rationality of their modern societies, "one period which saw [invented traditions] spring up with particular assiduity was in the thirty or forty years before the first world war. . . . [The] two main forms of the creation of tradition in the nineteenth century . . . reflect the profound and rapid social transformations of the period." That is, the very conditions of life in a modern nation-state demanded the invention of "traditions" to bind together the nation's subjects. "Quite new, or old but dramatically transformed, social groups, environments and social contexts called for new devices

1. Lytton to Salisbury, 11 May 1876, quoted in Bernard C. Cohn, "Representing Authority in Victorian India," in Eric Hobsbawm and Terence Ranger, eds., *The Invention of Tradition* (Cambridge: Cambridge University Press, 1983), p. 192.

to ensure or express social cohesion and identity and to structure social relations. At the same time a changing society made the traditional forms of ruling by states and social or political hierarchies more difficult or even impracticable. This required new methods of ruling or establishing bonds of loyalty."[2]

Bonds of loyalty worked, in the aggregate, at both the localized and nation-state level. For the latter, David Cannadine's study of state rituals around the British monarchy provides an instructive case in point. "Between the late 1870s and 1914 . . . there was a fundamental change in the public image of the British monarchy, as its ritual, hitherto inept, private and of limited appeal, became splendid, public and popular." In part this change related to the gradual retirement of the monarch from active politics, in part it concerned an altered domestic and international context. Indeed, as domestic changes heightened, so too did the appearance of stability through ritual; as international tension and decline increasingly marked Britain's position in the world, national ritual conveyed "continuity and comfort."[3] An even more successful phenomenon in this respect was the creation in France of Bastille Day in July 1880: although little notice had been given, "in Paris and many provincial cities and villages, crowds turned out in large numbers. . . . Thousands of mayors and other rural functionaries hailed local celebrations."[4] Bastille Day built on popular memories of the storming of the Bastille, which "remained vivid . . . through oral tradition, popular prints, a commercial panorama in Paris and dramatic histories by Jules Michelet and Louis Blanc, as well as a press campaign." Tapping this popular symbol, the new observance could measure its success in the extent to which it encompassed both official and unofficial activities. The celebrations drew support particularly from the urban working class; but it is important to note that

> local festivals did not arise spontaneously from all the people. Leaders and organizers emerged from groups of people most in touch with national politics and ideological thinking. These were usually educated local functionaries—the village mayor, the schoolmaster, the tax collector, the informal political groups

2. Eric Hobsbawm, "Mass-Producing Traditions: Europe, 1870–1914," in Hobsbawm and Ranger, eds., *The Invention of Tradition,* p. 263.

3. David Cannadine, "The Context, Performance and Meaning of Ritual: The British Monarchy and the 'Invention of Tradition,' c. 1820–1977," in Hobsbawm and Ranger, eds., *The Invention of Tradition,* pp. 120, 160.

4. Charles Rearick, *Pleasures of the Belle Epoque: Entertainment and Festivity in Turn-of-the-Century France* (New Haven: Yale University Press, 1985), pp. 3–4.

often centered in a village cafe, the kind of people who read newspapers and had some independence, economic and intellectual, from village priests and antirepublican notables. They often contributed money as well as time and effort.[5]

A marker of "France's emerging national civilization," this republican ritual, while not universally supported, nevertheless succeeded in allying local organization with national ideology.

Simultaneously with these national rituals, other popular forms of ritual and entertainment connected citizen and state at the local level, including such disparate experiences as sports events and elections.[6] Elections, in particular, should be viewed as a new form of collective public exercise, important not only as an obviously political act but for their ritual and ceremonial aspects as well.[7] Scholars have seen that "speeches, songs, processions and other election 'rituals' helped to define not only competing groups, but also the values of the broader society that bound the competing sides together . . . even as they engaged rhetorically in what often became a form of ritualized combat."[8] Indeed, competition remained key to the ability of national rituals to be interpreted in locally meaningful terms. Sports competitions, in much the same way as elections, defined a locally significant "Other" in a vocabulary that united its participants and possessed the potential, in many situations, to characterize the "Other" in national terms.[9]

These collective activities bound the individual to the European nation-state, thereby bringing a national ideology home through the more localized organizational networks of local village, political party, and the like. In this way the larger ideological framework could be mediated, once again, through face-to-face relationships. This aspect is particularly important since it explains how activities in the public

5. Rearick, *Pleasures*, p. 16; Hobsbawm, "Mass-Producing Traditions," p. 271.

6. For sports events, see Hobsbawm, "Mass-Producing Traditions."

7. I have been forced to realize the implications of elections by David Gilmartin. See reference to his excellent essay, below.

8. David Gilmartin, "Elections and Muslim Community," a paper presented to the Conference on the Political Inheritance of Pakistan, held at Cambridge University in July 1987, p. 13. See also Gilmartin's references to other works on the subject, including Stanley Suval, *Electoral Politics in Wilhelmine Germany* (Chapel Hill: University of North Carolina Press, 1985), and Kim Ezra Shienbaum, *Beyond the Electoral Connection* (Philadelphia: University of Pennsylvania Press, 1984).

9. See Hobsbawm, "Mass-Producing Traditions," pp. 288–89. He also notes that football—particularly once it had been "proletarianized"—"operated both on a local and a national scale, so that the topic of the day's matches would provide common ground for conversation between virtually any two male workers in England or Scotland, and a few score celebrated players provided a point of common reference for all."

sphere connected public opinion to the nation-state. Concerning elections, one scholar has noted that "the neglected ceremonies of politics showcase deeper structures of national thought. The rituals of politics touch on broad concerns about the delegation of power in a democratic society, the nature of the relationship between leaders and followers, the legitimacy of government, and the ways of establishing compliance to that government."[10] This is not to suggest that creation of the public sphere in western Europe addressed all problems of the position of minority groups in the nation-state. On the contrary, twentieth-century European history has produced all too dramatic examples of ethnic attacks, anti-Semitism, language conflict, and the like. However, the rhetoric of the public sphere, building on invented traditions conveying community solidarity, *appeared* to solve these problems. The most severe fissures had not grown large enough to belie the rhetoric when the model became available for emulation in the Third World. It is important to distinguish between the model (as well as the social legitimacy implied in that model) and the reality behind it. The appeal of the Western nation-state to those subjected to imperialism lay in its abstract qualities, not in its actual workings.

Wellsprings of authority and legitimacy clearly lay at the heart of collective ritual as it came to be shaped in the modern nation-state of the West.[11] It is not surprising, then, that the problems of reshaping Indian public arenas to function as the equivalent of the Western public sphere should revolve around just these issues. Rituals could be adapted; invented traditions could express the new nation through what appeared to be immutable cultural concepts such as Bharat Mata; even the unfolding of elections could appear to be "a political festival incorporating the elements of planning, pilgrimage, procession and other collective experiences that characterize both secular and religious rituals in the subcontinent."[12] With all this processual reinterpretation of symbolic behavior, however, certain basic premises of public arena activities

10. Jean H. Baker, "The Ceremonies of Politics: Nineteenth-Century Rituals of National Affirmation," in William J. Cooper, Jr., Michael F. Holt, and John McCardell, eds., *A Master's Due: Essays in Honor of David Herbert Donald* (Baton Rouge: Louisiana State University Press, 1985), p. 165.

11. See a discussion of the relationship between community and authority in C. J. Calhoun, "Community: Toward a Variable Conceptualization for Comparative Research," *Social History* 5, no. 1 (Jan. 1980): 120–27.

12. Walter Hauser and Wendy Singer, "The Democratic Rite: Celebration and Participation in the Indian Elections," *Asian Survey* 26, no. 9 (Sept. 1986): 942. The authors, however, have failed to see the significance of the reworking of collective ceremonies in this modern guise for the "invention of tradition" that it is.

could not be ignored or negated by the activists trying to remake them in the nation-state's image. Given that competition quickened most public arena activity, the identity or label assigned to the "Other" proved highly significant in conveying legitimacy. Most difficult to escape was the definition by religious identity of an "Other" that had been expressed through collective activities. Equally puzzling was the question of authority. Under the imperial regime the moral authority of Indian society had resided in public arenas, while power had resided in the imperial state apparatus. In the West the ideology of nationalism had successfully relocated authority in the public sphere. This proved more problematic to achieve in India, because it meant reuniting public arena activities and state structures. The nationalist movement attempted just such a reunification and appeared to have succeeded, so long as it could define a united India in contrast to an imperial "Other." The process became more difficult with impending independence, however, for the "Other" continued to be part of the nation, rather than outside it.

"Nation" and "Community": Ideology and the State in British India

The preceding narrative outlines changes in the relationship between state and community in urban north India. We will conclude by investigating the extent to which the pattern that has been uncovered may be seen as typical for the subcontinent as a whole (or at least for the cultural regions within the British Raj). No detailed analysis is possible here, although such an analysis would be required to do the subject justice. We can only speculate from the suggestive evidence available for these localities; much more work would be necessary to test the hypotheses advanced here.

Perhaps the most critical feature of the U.P. configuration was the implicit separation introduced by the British between state-focused institutional activities and the collective action of public arenas. As a consequence, the two realms of activity developed along very different lines. A virtually separate world, public arenas flourished, supported by the elaboration of a role for "corporations" initiated in the eighteenth century through the devolution of power from the Mughal Empire.[13]

13. See C. A. Bayly, *Rulers, Townsmen and Bazaars* (Cambridge: Cambridge University Press, 1983).

Activity by these "corporations" in pursuit of community interests began developing the potential for public arenas to operate as surrogates for the good ruler. This potential remained, waiting to be tapped as the British withdrew from an active role in popular culture. By the end of the nineteenth century public arenas had changed rather dramatically, shaping collective expressions of community values to fit the different reality of an imperial state interested only in representational community participation. We have traced, through processual analysis, the changed meaning infused in the symbolic behavior of public arenas around the turn of the century. From these changes came a construction of community identity that possessed the potential to move beyond the locality, to invoke symbols deemed significant in much of the subcontinent. This basic pattern seems to have held throughout much of British India, although provincial policies varied from place to place in important ways. Nevertheless, the public arena—a symbolically rich world informed by popular culture and consisting of collective activities on behalf of group interests—emerged throughout the British Raj in contradistinction to imperial institutions. That structural similarity, or artifact, united British India. Public arena activities differed, however, because they were shaped in each place by the interaction of specific provincial policies and the local content of popular culture.

Another similar artifact uniting the subcontinent was the role played by the symbolic language developed in U.P. This language, defining a reformist Muslim community, proved particularly effective in areas (often cities) in which resided clusters of ashraf Muslims conversant with Urdu and related culture. Even given the widespread dispersion of these two artifacts, to what extent can we find evidence that similar processes—creating from public arenas an ideology around constructions of community—occurred elsewhere? Perhaps the area most akin to U.P. is Bombay, at least in its urbanness and its concentration of ashraf Muslims. Given these resemblances, it is instructive to note important differences in developments there. In Bombay religion-focused activities in public arenas became circumscribed through government interference. Other constituent elements of identity emerged instead, perhaps because they could be fostered more easily around the smaller units within which the British administration permitted collective activities to occur.[14] Those who participated in "Hindu" public ceremonials, for

14. S. M. Edwardes, *The Bombay City Police: A Historical Sketch, 1672–1916* (London: Oxford University Press, 1923).

instance, tended to remain divided along linguistic lines that distinguished speakers of Marathi from those who spoke Gujarati.[15] Similarly, after 1911 the government confined Muharram observances within individual *muḥalla*s, discouraging efforts to forge identities shared by the myriad groups of Muslims residing in Bombay. In this way the range of actors normally encouraged by public arena participation contracted. So did the actors' frame of reference: few activities in Bombay reached beyond the *muḥalla*.[16] Elite leaders with citywide references remained in control, placing their highest priority on participation in state institutions.[17]

Thus, the interaction in Bombay of state interference in public arenas and limited ceremonial statements of religious community yielded very different results from community definition in U.P. A sense of community could not reach beyond the smaller boundaries of neighborhood and caste, and competition in Bombay came to be expressed through these smaller group boundaries. As a consequence, collective activities, when they emerged, referred not to an overarching identity expressed in religious terms but instead to linguistic identities and, ultimately, the Brahmin–non-Brahmin split. This is not to say that religious *modes* were unimportant, only that religious *identities* did not emerge as the most salient form of community. Indeed, South Asian popular devotionalism, common to the process of community identity formation, played a key role in Bombay, as scholarship on Mahar conversions to Buddhism, and even on the Devi movement among Adivasis, attests.[18] And of the non-Brahmin movement developed in the nineteenth century, Rosalind O'Hanlon notes that it did not reflect traditional caste antagonisms but was rooted "in the loyalties, symbols, and identities that were central to traditional popular culture."[19]

15. Richard Cashman, "The Political Recruitment of God Ganapati," *Indian Economic and Social History Review* 7, no. 3 (September 1970).
16. Raj Chandavarkar, "Workers' Politics and the Mill in Bombay Between the Wars," *Modern Asian Studies* 15, no. 3 (1981): 603–47.
17. See Jim Masselos's work, especially "Change and Custom in the Format of the Bombay Mohurram," *South Asia*, n.s., 5, no. 2 (1982): 47–67; and Sandria B. Freitag, "Roots of Muslim Separatism in South Asia," in Edmund Burke III and Ira A. Lapidus, eds., *Islam, Politics, and Social Movements* (Berkeley and Los Angeles: University of California Press, 1988). See also Ravindar Kumar, "The Bombay Textile Strike, 1919," *Indian Economic and Social History Review* 8, no. 1 (Mar. 1971): 17, and "From Swaraj to Purnja Swaraj: Nationalist Politics in the City of Bombay, 1920–32," in D. A. Low, ed., *Congress and the Raj: Facets of the Indian Struggle, 1917–47* (Columbia, Mo.: South Asia Books, 1977).
18. See Jayashree B. Gokhale, "The Sociopolitical Effects of Ideological Change: The Buddhist Conversion of Maharashtrian Untouchables," *Journal of Asian Studies* 45, no. 2 (February 1986): 269–92, and David Hardiman, *The Coming of the Devi: Adivisi Assertion in Western India* (Delhi: Oxford University Press, 1987).
19. Rosalind O'Hanlon, *Caste, Conflict and Ideology: Mahatma Jotivao Phule and*

Although the interaction of government interference and other forms of community ideology created a different pattern in Bombay, one basic similarity of process did exist: the underlying connection between the community invoked and the symbolic content of popular culture in the area. This connection also characterized South Indian patterns, which again shaped the relationship of local communities to the state. In the south, as in Bombay, communities became defined along the boundaries lines of the Brahmin–non-Brahmin schism. In part this seems to relate, once again, to the state structure. The dominant role played by Brahmins, first in Hindu state administrations and then under the British, as well as the inability of Muslim rulers to foster the paradigm of the good Islamic ruler in Maharashtra and the south, may go far to explain the differences with U.P. in general and the development of the Brahmin–non-Brahmin schism in particular.[20] Moreover, Muslims living in the south had emerged not as literate administrators replicating courtly culture but as local converts or offspring of traders.[21] Work on communities of converts suggests that, as in rural Bengal, the Islam of this minority often revolved around mediatory figures, particularly goddesses.[22]

Once again the shared popular culture of devotional religion provided the focus for collective activities.[23] Indeed, the central role played by the temple in ordering south Indian life—and the close connections between Brahmins and temple ceremony—may tell us much about the

Low Caste Protest in Nineteenth Century Western India (Cambridge: Cambridge University Press, 1985), p. 307. O'Hanlon's continuing investigations of popular culture promise to correct the overemphasis in *Caste, Conflict and Ideology* on the intellectual efforts of elite leadership to shape the public arena ideology of non-Brahminism.

20. See Susan Bayly, "Hindu Kingship and the Origin of Community: Religion, State and Society in Kerala, 1750–1850," *Modern Asian Studies* 18, no. 2 (Apr. 1984): 177–213. The presence of the Brahmin–non-Brahmin split may also relate to a social structure in which there were few groups to fill the middle levels of the ritual hierarchy.

21. See Mattison Mines, "Social Stratification Among Muslim Tamils," in Imtiaz Ahmad, ed., *Caste and Social Stratification Among the Muslims* (New Delhi: Manohar, 1973); Kenneth McPherson, "The Muslims of Madras and Calcutta: Agitational Politics in the Early '20s," *South Asia* 5 (December 1975), and "The Social Background and Politics of the Muslims of Tamil Nad, 1901–37," *Indian Economic and Social History Review* 6, no. 4 (Dec. 1969): 381–402; Stephen Dale, "The Islamic Frontier in Southwest India," *Modern Asian Studies* 11, no. 1 (Feb. 1977): 41–55, *Islamic Society on the South Asian Frontier: The Mappilas of Malabar, 1498–1922* (Oxford: Clarendon Press, 1980), and "The Mappilah Outbreaks: Ideology and Social Conflict," *Journal of Asian Studies* 35 (1975); and Robert Hardgrave, Jr., "The Mappila Rebellion, 1921: Peasant Revolt in Malabar," *Modern Asian Studies* 11, no. 1 (Feb. 1977): 57–100.

22. Susan Bayly, "Islam in Southern India: 'Purist' or 'Syncretic'?" paper presented to the Conference on Islam in South Asian Society, Ohio State University, April 1983.

23. For a suggestion of the importance of religious devotionalism in providing the framing worldview of popular culture, as exemplified in the folktale, see Stuart H. Blackburn, "Domesticating the Cosmos: History and Structure in a Folktale from India," *Journal of Asian Studies* 45, no. 3 (May 1986): 527–44.

particular ideologies of community that developed there, including the Brahmin–non-Brahmin split.[24] In Madurai, for instance, the seventeenth-century ruler Tirumala Nayak deliberately united two temple festivals to signify the unity behind two myths and to address the "real social antagonism" between "the local low-caste village people and cults, and the more classical high-caste city people and castes." All became united through their positive relationships with the goddess Minakshi, who is "the main focus of devotional attention."[25]

In the south, then, public arenas similar to U.P. in nature, if not in ceremonial (and, thus, ideological) content, seem to have emerged. Perhaps what most distinguished the community-building materials in U.P. from those in Bombay and the south was the relative linguistic compatibility of the peoples inhabiting the Gangetic plain and foothills; what would serve to define groups of them against each other would not be their vernacular languages but high-culture languages associated with religious identities.[26] Nevertheless, the underlying processes by which community could be defined through collective activity in public arenas seem to be remarkably similar in the south and in U.P.

U.P., Bombay, south India: these were all areas in which Muslims functioned as minority communities. What about the regions in which Muslims formed a majority (and hence represented a greater range of classes in the local population)? Would religion, rather than language or caste, emerge as the primary ideological vehicle there? The Punjab drew from much the same north Indian historical experience as U.P., creating an urbanized Indo-Islamic culture that resulted from its experience as part of the Mughal Empire. Areas of highest Muslim density, however, tended to be rural in the Punjab. A devotional style of Islam, focused on rural shrines, predominated in these areas. The Punjabi pattern was complicated by the fact that the *sajjāda nishīns* of these rural shrines also functioned as large landlords. Such landlords dominated local agrarian society. This fact proved to be the central issue, because the region was profoundly affected by the predilection of the provincial government for

---

24. See articles in *Indian Economic and Social History Review* 14, no. 1 (Jan.-Mar. 1977), Special Number on South Indian Temples, ed. Burton Stein.

25. Dennis Hudson, "Siva, Minaksi, Visnu—Reflections on a Popular Myth in Madurai," *Indian Economic and Social History Review* 14, no. 1 (Jan.-Mar. 1977): 115.

26. See the distinction between these two categories of language, and the potential for community delineation attached to high-culture languages, in Christopher King, "Forging a New Linguistic Identity," in Sandria B. Freitag, ed., *Culture and Power in Banaras: Community, Performance, and Environment, 1800–1980* (Berkeley and Los Angeles: University of California Press, 1989).

regarding only "agricultural tribes" as legitimate.[27] Provincial policies thus supported agrarian patterns rather than urban ones.

Against this rural pattern of mediation and devotionalism, urban Muslim reformists, ultimately supported by the Muslim League, attempted to juxtapose their vision of Islam, which was focused on individuals and their relationship to an Islamic community and was represented by the urban mosque.[28] Reformist agitation certainly motivated Muslims to opt for Pakistan as a putative Islamic state. But the cultural emphasis on mediation by the shrines and the landlords has remained to the present.[29] (Indeed, Pakistan, the independent nation shaped by this mediatory style, seems never to have reconciled the state's reliance on large landholders in the countryside with the reformist paradigm in the cities.) The critical elements in shaping collective culture in the Punjab thus related to the imperial state's actions in the province and to the particular nature of local popular culture, especially its emphasis on devotional religion and mediation.

Ideological continuity connected Bengal to U.P., as activists borrowed from U.P. the fully developed reformist ideology of "Islam in danger." Expressed through, and symbolized by, the Urdu culture elaborated in north Indian *qaṣbas*, the imported ideology took hold among Urdu speakers in Calcutta. This urban elite preached reformism in the countryside, emphasizing the Muslim identity shared by city and country dweller. But the Islam of Bengal, like that of the Punjab, emphasized a devotional, mediatory style exemplified by rural shrines. Indeed, the shared Bengali culture of the countryside had at its heart a rural devotional style common to Hindu and Muslim. The critical importance of this shared popular culture in shaping a sense of community in Bengal cannot be overstated.

27. David Gilmartin, "The Political Legacy of the Land Alienation Act in Twentieth Century Punjab," a paper presented to the Western Conference of the Association of Asian Studies, Tucson, 1978.

28. This analytical contrast between the values and worldviews represented by mosque and shrine is David Gilmartin's; see his *Empire and Islam* (Berkeley and Los Angeles: University of California Press, 1988).

29. For other work on the Punjab, see David Gilmartin, "Customary Law and Shari'at in British Punjab," in Katherine Ewing, ed., *Shari'at and Ambiguity in South Asian Islam* (Berkeley and Los Angeles: University of California Press, 1988), and "Religious Leadership and the Pakistan Movement in the Punjab," *Modern Asian Studies* 13, no. 3 (July 1979): 485–517. See also N. Gerald Barrier, "The Punjab Government and Communal Politics, 1870–1908," *Journal of Asian Studies* 27, no. 3 (May 1978); and Kenneth W. Jones, "Communalism in the Punjab: The Arya Samaj Contribution," *Journal of Asian Studies* 28, no. 1 (Nov. 1968): 39–54, and "Ham Hindu Nahin," *Journal of Asian Studies* 33, no. 3 (May 1974): 457–75.

At issue, ultimately, in Bengal was the nature of collective cultural expressions; these, in turn, related directly to definitions of the majority community. To the extent that that majority was defined as the rural clients of a (predominantly Hindu) Bhadralok class of urbanized land-lords,[30] its exponents opted for an integrative Bengali culture that was expressed through the products of both a high Bengali culture (self-consciously shaped during a "Renaissance") and shared devotional religious activity organized around shrine and goddess worship. To the extent that the majority was defined, instead, on the basis of shared Islamicness that also focused on peasant status, a very different kind of majority emerged.

Imperial policies pursued in the region provided the key to which definition of "majority" would prevail. Agitation around the Bengal partition of 1905 encouraged the development of a new political style among the Bhadralok that included terrorism and that distinguished itself from Muslim and rural values and interests. Though Rajat Ray and Sumit Sarkar may debate whether partition agitation or other, economic causes supplied the chief impetus for these developments, they would agree that the result was an increasingly obvious division be-tween urban and rural worlds and between those who identified them-selves as "Hindu" and those who called themselves "Muslim."[31] Look-ing at the countryside, Ray argues that rural peasant leadership seized the initiative at this point and—through the establishment of *anjuman*s to sponsor reformist sermons, schooling, and charitable activities to support Islamic causes even overseas—fostered "sectional patrio-tism."[32] Focusing more on the urban areas, Sarkar delineates the process by which this division became elaborated in the 1920s into a movement in which the "masses outstripp[ed] their leaders" and where the "specific features and collective mentalities" of the "subaltern

30. See S. N. Mukherjee, "Class, Caste and Politics in Calcutta, 1815–38," in Edmund Leach and S. N. Mukherjee, eds., *Elites in South Asia* (Cambridge: Cambridge University Press, 1970).
31. See Nirad Chaudhuri, *Autobiography of an Unknown Indian* (New York: Macmillan, 1951), and John McLane, "The 1905 Partition of Bengal and the New Communalism," in Alexander Lipski, ed., *Bengal East and West,* Michigan State Univer-sity Occasional Paper no. 13 (East Lansing, Mich.: Michigan State University, 1970).
32. Rajat Kanta Ray, *Social Conflict and Political Unrest in Bengal, 1875–1927* (Delhi: Oxford University Press, 1984). Unfortunately, the heart of Ray's argument rests on very traditional political history assumptions that "the emergence of sectional patriot-ism—especially Muslim separatism—was a process secondary to, and dependent on, the rise of nationalism. . . . Communalism was thus a secondary force set in motion by the confrontation of imperialism with nationalism" (pp. 3–4). The drawbacks to this approach have been discussed in detail in the Introduction to Part I.

groups" involved became sharply defined in distinction to "the domain of the elite politicians."[33] Popular notions began to define community not by a shared Bengali culture but by religious identity.

Through the early twentieth century, then, the kind of public arenas that developed, and the scope they came to possess, differed in the various cultural regions ruled by the British. Though the process was similar throughout the subcontinent (even where stunted, as in Bombay), the particular ideological content of community identity varied. Three different ideologies of community in South Asia proved sufficiently encompassing to move from localized referents to larger constructions (and, once politicized, to move back again to the locality): religious identity, linguistic affinities, and the caste-oriented division of "Brahman" and "non-Brahman." These identities often overlapped— language often carried a burden for religious identity, and religious devotionalism often served as the shared experience for "community" defined along caste boundary lines. Thus, the ideological content, though different, nevertheless operated according to a shared dynamic centered in popular culture. This dynamic made it possible, in the 1920s and 1930s, for regions with very disparate cultural patterns to coalesce around new ideologies. If we take communalism in this context to mean a politicized community activism focused on any group smaller than the emerging postimperial nation, we see two broad new ideologies developing in this period: communalism and nationalism.

Communalism, Nationalism, and the Postimperial State

By the turn of the century, activities in public arenas throughout the subcontinent had become even more effective, in part because of access to new communications networks (the railroads and a burgeoning newspaper industry), new organizing methods (such as subscription

---

33. Sumit Sarkar, "The Conditions and Nature of Subaltern Militancy: Bengal from Swadeshi to Non-Cooperation, c. 1905–22," in Ranajit Guha, ed., *Subaltern Studies*, vol. 3 (Delhi: Oxford University Press, 1984), p. 272. See also his "Hindu-Muslim Relations in Swadeshi Bengal, 1907–08," *Indian Economic and Social History Review* 9, no. 2 (June 1972): 161–216; Shila Sen, *Muslim Politics in Bengal 1937–47* (New Delhi: Impex India, 1976); and John Broomfield, "The Social and Institutional Bases of Politics in Bengal, 1906–47," in Rachel Van M. Baumer, ed., *Aspects of Bengali History and Society* (Honolulu: University Press of Hawaii, 1975). It is interesting that Dipesh Chakrabarty's work on the mill workers of Calcutta has as much to say about the up-country values and worldviews these workers brought with them as it does about Calcutta; see *Communal Riots and Labour: Bengal's Jute Mill Hands in the 1890s*, Centre for Studies in the Social Sciences, Occasional Paper no. 11, (Calcutta, 1976), and "Trade Unions in a Hierarchical Culture: The Jute Workers of Calcutta, 1920–50," in Guha, ed., *Subaltern Studies*, vol. 3.

campaigns to support voluntary organizations), and expanded political effectiveness (gained through protests and other organized activities). Although these support mechanisms, and the resulting popular activism, have generally been attributed to the Westernization or modernization of Indian public life, we have argued here that the significance of these elements related instead to their ability to nourish the special world of public arenas. This nourishment resulted in the dramatic development of a new vocabulary for expressing the ties felt among members of particular groups. Much of that vocabulary emerged from intragroup rivalries and debates over proper behavior (particularly relating to religious ritual) as practiced by ordinary people. These debates imbued with new importance personal acts that constituted statements of identity. In this way the style of an individual's personal practice took on a political significance it had never had before. The symbolic rhetoric forged around personal actions consequently coalesced into a public arena ideology capable of reaching beyond the locality.

Ideology, organization, mobilization: by the 1920s public arena activities had developed and shaped all three as potent forces. Those identifying themselves as "Hindus" or "Muslims" or "non-Brahmins" experienced a similar process as their ideologies evolved. Though the timing and tenor of the basic process by which the ideologies had developed differed, the techniques responsible for communicating them were shared by all activists throughout India. Because they were rooted in public arena activities, the methods of mobilizing and organizing, as well as the shared values and symbols that constituted the ideologies, bore little relation to the imperial state or its institutions. Instead, they implicitly challenged the very structure of the state by presenting an alternative ideology based in an alternative arena of activity that posited a very different relationship between nascent state and community.

Public arenas thus constituted a world of great significance. Even those Indians concerned with challenging the imperial regime within the structure set by state institutions could not resist the allure of public arenas and their potential for mass mobilization. Their very nature, resembling the world of the public sphere developed in the European nation-state, made public arenas a potent force for such activists. Moreover, public arena activities legitimated actions that, because they were based on popular culture and shared indigenous values, exerted a tremendous appeal. Indeed, this alternate world provided a moral authority of leadership expressed in a venue and rhetoric with which British administrators could not compete. As a consequence, the 1920s and 1930s are marked particularly by the attempt to realign public arenas and state structures, not only as a reflection of a previous indigenous pattern, but also as a world that could be inhabited only by Indians. However, to demonstrate effectiveness in this realigned world, Indian activists had to show that the symbols and causes valued in public arenas could be protected by the state.

The relationship between the nationalist movement's vision of a new Indian-controlled state and public arena values thus proved critical. We have paid close attention to the European model of the nation-state because nationalist politicians assumed that this model did, indeed, bring together the state and public arena activity by uniting participants as members of the nation. But just how closely did South Asian "nationalism" resemble its western European forebearer? The question is critical, because what really linked Indians together might be more accurately characterized as anti-imperialism than nationalism. That is, securing mass support proved easier when uniting people in opposition to a foreign "Other," than when unifying them in a single construction of community based on the western concept of nation. The movement that combined NonCooperation and Khilafat demonstrated both the potential of anti-imperialism as a shared ideology and its limitations, for the local reinterpretations of NonCooperation included the Mappila uprisings, the rural attacks of Chauri Chaura, and the urban demonstrations against the empire.

Like communalism, anti-imperialism possessed reservoirs of extralocal symbols and actions that infused personal choice with political significance. But to translate the elite issues that informed anti-imperialism into a true "nationalism" that reflected more broadly based popular concerns, activists had to turn to public arenas. Previously M. K. Gandhi has been credited with superhuman abilities for accomplishing this goal. Recent scholarship on Gandhi's thought and career, however, has suggested rather different implications and contradictions in Gandhi's role in popularizing "nationalism." Partha Chatterjee argues cogently that Gandhi's theories, in fact, constituted "a fundamental critique of the entire ediface of bourgeois society." Rather than encourage Indians to pursue for themselves the model of a participatory public sphere, Gandhi urged them to reject this model: "As a political ideal therefore Gandhi counterposes against the system of representative government an undivided concept of popular sovereignty where the community is self-regulating and political power is dissolved into the collective moral will."[34] That is, Gandhi's rhetoric recalled the underly-

34. Partha Chatterjee, "Gandhi and the Critique of Civil Society," in Guha, ed., *Subaltern Studies*, vol. 3, pp. 164, 162–63.

ing ties of public arenas, not those of the institutions of the imperial state. We would argue, however, that this was less the product of Gandhi's genius and more the reflection of values held by participants in public arenas. Just as Peter Worsley once noted that the charismatic leader is as much shaped by his followers as shaper of his movement,[35] so we would place the emphasis here on how Gandhi's message was reworked by his listeners to make sense of it in their own terms. And their terms had been shaped by experiences in public arenas.

How did public arenas shape a new kind of "nationalism"? By invoking the symbolic demeanor and rhetoric common to popular devotionalism, Gandhi tapped into an ideological reservoir typical of South Asia, not of western Europe. Shahid Amin traces the implications of this strategy through local reactions in 1921–1922 to Gandhi's appearance in Gorakhpur. Most important, Amin's analysis suggests that contrary even to Gandhi's intentions, popular reinterpretations of his message shaped it in ways peculiarly apposite to popular values.[36] Like the reinterpretation of Cow Protection ideology by Bhojpuris to fit the parochial concerns of the countryside in 1893, this reshaping of Gandhian rhetoric made it both recognizable (hence accessible) and significantly localized in its referents. Amin notes that of the six points Gandhi urged on his listeners, Gorakhpur kisans selected and conflated two of these to formulate a message appropriate to their own purposes: the Mahatma's "true followers" would "stop gambling, ganja-smoking, drinking and whoring"; this would lead to swaraj, which was imminent.[37] These messages became legitimized by rumors of supernatural occurrences that placed them firmly within the popular worldview. Thus, while ostensibly conveying a nationalist message that critiqued the basis of Western civilization, Gandhi's communications were appropriated by popular audiences. To see the significance in this translation of nationalist rhetoric, one need not subscribe to the Subalternist school's interpretation that it provided an ideology enabling "the political appropriation of the subaltern classes by a bourgeoisie aspiring for hegemony in the new nation-state."[38] Instead, we may find here evidence that popularly held values and worldviews could translate "na-

35. Peter Worsley, *The Trumpet Shall Sound,* 2d ed. (New York: Schocken, 1968), introduction to second augmented edition.

36. Shahid Amin, "Gandhi as Mahatma: Gorakhpur District, Eastern UP, 1921–22," in Guha, ed., *Subaltern Studies,* vol. 3, pp. 1–61. See also Hardiman, *The Coming of the Devi,* for discussion of a similar phenomenon among the adivasis.

37. Amin, "Gandhi as Mahatma," p. 22.

38. Chatterjee, "Gandhi and the Critique," p. 176.

tionalism" into an ideology made familiar in public arenas—the ideology of community.

But translated into locally significant terms, invocations of "community" possessed various meanings. In the Bhojpuri, Bengali, and south Indian countryside, it took the form of antilandlord and other agrarian class-based identities, as demonstrated in the Peasant Sabhas of the 1920s and the Mappila uprisings (a potential, we might note, that Gandhi worked hard to defuse). In the cities of U.P., the Punjab, and Bengal, "community" more often translated into the identities connected to religion. In the south and in western India, it became non-Brahminism. For many, then, politicization of nation-as-community led not to nationalism but to perceptions of a profound separation between one's own community and an indigenous "Other," with whom one's group competed for finite quantities of power and influence.

What marked the 1920s, therefore, were simultaneous efforts by two very different kinds of activists. On the one hand, those interested in popularizing nationalism attempted to translate a national-level ideology into locally meaningful terms. On the other hand, those interested in mobilizing around community issues attempted to translate local notions of community into a national-level ideology. Superficially it appeared that these twin goals could be accomplished by linking the emerging ideologies, by aligning state structures and public arenas. In this way the limitations imposed by the British Raj could be circumvented. By using community as a focal point but infusing it with the European meaning of "nation," activists hoped to emphasize the shared characteristics of the two ideologies, communalism and nationalism.

But these shared characteristics masked the very different intent of those interested in nationalism and those concerned with state support for community values. This inherent difference in emphasis inevitably emerged when leaders solicited public support. For "community" in popular culture too often drew its boundaries around a smaller group than would "nation." Indeed, the effort to make an all-India rhetoric familiar by tying it to local concerns carried within it important contradictions. In the politicized context of the 1920s and 1930s, the constructed community most north Indians chose was not "the nation" but a communally identified subgroup.

By the 1930s this development may have been inevitable, for the expectations that had been raised by nationalist activity in public arenas could not be met. For nationalists this "community" meant merely that state decisions would be made by Indians, not by representatives of the

British Empire. But to most supporters it suggested much more—that the nature of those decisions would be quite different; that informed by collective opinion, the state would actively pursue and protect community interests; even that once again the state would become a prime actor in public arenas.

The basic conundrum presented by these differing assumptions about the new relationship to be forged between state and community revolved around the position of minority communities within the realm. That is, the relationship between community and state could be finessed wherever "nation" could be equated with the community of the majority of those residing within it—wherever "nation" could be construed around the culture of the group. Finessing the problem, however, did not solve it, as recent secessionist movements in both India and Pakistan attest.

Indeed, Philip Oldenburg sketches the two notions of Pakistan held, respectively, by *muhajir*s (refugees from India) and Bengalis before 1971. It will not surprise us to learn that for *muhajir*s Pakistan represented a state that was to serve as a reference point for all Muslims in the subcontinent, in which Indo-Islamic culture would be fostered and protected (especially through the establishment of Urdu as the state language). This viewpoint was a logical extension of the public arena rhetoric on behalf of Muslim community developed particularly in U.P., an area always considered outside the likely borders of a Pakistan. Nor should it surprise us that the Bengali vision of Pakistan focused instead on the working of relational alliances that would enable Muslims to escape domination by a Hindu elite. Most telling is Oldenburg's analysis of language conflict at the heart of the dispute between East and West Pakistan. For *muhajir*s Urdu represented, in the words of Jinnah, "a language that has been nurtured by a hundred million Muslims of this subcontinent . . . and above all, a language which, more than any other *provincial language*, embodies the best that is in Islamic culture and Muslim tradition and is nearest to the language used in other Islamic countries." Bengali Muslims, however, did not want to trade Hindu dominance for north Indian dominance. They considered that use of their provincial tongue ensured their equal participation in the state, placing them at one remove from the status of disadvantaged minority.[39] When these two positions proved irreconcilable, once again

39. Jinnah is quoted in Philip Oldenburg, " 'A Place Insufficiently Imagined': Language, Belief, and the Pakistan Crisis of 1971," *Journal of Asian Studies* 44, no. 4 (1985): 716 (emphasis added). But Jinnah was speaking to an audience that had long struggled with the integration of Islam and Bengali culture. It is telling in this context to remember

the problem of the relationship of the state to the minority community was solved through geographic separation and the creation of the new nation-state of Bangladesh. That Pakistan continues to face separatist movements expressed through regional and linguistic identities, and posed in opposition to reformist Islam and Urdu, is telling for our analysis.

Similar evidence for India suggests that the confounding of nationalism and communalism has shaped in profound ways the postimperial Indian state. Indeed, events in the last decade indicate two related developments, both of which result from the fact that, in India, the importance attributed through popular culture to religious identity has been fostered especially by the increasing political dominance of a cultural elite embracing what we have called "Hindu merchant" values. Hindu merchant culture, important here for the auspiciousness it attributed to forms of charity and social action that supported the ceremonial world of public arenas, also provided an indigenous rationale for the elaboration of the ritual world that resulted from its separation from the state.

The conflation of Hindu merchant values and majority community interests has led to state support of reformism in general and Hindu reformism in particular. This support has done more than encourage communalism; it has also short-circuited the role of public arenas in bringing together elite and lower-class participants into overlapping and similar exercises. Efforts to constrain collective behavior within elite values led to a kind of cultural imperialism pursued by the elite against the lower classes. We have characterized this process as a type of "reformism," whose implications for independent India have yet to be investigated sufficiently by scholars. The new national elite proved generally unsuccessful in sanitizing popular culture activities in the 1930s and 1940s and therefore withdrew from them, to a large extent. Instead, they began to create (as had the British before them) new state rituals with a national referent. In independent India, then, public arenas have increasingly become a realm occupied almost solely by the lower classes.

---

that in the late nineteenth century Bengali reformist preachers, attempting to reach rural Muslims through printed media, had had to create "a curious hybrid [language] called Mussalmani or Islami Bengali, which made indiscriminate use of Arabic, Persian, and Urdu words" because they were dissatisfied with Bengali for this purpose (Rafiuddin Ahmed, *The Bengal Muslims, 1871–1906: A Quest for Identity* [Delhi: Oxford University Press, 1981], p. 724).

Thus, the relationship between community and state in independent India continues to be a significant issue, one that still turns on the legacy of the imperial state: a separation of public arenas and state institutions. But, ironically, the key element in the postimperial state has been the result of the reluctance of all actors to establish an equal distance between the state and each of its constituent communities, and of the independent state to serve, as had the traditional ruler, to unite its constituent communities within one common world. As N. C. Saxena has put it, full participation by minorities could be incorporated only if the various communities "negotiated" under a regime that, significantly, was "not identified, in the eyes of people, with any particular religious or linguistic group."[40] That is, Saxena has called for a society in which the public opinion of the public sphere would be equally accessible to all and could therefore exert a collective pressure on the structures of the state. It is this possibility that was forfeited in the 1930s. Once the regime, under the guidance of nationalist politicians, began to support the values of the Hindu majority and the reformist elite, public arenas could no longer unify majority and minority communities, elite and mass interests.

The implications of these developments affected both minority communities and the lower classes in independent India. Between the limitations imposed by imperialism and Hindu "corporations," few alternatives remained for minority communities. Those whose population was small had to be content with a return to the strategy of elaborating and enacting community within public arenas, at one remove from the power of the state. For those with sufficient population and political authority, the alternative became a demand for separate territory in which they might constitute the majority. For the lower classes today, tension remains between identifying with "the nation," as enunciated primarily in elite cultural terms, and identifying with the collective activities of ceremony and violence expressed through the long tradition embodied in public arenas. The varying definitions of "community" in the area now known as Bangladesh, as well as the contemporary demands of Sikhs, Adivasis, and others, display the complex legacy of the developments studied here.

40. N. C. Saxena, "Historiography of Communalism in India," in Mushirul Hasan, ed., *Communal and Pan-Islamic Trends in Colonial India* (New Delhi: Manohar, 1981), p. 309.

Appendix: Chronology of Political Events in U.P. and the British Empire

1555	Humayan recovers Delhi; Mughal Empire reestablished.
1556	Accession of Akbar.
1600	Charter of incorporation granted to English East India Company.
1605–1627	Reign of Jahangir.
1627–1658	Reign of Shah Jahan.
1651	Foundation of East India Company's factory at Hugli (Bengal).
1658–1707	Reign of Aurangzeb (after his death his successors are unable to prevent the gradual emergence of regional successor states).
1720s	Establishment of a successor state in Awadh.
1750s	Rajas of Banaras consolidate their hold and establish a small successor state in the Gangetic plain.
1757	Battle of Plassey; East India Company begins to rule over Bengal.
1794	Raja of Banaras signs an agreement with East India Company and loses direct control over his territory.
1809–1810	House Tax Protest, centered in Banaras.
1811	Riot in Banaras over sacred spaces.
1818	British defeat of Maratha successor state in Western India.
1833	Parliament deprives East India Company of all commercial functions; EIC still serves as ruler of India with indirect authority from Parliament.
1835	Macaulay's Minute on Education: EIC should concentrate on advanced instruction, which should be in English, Western literature, science, and philosophy; education strategy is designed to create Indian intermediaries to fill lower-level administrative positions; English is substituted for Persian as the primary language of government and diplomacy.

1850s   Series of clashes around urban ceremonies in areas previously dominated by Indo-Persian elite; these clashes are repeated in the 1870s, but on a larger scale and with greater frequency.

1854   Wood's Despatch expands and unifies Macaulay's theory of education to all levels of schooling (primary and secondary grades as well as advanced level); creates a Department of Public Instruction; provides support to private and missionary schools through grants and subsidies; and introduces a standardized examination system based on the British model.

1856   East India Company deposes the Nawab of Awadh and attempts to rule Awadh directly.

1857–1858   Mutiny/Revolt: mutiny of sepoys (Indian troops) recruited from Awadh leads, in turn, to widespread peasant rebellion in north India.

1858   East India Company rule is replaced by rule of Queen Victoria through viceroy.

1861   Indian Councils Act provides for some Indians to join the bodies of advisors (councils) to the governors of each province.

1870s   Further adjustments to urban power relationships between "corporations" of Hindu merchants and the Indo-Persian elite are expressed through the competition of festivals and other events.

1875   Arya Samaj founded at Bombay; Muhammadan Anglo-Oriental College founded at Aligarh.

1880s   Series of clashes around Hindu ceremonies in north Indian towns pits new Arya Samaj against traditionalist supporters who form Sanatan Dharm Sabhas.

1883–1884   Lord Ripon (Viceroy of India) establishes Local Government Act to provide network of district boards (in countryside) and urban municipal committees: these local governmental agencies are given control of education, sanitation, public works, and health and the authority to levy octroi, terminal, property, and other duties.

1885   Seventy-two Indians gather at Bombay for first session of the Indian National Congress.

1888–1893   Cow Protection movement.

1891   Banaras riot against new waterworks (and other technology).

1905   Partition of the province of Bengal into two administrative units, separating Calcutta from its hinterland; nationalist agitation results; British seen as dividing Hindu from Muslim Bengalis in crass attempt to "divide and rule."

1906   Muslim League is founded.

1909   Morley-Minto reforms (Indian Councils Act of 1909) recognize the principle of election to provincial and governor-general's councils; constituencies are seen as "communities," and Muslims are given "weightage" (more seats than they are entitled to by population): though voting in "general" constituencies with

Hindus, Muslims are to vote also for their own members in separate and wholly Muslim constituencies.

1910s
Civic ceremonial occasions, such as *Rāmlīlā*, begin to blend nationalist symbolism with long-standing religiocultural symbols.

1911
Delhi Durbar is staged by imperial government on occasion of coronation of King George V; partition of Bengal is rescinded; capital of British India is moved from Calcutta to Delhi.

1916
Lucknow Pact between Congress and Muslim League settles on a new constitutional plan that concedes the principle of separate electorates for Muslims but counterbalances the "weightage" given to them in Muslim minority areas with reduced numbers of representatives in majority areas; Muslims no longer to participate in "general" constituencies.

1919
Montague-Chelmsford reforms enlarge provincial legislative councils and stipulate that at least 70 percent of their members be elected representatives; franchise is extended by lowering property qualification; Lucknow Pact provisions are followed for Muslim electorates; "dyarchy" is established, in which law and order, land-revenue administration are reserved for British administrators, while Indian ministers are placed in charge of education, agriculture, public health, local government, etc.

1920
Hindi and the Devanagari script are adopted as the official language in the constitution drawn up by the Indian National Congress, on the grounds of its similarity to all other Indo-Aryan languages and its common use in north India.

1920–1922
Gandhi launches Civil Disobedience campaign (which is suspended after incidences of violence); the policy of non-cooperation is extended to the refusal by Congress to participate in elections designed by Montague-Chelmsford reforms.

1920s
Kisan movements express protest by peasants against landlords' repression, supported by the British imperial system; attempts to link this protest to nationalist movement are undercut by Gandhi and others.

1920–1924
Khilafat movement is launched by Ali brothers; at first it is coordinated with the NonCooperation movement with goal of pressuring the British government to restore Turkey to its pre–World War I status.

1923
Arya Samaj launches *shuddhi* (Hindu reconversion) and *Sangathan* (community defense) movements; Muslims respond, respectively, with *Tanzīm* and *Tablīgh* movements.

1922–1927
Series of staged, relatively small-scale urban riots occurs throughout U.P., pitting Hindus against Muslims.

1927–1929
Simon Commission tours India and proposes in a report in 1930 a new governmental structure; Congress boycotts two series of hearings and issues its own Nehru Report in 1928.

1930–1932	Round Table conferences held in Britain to discuss governance of India; first conference in 1930 is boycotted by Congress.
1930	Muhammad Iqbal proposes a separate state for Indian Muslims.
1930s	Large-scale urban communal riots (both Hindu-Muslim and Sunni-Shi'a) occur in most U.P. cities, including Banaras.
1930–1934	Second nationwide Civil Disobedience movement.
1931	Gandhi-Irwin Pact suspends civil disobedience and boycott of Round Table conferences, and in return all political prisoners are released; Gandhi represents Congress views at the second conference in London; the third conference is again boycotted by Congress, but the general outline of a new governmental structure has been established.
1935	Government of India Act results from Simon Commission and Round Table deliberations: dyarchy is abolished; government structure gives the provinces independence from the central government except for certain specified purposes; franchise is extended, and the principle of direct voting retained; a substantial portion of women is enfranchised (voters number about thirty million); separate electorates and "weightage" are retained—at first these policies apply to Untouchables as well as Muslims, but Gandhi vows to fast to death unless his alternate scheme is accepted; the resulting agreement, known as the Poona Pact, provides a number of seats reserved for the "Depressed Classes" in primary elections only.
1937	First elections are held under Government of India Act of 1935; Congress wins 70 percent of the vote, a majority of the legislative seats in seven of the eleven provinces, and a plurality in one other; to enforce party loyalty, the ministries it forms are Congress-only, admitting no Muslims except Congress members; by ignoring the Muslim League, passing legislation offensive to Muslims (e.g., relating to Cow Protection, Hindi, etc.) and doing little about agrarian reform and labor problems, Congress ministries alienate important segments of the population by 1939.
1940	Muslim League, under President Muhammad Ali Jinnah, demands creation of a sovereign Muslim state.
1942	War Cabinet Mission to India (to win Indian support for the war), led by Cripps, offers dominion status and a loose federatory format that recognizes Muslim League demands of "Pakistan," thus turning concept of Pakistan from bargaining ploy into possibility; Congress rejects the offer, characterizing it as a "postdated check," and demands that Britain "Quit India"; the resulting Quit India Movement consists of campaign of hartals (strikes), which turn to violence.
1945–1946	Elections return two main political parties, Congress and Muslim League, making it no longer possible to ignore League's claim to represent "Muslim" interests.

1947	Under new Governor-General Mountbatten, the Indian Independence Act is passed in July 1947, promising independence and partition of the subcontinent into two independent states; Jinnah characterizes the Muslim state as "moth-eaten" since Pakistan contains only some of the area originally demanded and consists of two unconnected territories—the Muslim-majority areas within Punjab and Bengal (the Bengali border between Pakistan and India follows almost exactly the boundaries of the 1905 partition); extraordinary levels of migration and bloodshed result as Sikhs and Hindus flee Muslim majority areas for India and many Muslims in India try to reach Pakistan.
1948	Gandhi is assassinated in New Delhi; Jinnah dies in Pakistan.
1950s	Territorial reorganization of Indian states follows regional cultural and linguistic lines; Pakistan adopts an Islamic constitution.
1960	Bombay is divided into two states along Gujarati and Marathi linguistic lines.
1963	Official Language Act of 1963 declares Hindi the sole official language of independent India; after protests (especially in the south) the act is amended to restore "recognized" status to English as well; Nagaland is created in the northeast to address Naga tribal demands.
1966	Sikh state of Haryana is created in Punjab (where Sikhs have become majority of population after relocation during partition).
1970s	New wave of communal riots breaks out.
1971	Bangladesh wins war of independence against Pakistan.

Glossary

The words listed below with diacritical marks have been transliterated following Platt's, with the exceptions described in the note on transliteration. Other words listed here and in the text without diacriticals have been found in *Webster's Third,* and hence have been treated as loan words, or could not be found in either source and have been presented as spelled conventionally in works on India.

Ahir	cattle-breeding and cattle-herding caste
Ahl-I Hadith	reformist Muslim sect
Ahrar	Muslim Congress party
Ajlāf (pl)	lower-class Muslim groups
Jilf (sg)	
Akhāṛā	guru-chela form of organization for performance and other groups
ᶜ*Alam*	flag of Husain (or brass replica of flag)
Alim (sg)	Muslim learned in Islamic law
Ulama (pl)	
Anjuman	organization
Arya Samaj	reformist Hindu organization
Ashraf (pl)	cultured, "respectable class" Muslims
Sharif (sg)	
Ashura	tenth day of Muharram
Auqāf (pl)	holdings contributed for the upkeep of religious institutions
Waqf (sg)	

Baniyā	Hindu moneylender or trader
Banjārā	long-distance hauler of grains and other goods
Baqar ᶜīd	observance of the sacrifice of Ishmael by Ibrahim
Barādarī	extended kinship network, "brotherhood"
Barāt	wedding procession
Barelwis	Muslim sect that defended customary practices
Bastī	urban colony, settlement
Bazaar	market area
Bhārat Mata	nationalist term for "Mother India"
Bhārat Milāp	procession, observance of *Rām*'s reunion with his brother *Bhārat* during *Rāmlīlā*
Bhumihar	landowning and aristocratic upper caste
Bilā faṣl	recitation of verses asserting the rightfulness of Ali's immediate succession on the death of Muhammad
Birahā	genre of folk music
Bisātī	lower caste of peddlers
Brahmin	Hindu priestly caste
Budmash	"bad character," urban hoodlum
Chamāhī	ceremony observed six months after Muharram
Chamar	Untouchable leather worker
Chār yārī	recitation of verses (by Sunnis) in praise of all four of the first caliphs
Chaudharī	headman
Chauk	central market
Chaukī	platform
Chaukidar	neighborhood watchman
Chehlum	tazia procession forty days after Ashura
Chela	follower, student
Chuṭkī	handful of rice set aside as contribution
Dacoity	organized banditry involving five or more participants
Dā'ira	tomb of Sufi saint
Dālān	ritual bathing place outside mosque
Dār ash-shīᶜā	land ruled by Shi'as
Dargāh	royal court; shrine or tomb
Dasehra	ten-day Hindu festival originally in honor of the goddess Durga
Deobandi	reformist Muslim sect
Devanagari	alphabet for Hindi based on Sanskrit alphabet
Divali	Hindu festival of lights held in late October
Durbar	official gathering of notables (adopted by the British from the Mughals)
Faqir	holy man

Fatwā (sg)	interpretation of Islamic law issued by a mufti in response to a petitioner's request
Fatāwa(pl)	
Ganj	small market town, base for rise of Hindu "corporations"
Ganpati	Bombay festival organized around the elephant-headed god Ganesh
Ga'ocharan	cow festivals, in which richly ornamented cows are paraded
Ga'orakshiṇi Sabha	Cow Protection Society
Ga'oshālā	cattle pound, cow shelter
Gharānā	organization of musicians
Ghats	steps leading to river's edge
Gosain	mendicant soldier/trader
Guru	teacher, leader
Hadith	sayings, actions of the Prophet
Hajj	Islamic pilgrimage
Hartal	work stoppage, strike
Hawelī	great house, palace
Holi	Hindu spring festival characterized by the throwing of colored water and powders
ᶜĪd	see *ᶜĪd ul-fitr* and *Baqar ᶜĪd*
ᶜĪd ul-fitr	celebration to break the fast at the end of Ramazan
Idgah	grounds set aside for the observance of *ᶜĪd ul-fitr*
Imāmbārā	building in which tazias are stored
Iqrārnāma	written agreement
Jameᶜ Masjid	major mosque of a town (in which Friday prayers are held)
Jāti	subcaste
Jhandā	long-bannered poles used in procession
Julāhā	Muslim weaver group
Juljhulni	festival for Krishna
Kanungo	subordinate revenue official
Karbalā	field traditionally set aside to symbolize the original battlefield of the events commemorated during Muharram
Kathā	exegetical oratory
Kayasth	Hindu scribal and administrative service caste
Khalifa	caliph, a successor to Muhammad as temporal and spiritual head of the Islamic community
Khatri	Hindu scribal and administrative service caste
Kisan Sabha	peasant organization
Kotwal	chief police officer for a city or town

Kotwalee	police station
Lathi	large wooden club
Lathiwala	one who wields a lathi
Madh-i ṣōḥbān	see *chār yārī*
Majālis (pl)	gathering, assembly, especially meetings during Muharram at which the story of Husain's martyrdom is recounted over the course of ten days
Majlis (sg)	
Marsiya	elegiac poetry composed for Muharram
Marwari	Baniyā from Marwar area
Mātam on Fire	Shi'a firewalking ceremony held during Muharram
Maulawī (pl)	learned men
Maulūd	anniversary of Muhammad's birth
Mela	fair
Mīr muḥalla	neighborhood headman
Mufti	interpreter of Islamic Law
Muhajir	Pakistani refugee from India
Muḥalla	neighborhood
Muharram	month during which mourning is observed, particularly by Shi'as, for the death of Husain and his followers
Muḥarrir	clerk
Mujtahid	authoritative interpreter of Shi'i Islamic law (recognized as competent to exercise private judgment in formulating authoritative answers to legal questions)
Munsif	lowest-ranking civil judge
Mushāʿara	gathering for recitation of poetry
Mutʿah	arrangement of temporary marriage among Shi'as
Mutawalli	(business) manager of mosque
Nagari	see Devanagari
Naṭ	barbers; "vagrant" caste
Nautanki	genre of street theater
Nautch	dance performance
Pairākī	swimming fair
Pan	betel leaf
Panchayat	council of elders
Pandri	tax
Pardah	seclusion of women
Pargana	administrative subdivision
Phatakbandi	tax levied by neighborhood to support chaukidars
Pipal	fig tree (sacred)
Pir	Muslim spiritual guide

Prabhāt pherī	nationalist procession
Puja	worship
Qadi (*Qazi*)	judge, law officer
Qaṣba	urban center, marked especially by presence of kotwal and qadi
Qur'an	Islamic scripture as revealed to Muhammad
Qurbānī	sacrifice of kine
Rais	person of authority, a notable
Rajput	military caste of Kshatriya varna
Rām	seventh divine incarnation of Vishnu
Rāmāyan	Hindu epic poem recounting the exploits and adventures of *Rām*
Ramazan	Islamic month of fasting
Rāmcharitmānās	version of *Rāmāyan* composed by Tulsidas in the vernacular, in the sixteenth century
Rāmdāl	army of *Rām*
Rāmlīlā	festival during which events in the life of *Rām* are dramatized (extends from ten to thirty days)
Rāmnaumī	the birth of *Rām,* observed by Vaishnavite Hindus
Ranki	wealthy Muslim traders and dealers in produce, hides, and leather goods
Rāvan	chief of demons, whose subjugation and destruction by *Rām* forms much of the subject of the *Rāmāyan*
Sabha	assembly, society, council
Sabhāpati	superior officer in Cow Protection hierarchy
Sabhāsad	local agent in Cow Protection hierarchy
Sabīl	refreshment stand
Sajjāda nishīn	Sufi pir, or his descendant presiding at the tomb
Sanad	deed or letter having the force of an edict or ordinance
Sanatan Dharm Sabha	traditionalist Hindu organization
Sangaṭhan	Hindu movement for self-defense
Sardārī system	spiritual guide
Shaggird	student
Shaikh	spiritual guide; often used to indicate status because used as title by descendants of Muhammad
Shariᶜa	Islamic law
Sharif	see ashraf
Shi'a (n)	minority sect in Islam; emphasizes belief that Ali should have succeeded Muhammad
Shi'i (adj)	
Shringār	temple renewal ceremony

Shuddhi	Hindu practice, movement providing for reconversion
Sītā	wife of *Rām*
Sunni	majority sect in Islam (from *Sunna,* "community")
Svang	early form of street theater, later called nautanki
Swadeshi	"Buy Indian" economic strategy of nationalists
Swarup	boy actors personating the gods in *Rāmlīlā* enactments
Tabarrā	stylized abuse (by Shi'as) of intervening three caliphs between Muhammad and Ali
Tablīgh	Muslim movement for conversion and reconversion
Tahsildar	subdivisional revenue officer
Talukdar	large landholder
Tanzīm	Muslim movement for self-defense
Taqlid	delegation of authority
Tazia	replica of the tomb of Husain
Taziadar	one who sponsors the construction and parading of a tazia
Teli	Hindu oil-pressing caste
Thakur	term of respect; upper-caste member of Kshatriya varna
Thanadar	subordinate police officer
Tilak	spot of color placed on forehead
Ulama	see alim
Ummat	term used by Muslims to designate the Muslim community
Ustad	teacher
Vakil	lawyer
Varna	four major divisions in caste system
Vishnu	one of principal Hindu deities
Vyas	narrator of the *Rāmcharitmānās*
Waqf	see *auqāf*
Waṣīqadār	pensioner of the East India Company and the ex-royal family of Awadh
Zamindar	small landholder

Bibliography

MANUSCRIPT SOURCES AT THE INDIA OFFICE
LIBRARY AND RECORDS OFFICE, LONDON

General Administration Proceedings for United Provinces [of Agra and Oudh]
General Administration Confidential Proceedings for United Provinces
Judicial (Criminal) Proceedings for North-Western Provinces and Oudh
Public and Judicial Files (series L/P&J/6–8) for United Provinces
[Revenue] Board's Collections for 1812, 1812–1813
Miscellaneous non-U.P. sources: Punjab Board of Revenue; Bombay Confidential Proceedings; European Manuscript Collection

UNPUBLISHED PAPERS AND DISSERTATIONS

Basu, Dilip. "Mallabir: A Calcutta Killer in Action, 1946–50." Unpublished paper.
_____ . "Mallabir: Life History of a Calcutta Killer." Unpublished paper.
Bayly, Susan. "Islam in Southern India: 'Purist' or 'Syncretic'?" Paper presented to the Conference on Islam in South Asian Society, Ohio State University, April 1983.
Blake, Stephen P. "Dar-ul-Khilafat-i-Shahjahanabad: The Padshahi Shahar in Mughal India, 1556–1739." Ph.D. diss., University of Chicago, 1974.
Breckenridge, Carol Appadurai. "Risking Incorporation and Worship in a South Indian Temple." Paper presented to the SSRC/ACLS Workshop on Risk and Uncertainty, Philadelphia, 1977.
Freitag, Sandria B. "Religious Rites and Riots." Ph.D. diss., University of California, Berkeley, 1980.
Gilmartin, David. "Elections and Muslim Community." Paper presented to the Conference on the Political Inheritance of Pakistan, Cambridge University, July 1987.

_____ . "The Political Legacy of the Land Alienation Act in Twentieth-Century Punjab." Paper presented to the Western Conference of the Association of Asian Studies, Tucson, 1978.

_____ . "Tribe, Land, and Religion in the Punjab: Muslim Politics and the Making of Pakistan." Ph.D. diss., University of California, Berkeley, 1979.

Hess, Linda. "The Poet and the People." Revised version of paper presented at University of Washington, Winter 1986.

Hjortshoj, Keith. "Kerbala in Context: A Study of Mohurram in Lucknow, India." Ph.D. diss., Cornell University, 1978.

[India Office.] U.P. Government. *Benaras Affairs, 1788–1810.* (Miscellaneous collection of documents printed and bound by the India Office.)

Jones, Kenneth W. "Sanatan Dharm: Hindu Orthodoxy in Defense of Tradition." Paper presented to the Mid-Western Conference on Asian Affairs, 1978.

King, Christopher R. "The Nagari Pracharini Sabha (Society for the Promotion of the Nagari Script and Language) of Benaras, 1893–1914: A Study of the Social and Political History of the Hindi Language." Ph.D. diss., University of Wisconsin, 1974.

Krishnaswamy, S. "A Riot in Bombay, August 11, 1893: A Study in Hindu-Muslim Relations in Western India During the Late Nineteenth Century." Ph.D. diss., University of Chicago, 1966.

Kumar, Nita. "Popular Culture in Urban India: The Artisans of Banaras, c. 1884–1984." Ph.D. diss., University of Chicago, 1984.

Lambert, Richard D. "Hindu-Muslim Riots." Ph.D. diss., University of Pennsylvania, 1951.

Lutgendorf, Philip. "The Life of a Text: Tulsidas' *Ramcaritmanas* in Performance." Ph.D. diss., University of Chicago, 1987.

Metcalf, Barbara Daly. "Conflict Among Muslims: New Sects, New Strategies, Old Paradigms." Paper delivered to the American Historical Association, 1978.

Oldenburg, Veena Talwar. "Lifestyle as Resistance: The Case of the Courtesans of Lucknow." Paper presented to the American Historical Association, December 1987.

Price, Pamela. "Resources and Rule in Zamindari South India, 1802–1903: Sivaganga and Ramnad as Kingdoms Under the Raj." Ph.D. diss., University of Wisconsin, 1979.

Stoddart, Brian. "The Changing Face of Colonial Administration in South India," 1978. Unpublished paper.

PRINTED SOURCES: OFFICIAL PUBLICATIONS

Archer, Mildred. *Indian Popular Painting in the India Office Library.* London: HMSO, 1977.

Butler, Sir Harcourt. *Oudh Policy—the Policy of Sympathy,* 1906.

Government Resolution on the Cow Disturbances in the Azamgarh District, 1893.

Government Resolution on Famine Relief, 1908.

"A History of the Province of Benares." Part 1. London: India Office, 1873.

Nesfield, John C. *Brief View of the Caste System of the North-Western Provinces.* Allahabad: NWP and O Government Press, 1885.

Nevill, H. R. *District Gazetteers of the United Provinces of Agra and Oudh.* Allahabad: U.P. Government Press, 1901–1911. *Supplements,* 1916.

Reports on the Administration of the United Provinces.

Reports on the Administration of the Police.

Roe, H. R. *Guide to Muhammadan and Hindu Festivals and Fasts in the U.P.* Allahabad: Superintendent, Printing and Stationery, U.P., 1934.

Selections from the Vernacular Newspapers for the North-Western Provinces. United Kingdom. Parliament. C. 63. 1893–1894; Cmd. 3891. 1930–1931.

Wage Census Reports.

PRINTED SOURCES: NEWSPAPERS, PAMPHLETS

The Leader (Allahabad).

The Pioneer (Allahabad).

The Tribune (Lahore).

Ali Khan, Mirza Sajjad. *Why 14,000 Shias Went to Jail?* Lucknow, [1939].

Dar, Pandit Bishan Narayan. *An Appeal to the English Public on Behalf of the Hindus of the North-Western Provinces and Oudh.* Lucknow: G. P. Varma, 1893.

BOOKS AND ARTICLES

Ahmad, Imtiaz, ed. *Family, Kinship, and Marriage Among Muslims in India.* Delhi: Manohar, 1976.

Ahmed, Rafiuddin. *The Bengal Muslims, 1871–1906.* Delhi: Oxford University Press, 1981.

Ali, Mrs. Meer Hassan [Mir Hasan]. *Observations on the Mussalmanns of India,* 1832. Revised and edited by William Crooke, 1917. Delhi: Deep Publications, 1975.

Ali, Mohamed. *My Life: A Fragment; an Autobiographical Sketch,* edited by Afzal Iqbal. Lahore: Sh. M. Ashraf, 1946.

Amin, Shahid. "Gandhi as Mahatma: Gorakhpur District, Eastern UP, 1921–22." In *Subaltern Studies,* edited by Ranajit Guha. Vol. 3, pp. 1–61. Delhi: Oxford University Press, 1984.

Anderson, Benedict. *Imagined Communities: Reflections on the Origin and Spread of Nationalism.* London: Verso, 1983.

Appadurai, Arjun. *Worship and Conflict Under Colonial Rule: A South Indian Case.* Cambridge: Cambridge University Press, 1981.

Ashplant, T. G. "London Working Men's Clubs, 1875–1914." In *Popular Culture and Class Conflict, 1590–1914,* edited by Eileen Yeo and Steven Yeo. Atlantic Highlands, N.J.: Humanities Press, 1981.

Baker, Jean H. "The Ceremonies of Politics: Nineteenth-Century Rituals of National Affirmation." In *A Master's Due: Essays in Honor of David Herbert Donald,* edited by William J. Cooper, Jr., Michael F. Holt, and John McCardell. Baton Rouge: Louisiana State University Press, 1985.

Barnett, Richard B. *North India Between Empires: Awadh, the Mughals and the*

British, 1720–1801. Berkeley and Los Angeles: University of California Press, 1980.

Barrier, N. Gerald. "The Punjab Government and Communal Politics, 1870–1908." *Journal of Asian Studies* 27, no. 3 (May 1978).

———, ed. *Roots of Communal Politics.* Columbia, Mo.: South Asia Books, n.d.

Bayly, C. A. "Indian Merchants in a 'Traditional' Setting: Benares, 1780–1830." In *Imperial Impact: Studies in the Economic History of Africa and India,* edited by C. Dewey and A. G. Hopkins. London: Athlone Press for the Institute of Commonwealth Studies, 1978.

———. *Local Roots of Indian Politics: Allahabad, 1880–1920.* Oxford: Clarendon Press, 1975.

———. "The Prehistory of 'Communalism'? Religious Conflict in India, 1700–1860." *Modern Asian Studies* 19, no. 2 (1985): 177–203.

———. *Rulers, Townsmen and Bazaars.* Cambridge: Cambridge University Press, 1983.

———. "The Small Town and Islamic Gentry in North India: The Case of Kara." In *The City in South Asia,* edited by K. Ballhatchet and J. Harrison. London: University of London, 1982.

Bayly, Susan. "Hindu Kingship and the Origin of Community: Religion, State and Society in Kerala, 1750–1850." *Modern Asian Studies* 18, no. 2 (April 1984): 177–213.

Bhinga, Raja of (Oday Pertap Singh). "The Cow Agitation, or Mutiny-plasm in India." *Nineteenth Century* (April 1894): 667–72.

Blackburn, Stuart H. "Domesticating the Cosmos: History and Structure in a Folktale from India." *Journal of Asian Studies* 45, no. 3 (May 1986): 527–44.

Bohstedt, John. *Riots and Community Politics in England and Wales, 1790–1810.* Cambridge, Mass.: Harvard University Press, 1983.

Brass, Paul R. *Factional Politics in an Indian State.* Berkeley and Los Angeles: University of California Press, 1965.

Brennan, Lance. "A Case of Attempted Segmental Modernization: Rampur State, 1930–39." *Comparative Studies in Society and History* 22, no. 3 (July 1981): 350–81.

———. "The Local Face of Nationalism: Congress Politics in Rohilkhand in the 1920s." *South Asia* 5 (December 1975): 9–19.

———. "Social Change in Rohilkhand, 1801–1833." *Indian Economic and Social History Review* 7 (1970): 443–65.

Brewer, John. *Party Ideology and Popular Politics at the Accession of George III.* Cambridge: Cambridge University Press, 1976.

Broomfield, John. "The Social and Institutional Bases of Politics in Bengal, 1906–47." In *Aspects of Bengali History and Society,* edited by Rachel Van M. Baumer. Honolulu: University Press of Hawaii, 1975.

Burger, A. S. *Opposition in a Dominant-Party System.* Berkeley and Los Angeles: University of California Press, 1969.

Burke, Peter. *Popular Culture in Early Modern Europe.* New York: New York University Press, 1978.

Buyers, William. *Recollections of Northern India.* London: John Snow, 1848.

Calhoun, C. J. "Community: Toward a Variable Conceptualization for Comparative Research." *Social History* 5, no.1 (January 1980): 105–29.

_____ . "Some Problems in Macfarlane's Proposal." *Social History* 3, no. 3 (October 1978): 363–73.

Cashman, Richard. "The Political Recruitment of God Ganapati." *Indian Economic and Social History Review* 7, no. 3 (September 1970): 347–73.

Chakrabarty, Dipesh. *Communal Riots and Labour: Bengal's Jute Mill Hands in the 1890s.* Centre for Studies in the Social Sciences, Occasional Paper no. 11. Calcutta, 1976.

_____ . "Trade Unions in a Hierarchical Culture: The Jute Workers of Calcutta, 1920–50." In *Subaltern Studies,* edited by Ranajit Guha. Vol. 3. Delhi: Oxford University Press, 1984.

Chandavarkar, Raj. "Workers' Politics and the Mill in Bombay Between the Wars." *Modern Asian Studies* 15, no. 3 (1981): 603–47.

Chandra, Bipan. *Communalism in Modern India.* New Delhi: Vikas, Vani Educational Books, 1984.

Chartier, Roger. "Culture as Appropriation: Popular Culture Uses in Early Modern France." In *Understanding Popular Culture,* edited by Steven L. Kaplan. New York: Mouton Publishing, 1984.

Chatterjee, Partha. "Agrarian Relations and Communalism in Bengal, 1926–1935." In *Subaltern Studies,* edited by Ranajit Guha. Vol. 1. Delhi: Oxford University Press, 1982.

_____ . "Gandhi and the Critique of Civil Society." In *Subaltern Studies,* edited by Ranajit Guha. Vol. 3. Delhi: Oxford University Press, 1984.

Chaudhuri, Nirad. *Autobiography of an Unknown Indian.* New York: Macmillan, 1951.

Coccari, Dianne. "Protection and Identity: Banaras Bir Babas as Neighborhood Guardian Dieties." In *Culture and Power in Banaras: Community, Performance, and Environment, 1800–1980,* edited by Sandria B. Freitag. Berkeley and Los Angeles: University of California Press, 1989.

Cohn, Bernard. "The Initial British Impact on India: A Case Study of the Benares Region." *Journal of Asian Studies* 19, no. 4 (1960): 418–31.

_____ . "Representing Authority in Victorian India." In *The Invention of Tradition,* edited by Eric Hobsbawm and Terence Ranger. Cambridge: Cambridge University Press, 1983.

_____ . "The Role of the Gosains in the Economy of Eighteenth and Nineteenth Century Upper India." *Indian Economic and Social History Review* 1, no. 4 (1964): 175–82.

Cole, Juan. *Roots of North Indian Shi'ism in Iran and Iraq: Religion and State in Awadh, 1722–1859.* Berkeley and Los Angeles: University of California Press, 1988.

Crooke, William. *The Popular Religion and Folklore of Northern India.* 2 vols. 1894. New Delhi: Munshiram Naoharlal, 1978.

Crow, Thomas E. *Painters and Public Life in Eighteenth-Century Paris.* New Haven: Yale University Press, 1985.

Dale, Stephen. "The Islamic Frontier in Southwest India: The Shahīd as a Cultural Ideal Among the Mappilas of Malabar." *Modern Asian Studies* 11, no. 1 (February 1977): 41–55.

_____ . *Islamic Society on the South Asian Frontier: The Mappilas of Malabar, 1498–1922.* Oxford: Clarendon Press, 1980.

_____ . "The Mappilah Outbreaks: Ideology and Social Conflict." *Journal of Asian Studies* 35 (1975).

Davies, James C. "Toward a Theory of Revolution." In *Anger, Violence, and Politics: Theories and Research,* edited by Ivo K. Feieraband et al. Englewood Cliffs, N.J.: Prentice-Hall, 1972.

Davis, Natalie Zemon. "The Rites of Violence: Religious Riot in Sixteenth Century France." *Past and Present 59* (May 1973).

Delves, Anthony. "Popular Recreation and Social Conflict in Derby, 1800–1850." In *Popular Culture and Class Conflict, 1590–1914,* edited by Eileen Yeo and Steven Yeo. Atlantic Highlands, N.J.: Humanities Press, 1981.

Dharampal. *Civil Disobedience and Indian Tradition.* Varanasi: Sarva Seva Sangh Prakashan, 1971.

Dumont, Louis. *Homo Hierarachicus: An Essay on the Caste System,* translated by Mark Sainsbury. Chicago: University of Chicago Press, 1970.

Eck, Diana. *Banaras: City of Light.* Princeton: Princeton University Press, 1982.

Edwardes, S. M. *The Bombay City Police: A Historical Sketch, 1672–1916.* London: Oxford University Press, 1923.

Ewing, Katherine, ed. *Sharī'at and Ambiguity in South Asian Islam.* Berkeley and Los Angeles: University of California Press, 1988.

Farquhar, John Nicol. *Modern Religious Movements in India.* New York: Macmillan, 1918.

Fisher, Michael. *Clash Between Cultures.* Riverdale, Md.: Riverdale Co., 1987.

Foster, George M. "Peasant Society and the Image of Limited Good." *American Anthropologist* 67, no. 2 (April 1965).

Fox, Richard G. *From Zamindar to Ballot Box.* Ithaca: Cornell University Press, 1969.

_____ . "Rurban Settlements and Rajput 'Clans' in Northern India." In *Urban India: Society, Space, and Image,* edited by Richard Fox. Duke University, Program in Comparative Studies on Southern Asia, monograph no. 10. Durham, N.C.: Duke University Press, 1970.

Freitag, Sandria B. "Ambiguous Public Arenas and Coherent Personal Practice." In *Sharī'at and Ambiguity in South Asian Islam,* edited by Katherine Ewing. Berkeley and Los Angeles: University of California Press, 1988.

_____ . "Hindu-Muslim Communal Riots in India: A Preliminary Overview." In *Berkeley Working Papers on South and Southeast Asia.* Vol. 1. Berkeley: Center for South and Southeast Asia Studies, 1977.

_____ . "The Roots of Muslim Separatism in South Asia: Personal Practice and Public Structures in Kanpur and Bombay." In *Islam, Politics, and Social Movements,* edited by Edmund Burke III and Ira Lapidus. Berkeley and Los Angeles: University of California Press, 1988.

_____ , ed. *Culture and Power in Banaras: Community, Performance, and Environment, 1800–1980.* Berkeley and Los Angeles: University of California Press, 1989.

Garrioch, David. *Neighbourhood and Community in Paris, 1740–1790.* Cambridge: Cambridge University Press, 1986.

Geertz, Clifford. *Interpretation of Culture*. New York: Basic Books, 1973.

_____ . *Local Knowledge*. New York: Basic Books, 1983.

Giddens, Anthony. *The Constitution of Society: Outline of the Theory of Structuration*. Berkeley and Los Angeles: University of California Press, 1984.

Gilmartin, David. "Customary Law and *Sharīʿat* in British Punjab." In *Sharīʿat and Ambiguity in South Asian Islam*, edited by Katherine Ewing. Berkeley and Los Angeles: University of California Press, 1988.

_____ . *Empire and Islam*. Berkeley and Los Angeles: University of California Press, 1988.

_____ . "Religious Leadership and the Pakistan Movement in the Punjab." *Modern Asian Studies* 13, no. 3 (1979): 485–517.

Gokhale, Jayashree B. "The Sociopolitical Effects of Ideological Change: The Buddhist Conversion of Maharashtrian Untouchables." *Journal of Asian Studies* 45, no. 2 (February 1986): 269–92.

Golby, J. M., and A. W. Purdue. *The Civilization of the Crowd: Popular Culture in England, 1750–1900*. London: Batsford Academic and Educational, 1984.

Gordon, Richard. "The Hindu Mahasabha and the Indian National Congress, 1915–26." *Modern Asian Studies* 9, no. 2 (1975).

Guha, Ranajit. *Elementary Aspects of Peasant Insurgency*. New Delhi: Oxford University Press, 1983.

_____ , ed. *Subaltern Studies*. Vols. 1–5. Delhi: Oxford University Press, 1982–1985.

Gupta, Ishwar Prakash. *Urban Glimpses of Mughal India: Agra, the Imperial Capital, 16th and 17th Centuries*. Delhi: Discovery, 1986.

Gupta, Navayani. *Delhi Between Two Empires, 1803–1931: Society, Government and Urban Growth*. Delhi: Oxford University Press, 1981.

Habermas, Jürgen. "The Public Sphere: An Encyclopedia Article (1964)." *New German Critique* 3 (Fall 1974): 49–55.

Hansen, Kathryn. "The Birth of Hindi Drama." In *Culture and Power in Banaras: Community, Performance, and Environment, 1800–1980,* edited by Sandria B. Freitag. Berkeley and Los Angeles: University of California Press, 1989.

_____ . "*Sultana the Dacoit* and *Harishchandra:* Two Popular Dramas of the Nautanki Tradition of North India." *Modern Asian Studies* 17, no. 2 (1983): 313–31.

Hardgrave, Robert, Jr. "The Mappila Rebellion, 1921: Peasant Revolt in Malabar." *Modern Asian Studies* 11, no. 1 (February 1977): 57–100.

_____ . *The Nadars of Tamilnad*. Berkeley and Los Angeles: University of California Press, 1969.

Hardiman, David. *The Coming of the Devi: Adivasi Assertion in Western India*. Delhi: Oxford University Press, 1987.

_____ . "The Indian 'Faction': A Political Theory Examined." In *Subaltern Studies,* edited by Ranajit Guha. Vol. 1. Delhi: Oxford University Press, 1982.

Hardy, Peter. *The Muslims of British India*. Cambridge: Cambridge University Press, 1972.

Hasan, Mushirul, ed. *Communal and Pan-Islamic Trends in Colonial India.* New Delhi: Manohar, 1981.

Hauser, Walter, and Wendy Singer. "The Democratic Rite: Celebration and Participation in the Indian Elections." *Asian Survey* 26, no. 9 (September 1986).

Havell, E. B. *Banaras, the Sacred City.* London: Blackie & Son, 1905.

Hein, Norvin. *The Miracle Plays of Mathura.* Delhi: Oxford University Press, 1971.

_____. "The Ram Lila." *Journal of American Folklore* 71, no. 281 (1958).

Heitler, Richard. "The Varanasi House Tax Hartal of 1810–11." *Indian Economic and Social History Review* 10, no. 3 (1972): 239–57.

Hobsbawm, Eric. *Primitive Rebels: Studies in Archaic Forms of Social Movements in the 19th and 20th Centuries.* New York: Manchester University Press, 1967.

Hobsbawm, Eric, and Terence Ranger, eds. *The Invention of Tradition.* Cambridge: Cambridge University Press, 1983.

Hunt, Lynn. *Politics, Culture, and Class in the French Revolution.* Berkeley and Los Angeles: University of California Press, 1984.

Isherwood, Robert M. *Farce and Fantasy: Popular Entertainment in Eighteenth Century Paris.* New York: Oxford University Press, 1986.

Jones, G. Stedman. "Working-Class Culture and Working-Class Politics in London, 1870–1900: Notes on the Remaking of a Working Class." *Journal of Social History* 7 (1974).

Jones, Kenneth W. *Arya Dharm.* Berkeley and Los Angeles: University of California Press, 1976.

_____. "Communalism in the Punjab: The Arya Samaj Contribution." *Journal of Asian Studies* 28, no. 1 (November 1968): 39–54.

_____. "Ham Hindu Nahin." *Journal of Asian Studies* 33, no. 3 (May 1974): 457–75.

Kaplan, Steven L., ed. *Understanding Popular Culture.* New York: Mouton, 1984.

Kapur, Anuradha. "Actors, Pilgrims, Kings, and Gods: The Ramlila at Ramnagar." *Contributions to Indian Sociology,* n.s., 19, no. 1 (1985): 57–74.

King, Christopher R. "Forging a New Linguistic Identity: The Hindi Movement in Banaras, 1868–1914." In *Culture and Power in Banaras: Community, Performance, and Environment, 1800–1980,* edited by Sandria B. Freitag. Berkeley and Los Angeles: University of California Press, 1989.

Kolff, D. H. A. "Sannyasi Trader-Soldiers." *Indian Economic and Social History Review* 8 (1971).

Kumar, Ravindar. "The Bombay Textile Strike, 1919." *Indian Economic and Social History Review* 8, no. 1 (June 1971): 213–18.

_____. "From Swaraj to Purnja Swaraj: Nationalist Politics in the City of Bombay, 1920–32." In *Congress and the Raj: Facets of the Indian Struggle, 1917–47,* edited by D. A. Low. Columbia, Mo.: South Asia Books, 1977.

Leach, Edmund R. *Rethinking Anthropology.* London: Athlone Press, 1961.

Lelyveld, David. *Aligarh's First Generation: Muslim Solidarity in British India.* Princeton: Princeton University Press, 1978.

Llewellyn-Jones, Rosie. *A Fatal Friendship: The Nawabs, the British, and the City of Lucknow.* Delhi: Oxford University Press, 1985.

Lutgendorf, Philip. "Ram's Story in Shiva's City: Public Arenas and Private Patronage." In *Culture and Power in Banaras: Community, Performance, and Environment, 1800–1980,* edited by Sandria B. Freitag. Berkeley and Los Angeles: University of California Press, 1989.

Macfarlane, Alan. "History, Anthropology and the Study of Communities." *Social History* 2, no. 5 (May 1977): 631–52.

McKendrick, Neil, and J. H. Plumb. *The Birth of a Consumer Society: The Commercialization of Eighteenth-Century England.* London: Europa, 1982.

McLane, John R. *Indian Nationalism and the Early Congress.* Princeton: Princeton University Press, 1977.

———. "The 1905 Partition of Bengal and the New Communalism." In *Bengal East and West,* edited by Alexander Lipski. Michigan State University Occasional Paper No. 13, 1970.

McPherson, Kenneth. "The Muslims of Madras and Calcutta: Agitational Politics in the Early '20s." *South Asia* 5 (December 1975).

———. "The Social Background and Politics of the Muslims of Tamil Nad, 1901–37." *Indian Economic and Social History Review* 6, no. 4 (December 1969): 381–402.

Masselos, Jim. "Change and Custom in the Format of the Bombay Mohurram in the Nineteenth and Twentieth Centuries." *South Asia,* n.s., 5, no. 2 (1982): 47–67.

———. *Nationalism on the Indian Subcontinent.* Melbourne: Thomas Nelson, 1972.

———. "Power in the Bombay 'Mohalla,' 1904–1915: An Initial Exploration into the World of the Indian Urban Muslim." *South Asia* 6 (December 1976).

———. "Some Aspects of Bombay City Politics in 1919." In *Essays on Gandhian Politics,* edited by Ravindar Kumar. Oxford: Clarendon Press, 1971.

Mathur, Poonam. "Notes on Banaras 'Ramlila.'" *N. K. Bose Memorial Foundation Newsletter* 2, no. 1 (1979).

———. "Observations on the Enactment of the Ramlila During October 1977." *N. K. Bose Memorial Foundation Newsletter* 1, no. 1 (1978).

Mathur, Y. B. *Growth of Muslim Politics in India.* Delhi: Pragarti, 1979.

Metcalf, Barbara Daly. "Hakim Ajmal Khan: *Rais* of Delhi and Muslim Leader." In *Delhi Through the Ages: Essays in Urban History, Culture, and Society,* edited by Robert Frykenberg. Delhi: Oxford University Press, 1986.

———. *Islamic Revival in British India: Deoband, 1860–1900.* Princeton: Princeton University Press, 1982.

———, ed. *Moral Conduct and Authority: The Place of Adab in South Asian Islam.* Berkeley and Los Angeles: University of California Press, 1983.

Metcalf, Thomas R. *Land, Landlords, and the British Raj.* Berkeley and Los Angeles: University of California Press, 1979.

Minault, Gail. *The Khilafat Movement: Religious Symbolism and Political Mobilization in India.* New York: Columbia University Press, 1982.

Mines, Mattison. "Social Stratification Among Muslim Tamils in Tamilnadu, South India." In *Caste and Social Stratification Among the Muslims,* edited by Imtiaz Ahmad. New Delhi: Manohar, 1973.

Mujeeb, M. *The Indian Muslims.* Montreal: McGill University Press, 1967.

Mukherjee, Rudrangshu. *Awadh in Revolt, 1857–1858: A Study of Popular Resistance.* Delhi: Oxford University Press, 1984.

Mukherjee, S. N. "Class, Caste and Politics in Calcutta, 1815–38." In *Elites in South Asia,* edited by Edmund Leach and S. N. Mukherjee. Cambridge: Cambridge University Press, 1970.

Nehru, Jawaharlal. *Selected Works.* Vol. 2. Bombay: Orient Longman, 1972.

Neuman, Daniel. *The Life of Music of North India: The Organization of Artistic Tradition.* New Delhi: Manohar Books, 1980.

O'Hanlon, Rosalind. *Caste, Conflict and Ideology: Mahatma Jotivao Phule and Low Caste Protest in Nineteenth Century Western India.* Cambridge: Cambridge University Press, 1985.

Oldenburg, Philip. " 'A Place Insufficiently Imagined': Language, Belief, and the Pakistan Crisis of 1971." *Journal of Asian Studies* 44, no. 4 (1985): 711–34.

Oldenburg, Veena Talwar. *The Making of Colonial Lucknow, 1856–77.* Princeton: Princeton University Press, 1984.

Pandey, Gyanendra. *The Ascendancy of the Congress in Uttar Pradesh, 1926–34: A Study in Imperfect Mobilization.* Delhi: Oxford University Press, 1978.

_____. " 'Encounters and Calamities': The History of a North Indian *Qasba* in the Nineteenth Century." In *Subaltern Studies,* edited by Ranajit Guha. Vol. 3. Delhi: Oxford University Press, 1984.

_____. Rallying Round the Cow: Sectarian Strife in the Bhojpuri Region, c. 1888–1917." In *Subaltern Studies,* edited by Ranajit Guha. Vol. 2. Delhi: Oxford University Press, 1983.

_____. "A Rural Base for Congress: The United Provinces, 1920–40." In *Congress and the Raj,* edited by D. A. Low. Columbia, Mo.: South Asia Books, 1977.

Parry, Jonathan. "Death and Cosmogony in Kashi." *Contributions to Indian Sociology,* n.s., 15, nos. 1–2 (January/December 1981): 337–65.

Phythian-Adams, Charles. "Ceremony and the Citizen: The Communal Yearbook at Coventry 1450–1550." In *Crisis and Order in English Towns 1500–1700,* edited by Peter Clark and Paul Slack. London: Routledge and Kegan Paul, 1972.

_____. *Desolation of a City: Coventry and the Urban Crisis of the Late Middle Ages.* Cambridge: Cambridge University Press, 1979.

Ray, Rajat Kanta. *Social Conflict and Political Unrest in Bengal, 1875–1927.* Delhi: Oxford University Press, 1984.

Rearick, Charles. *Pleasures of the Belle Epoque: Entertainment and Festivity in Turn-of-the-Century France.* New Haven: Yale University Press, 1985.

Reay, Barry, ed. *Popular Culture in Seventeenth Century England.* New York: St. Martin's Press, 1985.

Revel, Jacques. "Forms of Expertise: Intellectuals and 'Popular' Culture in France (1650–1800)." In *Understanding Popular Culture,* edited by Steven L. Kaplan. New York: Mouton, 1984.

Robinson, F. C. R. "Consultation and Control: The United Provinces' Government and Its Allies, 1860–1906." *Modern Asian Studies* 5, no. 4 (October 1971): 313–36.

———. "Islam and Muslim Separatism." In *Political Identity in South Asia,* edited by David Taylor and Malcolm Yapp. London: Curzon Press, 1979.

———. *Separatism Among Indian Muslims.* Cambridge: Cambridge University Press, 1974.

Rudé, George. *The Crowd in History.* New York: Wiley, 1959.

Ruswa, Mirza. *The Courtesan of Lucknow: Umrao Jan Ada.* Translated by Khushwant Singh and M. A. Husaini. New Delhi: Orient Paperbacks, 1961.

Sabean, David. *Power in the Blood: Popular Culture and Village Discourse in Early Modern Germany.* Cambridge: Cambridge University Press, 1984.

Sarkar, Sumit. "The Conditions and Nature of Subaltern Militancy: Bengal from Swadeshi to Non-Cooperation, c. 1905–22." In *Subaltern Studies,* edited by Ranajit Guha. Vol. 3. Delhi: Oxford University Press, 1984.

———. "Hindu-Muslim Relations in Swadeshi Bengal, 1907–08." *Indian Economic and Social History Review* 9, no. 2 (June 1972): 161–216.

Saxena, N. C. "Historiography of Communalism in India." In *Communal and Pan-Islamic Trends in Colonial India,* edited by Mushirul Hasan. New Delhi: Manohar, 1981.

Schechner, Richard, and Linda Hess. "The Ramlila of Ramnagar." *The Drama Review* 21, no. 3 (1977).

Sen, Shila. *Muslim Politics in Bengal, 1937–47.* New Delhi: Impex India, 1976.

Sharar, Abdul Harim. *Lucknow: The Last Phase of an Oriental Culture.* London: Elek, 1975.

Sherring, M. A. *Benares, Past and Present.* Delhi: B. R. Publishing, 1868. Reprint. Delhi: Oxford University Press, 1975.

Siddiqi, Majid Hayat. "History and Society in a Popular Rebellion: Mewat, 1920–1933." *Comparative Studies in Society and History* 28 (1986): 442–67.

Singer, Milton. "Cultural Patterns of Indian Civilization." *Far Eastern Quarterly* 15 (1955).

Singh, Bhola Nath, ed. *Benares: A Handbook.* Prepared for the seventy-eighth session of the Indian Science Congress, 1941.

Spate, O. H. K., and Enayat Ahmad. "Five Cities of the Gangetic Plain: A Cross Section of Indian Cultural History." *Geographic Review* 40:260–78.

Stein, Burton. *All the King's Mana: Papers on Medieval South Indian History.* Madras: New Era, 1984.

———. *Indian Economic and Social History Review* 14, no. 1 (January–March 1977). Special Number on South Indian Temples.

Stokes, Eric. *The Peasant and the Raj.* Cambridge: Cambridge University Press, 1978.

Summerfield, Penelope. "The Effingham Arms and the Empire: Deliberate Selection in the Evolution of Music Hall in London." In *Popular Culture and Class Conflict, 1590–1914,* edited by Eileen Yeo and Steven Yeo. Atlantic Highlands, N.J.: Humanities Press, 1981.

Tandon, Prakash. *Punjabi Century.* Berkeley and Los Angeles: University of California Press, 1968.

Taylor, David, and Malcolm Yapp, eds. *Political Identity in South Asia.* London: Curzon Press, 1979.

Thapar, Romila. *Ancient Indian Social History.* New Delhi: Orient Longman, 1978.

Thomas, David A. "Lucknow and Kanpur, 1880–1920: Stagnation and Development Under the Raj." *South Asia*, n.s. 5 (December 1982): 68–80.

Thompson, E. P. *The Making of the English Working Class.* New York: Vintage, 1963.

———. "The Moral Economy of the English Crowd in the Eighteenth Century." *Past and Present*, no. 50 (February 1971): 76–136.

Thursby, G. R. *Hindu-Muslim Relations in British India.* Leiden: E. J. Brill, 1975.

Tönnies, Ferdinard. *Community and Association,* translated by C. P. Loomis. London. Routledge and Paul, 1955. Originally published as *Gemeinschaft und Gesellschaft.* 1887.

Turner, Victor. *Dramas, Fields and Metaphors: Symbolic Action in Human Society.* Ithaca: Cornell University Press, 1974.

———. *Process, Performance and Pilgrimage: A Study in Comparative Symbology.* New Delhi: Concept, 1979.

Underdown, David. *Revel, Riot and Rebellion: Popular Politics and Culture in England, 1603–1660.* Oxford: Clarendon Press, 1985.

Vatuk, Sylvia. *Kinship and Urbanization: White-Collar Migrants in North India.* Berkeley and Los Angeles: University of California Press, 1972.

Weber, Eugen. *Peasants into Frenchmen: The Modernization of Rural France, 1870–1914.* Stanford: Stanford University Press, 1976.

Whitcomb, Elizabeth. *Agrarian Conditions in Northern India.* Vol. 1, *The U.P. Under British Rule, 1860–1900.* Berkeley and Los Angeles: University of California Press, 1972.

Wolpert, Stanley. *A New History of India.* New York: Oxford University Press, 1977.

Worsley, Peter. *The Trumpet Shall Sound.* 2d ed., aug. New York: Schocken, 1968.

Yang, Anand A. "The Agrarian Origins of Crime: A Study of Riots in Saran District, India, 1866–1920." *Journal of Social History* 13 (Winter 1979): 289–305.

———. "Sacred Symbol and Sacred Space." *Comparative Studies in Society and History* 22, no. 4 (October 1980): 576–96.

Yeo, Eileen, and Steven Yeo, eds. *Popular Culture and Class Conflict, 1950–1914.* Atlantic Highlands, N.J.: Humanities Press, 1981.

Index

Designer: Barbara Jellow
Compositor: Interactive Composition Corporation
Text: 10/13 Sabon
Display: Sabon
Printer: Braun-Brumfield, Inc.
Binder: Braun-Brumfield, Inc.